To
Helga & John
with best wishes
& in the hope you'll
find *something* therein
of interest !
— Eric
(May 05)

Religious Faith,
Human Identity
Dangerous Dynamics In Global & Indian Life

GW00726144

Religious Faith, Human Identity

Dangerous Dynamics In Global & Indian Life

ERIC LOTT

(Cambridge Teape Lectures)

ATC / UTC

Religious Faith,Human Identity : *Dangerous Dynamics In Global & Indian Life* — Jointly published by : **Asian Trading Corporation**, 58, 2nd Cross, Da Costa Layout, St. Mary's Town, Bangalore - 560 084. Tel : (080) 2548 7444, Fax : (080) 2547 9444, E-mail : mail@atcbooks.net Website : www.atcbooks.net and **United Theological College**, 63, Millers Road, Bangalore - 46, Tel : (080) 23332844 , E-mail : unitedc@giasbg01.vsnl.net.in Website : www.utcbangalore.com

Copyright : U.T.C.
First Published in 2005

ISBN 81-7086-341-4

To

the memory of my
respected professor
and
well-loved friend

Ninian Smart (1927-2001)

Contents

PART II
CRISIS-POINTS FOR GLOBAL IDENTITIES

PART III
CRISIS-POINTS IN INDIA'S CHANGING IDENTITIES

Acknowledgements

The following chapters are based on the Teape lectures given in India for the year 2000-01.

I am very grateful to those at Cambridge then administering this endowment (in particular Drs Martin Forward, Brian Hebblethwaite, Julius Lipner and John Sweet), for having invited me as Teape lecturer, especially as they had twice previously given me the opportunity to reflect in this Teapish way. 'Set Free by a Dancing God', the 1998 lectures at Cambridge, will also be published soon I hope. William Teape's original request was for the invited lecturer to look comparatively at the relationship of Christian theology and Indian religious thought, in particular the insights of the Upanishads. This is now usually interpreted in a very broad sense, as I also have done, though I am glad to say that at least in some places my reflections have been able to keep closely to the terms of the bequest.

The lectures, in various forms, were given in St Stephen's College, Delhi, Gurukul Theological College, Chennai (previously Madras), the United Theological College, Bangalore, the Rishi Valley Educational Centre (a Krishnamurti foundation), in Andhra Pradesh, and Eastern Theological College, Jorhat (Assam). In Bangalore, Rishi Valley and Delhi there were good numbers of people from a variety of faith-traditions. Subsequent discussions - with the Principal of Delhi's Hindu College, for example - were both enjoyable and valuable. So too were meetings with teachers and students at Jorhat, eagerly seeking new ways of understanding their identity as distinctive North Eastern 'first inhabitants' (Nagas/Mizos/Garos, etc) who now also profess Christian faith as part of their struggle to relate both to an Indian national context and to their global citizenship. I hope what I had to say gave some help in the configuring of their complex new self-identity.

I am immensely grateful for the kind hospitality received in all five centres, especially that of Dr Anil Wilson, Principal of St Stephen's with which the Teapes are specially related. There was lively discussion in each centre by way of response, but nowhere was there more clear awareness of the issues raised than in the arena where I spent many exciting years of teaching - U.T.College, Bangalore. I am particularly indebted to the convener, Dr S. Prabhakar, now Director

9

of the South Asian Institute for Theological Research, to Dr O.V.Jathanna, UTC Principal, and to those other members of Faculty and the wider community who were so generously welcoming.

In terms of my understanding of religious identities, my greatest indebtness is to Ninian Smart - professor, friend and fellow-cricketer - to whose memory I dedicate this book. It was in London in 1958 that I first sat as a student at a slimly youthful Ninian's feet. Later research too was under Ninian, when he had set up the department of Religious Studies at Lancaster. I will be only too happy if his influence can be seen in at least some of my thinking in the following pages. His sudden death in January 2001, while I was giving these lectures, and so soon after he had given his presidential address at the American Academy of Religion, was a painful shock. That he was a previous Teape lecturer too (published as *The Yogi and the Devotee* 1968) adds to the sense of occasion for me. I have fond memories too of long discussions in Bangalore in the early 1980s on issues of religious identity, and serendipitous journeys with Ninian and his wife Libushka that took us to meet strangely diverse religious characters in odd corners of Karnataka. I am grateful for these memories of my 'guru'.

Those who know me will be well aware of how indebted I am to my wife, Chris. In addition to the many ways in which I am dependent on her there is now her unstinting support during the writing of this book. A further cause for my gratitude.

January 2005

Preface

These lectures range quite widely through our religious worlds. And the paths taken in religious faith interweave with numerous other major highways traversing our global life. This means that tracking human self-identities and how religious faith can shape them calls for a rather complex analysis. So, by way of preface, I begin with a summary of the discussion to follow.

1. 'Identity' has increasingly become a *key category* for human self-understanding, nowhere more so than in looking at the role of religions in the world. Self-identity has to do with a sense of belonging within given boundaries, boundaries that provide a sense of continuity and integrity, and a story-enlivened sense of a significant past and a significant future destiny. Identities empower, and above all provide a sense of distinctive status in relation to others, in the first place the kinship of a shared status, but inevitably too the potential enmity of otherness.

2. Increasingly in late modernity the search for self-identity is seen as the individual working out a personal destiny, constructing a unique narrative, often through the breaking down of boundaries. Crucial here is the *tension between personal identity and corporate identity*. But this ambiguity is equally present within *religious* experience. Some believers will be quite happy with the secularist call for religion to be solely a private affair. Others will not. In religion, too, there may be tension, even antagonism, between the closely knit *inner* faith-group and wider communities *outside* that faith. Indeed it is religious symbolism that often furnishes the mythic materials for the most fierce demonising of the enemy other.

3. But there are also seminal compulsions within different strands of religious experience that make for forms of human *inclusiveness*. Faith does not only intensify feelings of being distinctive, it can also lead to more intense awareness of the wider human community. In this type of religion keeping faith private will clearly be impossible. A sense of belonging to God, for instance, may well include a heightened sense of being part of earth's life, for better or worse, even though there are spiritualities that at first glance seem to express an alienation from earthiness.

4. Contemporary events, especially since 11 September 2001 and the reverberations of the American aim to 'shock and awe' by way of global response, as well as alternating periods of intensifying and abating of both the Palestine-Israel and Pakistan-India conflicts, have compelled far more serious recognition of the *powerful significance of the role of religion in the shaping of human identities.*

Comment in western *secularist culture*, however, will more often be from perspectives that are inherently hostile to or dismissive of a religious worldview. Except when specifically denigrating religion, secularism has all too often reduced it to just an odd, probably obsolete, form of 'culture', allowed religion no life of its own. The extremist violence of 9/11 has moved at least a few more writers to recognise just how powerfully motivating within cultural and political life religion can be - even when it is not possible to distinguish precisely between religion and politics, or indeed between religion and culture. But this still leaves the contrast between sacralist and secularist views of the world, and the very different forms of self-identity these contrasting perceptions generate.

5. Others (in India for example) speak of '*secularism*' in a somewhat different way. A 'secularist' government is one with a pluralist social and political attitude, 'secularism' is a way of life not based primarily on belonging to a particular religious community. The secularising process goes much deeper than this though. No religious tradition can wholly disengage from this process, cannot avoid responding to modernity, and even incorporating insights from the 'secular' world.

The division, therefore, cannot be simply 'modern secular' versus 'religious tradition', or 'liberals' against 'conservatives'. The global system against which religious militants rage has great numbers of conservatives, even if 'neo-cons', in its ranks. These terms can be misleading. Yet, the crisis facing the world also results from what seem contradictory identities - the religious and the secularist. And it is 'fundamentalist' religion, and especially extremist Islam, with fundamentalist Christianity running a close second, that the secularist worldview sees as the most dangerous ingredient in our present global crisis.

6. It is rare (except among specialists in religious studies) to find serious recognition of the *diversity* of religious identities, diversities

even *within* what are commonly seen as single traditions - 'Hindu', 'Christian', 'Muslim', etc. Even terms for inner groupings, i.e. 'Saiva', 'Baptist', 'Shia', and so on, can refer to be widely contrasting worldviews. Nor is it only from outside that family uniformities are too easily assumed, uniformities that are often 'constructed' for political ends.

7. A divide of huge significance in religious life is that between the conservative and the radical, the *conformist* and the *transformist*. Within each tradition, along with boundary-making there is also a boundary-breaking strand. Generally, the religious *conservative* is locked into the dominant interpretation of tradition, with a self-identity based on what is believed to be a long-given, unchanging cultural life-style. Even the dominant social system - with its culture and political system - may somehow be seen as unchangeable, perhaps as sacred and absolute in its authority.

The religious *radical* on the other hand is likely to find resources within the tradition leading to a counter-cultural stance and a socially critical self-identity. Transformation rather than conformation is the primary aim. Or this may be worked out largely as *self*-transformation rather than *world*-transformation, depending on the undergirding belief-system.

So, the dynamics are complex, and the divide too can be misleadingly oversimplified, as religious faith engages with cultural and political life outside the tradition in many different ways. And this is especially so of radical faith's engagement with the changing world of modern secularism. Here the most 'conservative' in loyalty to the tradition and in resisting secular changes may be most 'radical' in actively seeking to transform that world. Hence the term 'fundamentalist' is often used of those seen as extremists in both their loyalty to tradition and commitment to world change. So, here we have a complex global phenomenon that warrants its own critical discussion.

8. Analysis of the role of religion in the shaping of human identity makes it necessary to give far greater weight than is usual to the peculiar *inner dynamic* of religious life, and the interacting *'dimensions'* that constitute religion. So, we need to recognise the distinctively *religious* dimensions of key forms of self-identity in the contemporary scene. At the same time, the interaction of religious

life with other historical and political realities, including other religious traditions, has to be given great weight. *Self-interpretation* within religions therefore becomes all-important and lays a heavy burden upon those leaders given the task of interpreting.

9. In recent decades a series of *crisis points* for human self-understanding have entailed differing forms of crisis for *religious self-understanding* also. Secularism, whether of a leftist critical worldview or a liberal accommodative worldview, though crucial in recent religious history, is only one such. Others include the burgeoning importance of nationalism, ethnicity, fundamentalism, globalisation, postmodernism, postcolonialism, eco-feminism, the issue of religious conversion. And some, such as the rise of Hindutva as a form of religious nationalism, issues of an Indian-Christian identity, the growing confidence of 'oppressed' Dalit (once 'untouchable') people in their own self-identity, are peculiar to India. All have had direct impact on the shaping of religious self-identities.

10. Nowhere - in spite of the present global confrontation between Islam and secularist modernity - nowhere have there been either more clearly distinctive human identities shaped by religion than in the *Indian subcontinent*, and - perhaps therefore - nowhere has there been more fruitfully vigorous response to the various cultural and ideological crisis-points of our time. The quite recent global fear of nuclear conflict between India and Pakistan is but one obvious example of a crisis-response.

Lying behind the dangerously threatening military stand-off in the Subcontinent are more deep-rooted tensions. Clearly, the Hindu-Muslim conflict is a major factor, but needs some unravelling. Hindu-Muslim relations in India historically have been far from violent conflict alone; the mutual inculturation too has been remarkable. In any case, India's religious history is the *world's richest source for exploring religion's fecundity*. If for no other reason, these lectures on the identity-shaping role of religion have turned for illustrative material not only to Islamic and Christian faith, but equally to the rich and varied traditions of Hindu, Buddhist, and even Sikh faith.

11. The critical tension between the religious conservative and the radical, between an attitude of cultural *con*-formation and one seeking *trans*-formation within the tradition as much as in worldly life, is also a *critical tension between given social identities and the*

new and higher Identity aimed for by engagement with the transcendent Focus of the concerned tradition. This critical tension is a central theme of these lectures. And it is at this point that Upanishadic (and other Indian religious) insights concerning Identity become so pertinent. Indeed, some form of 'identifying' with that Focus, even when this means stressing the unbridgeable difference between finite creature and the one infinite Creator, will invariably be part of religious aspiration.

12. It is, too, by engagement with that transcendent Focus - perceived in crucially different ways - that believers aim to resolve the problems relating to human *ego* and its compulsions to *power*. Yet the empowerment of ego is precisely what the nurturing of our self-identities usually achieves. Here obvious tensions emerge within the faith-process. It means that some form of *ec-stasy*, both personal and corporate, a 'standing outside' our given identities and their symbolisms, is in varying ways essential even within the goals of religious experience itself. Religion, at its differing levels, both creates social identities and counters the power of those identities.

13. On the road to that goal, however, in religion's shaping of human identities, various kinds of *dangers* emerge: when there is, for example, an absolutising of a tradition's institutions and its institutional authority. Or there may be the exploiting of religious symbolism and sentiment for crudely political ends. On the other hand, there can be the refusal to engage at all with social and cultural identities other than those within the religious community, which leads equally to a distorting of identities. Ecstasy as complete immersion of personal identity into the inner group identity may well provide a kind of self-liberation, but can also lead to a dangerous demonising of wide areas of human life, and thereby seriously limits the potential range of faith.

14. It is, therefore, not only human community that is endangered in these distortions of our religiousness. It is the *inner life* of the concerned religion too. Our understanding of the nature of Power, our response to Power, and consequently the character of our institutional power-structures, are fundamental to religious as to all human life, and certainly shape people's sense of self-identity. At every point, therefore, the *role of leading interpreters* of our faith-traditions is crucial.

All this suggests that my stance in this book is strictly neither that of a theologian of a particular faith, nor that of detached social or historical analysis, but somewhere in between. Mostly descriptive, I am clearly prescriptive too at key points. I am both an observer and a believer. Certainly an ideological bias – part of my personal faith - is not difficult to discern, along with my sometimes detached-seeming comparative approach. Religion itself usually engages in a similar dialectic, an in-between position.

The Epilogue with which I close is a suggested way of interpreting inclusively the shaping of self-identity within a particular faith tradition, Christianity.

My main concern throughout this book, then, has been to probe the distinctive dynamics of religion. Not that any purely *sui generis* character of religion is accessible to us. Detaching faith from its entanglements with the messiness of human history may heighten devotion, but leaves the researcher with a disembodied ghost. Faith always has its embedding milieu, however accommodating or critical the interactive process. Yet, far too much writing on religion is from a somewhat blinkered political or sociological or cultural perspective. Necessary as these interpretations of religion's role in human experience are if we wish to think intelligibly today about religion, ever present are the dangers of perspectival reductionism, as hegemonic as any political or cultural imperialism. The line between is fine indeed.

There has been substantial expansion of the material I presented in the original lectures. Yet I have mostly retained the style of the lectures: e.g. there is the inclusion of illustrative material from my personal experience of Indian religious life; and formal academic referencing, footnotes, and quotations from other writers have been kept to a minimum. That still leaves quite a number of key writings to which I have explicitly responded, sometimes in some detail. A more wide-ranging bibliography is appended.

Prologue :
Dangerous Polarities Post 9/11

In the first weeks of 2005, the terrifying power of the Tsunami wave dominated the imagination of people far beyond those South Asian shores where it had struck so devastatingly. The worldwide surge of responsive compassion still moved even distant hearts in unprecedented ways. A wave of human solidarity seemed for a while to sweep numerous dividing walls aside. In Sri Lanka, for instance, on both sides of the Tamil-Sinhala divide leaders spoke of the new opportunity for human togetherness in the face of such an awesome and utterly irresistible 'act of God', as it came to be called. For some, then, the Tsunami seemed to wash away lesser dividing identities. Among the perhaps 300,000 who drowned, were there not people of East and West, affluent tourist and vulnerable fisherfolk, pilgrim of faith and seeker of pleasure, all equally helpless in the face of the Tsunami's onslaught? Is it not at such crisis points, when a common transcending human identity is thrust upon us, that lesser distinctions lose their potency?

And yet, the rhetoric of a common human identity can become just that - mere rhetoric that ignores the continuing and harder realities of our divided human community. Thousands of visiting tourists died on those fateful shores; but many more thousands of fishing families perished, their homes and lives always so precariously balanced on that shoreline. Even tragedy can be used to hide the reality that the life of the poor is invariably more precarious, and that for them far fewer systems of protection are in place.

Nor did the Tsunami in any way touch the underlying causes of the conflicts that have raged so fiercely in the northern parts both of Sri Lanka and Indonesia's Aceh province of Sumatra (where as many as 200,000 may have died from the tidal wave). Indeed, with people so devastated and traumatised, government forces there seem to be taking the opportunity to quell with greater vigour the local Islam-based insurgency. There are reports of aggressive evangelism also seizing its chance.

We dare not ignore any push to a more inclusive human identity. Neither, though, can the basis of that inclusiveness be uncritically ignored; nor the inescapable fact that so much of the push to inclusiveness in reality increases the polarising of our humanity. And, at the heart of the increase both of pressure and polarisation, there is the role of religion to be much more rigorously reckoned with. The momentary drawing together in the face of Tsunamic terror changed very little.

It is especially when we attempt to trace how *religion* shapes human identities in our times that we are almost bound to begin with '9/11'. The eleventh day of September 2001 is now a defining moment in modern global history. No one will need reminding of the events of this date: extremist anti-American, anti-secularist, anti-Christian rage burst out in explosively destructive acts that reduced a proudly soaring World Trade Centre first to massive balls of all-consuming fire, then to pulverised heaps of rubble.

To argue that 'everything is now changed' claims too much, for that ignores the causal histories leading up to this atrocity. To say that 'nothing has changed' is to minimise the appalling dangers of the new political posturings and global confrontations, the terrifyingly destructive show of military might, which that event precipitated. In more ways than one 9/11 was a day of *falling*. Some have spoken of the falling away of the walls of American naivete. There was a loss of feeling invulnerable and safely distant from the rest of the world.

Others, more cynical perhaps, have seen in the rubble of those fallen towers the materials men hungry for global power needed to build new global neo-imperialist outposts for a 'new American century'. It gave impetus to the invasions of first Afghanistan, then Iraq, and threats against others. It enabled the deliberate manipulation of fear as a powerful weapon in the 2004 presidential election. As an act of terror in American and global life, therefore, 9/11 was eminently successful in creating further terror. The reverberations of 9/11 have sent shockwaves throughout the whole world. And the repeated showing of those horrifying but rivetting images on television in the first few days ensured that human consciousness was indelibly marked.

The Potency of Symbolic Acts
Human faiths deal especially in potent *symbols*. And there was very powerful symbolism in the dramatic collapse of the gigantic

twin towers. They stood as proud signs of the globalising economy, with its culturally homogenising impact, of which the United States is the initiating and driving centre. It was not only respect for those who died and the sensitivities of those who mourn that led to a virtual embargo on the further showing of these images throughout the western world. There was also the need to smother their symbolic and apocalyptic impact, to counter them with images of US invincible might.

And this, militarily, the US surely did - initially at least - in the 'shock and awe' of its (so far) two global counter-strikes. As far as possible, media images conveying vulnerability - even picturing the death or capture of its fighting forces - were carefully controlled. Only the Arabic TV station, al-Jazeera, showed such images, and itself soon became a military target. That the US/UK powers in defeated Iraq were later willing to show images of Saddam Hussein's sons' shell-disfigured dead bodies (and later the humiliating scenes, made globally public, of a cowed and disoriented Saddam Hussein having his hair and mouth examined for lice and disease) was yet another example of the double standards conflicts of this kind engender.

The response to 9/11 has produced terrifying counter-images. The subsequent, grotesquely asymmetrical, military encounters, as well as 'collateral' deaths even of innocent civilians numbering fifty times (according to some calculations) those killed on 9/11, have weakened the impact of the fall of the towers. The simultaneous September 11 strike at the Pentagon, military heart of US global power, may have been less destructive; but its symbolism at the time was equally effective. The weapons used were non-military passenger aircraft, turned against these centres of American power by a handful of men armed with pocket-knives, basic skills in piloting passenger planes, absolute belief in the justice of their cause and pathological hatred for the civilisation embodied in what they aimed to destroy. We can presume that the White House, strongly symbolic centre of US political power, was also an intended target. Even that particular date in September held symbolic significance for the avenging attackers, stirring hate-filled memories of oppressive acts by the enemy on that same day some years earlier.

The surreal *asymmetry* of the 9/11 'weapons' of destruction and the horrific armaments used in the 'counter-terrorist' response adds further potency to the symbolism. The devastating military humiliations in Afghanistan and Iraq serve for many merely to increase their conviction that it is 'the One God', to whose holy and unvanquishable cause they are committed, who will finally ensure victory against what they see as the rampant and evilly bloated forces of their secularist enemy. 'Allah alone is great' is the war-cry of each lonely 'sacrificer', each hugely outnumbered group of *jihadis*. Seeming imbalance of power, asymmetry in battle, heroic self-sacrifice, is of the essence - though reason leads us to ask how such one-sided defeats can but intensify a humiliated people's secret search for weapons of destructive power equal to those of the enemy?

It is as *symbolic public performance* that Mark Juergensmeyer interprets religion-based global violence in his wide-ranging analysis of this alarming phenomenon. The arguments of his earlier edition of *Terror in the Mind of God: the Global Rise of Religious Violence*, written a year prior to 9/11, have been impressively confirmed by subsequent events. He rightly contends that the increasing acts of extreme violence in our time in the name of one or other faith should not be seen merely in terms of *political strategy*. Clearly they *are* often extremist, politically based responses to political realities, at least as 'reality' is perceived within the worldview of the perpetrators.

Men of violence are never engaged purely in acts of symbolism. Iraqi insurgent resistance (in 2004) is no doubt inspired as much by calculations of which Muslim party will come to power if elections are held in January 2005 as they are by more lofty rejection of any such process imposed by an infidel invasion. Yet, in this struggle too, deeper patterns of faith and action emerge. At one level here too insurgent violence stems from an unshakeable conviction that their people are under attack from hostile, even demonic, powers whose victory would be catastrophic. Desperate counter-measures are called for. The terror threatening their world calls for a response of terror. But is that not precisely the claim made by those invading Iraq? And on both sides symbolic victories become all-important.

Symbolic they may be, but the sheer terror of these events is far from contrived. The powerful feelings aroused on both sides are all too real. Those anguished scenes in and around the school at Beslan in the southern Russian state of Ossetia, in September 2004 three years after 9/11, and the tragic slaughter of several hundred children, parents and teachers - hostage-takers too - can leave no one in doubt about how real was the terror and horror. But neither should we be in doubt about the preceding horrors of Chechnya and in the experience of the Ingush people. In Chechnya alone, separatist claims for the numbers of *children* killed since 1994 by State military action range from 20,000 to over 40,000 (perhaps one tenth of total deaths, though state secrecy about the dead, as in Afghanistan and Iraq, make exact figures impossible). As in the Balkans, among the Caucasian peoples too ancient Christian-Muslim, Orthodox-Catholic, and certainly inter-ethnic and ideological tensions, all in the context of lingering Russian hopes of wide-ranging state control, add to the potency of the brew.

Exactly which group perpetrated the Beslan tragedy is not the point here. Such repeated horror polarises, demonises, brutalises. And so came that act of un-Qur'anic barbarity against children, carried out clearly with the intention of creating maximum emotional impact. The greater the horror, the more clearly the world would see the intensity of their desperation - perhaps their victimhood too, whether from state or international aggression and its terrors. That such callously violent use of innocent children would prove counter-productive to their cause globally seems lost on them. To perform ever more powerful acts of global symbolism has become all-important, perceived as the only possible response to the aggression of their enemy.

Whether or not all al-Qaida and related militants are merely 'counter-terrorists', they are buoyed up by a vision of the victory of their own righteous cause, an ultimate victory to which such violent acts as are available to them, usually entailing self-sacrifice and probable martyrdom, are merely pointers. The sacrifice and the success of their acts of terror does result in the emotional empowering of groups within Islam - especially those, having left an increasingly precarious rural life, now powerless in their urban poverty. Such new-found emotional identity will have obvious political implications.

Even so, these acts are primarily intended as *symbolic performances,* dramatic violence that draws on the deep and dark wells of religious imagery for its power. New mass-media techniques, TV in particular, then make this performance *globally* symbolic.

Religion's Role?

So, we do not exaggerate if we describe 9/11 as 'apocalyptic'- implying it was both revealing and veiling, with the fiery and violent destruction marking a transition to some new epoch. The strong element of *political* protest was obvious; yet the powerful strands of *religious faith* are even more forceful, however shocking such an expression of faith may seem to others. Those belittling the role of religion may speak of 'insane fanatics', 'mindless gangsters', 'pathological thugs', 'brainwashed adolescent misfits', 'envy-driven', or some such dismissive description for all who adopt ways of terror. Terrorists may well include such types. But it is either stupid myopia or cynical spin that tries try to account for terrorism solely in such terms. And to refuse even to consider 'rational' causes of terrorism is itself dangerous irrationality.

Conspiracy theories inevitably abound in this skewed world. Many faithful Muslims flatly deny that people of their religion could have been the perpetrators of 9/11. Deliberate cruelty to and killing of the 'innocent' - non-combatant women and children in particular - contradict explicit Qur'anic prohibitions. It must, therefore - argue those of more naive faith - have been an Israeli-inspired conspiracy, part of the anti-Muslim global conspiracy threatening Islam. Other theories of intent to destroy Islam abound. True, the record of western imperialist manipulation of Muslim countries over the years is no less than appalling. Thoughts of a global conspiracy are only to be expected.

Theories of internal conspiracy within America, too, do not lack oddly inexplicable facts. In September 2000 the politically potent neo-conservative group Project for a New American Century, with which a number of leading advisors to American political leaders are associated, wrote a document entitled 'Rebuilding America's Defences'. This envisages greatly expanding direct American controlling power in key oil-producing and oil-transporting regions, including Iraq and Afghanistan. This document builds on an earlier one by leading ideologues of the group, which also argues for the control of space and cyberspace and the possible need to develop biological weapons able to 'target specific genotypes', thus changing 'biological warfare from the realm of terror to a political useful tool'. How uncannily prophetic is the suggestion too that a catastrophic terrorist action in a major American city would legitimate the global military action needed to create this 'new world order' believed to be of such benefit to western interests. There is, further, the inexplicable lack of US defence procedures (on 9/11) both before the co-ordinated hijacking of the passenger planes and in the considerable period between reports of those hijackings, so obviously a threat to key American cities, and the catastrophic crashes.

This, and much more (such as the material used in Michael Moore's openly polemical, but award-winning documentary *Fahrenheit 9/11*), is strong red meat to conspiracy theorists. But it must now take a very special kind of faith not to accept that 9/11's acts of vengeful destruction, though not in the true spirit of Islam, were done *in the name of Islam*, and that the enemy was identified as 'Christian'. In any case it was an act *deliberately intended to polarise and intensify enmities*. And that aim has been achieved.

Yet, even when fiercely critical of western ways, the great majority of Muslims are appalled by indiscriminately terrorising acts that kill the innocent. Most Muslims, humiliated or not, do not want to be part of this global 'war'. Even if committed to *jihadic* defence of their faith, the terrorising ways adopted by extremists who claim to act in their name are repudiated. The great majority of Muslims insist that the very name of their faith, the core vision of *'Islam'*, compels them to be essentially 'people of peace', as long as they are allowed to live according to their Qur'anic faith. Violent conflict abounds, though, and too often reaches the point where the 'innocent' are continually being killed on both sides. Israeli troops and Palestinian 'sacrificers' have regularly slaughtered each other's civilians, though the Palestian dead hugely outnumber Israelis.

In this globally crucial conflict in the Holy Land too there is such glaring *asymmetry* of military power. And normal sensitivities, as well as much else, are destroyed. Even basically decent people slide into accepting the equation, 'If our innocent, why not theirs too?' Or perhaps, 'No one now is innocent'. And so inner self-contradictions build up. For such acts, as well as finding ready-made legitimating imagery within the concerned tradition, also go against deeply held beliefs on both sides. Thus some of the basics of faith are threatened as much as the lives of the enemy. Yet, we cannot claim that these acts of extreme violence are outside the bounds of religion *per se*. They may be *bad* religion, morally unacceptable, and mixed up with political ambitions that contradict the highest religious aspirations. But that does not make them *non*-religion. Religion's complex link with violence is something we will need to look at.

Religion's Diversities

Here we have to take note of an important fact central to understanding the dynamics of religion. Religious people, even within one faith-family, relate to their tradition in very different ways, entailing very different commitments. *Diversity* is essential to the authentic life of any faith. From fundamentalists to anti-faith polemicists, far too few recognise this obvious fact. Within Islam, since...the impact of Saudi Arabia's militant Wahhabi movement has been globally significant. Yet, there are many other movements and potencies within Islam, some similarly exclusive and militant, others far more inclusive and world-engaging. The Muslim world is far from monolithic.

Just as it is very clear that large numbers of faithful Muslims find the indiscriminate violence of extremists abhorrent, so among those with a seemingly common grounding in Christian tradition there has been startling polarisation between, for example, those fiercely opposed to and those in favour of the massive military action against Iraq.

Even within America there is a deep divide. Alarming numbers of Southern Baptists, and those Christians locked into 'apocalyptic dispensationalism', tend to see an attack on any anti-Israel Middle-Eastern state, indeed any anti-Muslim action, as part of the divine plan prophesied in scripture. Other fundamentalist forms of Christian faith too are happy to accept anti-terrorist rhetoric as a call to an anti-Muslim crusade. Yet almost all other mainstream Christian bodies have been publicly, in some cases vehemently, opposed to the coalition invasion of Iraq - however much they recognised the need for a curtailing of Saddam Hussein's despotic ways. To believe in some form of effective global intervention where there is clearly inhuman oppression is surely inescapable in today's interwoven world - if only because the unjust human relations resulting from past 'intervention' is all too obvious. *What* form such globalist action should take is the key question.

Global Messianism

For, it is not only the apocalyptic end of the Christian faith-spectrum that *can* prompt dangerously invasive forms of 'global messianism'. Both President Bush and Prime Minister Blair share something in common here. There is no evidence that either personally believes that the human story is now in its final 'dispensation', that the imminent and violent climax centred in Jerusalem will include the destruction of all enemies of Christ - Muslims, secularists, multilateralists alike, and even those Jews who do not convert - and that there will very soon be a period of glorious 'rapture' for the elected faithful. But many millions do believe this, including presumably many readers of the best-selling series of 'Left Behind' novels by Tim LaHaye. Lahaye is not only a fiction-writer, but one of the leaders on the powerful Christian right that has made such an impact on American political life.

Yet, there is a global *messianism* implicit in both coalition leaders. The Bush regime believes that America has an inalienable right to ignore decisions made by the United Nations, or interpret them in their own way (even if, when in trouble, seeking UN assistance later). This conviction that it is able to take whatever unilateral action it deems necessary, even pre-emptive attacks, against any other sovereign state, is based not only on the total supremacy of American military power. It represents the sense of *special destiny* under God that lies deep in American political and cultural consciousness (and a century ago was central to British self-identity). This includes a widespread belief that America's own 'new world order' is that which is to dominate the whole globe.

The seeds of this conviction that 'we are a nation with a special destiny' can be seen more than two centuries earlier in statements by some of the pioneers of American Independence. As Thomas Paine put it: 'We have it in our power to begin a new world....a new world is at hand' (Armstrong 2000 pp.81-87). Even among the more secularist early fathers of America, a Christian eschatological worldview lingered. A crucial difference today is the felt need for a US-propelled global economy to function smoothly and profitably. In his devastatingly critical analysis of America's role in global economic affairs Will Hutton draws attention to this crucial national characteristic - a sense of 'special destiny' – that undergirds a global aggressiveness others often find so offensively arrogant (Hutton 2000).

All nationalist feeling includes this sense of being special in some way. It was certainly very clear in British imperialist posturing for at least two centuries. There is even some linkage to be found between imperialist ideology and missionary strategists. For example, a leading secretary of the 'Britain is the New Israel' movement, begun in the late eighteenth century and flourishing in Victorian and Edwardian times (born in Salem, South India) rose to a senior position in the Indian Civil Service in mid-nineteenth century, and went on to hold official posts in various British missionary societies (Wilson 1967). Even their vision of Britain as the true Israel was called 'The Identity'.

In his major address in America seeking to boulster support for the war against Iraq, Blair spoke of being gripped by a strong 'sense of mission' to re-shape the world. His words found strong resonance among his American audience. This belief that western powers can create a more just and 'democratic' world, though, is - for Blair at least - far too closely bound up with confidence in the transforming power of globalising modernity, the West's child. It is significant that a major ideological guru of Blair's is Anthony Giddens (whose ideas we look at in chapter one), for whom one aspect of modernity is that 'there are no "others"'. Even more problematic has been Blair's seemingly uncritical collaboration with the Bush regime's faith in aggressive military solutions. Act vigorously enough and evil regimes can be removed, unacceptable ills cured and the world made whole. There is the compulsion of a kind of messianic optimism, a moralising idealism, and a seemingly absolute confidence in the rightness of his cause (Naughtie 2004). All this is integral to what is essentially a shared *global missionary vision* that is a potent mix of naïve faith, imperialist militarism, and of course the crucial need for oil. The US/UK collaborative project to transform, by 'shock and awe', the Middle East's Muslim lands into their own 'democratic' image is more than a casual co-incidence.

Religion-based Identities

As expressive of religious faith, then, that apocalyptically violent act of 9/11, pregnant with symbolism though it may have been, veiled as much as it revealed. Some very confusing questions remain. What precisely *is* the role of religion in the various global conflicts of our time? What dynamics are at work when *religious* loyalties are at stake? Are ethical and humane considerations inevitably diminished when religious loyalty is primary? Is violence perhaps endemic to religious faith? Or is the key issue here the differing ways by which incipient violence is transmuted in religion? How is

Power perceived? And there are many more questions that will emerge as this book proceeds.

Religious identities - the way people are grouped and identified religiously - sometimes bear little resemblance to people's actual loyalties. As we shall see, though, events can sharpen these false identities, perhaps even give them credibility. Powerfully symbolic events, like ancient corporate memories, not only *unite*, they also *polarise* people.

Inevitably the corporate psyche of Muslims is still, through the long memory of stories told and retold, indelibly scarred by the brutal and relentless massacres of those *Christian crusades* in the early centuries of the second millennium. The crusaders, as 'cross-bearers', so grotesquely skewed the meaning of the death of Christ, that the soul both of Christendom and of the Muslim world was for ever scarred by those horrendous centuries. Repeated assurances (with the occasional Freudian slip) by western leaders that their post 9/11 invasions of Muslim countries are not part of an anti-Muslim crusade, have done little to allay Muslim fears of a global Christian conspiracy to destroy Islam.

The amazing spread of Islam has not been quite so dependent on the sword as earlier historians led us to believe. In India large numbers were converted to Islam by the charismatic preaching and impressive spirituality of Sufi preachers. Yet, as in Christian missionary history, all too often Muslim preachers - whatever their desire for genuinely spiritual engagement - were followed or even preceded by military back-up, and by their country's traders. In that religious and political power was in varying degrees both distinct and mutually dependent, the pattern of Muslim global mission was not completely dissimilar to that of European colonisers in later centuries, the Portuguese in particular. The conquest of faith was important for Muslim and Catholic colonisers, though both could benefit too from the spoils of conquest.

With the British - increasingly industrialised and with an insatiable commercial appetite by the mid-nineteenth century - exploitation of natural resources was more clearly and exclusively the imperialist goal. Muslim conquest was never impelled quite so directly, though commerce was crucial. So, the relationship of religious and political power, of sacred and secular mission, in those later conquests by

European powers became ever more discrete, even if the institutions of faith were still manipulated to legitimise political conquest.

On all sides of the Christian-Muslim-Hindu(-Sikh) divides, then, there are deeply embedded memories of almost pathological virulence. Corporate memory, mythically framed, is a potent factor in community faith and identity. Its dynamic can be both enhancing and damaging. And how faith deals with these and similarly negative corporate memories is surely a key issue in the shaping of human identities?

Today, however, the anti-Muslim crusade Muslims fear globally is a double-edged threat. There is now, they believe, militant *secularist faith* too seeking their destruction. If anti-Muslim intent on the part of secularised 'Christian' westernism and its globalising policies was a common Muslim assumption before 9/11, the aggression since then has made that fear far more inclusive, far more intense. Before the US/UK action in Iraq 'moderate' Muslim allies of western nations, those least friendly to extremist forms of Islam, voiced their fears that such action would spawn countless 'new bin Ladens', young men who will offer themselves to be glorious *fedayin*, 'counter-terrorists' in a *jihad* against the enemy that seeks to destroy their people and their faith. By mid-2004 their predictions were shown to be all too true. The revelations about nauseatingly inhuman treatment of prisoners at the Abu Ghraib jail, the attacks in 2004 on the Shia's holy city of Najaf - to destroy Moqtada al-Sadr's hardline resistance – and the even more violent attack on Sunni Fallujah, have further intensified and polarised Muslim and global feeling. Equally tragic is the intensifying animosity between Iraqi Shia and Sunni in their differing responses to the invasion and to the coalition-led election of January 2005. It is now the belief of many quite moderate Muslims, as of many non-Muslims worldwide, that the Bush regime has led America into being among the most dangerous of the 'rogue states' they have targetted.

America's inner cabinet of political leaders have rarely been so avowedly 'Christian' as the administration of George W. Bush, certainly rarely so committed to the 'vision thing' his father declared to be beyond him. In a crucial speech in June 2002 on his 'vision' for the future of Israel and Palestine, Bush the younger echoed the word spoken by God in Jewish-Christian scripture: 'I have set before you the way of life and of death: choose life', blithely assuming that there is the exalted status of divine sanction in his administration's account of what must be done if people in a far-off country are to live. Similar echoes of divine demands for absolute loyalty are heard in the words of his first major address to the nation following 9/11: 'Either you are with us, or you are with the terrorists'. Equally filled with faith-based allusions hinting both at a great divide and an imagined togetherness, was the inaugural speech as Bush began his second presidential term in January 2005. Here are all the seeds we need for a radical polarising of identities.

Dividing the world into people of the light and those belonging to darkness is a quite typical religious stance. It is how this mythic view is then interpreted that matters. In the case of a number in the Bush team, the evidence points to a simplist apocalyptic worldview with directly political and military forms of expression. Most compelling may well be underlying commercial interests. In any case, for a key section of the 'neo-cons' a faith-based worldview reinforces and directly nurtures the assumptions they hold both about the need for a dominant US role in global affairs and in particular about the legitimacy of military action in the Middle East. The enemy has been identified as a wide-ranging 'axis of evil' made up almost exclusively of Muslim countries, especially Iraq and Iran. Having become victims of that evil, the United States' government now believes it can unilaterally decide where and when the battle lines are to be drawn globally.

And so, faith-led, there has been a sharp shift by the American Right from its earlier global isolationism to its present aggressive policy of taking preemptive strikes even where it thinks a threat may develop. It does not matter that no Weapons of Mass Destruction (owned in abundance by the US and other privileged nations) were found in Iraq: there were thinking about acquiring them! This new global strategy is based on the absolutes of unilateralist certainty, and demands an identity of absolute patriotic loyalty. Religious convictions concerning a special national destiny certainly serve to reinforce this policy.

This stance by the world's superpower, in its sense of global destiny, its demand for absolute loyalty in its quest for global control, its terrifying violence, its veiling and revealing, its threat of the destruction of an 'axis of evil', is seen by many in more apocalyptic terms even than al-Qaida's destruction of the twin towers. Moreover, it seeks by self-reference to define our identities for us. Tragically and cruelly ignoring the ever-widening inequalities of wealth distribution and resource consumption, it divides the world into clear and very simple camps: those who threaten the 'free' world with terrorism, and those who join in the all-demanding battle against terrorists, a battle to be fought by every conceivable means, including the curtailing of freedoms, the leverage of massive strategic dollar deals, and the unrestrained use of maximum and unwavering fire-power.

Those not gripped by such apocalyptic certainties begin to see this 'anti-terrorist war', with its global display of military power, as just as much its *cause* of terrorism rather than its *cure*. To those for whom both faith and reason teach that war resolves very little, unbridled bomb-power seems just as dangerous to the world's future wellbeing as is the 'terrorism' it purports to be fighting against. Certainly the resultant hardening of polarised identities, within nations, between 'civilisations', has created an incalculable danger. If the aim of al-Qaida's 9/11 act was to provoke violent American retaliation against targetted Muslim regions, thus to unify Islamic global feelings against Jewish-Christian America, in particular on the grounds that there is a global Jewish-Christian conspiracy to destroy the Muslim religion, that act has been highly successful.

Religion's Ambivalence & the Need for Deeper Probing

So, then, what has resulted from the dramatic collapse of those towering walls of the World Trade Centre has been the further strengthening of the 'walls' of dangerously stark and simplistic identities marking the boundaries of who we are and who our 'enemies' are. On each side now are dangerously high numbers of people who see the conflict in terms of 'war' against 'evil forces of barbarism and terror'. Even four years later, throughout middle America, in part manipulated by devious but clever electioneering rhetoric, and so feeling threatened by secularist threat – the enemy within - to cherished 'moral values', as well as the stoked-up fear of alien ('terrorist') attack, the divide widened.

And yet, this is far from the whole story. We have already noted the deep divisions even within American attitudes, religious and secular.

Globally too faith-based traditions are not all divided along their given faith-identities. Hans Ucko writes as editor of an issue of *Current Dialogue* reporting a post-September eleven consultation on 'Religion and Violence' by representatives from various religions (No.39, June 2002, p.4):

> September 11 is a challenge to all religious traditions and not only to Islam....Following
> September 11, there have been powerful demonstrations of people of all faiths coming
> together to manifest solidarity between people of different faiths, to do whatever could be
> done to make sure that the definition of religion is not violence and hatred. Jews,
> Christians and Muslims came together, in and outside the US, showing that they wanted to
> hold on to each other; they wanted to strengthen each other in mutual support.

This is certainly not typical of all strands of Christianity, Islam, Hinduism, or Judaism, but it is a significant strand.

Throughout Muslim, Christian and Hindu worlds, then, we find *polarised positions* that range wide and are fiercely held. These differing faith-positions, differences in the interpretation of faith, lead equally sincere believers within the same tradition to contrasting global stances. America, in India and in the Muslim world, convictions about their nation's position in the world in very different directions. An identity shaped by the transcending element of faith *compels some to a self-critical stance that counters political power* and questions its commercial compulsions. For others, a *faith-based identity demands the certitude of simplicities, and the simplicity of self-certainty*.

The ambivalent role of religion, then - in the conflicts between Israel and the Palestinians, between Serbs, Croats and Muslims in the Balkans, between Pakistan and India, between Sinhalas and Tamils in Sri Lanka, or the confrontations in Northern Ireland, Chechnya, Somalia, the Philippines and in Indonesia – the ambivalent role of religious faith in the shaping of political posturings and community identities is one that calls for much more rigorous examination. And faith's role in shaping human identities is the question that looms large in the chapters which follow.

There are, of course, many complicating factors in this clash of identities and interests. National and ethnic loyalties, commercial interests (the role of oil in particular), the possible acquiring and possession of nuclear weapons, are among them. The further spread, sooner or later, of these most powerful means of 'shock and awe', and a consequent change in power-balancing, is inevitable. An apocalyptic response then could so easily precipitate Apocalypse Now. But above all are the potentially explosive feelings of a threatened corporate identity. And for Muslims, at the centre of the polarising of identities is the Israel-Palestine conflict, located in a land held to be 'Holy' by three religious traditions Jewish, Christian, Muslim.

The link of polarised identities and potential nuclear warfare is already part of the equation. This means that the unfolding of the future in part will depend on what happens in religio-political dynamics in Pakistan, in India, and thus on subsequent relations between these two sharply polarised nations. For both possess nuclear weapons that have been labelled, by militants on both sides, 'Hindu' and 'Muslim' bombs. Yet, pragmatic re-consideration by governments on both sides led to a change of rhetoric. From mid-2003, and again in 2004, talk has been heard of the urgent need for mutual compromise and for peaceful settling of the Kashmir dispute. The outcome of peace-talks remains to be seen.

In any case, events far beyond the borders of India and Pakistan are bound up with the persistent struggles within the Subcontinent. Polarised national self-identities there had become dangerously dependent on hatred of each other, with Pakistan's Islamic orientation and India's newly militant Hindutva the grounding focal points of that enmity. Delineating opposing identities of ally and alien, friend and enemy, had rarely been made so starkly, especially given that the complex ethnicities of both sides share so much. The need to probe deeper into faith's role in the shaping of our human identities has rarely been more crucial.

Part I : The Dynamics Of Religion & Identity

Chapter 1
Self-Identities, Sacred Identities

(1) The Shaping of Human Identities

Long before those fateful September attacks in the United States, 'identity' had become a key category for defining our human self-understanding. 'Fuelled by political struggles as well (as) by philosophical and linguistic concerns, "identity" emerged as the central theme of cultural studies in the 1990s' (Barker 2000: 165). We have here, then, the interpretive key for a very wide range of discourse. This inevitably means that emphases differ widely as to what constitutes 'identity', and there is even greater divergence about what is *desirable* as the basis of such core-identities. But there are some simply expressed dominant themes - that we will need to return to in various contexts later.

(a) 'Identity' refers most basically to human experience of *who we are* and where we *belong*. It is about being identified with, as well as aligning ourselves with, a distinctive way of life and the people who share the values of that way of life. What is worn, how hair is styled, ways of speech, forms of greeting, bodily gestures, as well as what we eat and drink, our moral attitudes and social relationships - all mark us out as belonging to a particular kind of people. This reference to others, to relationships, still has to be a primary factor, in spite of the growing complexity of such corporate alignments, and the tendency in modern culture to individualise, to be more concerned about 'my self-identity', and often to be deeply confused about our corporate identities.

(b) Secondly, affirming a common identity entails some degree of *contrast with others*. As the term implies, 'identity' intends some form of unitive integration. But the paradox is that identity, whatever our intentions, always entails some form of differentiation. In making

33

clear who we are and where we belong, we implicitly set ourselves in some measure over against others who are different. Alignment inevitably creates some kind of alienation.

(c) Then, the greater the perceived *crisis* at the point when identities are forged and affirmed, the more marked the contrast. In response to the attack by a small group of militants on 9/11 (11 Sept 01), the American President and others in his administration immediately used language that intensified the sense of contrast between 'our people', 'our democratic freedom', 'our good and civilised values', and 'the evil of the enemy'. That enemy was broadened to include all possible supporters of the al-Qaida terrorist network, a wide 'axis of evil', demonised as barbaric forces of hatred and oppression, against whom there was now to be unrelenting war. Such polarising, even demonising too, is often found when identities are shaped or re-shaped at critical points of our histories.

(d) Fourthly, *symbolism* will invariably be prominent in the affirming of identities - ethnic, national, certainly religious, or those based on class, gender, eco-vision, and many more. The role of the flag, for example, is central in the strengthening of nationalist identities. So, we saw fervent corporate devotion to the Stars and Stripes ('Old Glory') at the time of the 9/11 crisis and as part of the re-affirmation of American identity. In those primal cultures that are totemic, the community's identity shares inseparably in the life of the totemic emblem, often an animal or natural object with which the life potency of the tribe or clan is identified. Along with symbols, of course, various forms of ritual and other re-presentative performance have been essential to the process of identity-shaping. Symbols are both expressive and impressive. They both represent and re-affirm, they sharpen a distinct sense of who we are.

(e) The *body* is given primary, paradigmatic significance in identity-shaping, because of its central place in the materiality of human existence, its relational significance, its role as a boundary to the self, its function in expressing identity through dress, ornament, hair-style and body-marks. The growing fashion throughout modernised society of tattoo-marks and rings in every possible part of the body, though intended to mark out very personal self-identity, is astonishingly similar in principle to the shared customs of many tribal communities. The body has again become a very open point of differentiation. Naturally, the meaning of the body has been explored by feminists, eco-visionaries, and perhaps especially those who wish to distance themselves from the mind-centred humanness typical of western Enlightenment attitudes revealed in such identity-statements as that of Rene Descartes (1596-1650), 'I think, therefore I am'. It was this trans-corporal exalting of the mind far above the body and nature generally that laid the foundation of the early-modern philosophy of science that late-modernity challenges in various ways (on body and self-actualisation, Giddens 1991: 56-63, 99-107).

(f) Whether to see identity primarily in *personal* or in *relational* terms - or in terms of the dynamic created between these two poles of experience - is a major divide in the identity debate. In numerous writings on identity issues, culminating in her recent *Understanding Identity*, Kath Woodward highlights this tension (Woodward 2002). The social and political theorist Anthony Giddens' very influential *Modernity and Self-Identity* (re-issued almost every year since 1991) assumes a far more easy resolving of any such tension. In analysing what is normative in modern perceptions of our humanness, Giddens gives such weight to the individual's self-constructed, very personal identity, that the corporate dimension of that process ('life-politics') seems merely tacked on rather than implicit. Giddens obviously *intends* social engagement, relationality, to be intrinsic to the 'reflexive' life of the self in its identity-shaping, with our modern global context now innate to consciousness. But individuality dominates the picture, and the impact of globalist powers is strangely ignored. Others, such as Jorge Larrain (Larrain 1994), go much further than Woodward in giving priority to this corporate dimension, and also recognise the squeeze of global forces. In any case, without extreme distortion of human realities it is impossible not to conclude that 'identity is relational' (Woodward 2002: xii).

We shall look later at Erik Erikson's analysis of identity-formation within the human psyche. Here we note that though psychology is his field, and therefore it is the individual psyche that is of primary concern, the corporate dimension is crucial. Identity is 'a process located in the core of the individual and yet also in the core of his communal culture' (Erikson 1951).

(g) Within 'late modernist' perceptions of self-identity, there is a prominent role for the *narrative* each is to construct if there is to be meaning for life. We need a sense of where we have come from and what the destiny of our particular history is to be. It is in the creating of this life-story that, at least within the ethos of late modernity, it is believed each can 'control' events. Our 'myths' define who we are and determine what we will become. Thus the self is thought to become an agent in the historical process rather than merely swept along by it. To the extent that we 'construct ourselves', it is believed that we are liberated, autonomous selves. Subjectivity is truth; objectivity highly suspect.

Existentialists such as the 'melancholy Dane' Soren Kierkegaard (1813-1855) have clearly made their mark on this 'late modernist' way of seeing things, though Kierkegaard's intraverted self-doubt has been left far behind. Perhaps as a more direct antecedent we should point to Friedrich Nietzsche (1844-1900, another child of devout Lutheran Christian parents) and his emphasis on the will - rather than reason or sentiment - the will to 'become what we are', to move beyond the herd instinct and onto the level of 'superman', doing away with (the Christian) appeal to self-denying meekness and instead developing the 'will to power' (Nietzsche 1979).

Nor should the impact of much earlier Indian thought be forgotten - on nineteenth century European Idealism for example. Become what in reality we already are, or 'as we act, so we become', the self thus creating its own destiny - these are central themes in Hindu Vedantic spirituality. The 'idealist' strand goes further though. Sankara , in the eighth century, became the Hindu community's leading philosopher of a non-dualist worldview. Influenced by late Buddhist views that reality is to be understood at two levels, that at its centre is the mystery of Emptiness, and even that the perceived world is the creation of the perceiving person, Sankara introduced his most systematic interpretation of the Vedic tradition (his commentary on the Vedanta-Sutras, or Brahma-Sutra-Bhashya) by stating that Subject and Object, in the ancient Vedic vision, are 'as unlike as light and darkness'. The inner self becomes the cosmic Self, all is found within the One.

So, then, there are striking, though very differently framed, precedents for the late modernist emphasis on subjectivity, on creating our own story, even our own reality. The process of creating our own life-story is seen as one of ever-changing fluidity and of tradition-breaking iconoclasm. Like the Buddha (though certainly not the Hindu Vedantins) late-modernity sees *no enduring core of selfhood* as the basis for true identity. A uniquely existential self is created and continually re-created. Clearly, religious concerns overlap strikingly at various points here, but diverge as much as converge, as with other positions in this introductory list.

(h) Then, even when the emphasis is on a corporate rather than individualist self-identity, late-modernity increasingly assumes that all our identities are *invented* and, if necessary, *re-invented*. Distinctions of nationality, of race, of religion and other group-affiliations are all created as a result of political and cultural dynamics. Consequently, they can have only relative never absolute status. This can create a fundamental clash between a modern secularist and a religious worldview, especially when religious faith is believed to be based on divine authority. But other group-loyalties too - especially right-wing nationalism - often clash with relativists for whom the nation has merely been 'invented'. And religion's contrast with late-modernism is not quite so clearcut, as we shall see in a moment.

(i) In speaking of the 'tensions' involved in identity-shaping, or of alignment leading to alienation, we find also the frequent encounter between an *inner, special group* and *larger human communities*. Such an exclusivist attitude by an enclave with a highly developed sense of being different, having a chosen destiny, can be specially characteristic of a religion-based identity. But it is often found in other kinds of groups too - from artists and poets to extreme political activists. In fact in many arenas of political struggle - including politics of gender and globalisation, as well as ethnic and nationalist movements - 'identity-politics' have given urgency to people's felt need for empowerment, their need to strengthen a sense of shared roots, shared destinies, shared revolutions, shared self-determining.

(j) Even so, much of the language of 'identity' has evolved within the less activist disciplines of philosophy and psychology, as well as sociology. And this to some extent explains the tension within our understanding of what 'identity' means. In particular, as psychological theory and practice have filtered through to popular culture in the West, the counselling profession has become the new pastoral priesthood. Here concerns are largely attuned to the emotional needs of the *individual,* perhaps traumatised by the childhood repressions of which Sigmund Freud spoke, perhaps bewildered by the rapid fragmentation of accustomed communities and their replacement by ever-changing new groupings, new loyalties. Personal self-identity is perceived as in crisis. Even recognising this social milieu as the arena within which a person struggles, the focus remains clear.

And when the focus is on the individual psyche and its needs, 'identity' primarily has to do with a well integrated personal ego, a strong sense of individual subjecthood and of continuity within one's own self-being. Integration is then to be seen as adapting to the pressures of society in the most comfortable possible way, the ability to retain a secure inner selfhood while having to live out numerous very different roles. No doubt there are still those 'roles' we have to play as given by others and by life's circumstances. Whether understood as self-created or not, my 'real identity', it is believed, is that inner core of selfhood able to retain its integrity in spite of the pressures of modernity's ever-accelerating pace of change. An inner self-identity remains, unfractured by the demands of the many new roles of life today. Here the sustaining narrative is concerned primarily with ego-boosting. There is the strange anomaly that in 'cultural studies', with their strongly postmodernist assumptions, and even in the writings of sociologists, while rank individualism may be rejected, in the struggle between the personal and social dimensions of humanness our selfhood is rarely seen in terms of the binding relationships of community, or as innately embedded in corporate contexts. Perhaps the ghost of Karl Marx still frightens western liberal secularists.

(2) Modernity, Religion & Identity

We can now look more closely at Anthony Giddens' outstandingly popular account of how modernity aspires to self-identity. Here we have a clear example of how the individual, at least at the perceptual level, is able to take centre stage in a secular world. Giddens was for some time Director of the London School of Economics, an institution renowned a generation ago for many of its teachers' uncompromising leftwing stance on socio-economic matters. Among other things he has also been a socio-political 'guru' to Britain's Prime Minister Tony

Blair. Other writings in Giddens' prolific output should no doubt also be taken into account (in particular his *The Consequence of Modernity*, 1990), but it is in *Modernity and Self-Identity* that we have the most full treatment of the meaning of self-identity in what he calls 'high' or 'late' modernity. (The term '*post*modern' is restricted to more esoteric post-structuralist cultural critique in the arts and literature). Late modernity's essential dynamics are seen as undercutting all tradition, and as having global impact in ways quite foreign to the traditions of pre-modernity, including religion. Rejecting those earlier interpretations that saw the innate structures of human life continuing through new configurations, Giddens sees modernity as essentially discontinuous with the past.

Giddens at least begins by affirming the importance of corporate life - even modernity has to be 'understood on an institutional level'. And he ends with a chapter on 'life-politics'. Society and its structures, after all, can hardly fail to be of primary concern to a social and political theorist. It is the *individual's personal life*, though, that in the greater part of this book is central, echoing accurately a late-modern view of things. Such individualism is of necessity 'interlaced' with the 'transmutations' effected in our social being by the modernising process. Indeed, modernity is at its heart characterised by the dialectic of two 'increasing interconnections'- 'globalising influences on the one hand and personal dispositions on the other' (Giddens 1991:1).

'Globalising influences', though, are very different from trends that might make for a human identity innately dependent on human togetherness, on that common sense of community and fraternal solidarity which can reach a global scale. Giddens' analysis of the intrinsic marks of modernity, especially in chapters delineating the 'self' in our human self-identity, suggests a movement towards ever greater focus on *personal emancipation* from the bonds imposed by corporate life and the structures necessary for embodying this. The *individual*'s freedom has become the all-important goal - freedom to create a personal life-agenda, to break through all inhibiting boundaries that past tradition may set to self-liberation. Modern communications have even removed the old boundaries of time and space. *Any* place now can become 'phantasmagoric', as influences from far off penetrate and reconfigure how life is experienced in that place.

Modernity's defining aim is the cultivating of individual control of the future, the creating of a personal history of increasing self-emancipation. Globalisation is in effect what results from this modernising process. Thus, personal and local self-determination, with reflexive relationships built into this, become transformed into the global according to Giddens. This means that personal reflexivity and globalisation are virtually equivalent concepts.

Critics of Giddens

There have, rightly, been critics of Gidden's rather rosy view of the globalising process – as being of a piece with late-modernity, and including the break with past tradition and the dominance of individual choice. The new globalists are in reality not just people helping us to break with ancient taboos and work out new and liberating life-narratives. More sinister forces are at work too. A closer and more critical approach to the process is attempted below in the chapter on globalisation.

Here we note very briefly that more radical critics of the globalising process, such as John Tomlinson in *Globalisation and Culture* (1999), see as far more problematic the way this process 'annihilates' space and time, making both the distinctive location of peoples and their distinctive histories no longer significant dimensions of their lives. The 'glocalisation' of which 'new internationalist' and one-world ideologues may speak is impossible within a global life where the local is so obliterated. When it is the globalising outreach of very powerful economic and political institutions over which local life has no control, when those alien power-bases begin to control how communities and individuals see the world and their place in it, and when these global forces are still largely West-based (even if no longer overtly 'imperialist'), in what sense is there still any meaningful 'reflexivity' of relationship – between local and global, between individual and institution? We certainly, then, have to question if Giddens is correct in arguing that such 'reflexivity' - in the dynamics of modernity - though initiated by the West, makes for the 'evaporating of the privileged position of the West' (1991: 53). It is just not possible for a movement so thoroughly western in its origins and essential power-bases to be the means of liberating all 'others' from the dominance of western influence, so that there no longer are any 'others'? As we noted earlier, Giddens actually contends that in modernity 'there are no "others"' (1991: 175).

It is within this framework that we have to set Giddens' account of the 'modern' person's search for freedom from the bonds of the past and the accompanying concern for the elimination of *risk*, or rather a satisfactory dealing with risk. He acknowledges that new dangers are in fact created by the modernising process, especially dangers to the environment. 'Modernity is a risk culture' (1991: 3). Nor is the elimination of doubt an option, for choosing between various options and the doubt this necessarily entails, is crucial to life today. *Trust*, including trust of others, becomes a necessity.

Thus there is for Giddens, as we saw, a *self-reflexive* interacting process of change continually at work, making the self's active participation in these changes the key to things. Nothing is fully determined from outside the individual. With the individual as the primary unit, this interacting process is taken somehow to be the basis for a new global order, an all-embracing human interconnectedness. By way of undergirding support for his thesis, Giddens refers almost entirely to psychology and personal therapy, and to existentialist philosophers, rather than to more community-conscious, let alone more radically socialist, sources. Relationality, mutuality, in its ever-widening scope, is in reality not at the centre of the modernity he expounds.

Strangely, this account of a key strand of modern life is at points akin to assumptions in the spiritualities developed within a number of mainstream religions, as we shall see especially in relation to Hindu and Buddhist 'high' traditions. Important differences remain, though, as we shall see.

Giddens' analysis is in many ways brilliantly accurate of key features of 'late' modernity. Little wonder, though, that other responses to this process, such as those by Richard Sennet and Christopher Lasch, have been deeply critical of modernity as being thoroughly 'narcissistic', with a self-absorbed love of personal being - the 'me, me, me' view of the world - that in the end becomes self-destructive of what it is to be a post-infantile human (Sennett 1977, Lasch 1980). Giddens is no doubt correct in finding any such gloomy and sweepingly negative critique too onesided. There is more to modernity than any single focus. To disregard the plurality is to distort the wider picture and miss the truth. Yet, it is impossible not to conclude that in this account of self-identity in modernity, those like Giddens who emphasise the benefits of our globalist present have been *over-complacent* regarding its dangers both to human community, and thus to personal being.

Another critical point arises precisely when we refer to the fact of *plurality* in the world. Roland Robertson among others quickly responded to Giddens along these lines (Robertson 1992). However, it is not easy to understand Robertson's contention that the problem of the 'Other' arises only in a globalised world, even if modern globalisation is responsible for the peculiar sense of threat to their identities widely felt by communities today. Feelings of threat from and hatred of other groups, though, are very ancient.

Can we remain complacent, let alone triumphalist, about the prospect of modernity's conquest of our amazingly varied human traditions, religions and cultures, all becoming pervaded and eventually replaced by modernity's homogeneity? As we noted, in modernity 'there are no "others" ', which can simply mean that all are expected to be as we are. Or, if the process of 'reflexivity', by which people incorporate modernity's new vision and respond to its dynamic, is conceived as itself characterised by amazing diversity, does the modernist viewpoint seriously reckon with the quite radically *divergent* perspectives involved? Can the late-modernist allow room for a perspective in which the goal of each individual's self-narrative and personal control of the future can never be the dominant feature? If not, is the modernising process not just a new cultural imperialism, a more subtle continuation of the old?

When a culture's focus is on community, 'identity' has more to do with a strong sense of *belonging*, of being well integrated into and a significant sharer in wider corporate life. The sustaining narrative draws in the journey, with all its 'imagined' history, of a wider community in which the self is a participant pilgrim. Then, the boundaries set by various kinds of kinship, and our sharing in the binding life of a community acquire the highest value. This may well mean seeing that community's place, its history, its traditions and culture, as sacred and inviolate - though, as we shall see, the dynamic of reconfiguring change, however slow and hidden, has also in reality been characteristic of all cultures, all religious traditions.

Identity-talk, then, can refer to either of these two poles of our humanness: personal self-identity or corporate social identity.

Counter-Movements to Dis-Location

It is not only our earlier community boundaries, the boundaries of sacred time and place, that disappear in late-modernist culture. All sense of belonging to a particular place, with all its grounding potencies, have been broken by modernity's rapidly increased mobility and speed of travel. We move so fast, earlier gods are left behind. There is an inevitable dis-location of peoples and their cultures as aggressive globalisation, with its powerful economic pressures, impinges ever further upon people's consciousness. Everywhere, indigenous people's sense of belonging to a common sacred history, their sense of a cohering self-identity is threatened - though far from utterly lost.

For there have been, and still are, significant *counter movements* to this process. Some diasporic communities have been determined to protect their particular history, and keep the boundaries clearly visible. In the case, for example, of traditional Jewish communities not only are there the metaphorical boundaries set up by the requirements of *kosher* purity. It can also entail the literal erection of the *eruv* boundary (involving a light wire affixed to poles where a natural boundary will not suffice) in the midst of modern city life. Its specific purpose has been to enable infants, aged and disabled people to be taken to Synagogue without contravening the boundaries set to Sabbath activity. Other ethnic groups, feeling the threat of alien incursion, have vigorously, even violently, asserted the sacred worth of the land and blood to which they belong, often engaging in forms of 'ethnic cleansing'. Ethnic identities have sometimes been viciously exclusive, as Jewish people have especially experienced through the ages. How tragically ironic that it is this community that has now caused the dislocating exclusion of Palestinian people!

In India, while increased mobility across that widespread and strikingly diverse country may have modified many local traditions and the identities these have engendered, other-resistant boundaries of language, caste, tribe, and religious community still stand firmly fixed. At the same time, there is the culturally resurgent and politically sinister phenomenon of an intensified sense of 'Hindu' identity (see chapter 14 below) - in distorted ways corresponding to 'Christian' and 'Muslim' globally inclusive identities - that in part was created precisely by the recently increased middleclass mobility, enabling people to visit sacred places throughout the land, and so feel they belong to this wider sacred world. But there are other dynamics at work too in this process of remaking boundaries, as we shall see later.

Rhetoric & Reality in Modern Secularism

So, then, religious communities have struggled in a variety of ways to keep their faith: perhaps in what they have seen as its most pure and therefore most distinct form, or perhaps in its most pertinent and so more accommodative form. In spite of modern liberal society's rhetoric of 'cultural pluralism', more often the reality has been that distinctive traditions are expected to be absorbed within a subtly but relentlessly monolithic secular liberal framework in which all boundaries disappear. And hardline secularists have actively worked to weaken any faith-based identities.

Much opposition to faith-schools in Britain, for instance, takes it for granted that education grounded in any way in a distinctive religious tradition can never be other than harmful to the health of wider human society. France's anti-headscarf (*hijab*) legislation in 2004, making illegal the wearing of the head-scarf by Muslim girls at state schools seems almost unbelievable to multi-culturalists, religious or secular. It is, though, a glaring example of the exclusiveness and intolerance of a certain kind of secularism. That other obvious forms of religious affiliation were outlawed in the same legislation is of little import. An overtly Muslim identity was the target. This, the French form of secularism believes, makes wider belonging, an inclusive French identity, impossible. At the other extreme, there have been forms of fascist political control offering a 'cultural pluralism' that is merely the separateness of *apartheid*, with its all too clear marking off of difference and identity.

We have already seen that a key strand in modern secularism urges us to forget all these narrow boundaries created by conditioning from the past and to see either the 'individual person' or perhaps our 'common humanity' as primary categories for self-understanding. Giddens makes no reference to G.W.F.Hegel (1770-1831). Yet it was he, according to the powerful leftwing ideologue J. Habermas (Oberoi in Marty Vol.5, 102-109), who 'inaugurated the discourse of modernity', finding individualism to be modernity's primary value. Subjective freedom, the right to criticism of all tradition, each person's responsibility for their own actions, and the ability to know one's own identity without reference to given roles grounded in religion - these, argued Hegel, comprise the very 'dialectic of enlightenment'.

There is, though, a sad irony here. While weakening the sense of shared community being, key institutions of modern life - for example, increasingly powerful global corporatism, state militarism and the skewed forms of 'democracy' these engender - for all their rhetoric of 'individual choice', in reality allow less and less significance to the individual. Again, in spite of neo-liberal rhetoric, is not modern Corporatism and its growing global power closely akin to the Communism of Lenin/Stalin? Now, though, the value and status of the individual is subservient, not to the state, but more subtly to the corporation as a profit-making body. Yet, such is directorial power that even accountability by corporation bosses to the shareholders often seems non-existent. Hugely inflated self-awarded rises in salary are normal. When things go wrong - near bankruptcy, loss of participants' pensions, even unlawful dealing - the usual response seems to be a massive golden handshake for the concerned managing director, and the humble share-holder is left victimised. But the huge number of the world's people who hold no share, no stakehold, in any company at all remain powerless, as the divide between affluence and poverty actually increases, locally and globally.

From both sides - that of religious and secularist faiths - the struggle for a sense of identity, both personal and corporate, becomes more intense. So, on the one hand a prominent (but certainly not the only) strand of the secularist world becomes increasingly self-absorbed and oriented to the satisfying of the ego's demands - its demands for instant pleasure, for increasingly intense sensory excitement, for endlessly changing consumer goods. And self-identity can then become increasingly dependent upon such ego-feeding. On the other hand, anti-secularist traditions by way of reaction often become more and more isolated, turning in on themselves and making the resources of the tradition so absolute that self-identity becomes one with that tightly bounded community's identity. Selfhood becomes entirely dependent upon belonging to the special group. And in both extremes the necessary dialectic between personal self-identity and corporate self-identity is lost.

(3) Breaking the Boundaries in Religion

There is, then, a two-sidedness *intrinsic to religious faith* in the way each relates to the boundaries referred to above, boundaries of place, of time, of people. With each kind of boundary in faith-worlds there is both a building up and a breaking down. Sacred places, with their special restoring potencies, loom large in all faith-traditions. Often this has led to the land itself, a whole country, becoming sacrally potent for those of the tradition. Yet, pilgrimage to the sacred place involves too a breaking away from any static view of belonging. The movement from home to sacred place of pilgrimage entails a weakening and a re-visioning of the foundations of the everyday place of living and working - made clear in the articles on 'Pilgrimage' and 'Shrine' in Eliade's *Encyclopedia of Religion* (1987, 1995). The pilgrim, then, is a kind of temporary holy wanderer. So, the next step is the embracing of permament impermanence, either as a wanderer who transcends all boundaries, or as a monk confined by very different boundaries of place, as well as of community.

It is a similar case with the boundaries of time, and the special history and culture this engenders for a community. Normally, in traditional societies, inherited norms - language, life-style, and especially stories of sacrifice on the part of the ancestors - all are seen as integral to the sacred tradition. Yet, within religion itself there will often also be moves pushing heroic souls beyond such cultural boundedness. In this way the boundary-breaking of modernity and religious faith do strangely coincide at some points.

For one thing, religious faith, visionary faith, can prove very counter-cultural. It has often led people to resist the identity imposed upon them by the dominant group, and to say 'No, we refuse to accept the mould you wish to shape us in. We are not who you say we are, or should be. Our identity is different'. Communities of Dalits, *bhaktas* such as Kabir, non-conformist Christians, Muslims resisting the pressures to conform to modern secularism - these and numerous others too are examples (in the following pages) of counter-cultural resistance.

Affirming a faith and an identity that refuses to conform may well lead to accusations of madness, certainly of fanaticism. Accusing non-conformist deviants of being 'mad' when there are ways of thinking and acting that are not thought normal, acceptable, rational, tell us much about expectations of human identity. Here the polarising of perceptions becomes extreme. Of course, people mourning the loss of an earlier life-style and its traditions may well speak of the 'madness' of modernity and its changes. But it is when people are radical visionaries, religious in new and non-conformist ways that they have appeared utterly 'mad' to those not part of such a faith. Jesus was thought to have become mad even by his own family as well as by his detractors. Muhammad wondered whether perhaps he was becoming mad, until his faithful wife, some years older than himself, and other friends reassured him. Mystics and ecstatics, in both religions have been considered insane. Shamanism and spirit-possession in primal faiths are perhaps the most obvious instances of abnormal states of identity-experience. They may well take on a different persona, their very self-identity changes.

It is, though, among *Hindu* holy men that we find the most prolific and pronounced instances of divine 'madness' (Kinsley 1973; McDaniel 1989). A wide range of literature could be quoted here, relating to devotees of Krishna, of Siva and especially of the female deity Kali. There have been the Rajput princess Mirabai, the usually quite down-to-earth Maratha-speaking Tukaram, in Tamilnadu the Saiva Nambi Aruvar and the Vishnu-devotee Peyalvar ('drowned in madness?'). In Bengal there was the Krishna-lover Chaitanya as well as the Mother Kali-possessed Ramprasad and the more famous Ramakrishna. These and many more speak of their love-intoxication, their wild dancing, their laughing and weeping, their madly uninhibited behaviour. It is, though, the outrageous manner and actions of the deities themselves, and devotees' identifying with this, that lie behind the 'madness' of believers.

Just one quotation, from the 19th century Bengali Ramprasad, especially significant in that he and Ramakrishna had at least some exposure to western views of what was acceptable as proper and reasonable religion.

> Make me mad, O divine Mother...
> Make me drunk with the wine of your love.
> O Mother, enchanter of your lovers' hearts, immerse me in your love's ocean.
> In this your refuge for lunatics, some laugh, some cry,
> and others dance in excess of joy...
> ....mad with love, O Mother, crown of lunatics!

As with cultic spirit-possession in primal faiths (when, for example, a possessed 'outcaste' woman is able in ritual ecstasy to heap ridicule and insult on Brahmin men, without fear of retaliation because the Power is within her), it is as though the God-identity of the ecstatics sets them free from normal community constraints. They move beyond the expected ways of the world. When their own individuality is most identified with the Focus of their devotion, there is also ecstatic liberation from many of the usual boundaries accepted by the community. No longer do they conform to the community's perception of what is normal. But this extreme non-conformity, this rejection of expected identities, is such that even within the faith-community there are those who find too many boundaries broken, as well as those who find precisely the unpredictability, the 'madness', to be the most powerful sign of true identity with the divine (Kinsley 1973).

(4) A Converging of Religious & Late-modernist Viewpoints?

We now return to an earlier point – that there are numerous ways in which religious and late-modernist viewpoints converge. (a) One crucial form of the dual character of religious faith has to do with its personal and community dimensions. *Faith-based self-identities have to do with both personal inner subjectivity and with corporate subjectivities*. Think of the great traditions most committed to inner transformation - perhaps, like the Buddhism of the Elders (Theravada), committed to the uprooting of all ego-fostering desire. We cannot imagine that new inner orientation and its world-transcending new identity without the accompanying identity *of* and *with* the wider community of seekers, a binding identity with that community's sustaining narratives. Buddhism's 'three jewels' involve going for 'refuge' to the *sangha* or congregation along with finding refuge in the Buddha and his new Way.

But the converse is also true. Those traditions most overtly aiming at a strong sense of community togetherness, as with Judaism and Islam, also have strands of intense focus on the individual. The dialectic can only be maintained, though, by that dimension of religious life which the modern secularist finds most difficult to reckon with - the *transcendent Focus* that the believer sees as beyond all our lesser identities. It is this transcending Identity that will in one form or another be the basis of, will provide value to, those identities. Though they are 'lesser' identities, they are yet seen as of lasting significance in the path to that Identity which is the final goal of faith.

(b) It is at this point that a religious and a late-modernist view of life differ, though we have to note too where they concur. For, just as does a critical religious perspective, late-modernist (and certainly post-modernist) cultural criticism rejects *any absolute status* to all our institutions and authorities and the many kinds of social and self-identity based on them. Late-modernism radically relativises all our identities with its de-constructivist stance. 'Identities are discursive constructions which change their meanings according to time, place and usage'. This may be seen as primarily a 'cultural' or 'social construct', or as the individual attempting 'to construct a coherent identity narrative', a life-story by which (quoting Anthony Giddens, who we have seen to be fairly moderate in postmodernist terms) 'the self forms a trajectory of development from the past to an anticipated future'.

For, self-identity is 'the self as reflexively understood by the person in terms of his or her biography'. The power to construct one's own history and destiny is emphasised, and so human agency rather than passive subjection to other forces. Yet, there is nothing that can be identified as the essence of selfhood. Rather like the 'elder' Buddhists with their doctrine of 'non-self', the postmodernist critic denies a substantial core of being to *any* of our self-identities. Identity is *never* a permanent feature of our being; it is merely a 'mode of thinking about ourselves' at a particular time and place (Barker 2000: 166).

So, then, there is significant convergence between an early Buddhist and a late/post-modernist view of how things are. No doubt this accounts for the quite large numbers of more reflective late-modernistic westerners who have rejected traditional Christianity, as well as confidence in any traditional institutions of the West, and have embraced Buddhistic ideas.

(c) In passing, we can note how often modern 'cultural studies' completely ignore the fact of *religion* as an identifiably distinct human reality. It is not just that 'culture' is assumed to cover all human experience. There is virtually no reference at all to those dimensions of cultural experience that are distinctively religious. Both Woodward (2002) and Barker (2000) are intended as comprehensive textbooks, yet both completely and typically fail to recognise 'religion' either as a distinct category or as expressing distinctive insights to be noted in understanding either identity or culture.

(d) Yet, a clear contrast remains between a typically religious view of selfhood and its related self-identities on the one hand, and that of late-modernist secularism on the other. For all the seeming overlap between, for example, the Buddhist critique of the self and the late-modernist view of its constructed and relative character, the differences are great. Yes, permanently fixed selfhood is denied in, for example, two of the three Buddhist 'jewel' doctrines describing the true state of things: *anicca* (Sanskrit *anitya)* or impermanence, and *anatta* (Sanskrit *an-atma)* or non-self, with only the final goal of *nirvana* and its state of ego-less equanimity seen as ultimately unchanging. Even so, the stages of the ethical path leading up to this (and so too the various identities that emerge along the way, including that of 'position-less' monk in the Buddhist congregation 'on the Way') are endowed with the very highest spiritual significance. Especially the special 'refuge' life in the 'togetherness' of monks is pregnant with ultimacy, or at least is the pen-ultimacy that leads to *Nirvana*. And this is one of the most radical of anti-essentialist religious positions.

(e) For many other traditions too the 'stages' of life and their associated self-identities are certainly not seen by believers as 'wholly social constructions' in the manner late-modernism contends. True, what the believer imagines to be the case is not necessarily any more than that - an *imagined* state of being. On the other hand, to disallow *per se* any objective ontological status to faith's imaginings is surely the same as equating mythic being with false being, and faith becomes false consciousness with no possibility of being a window into truth. Some Christian theologians (perhaps Don Cupitt and his 'Sea of Faith' followers) have been so impressed by postmodernist ways of seeing the world that identity-creating narrative itself, divested of all objective significance, has become everything. Even the 'God' of whom the narrative speaks is no longer to be identified with any corresponding ontological reality.

(f) One more shared perspective between critical secularists and critical religious believers can be identitied. Not only are we - sometimes at least - both aware of the conditioned character of our human life. Secularist and religious faith alike can also be gripped by the paradoxical vision both of the ultimate value of the individual person and a more globally inclusive humanness. Here we have two seemingly polarised categories: individual personhood and our wider shared humanness, expressed in but transcending all its corporate forms. As my argument unfolds - based on a critical analysis of the potential for religious faith to function in human life both positively and negatively, creatively and destructively, delightfully and dangerously - it will be very clear that these two categories are crucially part of our *religious* self-understandings.

(g) Before leaving this reflection on secularist and religious attitudes, at least brief mention should be made of a very explicit contrast. Central to faith has always been its refusal to accept the boundaries of this *saeculum*, this world. Belief in a world beyond, and its promised delights, even though prompting radical action in this world, is very obviously central to those Islamists convinced they must offer up their own lives along with those they kill as part of their 'struggle' for Allah's way. The medieval Christian crusaders so hateful within their corporate memory were of similar faith. Much later, affirming 'I am a pilgrim here below, this world is not my home' was a sentiment typical of the Victorian Christian. And in varying forms, finding one's true identity in some eternal realm beyond the usually experienced limits of mortal life is invariably part of faith. To the extent that this eternal dimension of faith is lost by contemporary Christianity for example, perhaps even declared to be unnecessary to faith, we really do see the impact of modern secularism.

Yet, finding one's identity - personal or community - bound up with the concerns of this world, believing we do have a home in and belong to this world, is not in itself the result of modern secularisation. Even India's most God-obsessed *bhaktas* were at times surprisingly given to 'non-renunciation', to use T.N.Madan's phrase (1987). Identifying with the world's concerns, this-worldly confidence, has been part of all manner of faiths from their founding. If, though, a sense of that final fulfilment in eternity is lost, faith in a typically religious way would seem to have been washed away by the rising tide of a full-blown secularist perspective.

Conclusion

There is, then, this important overlap of late-modernist and one typical religious (especially Buddhist) analysis of what it is to be human. Our life is inescapably *conditioned by* and therefore *bounded by socially and culturally shaped identities*, however complex the delineating of these boundaries may prove. On both sides, of course, there are limits to how far we are to take this recognition of our cultural conditioning. Giving universal value to *any* of our positions is ruled out by the radical relativist. Hardline secularist faith, though, rarely recognises how tribalist (to use Ninian Smart's term: 1968:102) are the universalisms it tries to press on all others. Gayatri Spivak and other postcolonial writers have rightly been critical of the universalist assumptions implicit in the western-oriented education they received, usually in India.

Religious believers too will often absolutise and so universalise the particular life-style of an earlier age - perhaps the co-incidental culture of the age of revelation. Believing Arabian culture of the eigth century (or the Prophet's view of it) to be binding for all time and all places is an especially powerful factor in Arabic Islam. A similar stance is endemic too in Jewish, Christian, Hindu and Sikh faiths. The question arises, is this form of faith confusing a particular cultural history with the absolutes implicit within their sacred revelation? That such faiths believe it necessary critically to judge from the perspective of that sacred vision all life adjunct to it - social, cultural, political - in itself is not the problem. Finding absolutes in the cultural life of a prior age, with all its historical conditioning, is the issue.

Both the person and humanness are, though, defined in peculiar ways within differing traditions. In focussing on a distinctive stance of a religious as against a secularist worldview, we must not lose sight of the diversities within both. So, I reiterate: People of faith in different traditions have very distinctive perceptions both of their own and of the world's identity. Even among themselves, and not only between each other, traditions differ as to whether our most important 'identity' is to be discovered in belonging to the group, or in being an authentic individual. As we saw, both kinds of identity are shaped by a dialectic between them, an interplay of poles of human existence in which there is also the crucial role of sacred Focus and sacred Community. On the one hand Hindu, Buddhist, Jewish, Christian, Muslim, Sikh - all at times give maximum importance to *belonging to a community*. True self-identity, our traditions claim, is created by belonging to the body of the initiated, the believers, those committed to the Way, those who are the pure, the enlightened.

Yet each tradition, in differing ways and to different degrees, also has a strand of experience in which self-identity is very much what takes place *within personal selfhood*, an engagement with transcendence that goes beyond just breaking through the bounds of individual existence and becoming part of the believing, distinctively sacred community. And even when great stress is placed on the need to be other than the 'world', different from the 'infidels', unlike the 'unenlightened', far removed from the 'impure', believers are convinced that their way of faith is what *humanness* should truly be. The aim may well be to move on - though this is not always made explicit - by means of faith's transforming work, to a more *inclusive humanness embracing the whole world*.

On this point too, inevitably, faiths differ greatly, and here description needs to become discriminatingly critical. The identity of the Transcendent, and ways of identifying with that Transcendent, differ from faith to faith (even within one tradition), and these ways of divine identifying are crucial to the dialectic. Even so, secular modernity is not alone in placing emphasis on finding true self-identity in being either an authentic individual or in finding our true humanness. Nor is this simply the impact of secularist thinking on religions, even if the language here is not that of traditional religion. Indeed, the precise opposite could be argued: the roots of secularist emphasis both on the sacred value of the individual and the need to be fully human lie in religious experience. This, though, is a thesis that cannot be argued any further at this point.

(5) When Faith Questions All Identities

In all religious traditions, then, we find the most highly regarded human identity is that sense of *selfhood* (or of non-selfhood in the Buddhist vision of these higher realities) *able to transcend all undergirding prior identities*. Certainly this is believed to be so in the life of their 'saints', or those seen as most perfectly representing believers' aspirations. Maybe we have to limit identity-transcending to faiths with a soteriological emphasis, those within Hindu, Buddhist, Christian, and Islamic traditions which usually take for granted the need for some form of change in how life is seen and lived. Without divine grace perhaps, or transforming insight, a new life-direction, more complete commitment to 'the Way', our human identities have not been as they should. To aim explicitly for non-selfhood as 'elder' Buddhism does is to take this goal to its logical extreme. The other great spiritual systems of India, i.e. classical Hindu belief-forms, speak rather of a higher selfhood that must move beyond all ego-linked limitations of 'name and form'. And this in a religious culture - the Brahmanic tradition - in which purity of name and correctness of form are absolutised in the sacral order of *dharma*.

In religious vision, then, there proves to be an even higher order, where no prior identities given by nature or culture must be allowed to define who the innermost person essentially is. Nor is it merely the classical Sanskritic spiritual systems that aim for such lofty de-conditioned goals. Vernacular devotion too is replete with similar sentiments. Here is one example from Tukaram, the seventeenth century Maratha shopkeeper-saint devoted passionately to Vitthala (Krishna):

> Cursed now be name and form;
> These the guilt I carry bound up with me.
> Let us take the dust of the saints' feet
> to rid us of this burden of clay.
> Pride in worthless claims brought me to misery.
> Tuka says, our joy in the Formless is true and beyond all names.
>
> Every form is destroyed by time;
> The Name of Hari alone is beyond its power....
> Tuka says, God has made me weary of the very name
> of the disguises of the soul.
>
> Despise pigs and dogs for their bodies,
> but show them respect for their souls.
> So I have learned to sweep away 'I' and 'mine'...
> Despise home, wealth and country;
> Embrace in spirit beasts and trees...
> (Abhangs 865, 867, 876: Fraser and Marathe 1909, 1983).

As with all religious poetry of passion, there are many paradoxes, many seemingly contradictory sentiments to reckon with for a more complete picture of Tukaram's spiritual struggle. For all his aim of sweeping away 'I' and 'mine', he sees all too clearly that they still compel so much powerful feeling in his life. And we cannot leave out a point that in different ways is quite prominent in his theology: 'You have found a place for my name and form, or who would call you God?' (Abhang 456).

In a very similar way Christian scripture (the Apostle Paul at least) urges those 'in Christ' to disregard their given male and female identities, the fact of their being either slave or free, Jew or Gentile (Galations 3:28). At the transcendent level of faith there are to be no such distinctions, for there is a newly created identity, a 'new creation' that relativises all old identities. The new 'body' of those united together 'in Christ' is now the supreme reality. All those self-boulstering support systems such as family pedigree, ethnic purity, or even institutionalised religious disciplines, can even be described - with the typical hyperbole of faith - as so much 'refuse' (Philippians 3:5-8).

Yet, again and again it becomes clear those God-given old identities still 'find a place' in the new, equally God-given, faith-identity. Life of the old creation, 'under the law', 'life in this body', the life of 'this world', may at times seem to be given little value. Elsewhere its claims become very great, even if not absolute. Our human identities as men/women, husbands/wives, masters/slaves, rulers/citizens, even as Jews and Gentiles (an immensely important issue for the first Christian apostles), are still given great significance. Indeed, the new identity demands that all such prior but now lesser identities are lived out with even greater awareness of the value and blessedness possible within such 'orders of creation'. Over all there is their 'higher calling'. (What are here referred to as 'lesser identities', some would no doubt call 'roles'. But insofar as a 'role' determines the way people see themselves and others it clearly takes on the character of an 'identity'.)

So, a *dialectic of faith* operates that is found in not dissimilar form in a number of religious traditions. Hinduism's 'ways' both of *jnana* (knowledge, or enlightened awareness) and of *bhakti* (devotion, loving trustfulness) may express the dialectic differently, but they also point to a distinctive identity by which other forms of cultural and social conditioning are believed to be transcended, though not entirely superceded. In Islam there is sometimes resistance to the idea of a born-again experience where the new identity transcends the old, at least for the Muslim brought up in the tradition (V. J. Hoffman in Marty 1995: 220-24). There is no doubt, though, as to how radical is the new identity expected of one becoming a Muslim, and the contrast between life before and after entry into the new faith. And there is certainly no doubt about how prior human identities are thereby to be transformed. Even the climactic experience of Hajj, the pilgrimage to Macca, is often likened to a fresh birth, a newly purified identity, with new attitudes, values and relationships expected as a result.

Some Muslim writers call for a self-identity determined by a living engagement with and so a more dynamic conformity to the Qur'anic model than they find in a legalist view of the *shariah*. Yet, it is resurgent challenge of militant Islam that is most effective in resisting the absolutising of the modern nation-state's identity and the new globalising identities based on a consumerist capitalism which makes life-transforming faith in a transcendent Being as difficult as a 'camel going through the eye of a needle' - to use the Jesus-image of the dangers of wealth and materialism.

(6) Mistaken Identities According to Upanishadic Insight

It is the Upanishadic and Buddhist traditions in particular that assert *the provisional nature of all our institutionally inherited identities*. Not to recognise such limited provisionality is to be dangerously deluded. It is not just inherited corporate identities, but any sense of belonging as individuals we may have either by nature or nurture, that are called into question. Such conditioning potentially can lead to a dangerously *mistaken identity (bhrama* about *brahman* according to Vedanta). The names we are given, the roles we play, the forms we assume, are all part of a *nama-rupa* provisional level of existence that needs to be transcended by the recognition of another higher identity.

Not that the Upanishads present us with a clear view of the material world in itself as illusory, a deluding mirage. *Maya*, in the sense of a veil of ignorance so all-embracing that creation and all creaturely being is vitiated by this cosmic nescience, is almost never found in these seminal texts of Vedanta, even if later interpretation tended in this direction. The Upanishads, though, do make it clear that the reality of the world and of our own being is a *mystery*, not superficially obvious.

To the theistic interpreters like Ramanuja and Madhva, that the world is *maya*, or that God creates the world by means of *maya*, simply means that it emerges mysteriously from God's miraculous power. Even so, every Vedantin, or Upanishadic interpreter, took for granted that in our unenlightened state we all remain misguided by a fundamentally *mistaken identity* which does vitiate, dangerously, our whole existence. We mistake sensory bodily experience for the real thing. We mistake the changing, transitory world of the senses for the unchanging, eternal world of the true Self. But then the being and nature of that Self comes into question (Lott 1980, ch.5).

For a theist like Madhva the mistaken identity meant failing to recognise the sovereign grace of God, not realising that only God is the eternally self-determining One, and that we are eternally dependent upon God's power and grace. This seems so close to the monotheist strand within Christian and Muslim theology. Far from determining one's own selfhood and its destiny - the self-identity modernity seeks - our true destiny, our true identity, is to be God-determined. Human selfhood and God's Selfhood are sharply contrasted. Even a *pre*-determining of the soul's destiny is envisaged, a position given great prominence in fifth century Augustine and sixteenth century Calvin. In both Hindu and Christian traditions, though, other strands of faith - as with Sufi faith even within Islam - find that 'determining' divine selfhood *within*, so lessening the tension between divine and human identities.

A century or two before Madhva, the great Ramanuja's understanding of 'true identity' similarly differs from Madhva is giving great emphasis to continuity of being, 'inseparability', between God and that creation which is eternally dependent on him. Failing to know and be in this *inseparable love-relationship* is the basis for our mistaken identity. For the arch-non-dualist Sankara the mistaken identity is two-fold: yes, there is the failure to distinguish the Self and conscious subjecthood from non-self and sensory objecthood; and there is the failure to realise that ultimate and liberating Identity, the oneness, of our own inner selfhood (*atman*) with the cosmic Self of all, *Brahman*. Thus key-verses for Sankara's non-dualist interpretation are the 'identity texts': 'That thou art', 'I am *brahman*', and suchlike.

And we should note the range of these Upanishadic identities, not all taken up as crucial by Sankara. For example: 'I am *annam*' (food, rice), or 'He is *rasah*' (joy-giving essence). For other interpreting perspectives such texts as these could become the key to new identities. The important Ramanandi sect, for example, still prominent at Ayodhya, based their own life-identity on the declaration that the Supreme is *Rasa,* the invigorating, joy-inspiring essence of all (van der Veer 1997). All Upanishad-interpreters, though, were agreed on the dangerously seductive power of our mistaken identities.

Admittedly, the need to break with, to supercede all our socially and culturally conditioned worlds, and to break through into some more transcendent level of being, to attain a higher identity, is a little more ambivalent in the Upanishads than in Theravada Buddhism. For the Buddha, even the identifying of a part of our being as 'the self' (*atman*), that at its core is somehow unchanging and eternal, was a mistaken identity. Nothing substantially identifiable in this way has lasting character. Everything is subject to flux and change. No continuing belonging is possible. There is no other reliable identity than that provided by the three-fold Refuge - the Buddha, his Dhamma, and the Sangha of enlightened, place-less monks (*bikkus*) sustained by the alms of others. Only an utterly new quality of inner being can ensure liberation from our conditioned past, in particular from our compelling thirst for ego-hood with all its demanding, self-indulging desires, and set us free for lasting peace and bliss.

The Upanishads, on the other hand - especially if we give room for the Bhagavad Gita as having Upanishadic status, which it rapidly came to have in Hindu regard - the Upanishads did come to give normative room for the identity-creating role of inherited culture, i.e. the *dharma*, understood as an all-encompassing right ordering of life. Soon after the glorious vision of all creation embodied within Krishna, and before the final 'highest secret' about divine love, we have several chapters describing the way things are ordered, from demonic life to truly good life. The three 'qualities' (*gunas*) determine of what kind we are, what kind of food we eat, how we behave, what our social status is. The dharmic givenness of life is comprised of varying degrees of intermingling of these three eternal qualities of nature.

The impression should not be given that this is entirely a static worldview, with no scope for aspiration to change. Why, even a Brahmin is not one merely born as such, but a person who acts in a Brahmin-like way. The *dharma*, at least in principle if not in social practice, does allow scope for dynamic change of identity. And change of identity, at least from a religious perspective, is very sharply expressed in other places in the Gita. In earlier Upanishads too, it is clear that those who come to a teacher for enlightenment are not from the Brahmin community. There are numerous Kshatriyas who set up as enlightened teachers themselves (to the extent that some scholars see a sort of Kshatriya revolt against Brahmin dominance here); and there are Sudras and women who find place in this Upanishadic movement for inner liberation and new identity. This inclusiveness is precisely what the Gita declares to be an immediate feature of liberation from a *bhakti* (loving devotion) perspective. Just before the great Vision, Krishna speaks as follows (9.30-34, see also R.C.Zaehner's translation):

> However evil a person's occupation may be, but worship Me with love
> And serve no other; then that person is reckoned as good...

> Very soon will that self be justified and win eternal peace
> ...None who worships me with love is lost to me

> Whoever make Me their refuge, low-born though they be,
> Yes, women, middle-rank workers, even serfs will walk the highest way.

> How much more, then, Brahmins, full of good merit, and royal holy seers,
> if they are my bhaktas...

> On Me your mind, for Me your loving service,
> for Me your sacrifice and reverence...

What emerges from this picture of the identities created by *bhakti* religion is the kind of two-tier existence often found in religious life, though maybe in differing forms. The power of the *bhakti* experience to create a new identity cannot be in doubt. What is in question, and has been in almost all *bhakti*-like movements within Hinduism, Christianity, or any other religion, is the extent of interaction between these two tiers. In fact the same question can be asked of religious experience in a non-*bhakti* context; and I should certainly not give the impression that Upanishadic wisdom invariably culminates in *bhakti*. This would push my own prejudice a little too far. The more general question is, then, has the experience that one's ultimate identity is to be found in relation to a wonderfully loving God, or the sense of inner identity with the transcendent Self, or of breakthrough into Nirvanic being - does this experience dynamically interpenetrate and eventually transform other levels of being? What is to be the dialectic by which our different identities relate to each other?

For the Upanishadic world of the Hindu this means more precisely: Is it the inner realisation of transcendent identity, or the *bhakti* experience of transcendent love, that impinges most strongly on the given structures of *dharma*? Or is it the case that the social role of either is in the end determined by what is given in *dharma*? Some might argue that the 'way of transcendent knowledge' is in more sharply dialectical relationship with dharmic social structuring than is 'the way of loving devotion', especially because the former was more likely to result in a world-renunciatory position than the latter. The truly enlightened one will necessarily be a world-renouncer of some kind, that *sanyasi*-identity being beyond the constraints of normal social identities. Yet, said the greatest exponent of this transcendent way, the renouncer has the freedom also to engage voluntarily with the world. Certainly, such stories of Sankara as we have suggest he engaged quite vigorously in restructuring dharmic life as a bulwark against the successes of Buddhism. There is no doubt, though, of the sharper break between doing and being, between the duties of *dharma* and enlightenment realised through *dhyana*, or the inner contemplative way of 'knowledge', than is the case at least with non-ecstatic forms of *bhakti*. Once the self is set free from its delusory state, said Sankara, all other identities, all other social loyalties lose their claim on us. We are free either to do or not to do our dharmic duties.

Yet, Sankara still retains the strangely *dharma*-bound position that only the twice-born are able to attain ultimate liberation. The *bhakti*-theologian, Ramanuja, on the other hand set no such limits to the finding of ultimate self-liberation: even one of his early Gurus was a Shudra, and later when exiled to the Mysore region, he opened the doors of Vaishnavism to numerous 'low-caste' peoples. True to *bhakti* insights, lowliness of birth is no barrier to that ultimate identity, for had not a number of the 'love-drowned' saints of the past been from lowly castes? Even so, in terms of Sri Vaishnava insitutional identity, conservative Brahmanic dominance within the community remained. Among those earlier God-lovers, the Alvars, whether they were from Brahmin or non-Brahmin castes seemed to make little difference to the way their faith-identity engaged with their lower social identities. Not that they continued to see themselves in terms of those social identities. Those lower dharmic roles are simply ignored.

Nor was this because the world was believed to be in no way transformable. True, we often find the world and the body described in very derogatory terms, though far more so in the poetry of the Tamil Saiva saints than their Vaishnava counterparts. It is not in the world or in this particular body that our ultimate identity is to be found. Yet, do they not also speak of the macrocosmic world as the glorious 'body' of God, inseparably related to its creator-Self? This was to become in fact the key hermeneutical image in their community belief-system, especially as expressed later so powerfully and systematically by Ramanuja.

So, the lack of obvious impact of the higher identity - i.e. finding our true being in the love of God - on our lower social and dharmic identities, is not due to a consistently negative view of the world. Just listen, for instance, to some ecstatic words from the most revered of the 'loved-drowned', Nammalvar, 'Our Alvar' (in Tiruvaimoli V.2), in the eighth or ninth century:

> Rejoice! Rejoice! Rejoice! Gone is life's curse,
> Hell's agony destroyed;
> Death has no place here;
> Even the power of the dark age is eclipsed.
> See for yourself!
>
> Those beloved of our discus-wielding Lord, come to stay,
> Uproot disease, hatred, poverty and pain
> which conquer this earth.
> With melodious songs they leap, they dance in ecstasy,
> and fly all over this earth...

That life in this karma-bound world is untransformable is clearly not a necessary part of *bhakti* belief. Generally, though, once the higher life-identity is experienced, other lesser identities, lower loyalties, life-duties in the world at large, are hardly referred to except in terms contrasting the two and seeing all those lesser roles in the mythic terms of the new reality.

This, though, was not the case with such *bhakti* movements as involved entirely or predominantly non-Brahmin castes. The Lingayats of Karnataka, for example, gave such theological weight to social ethics - the importance of work, the status of widows and women generally, the sharing of experience, the insignificance of caste status - that there is little doubt about the power of the higher identity to reshape those lower identities. Throughout their poetic writings, though, the key remains that absolute claim of the 'Lord of the Meeting Rivers', expressed through his symbol, the Lingam, with whom constant togetherness is aimed for. Even more strikingly counter-cultural was the *bhakti* of North Indian *'nirgunis'*, such as Kabir and Nanak, those whose faith-focus was beyond image and concept.

Chapter 2
Dangerous Identities?

(1) Further Definitional Refining

The main concern of these lectures, then, is the ways - sometimes differing, sometimes converging - that religious faiths shape human identities. We still need, though, in part as a result of material already looked at, more formal clarity concerning what we mean by 'identity', and how we define human identity. Definitions themselves are forms of identity. When we define a word (an object, concept, category, phenomenon), we set boundaries to the meaning(s) with which the concerned thing can be referred to. We focus on and identify its essential character in ways that make sense within our world of discourse: what connotation it has for us. So, the more rigorous the aim for the defining clarity of objectivity, the greater the danger of epistemological reductionism. Identifying ourselves and others, or defining what it is to be essentially human, involves a similar limiting.

At the simplest level, our identities define who we think we are and who others think we are. And they concern what people see as essentials, as ultimacies. Such definitions can set up some rarified boundaries, boundaries that may not be at all obvious to others. When Rene Descartes (1596-1650), for instance, one of the founding fathers of the Enlightenment's scientific way of seeing the world, defined the new approach to knowledge and reality in the words, 'I think, therefore I am', he pointed in effect to a new form of human self-identity - the (in)famous 'Cartesian dualism' of disembodied self-conscious mind as essential to human identity over against the limitations of embodiment. No doubt the intention is to lift us far beyond our usual corporate traditions and their attendant identities and into the freedom of limitless modernity. But the age of Enlightenment, the scientific spirit, too has created its mutually exclusive communities, its clearly defined and very binding identities, including those who place themselves firmly over against both the individualist and the disembodying tendencies of Descartes' definition of what we really are. An important strand of late modernism (and certainly eco-feminists) is critical of Enlightenment 'modernity' precisely on this loss of unitive embodiedness.

Religious faith too affirms basic statements of belief that stand as self-definitions, who we *really* are: faith-statements such as 'In the beginning God created...', or 'I am Brahman', or 'I no longer live, it is Christ who lives in me...', or 'Allah is One, Allah is great, Muhammed is the prophet...'. As we shall see, these transcending identity-statements of our religious faiths, though able to move us beyond the limitations of prior identities, can in turn create their own new corporate loyalties, even if they also have the potential to go on compelling the believer to a life 'beyond identity' (Ninian Smart almost used this as the title of his 1980 Gifford Lectures, *Beyond Ideology*). In this process also there will be, even if unconsciously, reference to those factors in human experience that provide self-*continuity*, both across time, binding us to those with whom we identify, and through time, binding us to past expressions of the tradition we share. Further, such self-defining at some point will always be by way of reference to what we believe *others* to be, both by way of identifying with some and by differentiating ourselves from others. As noted ealier, there is both *alignment* and *over-againstness* involved.

The sense of the self as being *free* in some way to act, to work out a chosen destiny, and so be a significant agent of action, not just helplessly subject to the forces of fate, was a key issue for ancient as well as (post)modern thinkers. The fierce theological tussles within the Christian and Muslim communities (and differently posed, even within Hindu tradition) have often been about precisely this question of freedom of action, human agency in relation to divine agency, human identity in relation to divine identity. Recent post-theological discussion may put things very differently, but in the end the issue still concerns the nature of the human self - a basic common assumption being that without a sense of self-determination and responsible agency, perhaps by way of 'constructing our own story', there can be no sense of continuity of being, no sense of self-identity (Giddens 1991; Woodward 2002).

Even when the emphasis is on *personal* self-identity, identity is at key points shaped by cultural tradition, by a shared value-system, by commonly understood symbolic worlds. The easier we can communicate with another, non-verbally as well as by way of spoken language, not only is the sense of identity with that other enhanced, personal identity too is sharpened. The influential social anthropologist, Robert Bellah has been among those pointing to the dangers of western, especially American, focus on individual identity, as though the self were 'absolutely empty, unencumbered and improvisional'. This 'obscures personal reality, social reality and particularly moral reality, that links person to society' (Bellah 1985: 80). Here is another confirmation of Giddens' analysis, though more directly critical of this self-absorption, as we noted others have been too. Modernity may be obsessed at the psychological level with *personal* desire and feeling, and at the economic level with what the *individual* chooses and consumes - in both cases there are delusional aspects to this - but in wider global tradition self-identity is decisively and overtly group-related. People identify themselves (and others) by reference to that group and its traditions to which they see themselves (or others) as most significantly belonging.

And yet, it is confrontation by the 'other', and especially a sense of alienation from the other, that intensifies both personal and group self-identity. The formation of self-identity, therefore, inevitably entails some measure of confrontation between groups who have very differing identities. Differentiation is essential to our creatureliness, our humanness.

Few religions, though, will expect their followers to act as though those 'others', the 'world', the wider human community, did not exist. Devotional hyperbole may well often speak of the world as 'nothing', or, like the Apostle Paul writing of the marks of his earlier very respectable rabbinic identity, as so much 'refuse' in view of the new Identity 'in Christ' (Letter to Philippians). But the linkage with those worlds outside devotion can never be so easily broken. And so we find the same Apostle, for example, at every point in his letters showing unconsciously just how indebted he was culturally and conceptually not only to Jerusalem, but to Rome, Athens, and perhaps even the world of the Gnostics.

Sociologists of religion (e.g. Mol 1976, 1978) have quite rightly differentiated three main types of identity within religious worldviews: *personal self-identity, distinctive group identity, and wider social/human identity*. Naturally, these three general types take very different forms in different contexts. Person, faith-group, human society are seen in many varying ways, and relate to each other in varying ways too.

Such a typology of identities with a religious focus can be readily linked (as by Hans Mol) with the classical sociological theory of religion as 'cosmisation in a sacred mode'. The construction of a religious world is the same, sociologically speaking, as the constructing of any other social world. There is a dialectical process involving three modes: religious consciousness is (mythologically) externalised; this construct is endowed with objective reality beyond the believer's own being; that objectified world is by faith and 'commitment' internalised, especially by way of ritual ensuring that consciousness keeps on being filled with, and occasionally even overwhelmed by, the reality of that faith-world (Berger 1969). In this way, personal identity becomes inextricably bound up with the identity of the faith-group, which is experienced as a *sacred* group. The relationship of that sacred identity with wider society may be one mainly of contrast and conflict, or it may involve a surprising amount of interaction and complementarity (Mol 1978: 9). A religious group with a clear sense of its sacred identity will usually seem to be more concerned to confront, to be critical of that wider humanity. In reality, there will be both conscious and unconscious engagement with and various forms of dependence on the 'other', the world of the 'profane'.

People's sense of difference, then, even within religious contexts, is worked out in very contrasting ways. This ranges from mutually tolerant accommodation learnt over time, to violent antagonism. Modern society - sometimes with an astounding degree of self-deception in view of the phobias that abound - boasts of its ability to be tolerant of differing identities. This may often be explicitly in contrast to the hate-fired intolerance thought to be typical of religious communities. And there have been many times in our religious histories when, embroiled in political struggles for power, religion has been party to ruthlessly bloody scenes. In British internal history, for example, when sixteenth century Protestants were burnt alive by the Catholic 'Bloody Mary', or Catholics were hung drawn and quartered by those espousing the anti-Roman Protestant cause both before and after Mary, the intolerance was unrelenting.

A thousand other instances could be found, and in the histories of almost every civilisation. Each group seemed so sure of the absolute right of their own cause, so utterly convinced of the evil of the other. Yet, that religious faith was entangled with the machinations of those dedicated to political power is too often overlooked, as is also the equally ruthless aggression of numerous 'secularist' regimes of modern times. The tolerance of the secularist eschewing religious faith, in times of crisis perhaps based on racial or ethnic difference, can so easily switch to confrontation and violence. Even so, why the believer might come to hate rather than respect another form of belief, why faith-based identities can become hate-based, is a serious issue calling for further examination as we go along.

In general, the more 'primal' and less complex a society, the more integrated and in some ways the more sharply defined that identity. Yet, it will not become a self-consciously defined identity until there has been exposure to and confrontation by other communities and the differing identities there encountered. Almost all 'primal' communities have in fact experienced such confrontation. Corporate identities based on clan and totemic loyalties, for instance, have been well aware of how distinct they are from other totemic groups. And with competition for resources, the 'other' has so often become a life-threatening enemy.

Innate to modernity is the potentially fracturing experience of multiple, often seemingly unrelated inner identities - defined by family, business, sporting passion, musical interest, leisure hobby, local region, political party, language, race, and a wide range of voluntary associations - a conglomerate of identities that from hour to hour may see one or other as surfacing to temporary dominance. Many are the worlds that for a time define who we feel ourselves to be.

Even in the ultimacies of religious faith, such is the growing impingement of plurality that witness to being part of a *multi-faith identity* is increasingly found. Western Christians such as Pierre Johanns, Bede Griffiths, Sarah Grant, Diana Eck, and many others too numerous to list, have discovered in their encounter with Indian religious life that their faith has come to incorporate new dimensions. They have crossed boundaries and become more religiously inclusive, less sharply defined in their selfhood.

Such moving across boundaries is far from confined to recent times. Indeed, modernity brings special dangers to inclusiveness and tolerance. In terms of clarity of self-identity, modernity's pluralism brings with it the danger of such loss of a coherent grounding for a clear sense of who we are and where we belong, that self-identity is threatened. There is a loss of the necessary sense of being corporate beings, integrated in an embodying community. And so the search for a more distinctive sense of such self-identity is commonplace in social and cultural studies.

On the other hand does not contemporary world history suggest that *any* too sharply developed sense of group identity is *dangerous* - dangerous to those of other loyalties who happen to be in a confrontatory situation? Do not people with the most strongly defined group identities tend to be militant nationalists, ethnic cleansers, terrorists, insurgent tribalists, exclusive fundamentalists, global bullies, and suchlike difficult people whose group psyche may well be dominated by paranoia, by fear of threat from the enemy other, whether there is evidence of this or not, and an unwillingness to make conciliatory accommodations? Has this not been the case with the conflicts in the Balkans, Northern Ireland, Israel, India, Indonesia, Sri Lanka, the Philippines, Spain, various parts of Africa and elsewhere? Each of these regions has its particular historical causes. But in each there is a clash of sharply defined identities, and the emergence of (usually) minority communities feeling alienated, subject to humiliating discrimination.

Strong religious loyalties are clearly part of almost all those histories and their violence. Making religion the sole scapegoat, however, misreads reality. As Parekh implies, a certain kind of secularist worldview, 'fundamentalist secularism', is equally exclusive of those whose worldview is alien. At least for a number of 'extremist' minority groups, what creates their sense of alienation and so their extremism is the overwhelming perception of the threat to their existence, certainly to their distinctive identity, posed by such diverse hegemonic juggernauts as globalising western secularist culture, trans-national corporations (manipulating amounts of capital far greater than the gross national budget of most developing countries), American and North Atlantic military power, political regimes of right, or left, or those based on despotic and dynastic power. The acquiring of supreme power in relation to others creates a bloated self-identity that not only alienates, but in its dangerously insensitive attitudes to the reality of others is itself 'alienated'. No doubt a clearly defined self-identity is what enables decisive and effective action in relation to others. In itself, though, the self-confidence of power is rarely such a fine thing.

Just how paranoid are the many groups who perceive their own identity as dangerously threatened? It is clearly the case that militantly expressed group identities often actually *are* endangered by others just as they claim. They *are* victims to the overbearing ambitions of others. It has been the aggressive ego, the domineering identity, of others that *has* made their militancy an inevitable response. The very existence of their ethnic or religious community may well *be* at stake: the Kurdish people's struggle with Iraq, Iran and Turkey for a homeland of their own; the Tibetan Buddhist people's struggle with an occupying regime antagonistic to their religion and culture; the Palestinian community - though Israelis would make the same claim of their own vulnerability; the Dalit people's struggle in India. And there are many more.

Mythic interpretation of these quite real vulnerabilities is inevitable. Elsewhere the fears are sometimes more delusional, not merely myth-construed, but mis-construed, connected in very skewed ways with historical realities. Not that 'myth' has nothing to do with 'history'. By 'myth' we should rather intend those explanatory narratives by which a community is persuaded of its distinctive character and its hoped-for destiny. The experienced 'history' of that community will clearly undergird its myth-making. By 'history' we have come to think of those narrative accounts of our past that have an empirically verifiable basis. In reality those accounts will always have some measure of interpretive, mythic narrative. But if we take just three examples of dangerously 'myth-construed history': Was the Jewish presence in 1930s Germany really such a fatal threat to the 'Aryan race' as imagined by Nazi leaders? Has Serbian identity in the Balkans, undergirded by the rich traditions of Orthodoxy, really been so mortally threatened, at least in the past century, by the Muslims of Kosovo or Bosnia? Or can the roughly 2.5% Christian population in the Sub-continent in itself constitute any serious threat either to Hindus or to Muslims as Hindutva nationalists and Islamic militants seem to believe?

In each of the above cases, however, what may well be feared is the *international* connection, the power-relations, by which the status of the small group within the larger community can be artificially boulstered, as well as the sheer symbolic impact of their presence.

And in global terms, when we look at the history of the humiliating treatment region after region in the Muslim world has received at the hands of western nations in the past two centuries, that Muslim world's strong sense of being the victim of a western, and therefore in Muslim eyes 'Christian', conspiracy to destroy Islam hardly looks like a delusion. Similarly, given the militancy of Islamic faith and of Christian nations globally , and Muslim and British rule in India for so many centuries, it is hardly surprising that a certain kind of Hindu, when politically directed, sees a distinctive Muslim or Christian identity in India as a threat. In any case, we already see how closely *identity* and *religion* can be entwined together, especially when religion acts as a boundary-maker and boundary-marker. But it is also clear just how much nuancing is called for in delineating that religious dimension in identity-shaping.

(2) Faith's New Identities & their Inner Tension

Religion can often act as a legitimator for old identities, a boundary-marker for people's long-held corporate sense of where they belong. There is, though, that quite opposite possibility: a strong *new* sense of identity, of who we are and what we are to be, perhaps an explicitly religious identity, that entails a startling break from previously accepted boundaries. The new spiritual identity may well even renounce basic elements in inherited worlds of meaning. In many cases such a breakthrough has come from a discovery of some newly compelling strand from *within* the tradition; the new identity springs from the dynamics of engaging with lost or moribund roots. In this way Mahavira, great teacher for the Jain community more than two and a half millennia ago, found a new 'heroic' way within a long prior tradition of ascetic struggle for inner purity and liberation. Jesus discovered a radical new way, in large part from within the earlier Hebrew prophetic tradition. Basava, in twelfth century southern India, saw the age-old Linga of Siva (in origin phallic, but long having no such connotation for most Siva-worshippers) with empowering new moral and spiritual vision - the list is endless.

What these new movements are not, though, is a mere reviving of the old. New forms of religious vision, and so new identities, emerge from hidden roots within some stream of the earlier tradition only by way of engagement with other streams of cultural life. The massively significant new paths taken within Europe's sixteenth century Protestant reform movements, as well as in the innumerable new groups later to spring from them, resulted initially from the tensions set up by the impact of Enlightenment insights upon medieval Christendom's religious life. Assumptions previously unquestioned concerning inherited sacral structures, modes of power and authority, the processes of sacramental life, the enchantments seen as part of our earthling nature, were all now questioned. Now authority was, in ostensive confessional statements at least, vested in the sacred written Word alone, linked with the doctrinal system articulated on the basis of that Word. Power was held to be available through the individual's faith, consciously linked with the efficacy of divine grace directly experienced in the believer's heart. Or it may well have been a combination of these in the life of the community of true believers that became the means for the outworking of a new sense of what Christians are and should yet become, what is to be their new sense of identity, personal and corporate. Much, too, was shaped by way of sharply critical differentiation from the mother-church of Rome, now perceived as the 'enemy', the accursed 'whore of Babylon'.

Inevitably, with such a radical project of liberation from earlier institutional norms, reformers differed vigorously among themselves, and their breakaway movements in time spawned countless more mini-breakaways. But while engagement with insights given prominence by the European Enlightenment, a secularising movement, may have been the reason for reform, it was to new perceptions from within the sacred traditions that reformers turned as the authoritative legitimation for change. And now the 'enemy' became not only an 'evil, unbelieving world', but that source of more subtle danger, the unreformed Roman church, still unpurified by faith, and so seen even as the 'anti-Christ'. Reform movements within a tradition usually generate such dual, even multiple, frontiers of engagement. At least initially, the new sense of separate identity is likely to lead largely to frontiers of enmity.

In other cases the new identities emerge from struggle through disillusionment with all prior traditions. The Prophet Muhammed, for example, though clearly engaging with Jewish and Christian faiths, and in various ways indebted to them, in his revelatory visions mainly struggles against the 'animistic polytheism' of Arabian cultural life of the time. The pre-Muslim sacred Kabah stone remains a central focal point for Arab (now Muslim) identity. Now, though, central to the climactic sacred moment in Muslim faith, the Hajj pilgrimage, the Kabah is symbolic of a very different identity and supporting discipline focussed on the One God, Al-lah.

Similarly, Kabir, that extraordinary fifteenth century weaver from Varanasi so uncompromisingly devoted to a transcendent and yet all-pervading Lord Ram, was without doubt shaped in unconscious ways by the impact of Muslim Sufis as much as by Hindu esoteric Natha-yogis. Yet, the main burden of his roughly poetic outbursts - in turn stridently critical of all hypocrisy, caustically satirising any behaviour bereft of faith in God's presence, and then lyrical in exalting the mystery of divine love - is that being neither 'Hindu' nor 'Muslim' carries any weight at all in attaining an authentic spiritual identity.

> Pandits read Puranas, Vedas,
> Mullas learn Muhammed's faith.
> Kabir says, both go straight to hell
> if they don't know Ram in every breath.
>
> I'm telling you my own truth;
> madmen follow others' dreams.
> Hidden and visible - all one milk.
> Who's the Brahmin? Who's the Sudra?
> Don't get lost in false pride.
> False is the Hindu, false the Turk.
>
> (Vaudeville' translation of verses 83 and 26)

Many other faith-gripped saints, sants and seers of earlier India were equally adamant that the outwardly identifying marks of their faith were not of the essence. Distinguishing symbols were dismissed as seemingly peripheral, even though for the great majority of the 'faithful' it was precisely that symbolic tradition that made them what they were. Some twenty centuries before Kabir, the Buddha, after a long period of intense struggle in response to contrasting spiritual disciplines and their symbolic forms, reached that supremely quiescent moment of insight based on the 'middle way' of calm meditation. His new middle-way identity was based neither on the 'heroic' rigorous self-mortification of Mahavira and the way of the 'victorious' Jinas, nor on the way of earlier sacrifice of other life-forms (as prescribed in the Vedas for example) by which all desires in this world and the world to come were believed to be realised.

Yet, so much in the Buddha's new 'noble-*dharma*' - his eight-fold *'yoga'* discipline, his emphasis on the corporate monastic life of the *sangha* (community), even Buddhist symbols such as tree, umbrella, footprint, stupa - suggest his engagement with other spiritual streams vigorously swirling round in his time. There is no doubt that symbolic forms still remain part of his new Way. But the 'self-identity' to which he finally pointed was to be based on a renouncing of all ego-based desire and even any permanent sense of selfhood - a central expectation in much Vedic faith preceding him. And this raises a continuing question mark against all our human search for and dependence on a strong sense of self-identity.

Yet, the Buddha's expectation that every true follower of this self-liberating Way would also be bound in loyalty to the community of fellow-followers, the *sangha*, brings in a certain very clear sense of corporate identity. The same was true of Kabir and Tukaram, both outstanding individualists, as too with the earlier God-lovers of South India. Unexpectedly, again and again we find them glorifying the 'precious fellowship of the saints', the community of other God-lovers whose presence is liberating and transporting because it is there that personal identity is lost in a renewed sense of identity with God.

Then Sikh faith too emerges from creative engagement between prior religious traditions, in this case the devotional fervour of *bhakti* forms of Hindu faith and Islam's faith in the one God, especially as expressed in the passion of North India's Sufi experience. How significant that the songs of Kabir (1440-1518) are prominent in the Sikh scriptures and liturgical life. This is far from suggesting that Sikh faith is no more than an amalgam of Hindu *bhakti* and Islamic faith, a claim that quite naturally angers Sikhs. But this point of creative encounter was certainly the historical context for the emergence of that new religious and community identity based on the experience of Nanak (born 1469) and the following nine Gurus of Sikh tradition. No doubt there are other ethnic, social and historical factors, as with the emergence of all new religious identities. Both the influx of the agricultural Jat community, with their distinctive culture and history, and the hardening of Muslim policy under Mughal emperors such as Aurangzeb, are factors to reckon with in understanding the changes that took place during the two hundred years of the first ten Sikh Gurus. The dynamics of religious life can never function in some wholly discrete spiritual vacuum unconnected with the stormy world of power-struggles, social conflicts and economic realities. In passing we note here in Sikh faith-experience too, as with that initiated by the Buddha and Muhammed, the great emphasis on personal faith being part of the corporate identity of believers.

Yet, whatever the initiating stress on the need for breaking with old loyalties and being shaped by new identities, there are sad ironies in store. All too often within the established faith-community *conformity* becomes the dominant value. Identities *are* shaped by a staunch conservatism concerned primarily to legitimate the givens - the taboos, the required morals, the cultural conformities - developed within the community. Self-identity is likely to be nurtured as much by the need to cultivate those conformities as it is to the counter-cultural thrust of the originating vision. The point here is not that community loyalty is necessarily an evil, but that becoming conformist may well contradict the originating vision.

This conformist tendency, though, is never the whole story. The liberating experience of countless people - newly industrialised workers, farming communities, small shopkeepers and the like - as Methodist evangelical fervour swept Britain from the middle of the eighteenth century is most effectively expressed in the songs of Charles Wesley (1707-88). Brother John Wesley, whose birth tercentenary fell on June 17th 2003, with his energetic preaching throughout the land (40,000 sermons, 225,000 miles on horseback, still at it well into his 80s!) was no doubt the public inspiration, the systematic teacher and the organising genius that secured the movement's lasting effect. But it was the poetry of Charles that continued to touch people's heart more powerfully. Three verses from two different hymns make it very clear on what the believer's sense of self-identity was to be based (first from 'Jesus, lover of my soul'):

> Other refuge have I none,
> Hangs my helpless soul on thee;
> Leave, ah, leave me not alone,
> Still support and comfort me.
> All my trust on thee is stayed,
> All my help from thee I bring;
> Cover my defenceless head
> With the shadow of thy wing.

Thou, O Christ, art all I want;
More than all in thee I find;
Raise the fallen, cheer the faint,
Heal the sick, and lead the blind.
Just and holy is they name,
I am all unrighteous ness;
False and full of sin I am,
Thou art full of truth and grace.

(And from 'Where shall my wondering soul begin?'):

Outcasts of men, to you I call,
Harlots, and publicans, and thieves!
He spreads his arms to embrace you all;
Sinners alone his grace receives:
No need of him the righteous have;
He came the lost to seek and save.

No doubt it is possible even when gripped by such a faith to live as though very different social and cultural conformities constitute the 'support' and 'stay' that actually create one's sense of identity. Less than a century later the dominant ethos of the Wesleyan Methodist community, by then a thoroughly institutionalised 'church', far from identifying itself with the 'sick', the 'blind', far from the tolerant humility to be expected of those sensing they are 'false and full of sin', or living out the liberated life of grace-led sinners, all too often conformed to the dominant middle-class self-righteousness of Victorian Britain. Only on its ministering fringes was that early identifying still found.

Contrasting exceptions continually broke through of course, and from time to time this led early in the 19th century to break-away movements of those who found the need for a self-identity based differently, shaped differently. One such was the far more socially radical Primitive Methodists centred in the North. When they held their day-long emotion-charged camp meetings, imported from the American West, mainly for the unchurched, and accepted women as preachers and ministers, the increasingly starchy Wesleyans found such developments offensive and threatening. Increasingly, though, it was the Primitives who touched the lives of the less privileged in society. A different example was the thoroughly non-conformist Cornish tin-miner, Billy Bray. He was one of those springing out of that para-Methodist movement of my own rural region, North Devon, the Bible Christians whose great emphasis was on ecstatic inner piety and an overwhelming sense of divine love. They also, in their early period encouraged women's ministry, though later pressures to conformity and the move to unite with Wesleyans led eventually to a return to all-male ordination. Billy Bray was the antithesis of such moves to cultural and social conformity. Given to uninhibited ecstasy, he was for ever breaking into song and dance, even in the staidly inhibiting presence of the privileged classes.

So, then, there are two forms of tension to be reckoned with here: the first is between the liberating new self-identity expected by the visionary initiators and their equal emphasis on community loyalty. As we saw, in spite of the pull to conformity, initiating vision can never be written off completely. Then, impinging on this is the tension between the expectations of faith and the conforming pull of dominant cultures, whether this be the developed ethos within the faith-community, or the hegemonic influence of the dominant culture. Faith-communities may be able to retain their counter-cultural life, and indeed may find their major nurturing strength precisely in standing out as different. For other faith-communities, what prevails is the pull to a conformity led by the dominant group. Again, though, human identities in relation to religious vision can never be simplified. The role of faith is complex and crucial. And at all times the religious vision in believers' life contains the potential for a sharp breaking with dominant conformities, a breaking away from the dominant community, and in important respects even involving liberation from the nurturing community of fellow-believers.

(3) Dangers in Religious Identities?

So, then, when do religious identities become 'dangerous'. Already we have two preliminary reasons for speaking of 'dangerous identities' where religion is concerned: First, there is ultra-conservative resistance to change. It is quite rational to want to protect those elements of tradition whose value is proven. When, though, this conserving attitude turns to uncritical veneration, in which custom is given sacral status locked into hierarchically structured religious institutional life, when conformity becomes a divine duty and critical scrutiny a sacrilege, such conservatism carries obviously large dangers, not least in the eyes of those who believe in religion's liberative potential.

Secondly, to the narrowly conservative believer, that non-conformist dynamic, claiming to be part of the same religious tradition, for that very reason will invariably be seen as a danger, an enemy within the ranks. The urge to change, perhaps to a new vision of transcendence from within the old religion, far from being acknowledged as an authentic discovery within that tradition, will more probably be seen as anti-faith sacrilegious heresy. Indeed, the fact that our identities, religion-based or not, are always part of a process of continual change, the fact that identities are always 'dynamic, processual, and contextual', to use the description of a Polish political anthropologist (Mach 1993: 5), in itself will be fiercely resisted by deeply conservative people, especially those whose identity is determined by a fundamentalist stance. But the term 'fundamentalist' is one loaded with confusion, and will need closer examination. At this point I simply mean that stance which sees any element of the unpredictable within religious life - in reality an essential part of the dynamic of religion - as one to be denied and resisted, as is done by those who look primarily for continuity, security, the familiar and controllable within their religion. This, though, is but one element within a 'fundamentalist' stance, and probably not the most familiar.

Then, there are other grounds within the very dynamic of religious life for speaking of its 'danger'. It is not just that all our religions - Primal, Hindu, Buddhist, Jain, Jewish, Christian, Muslim, Sikh - in greater and lesser degrees have their deep ambiguities, that all our faith traditions have had their darkly destructive moments as well as their stories of power to redeem and transform. Deeper still, there is the fact that the very heart of religion has always been concerned with what is 'dangerous'. It deals with that mysterious dimension in human experience which in the 'primal' forms within all our traditions is believed to carry a potency that is unpredictable, uncontrollable, and therefore perilous, able to harm as much as to heal and enhance.

Friedhelm Hardy's penetrating and erudite account of 'the Religious Culture of India' gives great prominence to the perceived dangers in India's faith-worlds, especially at all manner of boundary-points, and to the 'safe havens' by which to counter the diverse threats of these mythic powers (Hardy 1994).

With the growing faith of modernity in the rational and urbane, in our ability to tame and control, even our religious thinking can so easily lose sight of the Sacred as this scarily untameable Other. Yet, religion in the raw - and at deeper levels even our well-tamed religious life - has pre-eminently to do with this primordial Power (*sakti* in the widely ranging levels of Hindu). Precisely because it is dangerously unpredictable, the structures of religious traditions have assumed such Power can only be approached and handled by sacrally qualified functionaries who, it is hoped, are able to channel its potency in life-enhancing ways. And already we see cause for tension between conformity and the boundary-breaker.

Many today will see all these dark forces solely as projections of the human psyche and its conflicts, demons of the soul that lack any objective reference. In itself, though, this does not reduce their 'danger' - especially when it is clear that our demons can become corporately and institutionally embodied. In any case, it is often in the encounter with this unpredictable strand of religious experience that faith has been led to its most liberating moments. It is true that much religious practice has, inevitably and perhaps rightly, to do with establishing order, averting the dangers of the chaotic powers beyond the boundaries of properly ordered life, ensuring conformity to the righteousness of established norms. Yet again and again in our religious histories the exact opposite has happened. Religion has been a compelling impetus behind non-conforming rebellions of individuals and groups, when the givens of their tradition have been broken with, when the unthinkable has been thought, the unspeakable spoken, the untouchable touched. And of rebels, with their counter-cultural ways, the established powers will always say (along with Shakespeare's Caesar): 'Such men are dangerous'.

The 'Renouncers' of Indian Religion

There are, then, very divergent ways in which religious identities signify *danger*. For instance, one of the most important ways, especially in the Indian context, by which counter-cultural and non-conforming identities have been worked out religiously is through *renunciation,* often quite formalised in religious life. Indian sociologists (notably T.N.Madan), as well as other interpreters of Indian cultural and religious life, have reflected on ways in which *sanyasa* has worked in Indian society. The point to note is that renouncers have very often been greatly feared by social conformists as thoroughly *dangerous* individuals. In essence this is one of the questions sociologists debate: to what extent is this way of renunciation in conflict with other institutional structures of Hindu tradition - caste *dharma* or the sacrally given ordering of society, for instance? Did it, does it even now, necessarily mean that all normal social connections are given up?

Here we have one of the key points debated within the Bhagavad Gita. The Gita proposes the happy solution of renunciation-in-action, or breaking the bondage of attachment to the results of our deeds both by yogic detachment and by dedication of everything to God. The result is that many renouncers, in the Indian tradition as elsewhere, have seen their self-identity in terms of very specific social action, sometimes fiercely counter-cultural, sometimes quite conformist. I. Selvanayagam provides important background material to India's early counter-cultural movements (*sramanika* 'struggling' renouncers against *brahmanika* establishment conformists) leading up to the Gita's renunciation-in-action, as well as his own critical response (Selvanayagam 1996). When a culture holds that radical renunciation enables the acquiring of unusual inner powers, powers for both good and ill, the renouncer will naturally be feared.

In our ways of thinking today, talk about 'renouncers' may seem very distant from what most regard as seriously *dangerous* forms of religion. This may not actually be the case though. The most feared global renouncers of today, those rejecting the dominant norms of modern life - social, cultural, economic - are not the secularist and occasionally violent antiglobalisers, but the desperate and destructive renunciation of Islam's 'suicide bombers'. That their unpredictable ways have a *faith*-based commitment makes them specially alarming in the minds of those less extremist in their critical response to the dominant life-style of our times.

In any case, India's age-old renouncers are a good example of how faith that questions normative social life can often appear to the conformists as threatening the general well-being of society. Remember that the Gita too gives considerable weight to just this concern for 'community well-being', the 'integration of the world's life' (*loka-samgraha*). Which is precisely why renouncing the usual duties of life should not be taken literally, according to this central

Hindu text with its remarkable mix of the radical and the conservative - this was by way of response to the spread of Buddhist ideas, including the call to those serious about ultimate things to leave the world and join the monkhood. To what extent is this too the concern of those today for whom the most dangerous religious loyalties are those which in any way question the integrity and authority of the Nation-State? Such movements rapidly become socially damaging 'cults' to be resisted vigorously. Different again is to see any authority threatening individual freedom as the ultimate danger. Resistance on this point though has been based as much on religious faith as on liberal secularist values. Reasons for seeing 'dangers' and criteria for 'well-being' may differ greatly. They can be, though, crucial to what people see as being a 'dangerous' religious identity.

And yet, we are still a long way from coming to grips with the greatest dangers possible in identity-formation, dangers that can be socially explosive when an identity is shaped by *powerful religious myth and its symbolism*. The language by which we describe such a process is greatly indebted to psycho-analysis, a discipline that naturally tends to focus more on the dynamics of individual psyche-making. Corporate identities tend to be mere stage-sets against which the true life-dramas of individuals are played out. Some prominent schools of psycho-analysis - those indebted to Melanie Klein, for example - allow very little significance to culture and the external world. Sudhir Kakar is effectively critical of this kind of reductionism: 'Interpretations are almost exclusively oriented towards a universal infantile fantasy life (especially the primal mother, both good and frightening), leaving little room for the effect of cultural differences on mental life' (Kakar 1997).

This distorting reductionism fits western modernity's self-indulgent and socially disastrous emphasis on the individual, even if such an emphasis is in reality largely rhetorical. It also fits the capitalist ideology of the ultimacy of 'market forces', in which free choice for the individual is ostensibly sacred dogma, while in reality the power-growth of giant corporate institutions is what determines even what people are taught to choose. The political theory that says 'there is no such thing as society', is of a piece with the reducing of authentic identity to the individual psyche. And both express an ego-inflating individualism that destroys community identities and shows little sign of building up those new forms of community able to enhance our humanness.

Within psychology's account of how identities emerge, Erik Erikson's ground-breaking psycho-analysis forty years ago of identity-formation, as we noted earlier at least gives clear recognition to the interaction of factors that are 'subjective and objective, individual and social...' (Mach 1993: 3-4; Woodward 2002). And it is the interaction between these two foci of human experience that makes *crisis* commonplace in the search for integration and identity. 'Identity formation', says Erikson, 'thus involves a continuous conflict with powerful negative elements. In times of aggravated crises these come to the fore to arouse.... a murderous hate of "otherness"....' Mach, more concerned for the political dimensions of our social life, puts it thus: 'Identity crisis (involves)....fear of intrusion of strange elements within one's own domain and (is seen) in attempts at defending one's own distinct character defined in opposition to that of others' (Mach 1993: 7).

Our identities, then, though most empowering when most clearly defined, also involve an 'othering', a seeing of others as over against ourselves, even to the extent of being threatening enemies. And now the element of danger is hotting up. It is when the other is identified as essentially *demonic* and an *evil enemy*, and essential to our own identity is the need to resist, oppose, and if necessary destroy that enemy, that the *mythic* identities capable of being shaped by religious imagery become most dangerous.

(4) Religion's Violent Imagery

So, then, when the sharpening and strengthening of our own identity is achieved by the harsh demonising of the 'other', it is *religion* that most readily provides the *myths and symbols* by which such identities are communicated. Identity-forming is all about the effective configuring of symbols, the integrating of communally convincing imagery, from those corporate memories that make up our deepest consciousness. And religious tradition is a very fertile source for the furnishing of our symbolic worlds, even in their most pathologically extreme form.

This brings up several further points:

(a) Religious tradition may well furnish the 'symbolic worlds' in which extremist groups make their home, but it is never the sole builder. It is hardly possible to see, for example, the actions of those perpetrating the massively destructive acts of 9/11, including their own self-destruction, *solely as religious* acts. I have already argued that such atrocities cannot be ruled out *per se* as religion-based, or as inextricably linked with faith. Indeed, the secularist view of such acts as *pathological* is also not entirely off the mark, though we have then to ask what are the factors causing the soul-wounding, or mind-warping, rather than assuming - with the hardline secularist polemics - that religion itself is essentially pathological.

(b) Religion-refuting critics, to confirm the religious basis of such violence have made much of the anticipated delights in paradise with which the 'suicide bombers' motivate themselves for such self-sacrifice. Only the Muslim religion, it has been claimed, with its distinctive depictions of the blessed afterlife of martyrs for the faith, could have led to such 'suicidal' acts with seemingly calm assurance by young men and their mothers too.

This comment ignores the fact that in other non-Muslim contexts similar 'suicidal' acts aimed at damaging the 'enemy' have taken place without any such special blessing anticipated in the afterlife. The actions of those numerous Buddhist monks setting themselves ablaze in opposition to a variety of political situations in East Asia may be part of a very distinctive belief-system; but it is not one in which endless felicity in paradise is prominent. Similarly, the young Sri Lankan Tamil woman, from a relatively 'low-caste' Hindu background, who destroyed herself in the explosion with which she killed Rajiv Gandhi, Prime Minister of India, would probably not have been thinking in terms of the joys of an afterlife, nor in terms of how such a violent act would affect future rebirths. The main compulsion for her willingness to sacrifice herself as she blew up the 'enemy' was her absolute belief in the Tamil ethno-political cause, steeled by the need for revenge, we are told, for what had happened to her own family at the hands of Indian military personnel in Sri Lanka. No doubt a further reinforcement to her resolve was the belief that her matyrdom will be remembered, even sacralised, not only by her own family, but within the whole community engaged in what has been seen as a struggle to the death for their Tamil identity.

(It so happens that I had been giving a lecture at precisely the same place, Perumbudur in Tamil Nadu, not long before this horrific incident. It was a seminar of Sri Vaishnava Hindu scholars, and my subject was the sophisticated way in which Ramanuja, born at Perumbudur in 1017CE, and revered formative teacher of the Sri

Vaishnava tradition, taught that the universe is the 'body' of the all-pervading Self).

(c) This question of religion and violence must, though, be taken a little further. For, in the words of Juergensmeyer, the 'shadowy presence' of violence is there 'at the deepest levels of religious imagination'. And, as he rightly goes on to say, it is invariably the case that 'images of death (and violence) have never been far from the heart of religion's power to stir the imagination' (Juergensmeyer 2000: 6). In other words, this violent dimension of our religious traditions touches something at the dark core of human need. Expanding on a theme of Sigmund Freud, Rene Girard suggested that sacrifice results from the imitative ritualising of impulses to violence against rivals. In this way violence is 'tricked' into 'spending itself on victims whose death will provoke no reprisals' (Girard 1977). With human sacrifice as quite probably the earlier way, in time there was an animal substitute, which became one of the most basic and widespread of religious acts. The sacrificial victim, violently slain, not only vicariously bears away the guilt of the sacrificer. The victim sublimates, transmutes, channels off his murderous impulses too.

As usual, single explanations rarely do justice to the full range of phenomena to be accounted for. Other kinds of religious violence and symbols of violence seem far removed from ritual sacrifice. Then there are the very different *forms* of 'sacrifice' religious people come up with, from deliberate and heroic martyrdom to transmuted forms of self-sacrifice such as renunciation, fasting, the sacrificial offerings of charity, of scripture-reading, of 'the broken and contrite heart' (a sentiment found from Hebrew Psalms to Tamil Saivism), all of which seem equally unrelated to ritual sacrifice.

(d) There is, too, the God-dimension of religion that anti-faith reductionist theory, whether Freudian or not, will invariably see as the mere projection of some other psycho-social human need. What new factor is present when an all-creating, all-sustaining divine Being characterised by the highest qualities the human spirit is able to conceive is the sacred Object of any sacrificial offering, and when what is 'pleasing' to that Person is the main motive? At least for the Hebrew Psalmist, as for a number of Hebrew Prophets, it meant that it was not blood-sacrifice which pleased God, but the life-offering of humility, obedience, justice and mercy. A new vision of God brought a new ethical vision dominated by, in many respects, a strikingly humane religious ethic. It took the final fall of the central Temple, the result of attempting violently but hopelessly to resist the might of Rome in the first century, to bring the ritual sacrificial system of the Hebrew people to an end. Or rather, sacrifice was transmuted to the offering of prayer and life in the local Synagogue.

A similar transmuting took place within Brahmanic Hinduism, especially in its Vaishnava stream. Here, though, the cause seems to have been the resurgence, affected deeply by the Jaina and Buddhist movements, of indigenous feelings of *ahimsa*, the sense that injury to animal life in particular is *taboo*. Thus, earlier Aryan and other tribal rituals of animal and perhaps human sacrifice were replaced by more gentle offerings to Agni (the Fire at the centre of life and home, the 'Priest' who linked earth and heaven). And - as with Hebrew faith - in Hinduism too, the offering of a good, obediently *dharmic* life was seen as 'that which is pleasing to God', a phrase we find regularly in the writings of that great Vaishnava theologian, Ramanuja, for example. He is repeating a theme of the Gita. On the battle-field in the great war of Bharata, deeply doubting his *dharmic* role as warrior-prince, Arjuna is told that everything he does as part of his life-*dharma* is to be offered with loving devotion to God.

(e) Juergensmeyer argues that more basic than ritual sacrifice is the religious theme of cosmic warfare. It is 'the enduring and seemingly ubiquitous image of cosmic war from ancient times to the present' that gives meaning to rites of sacrifice. 'The sacrificial victim represents the destruction endemic to battle. Like the enemy - and like violence itself - the victim is often categorically out of place and therefore a symbol of disorder' (2000:170). He points to this dislocation in many types of 'victim' - from Indian widows who in the act of *sati* sacrifice themselves on their husbands' funeral pyre, to the usual personal type of young Arab offering himself for 'suicidal' bombing. The widow no longer has her proper place; the bomber is often a shy, not very sociable youngster between childhood and manhood. But it is in the context of conflict seen as part of the wider war between the forces of good and of evil, perhaps cosmic in range, that sacrifice is seen as most needed and most divinely fruitful. Without the transmuting moves to mythic drama, without re-interpretation in terms of a spiritual struggle against evil, it is perhaps inevitable that the cosmic war becomes played out on various battlefields very much part of this world.

(f) There are, though, other restraining faith-factors often missed by interpreters intent on placing violence at the centre of religious tradition. Judaism and Islam, for example, speak as much of mercy as they do of justice, as much of peace as they do of war. The compelling figure of the self-sacrificing Jesus, with his unequivocal stance against violence, even when the 'enemy' provokes such a response, stands as a continual counter-restraint to Christian aggressiveness. Perhaps, then, we need to look more to historical contexts and politically driven exegesis, as reasons for a tradition to over-ride its counters to blood-lust, so that mythic warfare becomes expressed in the most literal possible form.

I take up this issue of violence in religion again towards the end of the next chapter. Before closing this section, two further points might be mentioned. It is surely wide of the mark to suggest, as some have, that Islam's lack of a full-blown ritual sacrificial system is the reason for the tendency to take so quickly to violent *jihad* against perceived enemies of Allah. The argument is that there is no ritual way of working through resentments and animosities. But this is hardly convincing in view, on the one hand, of the very different histories of, say, Buddhist cultures, which usually have been far less prone to violence, yet also have no ritual sacrifice. Along with the 'strugglers' of the various early Indian *sramanika* movements, Buddhism did take up a radically transposed form sacrifice in the self-renunciation called for in the Noble Eight-fold Path (Selvanayagam 1996). Then, Islam too does continue a form of sacrifice both in life surrendered to the Will of Allah and even in the ritual way of all animal-slaughter.

Further, has it been the dominant traditional Christian interpretation of the death of Jesus as a substitutionary sacrifice, once and for all taking away the believer's sin and guilt, that has led Christian culture so often to be violent against perceived enemies - in spite of the very clear directions of Jesus himself that 'enemies' are never to be acted against in such self-protective, self-projective and violent ways? Perhaps. In both these cases, though, contextual factors of political, economic and cultural histories, as well as of exegetical interpretation, have greatly influenced the ways the Abrahamic religions have developed in general, and how they have worked out in particular both their attitude to sacrifice and their sense of sharing sacrificially in God's battle against evil - which is how they have seen their violence against others.

Religious traditions have emerged from long periods of interaction with a wide range of diverse human experience. The question of whether a religious act is socially and ethically intolerable is clearly one that has to be engaged in by the wider human community as much as by the concerned religious community, and from a variety of perspectives. But whatever may be the wider human response to terrorist acts done in the name of a religion, the often anti-religious 'reducing' of religion by those for whom a secularist perspective is the only option is precisely one of the factors making for feelings of alienation, and so increasing the possibility of the 'pathological', within traditional religious communities. This issue of seemingly contradictory forms of discourse, especially when we aim to convey the distinctive religious dimensions of our life as humans, clearly looms quite large in this matter of our identities. We identify ourselves in contradictory ways.

(5) The Identifying Power of Symbols

It would be ludicrous to suggest that religious imagery and symbols in themselves are in some way a danger to human wellbeing. The identities that make up our humanness as well as our religiousness are so dependent on symbolic embodying it is impossible to imagine either in completely non-iconic form. Vivid imagery is innate to human consciousness and all our faith-experience. Yet, even within religion we often find symbolic forms being suspect, perhaps seen as dangerously seductive. This suspicion ranges from the fierce revulsion by Hebrew, Muslim and Protestant traditions against 'graven images' - symbols given the sacral status of divine embodiment - to the search of transcendentalist Vedanta to find that Being who is beyond all 'name and form'. And poets of divine love East and West often ridicule fellow-believers whose faith seems unable to penetrate to the living Presence behind the imagery.

We might look briefly at the devotees of the 'great God' Siva known as 'Linga-bearers' - *linga* originally meaning 'phallus' or phallic representation, but later often just 'identifying mark'. It is the devotee's constant attachment to this symbol of Siva's presence, the Linga, that definitively identifies the 'Linga-bearer'. The 'image' is central to faith, but is very different from the usual iconic forms of the Hindu temple. Indeed, the 'identifying mark' (linga) is almost non-iconic in that it certainly is not in human form.

Among the 'linga-bearers' too there are numerous other explicitly sacral means, including the sacral mediation of itinerant teachers and gurus, all central to Lingayata identity. Here this special identity overlaps with other Hindu faith. For this linking of *the sacral identity of the Guru with seekers' self-realisation* is perhaps the most important means by which true identities are sought, not only in *bhakti* sectarian religion (such as earlier Lingayata), but in most forms of Hindu spirituality. For the Guru shares a measure of identity with God. Identities of a lesser kind figure prominently in social communication: making clear one's membership of a *bhakti* sect by its particular outward symbols, such as the special way of painting the Vaishnava *namam* (naming), being the two feet of the Lord imprinted vertically on the forehead, with the red mark between showing the Lady's role in the divine identity. Such slight differences immediately mark a person's group identity, which at the social level might be a matter of great import.

Within any *bhakti* group, though, it is the identity of God the mysterious Lover behind and beyond all others, even behind and beyond the figure of the Guru, that is the ultimate Focus. This supreme Being will always be identified in distinctive mythic and symbolic ways - the Lord of Meeting Rivers, Fluteplaying Krishna, the One who lies on the Sea-serpent, the Lord of Dance, and so on. It is this that determines the community's highest identity. Along with imagery, names too become crucial. A symbolically framed name often becomes a secretly initiating Name. Naming God is both the point of entry into the initiate's new identity, and - through constant repetition of the Name - the means of sustaining that identity.

The religiously and socially radical Kabir (15th century) referred to earlier is a fascinating case. Probably from a 'low-caste' weaver and nominally Muslim background, he regularly refused to be identified as either Muslim or Hindu. And this reflects the indefinable character of the great Name, the supreme Being he taught - often referred to as *Nir-guna* (without qualities, i.e. not qualifiable) just as Guru Nanak was to speak often of 'the One without form'. The given identity of any already established religious community could not embody the liberated identity that was Kabir's (and Nanak's) because the Object of his faith was beyond such identities. The unslottably radical newness of both God and the faith this God inspires dramatically fills his poetic writing. Not that faith is all sweetness and light. As with the southern love-poets, the pain of separation from God is also a frequent theme. Here are a few typical couplets, selected almost at random, expressing both the ecstasy and the agony:

Invoking the Name of Ram
  my body was consumed;
In the Name of Ram,
  my spirit was merged...
If the Lord himself sets you afire,
  who will save you?...
If Ram is there,
  He will save you.

God, You are my Mother
  and I your child...
If the child is in pain,
  Will its mother not feel pain too?
....Ram is my Husband,
  I his little wife;
Ram is great,
  and I am so small...

You are the Ocean,
  and I - a fish in the water:
In water I live,
  yet for water I pine..
I beseech you,
  turn your face towards me, my beloved.

           (translation by Vaudeville 1997: 258-71)

As with almost all India's love-drowned devotees, quite regularly and surprisingly we find him exalting the 'fellowship of the saints'. With those revered soul-mates, though, Kabir's one concern was for an inner passion for a God who pays no heed to the customary boundaries of human society. Before all these conventions, therefore,

Adam, the first man, never found out
  where Mama Eve had come from!
Then there was neither Turk nor Hindu...

neither cow nor butcher...
neither family nor caste...

It is hardly surprising that in the eyes of today's proponents of Hindutva who aim for a sharply identifiable uniformity for the Hindu community, especially as over against the Muslim tradition, the Kabirpanthis, socially resistant 'followers of Kabir's path', are seen as a deplorable threat. But he is equally anathema to militant Islam.

Kabir clearly had significant influence on the emergence of Guru Nanak's faith, to whom the Sikh community, which itself is 'neither Hindu nor Muslim', traces its lineage. In this Sikh tradition that sprang from Guru Nanak, and from the following nine Gurus whose voice and corporate presence became embodied in the Guru Granth Sahib, the identifying power of outer signs - their five K-symbols - became just as crucial to their sense of who they were, as were the lingas, ash and suchlike with the Lingayats. So there is a massive emphasis on the icons of faith. Yet, in the life of both, central to faith is the distinctive vision of their God-beyond-embodiment, beyond iconic expression or verbal description. In both cases, therefore, this great emphasis on symbol-transcendence is strangely paradoxical. Sikh symbolism at face value is so martial, reflecting the historical need, as perceived by Guru Govind, to be ready for sacrificial battle for the community and its faith. Yet Sikh devotion within the supportive context of these military symbols is focussed on wonder at the gentle power and merciful grace of God. The grounding symbol of the Saivite Linga-bearers in its primordial origins is phallic, and yet in Lingayata (and much other Saiva) devotion there is not the least recognition of any sexual connotation. It is even claimed that their Linga is an-iconic. The mysterious liberating power of 'the Lord of the meeting rivers', along with loyalty to his teachers and devotees, is all.

To what extent has this also been the case with Christian devotion to the Cross? Christian identity has been closely bound up with this symbol, though Christian theology here gives great weight to its grounding in acts of history. The first paradox is that what historically was a public gallows for anti-Roman criminals becomes the symbol of liberation, what was a cruel death became symbolic of the saving love of God, however interpreted doctrinally. But the most serious transition in interpretation is when this symbol of self-denying love

89

became, in the emperor Constantine's fourth century struggle for supremacy, the 'sign by which we triumph', that is against our enemies in battle. To 'take the cross' for medieval European crusaders meant marching into battle against Muslims and Jews, surely contradicting the faith-identity inherent to their primary symbol. Yet, it became powerfully effective as a triumphalist symbol.

These are not the full stories though. In all our religious devotion the range of response to our focal symbols can be surprising. Maybe there always remains some linkage with more 'original' worlds of meaning from which the symbols came: the Linga as creative power, the Sikh five central symbols as the call to absolute loyalty, the Cross as the death of one who suffered obediently and 'loved even unto the end'. But we should not miss the dangers of the power of our symbols. In particular they also have great power to elicit loyalty exclusively to the community identified by the symbols, and so that community's claims come to over-ride all other claims. Militancy, and not merely as a life-defensive strategy, in relation to other faith-communities has at times been the dominant response to all symbol-loyalty. Which points again to the paramount import of *interpretation* within our faith-bodies. Elaborating the meaning(s) of faith's grounding symbols is crucial for faithful inner orientation to the Beyond to whom those symbols point.

So then, our identities at all levels are inextricably bound up with and sharpened by the dominant symbols within our belief-system. No doubt we can extend this symbol-talk, as anthropology does, to include most of human life. All religion and culture can be spoken of as 'symbol-systems', every part of which signify meaning for those who share the life of those traditions. But we do not need here to enter into the complex discussion about how these symbol-systems function, how they differ from signs, and so on (cp Mach 1993). It is sufficient to restate the obvious: symbols are of immense importance in the shaping of identities, especially religion-based identities.

Even in spiritual systems such as Vedanta, Yoga, or the Dhyana of the Buddha, that emphasise so strongly the nurture of a new *inner consciousness* and the cultivating of inner qualities - perhaps even culminating in a pure consciousness beyond all qualities, all differentiations (as with non-dualist Vedanta) - there is no escaping the pivotal identity-creating role of symbols. The leading classical non-dualist, Sankara, may speak of the point where 'all spiritual means (*sadhanas*) are given up (*sanyasa*)' (Lott 1980:169ff). But the creative role of images is crucial, even if they be never more than 'indirect pointers' (as Sankara held) in reaching that desired moment of transcendent freedom. In Vedanta generally, it is not only the obvious iconic entities - Fire, Sun, Moon, River, and suchlike powers of nature - but more esoterically the various *pratika* images - Mind, Breath, Soul, and so on - that are to be meditated on with the aim of leading on to liberating vision of the supreme Self within both the icon and the seeker.

Symbols, then, though very much outward identifiers, also have this powerful role in creating new forms of inner consciousness. Indeed, these potent images spring up originally from the depths of human consciousness. Carl Jung's theory of 'archetypes' perhaps places too much emphasis on the primal unconscious as the source of our symbols. This does not wholly explain the dynamic. Our distinctive histories, and the widely differing human stories within these histories, also determine the functioning of symbols. That they are immensely powerful at the depths of our being, though, is undeniable.

And this is all the more mystifying when people look at the dynamics of religion from the outside and see our diverse religious symbols as serving merely to externalise, perhaps to politicise, religion and consequently to make our religious identities divisive one from another. But we have already seen how every identity always both incorporates us into a community, and by so doing distinguishes and divides us from others. The delineating community boundaries are such that if I identify myself as Christian, then I am not Muslim; if I am Sikh, I am not Hindu (as Sikhs themselves insist vehemently). And it is especially the externals, the outward symbols, maintaining that identity - Cross, Crescent, the five Ks of Sikhism, as well as many other less prominent symbols - that publicly distinguish and divide one religious group from another. Belief-systems are secondary in this matter of external identity, though the fact that symbols are always inextricably locked into beliefs - however wide interpretation of belief ranges - warns us against the indifference to belief of some anthropologists.

For Hindus, though divided into numerous groups with their own distinguishing symbols - Trident, Ash, *Namam*, Sacred Thread, and

91

so on - there is the Cow which functions symbolically as the most unifying Hindu sacral entity, reinforcing claims for a common Hindu identity. It is these central symbols that become such powerful rallying points for defending the community and its faith against perceived threats from others. 'Take the Cross' was the rallying cry for crusaders seeking to purge Europe and their 'holy land' of hated aliens. 'Protect the Cow', depicted as earth-like, as mother-like, has been a rallying cry for Hindus seeking a unified front against those seen as a threat to their existence as Hindus.

So it is all too easy to see our external identifying symbols not only as dangerously divisive, but even as inspiring militancy against other communities. When institutionalised, politicised, used solely as strategic devices for enhancing institutional power, then our religious symbols truly are dangerous to the life of the wider human community. Yet, without these symbols we have no religious identities at all, we are religiously rootless.

A crucial question for a number of religious traditions is the sense in which sacred scripture, often the source of symbolic imagery, is itself to be regarded as symbolic. Is there a Word beyond the words? Within Protestant Christianity, for example, there have flourished many groups with extreme literalist reverence for scripture as itself the Word of God. A basis for faith of this kind clearly entails a particular kind of 'fundamentalist' identity. Mainline Protestants too, such as Martin Luther, may have insisted on *sola scriptura* as the foundation for faith and its theological edifice, yet it has always been the transcendent Christ who is finally seen as the Word, resulting in a 'canon within the canon' in matters of exegesis. The term 'symbolics', in fact, was used extensively within the Reformed tradition to refer to the task of identifying the true Word beyond the words. Any other view of scripture verges on the idolatrous. Much Catholic exegetical tradition has been in essence similar.

As with other faiths, in the 'high' traditions of Hindu faith, all of which extol the Vedas as 'trans-human', 'eternal', 'infallible' and so on, considerable differences are to be found as to how these revered texts function and therefore as to what their revelatory character is and how they are to be interpreted (Coward 1988). They may be taken as primarily effective for action - especially ritual, sacral action - and their very sound deemed efficacious to that end, with particular texts powerful in effecting particular human desires. Clearly, this can be close to a literalist approach - and may well be how texts are often utilised by Hindus at a popular level, virtually as instruments of magic. But there is another widely practised approach that looks to scripture for inner illumination rather than for tangible benefits. Becoming aware, 'knowing', takes precedence over 'doing' and the effecting of worldly purposes.

Even here we find differing views. More transcendental non-dualists, looking for the realisation of the Self's oneness above and beyond all, also look in scripture for that which is beyond all words, that which can only be indirectly pointed at. Thus Sankara interprets Taittiriya Upanishad 2.9 (Lott 1980: 74-5). Here is a symbolist view *par excellence*. Even the 'infallibility' of scripture is said only to refer to its liberating potency, not to every aspect of worldly life. Hindu theists, on the other hand, giving greater weight to objective being as necessary to the subject-object 'inseparability' that is reality, often - but not always by any means - do not sit so lightly to the actual words of scripture. In particular, what is said about God, and what is to be done, are to be taken at face value. But the potential literalism of this is far from the position of many of Hinduism's 'love-drowned'.

In any case, what is crucial both for the inner vitality of a religious tradition as well as for relationships between religions, is the way in which our symbols are reflectively interpreted within traditions. Again, the importance of interpretive leadership cannot be stressed enough. And in our interpreting, two seemingly very different forms of sensitivity, of interaction, are called for. On the one hand, focussed on the fundamental Identity at the concerned tradition's centre, the interpreted meaning of the symbols we live by has necessarily to go on aiming for the development of the primary *higher identities* those symbols point us to. On the other hand our interpreters cannot but be aware of the *context* within which those symbols can continue to speak meaningfully to us, a context in which so many other identities lay claim upon us, not least the claims of other religious identities. How to be faithful to our primary identities, yet respond creatively to these many other identities, is the challenge to religious teachers today. Without this two-way interpretive process transforming inner consciousness, there is serious danger of religion becoming obsession with the outward symbols of institutional power, and faith-based identity becoming merely the corporate expanding of ego.

Chapter 3
Religion's Distinctive Dimensions

(1) The Identifying *Dimensions* of Religion

Religiously shaped identities, then, are complex. There are is even great diversity *within* what we think of as a religious tradition. Which leads us to the *complex character of religion itself*. All religion, no doubt, has to do in some way with the *Sacred*, a power-pregnant dimension of human experience of the world that mysteriously transcends the mundane. It is just here that a religious perspective differs from full-blown secularism.

Not that a non-sacred, non-transcendentalist worldview is wholly modern and western. There was a strand of ancient Indian thinking that limited itself to the boundaries of this world (*lokayata*), with sensory experience being the only reliable source of knowledge, and the satisfaction of the senses the only worthwhile goal of life. It was from out of this worldview that the *Kama-sutra*, the manual of erotic sexuality, emerged. Indian cultural tradition has not been solely about the mysteries of the Transcendent. The erotic can, of course, be seen as sacred and of ultimate value; this too is part of Indian spirituality. But where the boundaries of value are the material senses and their satisfaction, there will be little sense of the 'sacred' and its ultimacies.

Mircea Eliade, along with many others who emphasise the singularity of that which is at the core of any religious phenomenon, claims that it is this 'element of the sacred' that is the 'one unique and irreducible element' in religion (Eliade 1958, Foreword). Yet, all we can say of the sacred is that 'it is the opposite of the profane'. No other definition will 'cover the labyrinthine complexity of the facts'.

There is no end to the debate that can ensue from such a vaguely negative methodological starting point. Should there not be far more rigorous definition, less intuitional or 'theological' assumptions, as the basis for any properly systematic study of religion? Such is the argument of those religionists committed to more rigorously empirical method (e.g. Baird 1971), an approach that has gained ground in many University departments of religious studies increasingly in the last quarter of the twentieth century. This rejection of the more empathetic approach of moderate forms of phenomenology is itself perhaps a symptom of growing secularist hegemony in western intellectual life.

The unique *sacredness* at the centre of religious experience and the shaping of religious identities, for all their diverse manifestations, is crucial. Yet, a de-sacralising, dis-enchanting process is seemingly intrinsic to modernity and its secularities. Such disenchanting, though, has not led all humanity to lose the sense that anything is sacred. It has rather led to a conflictual polarising of sacred and profane, of religious and secular identities, in more starkly oppositional form than ever before. No one can argue that the secularising process gives us a complete lack of diversity. Even so, the globalising spread of modernity is producing on the one hand an homogenising of human culture equally the opposite of the 'labyrinthine complexity' seen in manifestations of the 'sacred'. And, by way of reaction and resistance to western secularism, there is in some ways a growing 'fundamentalist' uniformity within several disparate religious traditions.

The question is, then, in what ways are we to *understand the dynamics of the 'sacred'?* Gerardus van der Leeuw became known as the 'father' of a phenomenological approach to religion (van der Leeuw 1938). With its view of the *sui generis* character of religious experience, or what amounts to the autonomous functioning of religious subjectivity, many historians of religion have rightly been critical of phenomenology's insufficient attention to historical contexts, and thus to the very distinctive configurations religious phenomena take as a result of devotees interacting with their contexts.

Rudolf Otto, looking for religion's defining category, had earlier pointed to the experience of the *numinous*, faith's encounter with sacred power as both awe-ful, even terrifying, and yet fascinating (Otto 1923). Clearly this concentrates too much on one kind of faith-experience. Van der Leeuw also identified sacred *power* as religion's key; but his delineation takes into account the wide range of perceptions of and responses to that Power at the heart of faith, whether as seeking to avoid, manipulate, submit to, be attuned to, enjoy personal union with, even reject except in the transmuted terms perhaps of self-sacrificial love, or of an absorption transcending all egoity and personal power-goals. These differing forms of response implied in van der Leeuw's analysis could perhaps be taken as suggesting also our differing religious identities, though I will not follow this through here.

The years 2000-2001 saw the death of two scholars in the history of religions who, along with (but in very different ways from that of) Eliade and van der Leeuw, also made an outstanding impact on our understanding of what comprises 'religion'.

(a) *Wilfred Cantwell Smith*, whose name is linked primarily with the Centre for the Study of Religions at Harvard University, originally approached the study of religion, in India, from a sociological perspective. But even by the time of his quite early (1962) seminal work, *The Meaning and End of Religion*, Smith had worked out what were to be his central themes, urging us never to see any religion in objectifying or 'reified' terms. We should not try to delineate precisely the objective boundaries and character of what 'religion' is. Even to speak of 'a religion' is to distort the fluidity of its actual life. Smith allowed that there are certain identifiable givens in any 'cumulative tradition', but the key to understanding that tradition will always be the subjectivity, the transcending *faith*, of its participants. Faith-people share in the life of their tradition in many different ways, their countlessly diverging needs and aspirations being part of the shimmering flow that is human history. Because religious experience belongs to that of persons of faith within an ever-changing historical process, that faith-experience is necessarily elusive. And in turn this means that there is certainly no fixed or normative religious identity within any one tradition.

For Smith, the notion of a rigorous 'methodology' in matters religious was ludicrous. Attempts at precise definitions are doomed by the incommensurability of such an approach with the elusiveness of *faith*. Even identifying and delineating *types* of religious experience, he felt, introduced an artificiality that was highly questionable. Faith - the transcendent factor common to all religious experience - essentially involves a dialogical process. And this means that change and fluidity is also characteristic of the various histories of 'faith' - for Smith much preferred the singular, rather than speaking of 'faiths' in the plural. That which our traditions move towards, as well as the transcending 'faith' that somehow integrates all religious life, was to him more important than the historical forms from which they have come.

Clearly, then, Smith's passionately argued analysis of religion includes a strongly idealist strand, an assumption of a transcending coherence lying behind the fluidity of religion and the varieties of its historical forms. Understanding religious life in such fluid and elusive terms might lead us to think that religious identity too is equally elusive. However, Smith had to recognise that while 'faith' cannot be precisely or objectively formulated, both the various forms of *belief* and of *institution* that faith takes in our religious traditions obviously can be. Faith and belief, faith and social form, he argued, have to be carefully differentiated, though even the cognitive beliefs of people may not actually be expressed in a tradition's formal credal statements. So, while the essential identity of a religious person can be defined only by reference to transcending 'faith'- the essence of all religious experience - there are other lesser levels of identity to be found.

(b) In some basic respects, we can see similarities between the position of Wilfred Cantwell Smith and that of *Ninian Smart* (who sadly died suddenly early in 2001, just after completing his year as President of the American Academy of Religion, and as these lectures of mine were being given). They also diverge significantly. Smart was originally schooled in Oxford's philosophical tradition of logical and linguistic analysis. He rapidly moved on, though, from such an 'off the ground' cerebral approach, realising that it is futile to discuss either the meaning or the truth of religious statements apart from the religious context in which they are grounded. So there followed a period of systematic exposure especially to Hindu and Buddhist traditions. His analysis then became that of a phenomenologist, finding patterns akin to, yet also distinct from, the 'essences' of continental scholars such as Gerardus van der Leeuw.

Smart, then, was far less wary than was Smith of analysing the structures of the sacred and identifying key *types* of religious life. Both agree that we have to recognise fluidity within traditions. We should not too easily identify people's religious identity on the grounds of the general tradition they relate to. Smart's greater phenomenological interest, though, led him more readily to identify typical and essential patterns of religious life, even if these do cut across the boundaries of our traditionally identified religious communities. Such deeply embedded differences within what is usually seen as one religion will obviously impinge heavily on a typology of religious identities. Both Smith and Smart give great weight to the *transcendence* typical of religious experience, though it is Smart who is usually more concerned, as a methodological need, to point evocatively to the sacred Object central to that experience.

Basic to Ninian Smart's understanding of religion is its *multi-dimensional* character. First suggested in the 1960s, it was an analysis that he was to explore most fully in his *Dimensions of the Sacred: An Anatomy of the World's Beliefs*, in 1996. To neglect any of these numerous 'dimensions' in describing 'religion' is to distort the nature of religious traditions. It is to distort how they function, and how their adherents participate in the life of those traditions. He proposed six essential 'dimensions' as typical if any cultural tradition is to be called 'religion': the *ritual, mythic, doctrinal, social, ethical* and *experiential* dimensions. Or we might word it as five ways of experiencing the Sacred Power - through sacred act, story, belief-system, community, and life-values. This analysis of Smart's is still convincing in spite of adjustments and additions that can and have been made. It also leads to possible ways of looking more closely at faith-based types of self-identity.

Clearly the 'dimensions' do not always have the same balance, overtly at least. In mainstream Islam, for instance, the 'mythic' element in their religion's undergirding narrative is usually far less obvious, less luxuriantly expressed, than in most forms of Hindu tradition. In Pentecostal Christianity, as in some *bhakti* streams of Hinduism, inner experience is given far more weight than any other aspect of religion, though the social dimension - in terms of the fellowship of believers, akin to the Hindu God-lovers here - can also be surprisingly strong. But even within Islam, Sufis look to inner experience, even ecstasy, as all-important. Lutheranism has usually given greatest weight to doctrine and its faith-confessions, though its liturgical ritual too is vital to its sense of tradition, and it has had its periods of pietism. In reformed Protestantism the doctrinal, ethical and so didactic dimensions are seemingly paramount. And there are many other ways in which the dimensional balance differs (Lott 1987 for more extensive confirmatory examples of these invariable features of religious life*).*

To these six dimensions I add four invariable characteristics. Smart was well aware of these aspects of religious life, but did not include them as 'dimensions' as they function in rather different ways. They do, nevertheless, have to be reckoned with if we are to understand those dimensional facets of religious life and in particular the forms of self-identity related to them.

(i) There is an *organically related interdependence* of the various 'dimensions'; the meaning of each is locked into all the others: myth interprets ritual, is embedded in doctrine and undergirds social relationships; social identities are shaped as much by the performance of ritual as by the telling of myth and the observance of an ethic. The permutations are almost endless. Religious life is a complex organism. So this means that the integrating sense of self-identity of religious people has multiple sources and is multi-faceted.

(ii) All the dimensions of religion function too as part of a *dynamic process of continual change* - one of Smith's key themes as we saw. This historical and experiential fact, though, is rather at variance with the way in which traditions, on their conservative side, often see themselves as being 'from the beginning' unchanged and unchanging. In reality, even within them radical reform movements emerge from time to time, deeply critical of the way things have been in the tradition, and claiming to recapture some more pure and original form of faith. This reforming element is as typical of Hindu tradition, with its traditional belief in its unchanging *'sanatana dharma'* or 'everlasting sacral order', as it is of the history of Christianity, with its more obvious protesting and reforming, especially since the sixteenth century and the flowering of Europe's socio-cultural Enlightenment.

Even the deep divide within Islam between Sunni and Shi'a resulted from a movement for critical reform of the growing self-indulgent life-style of the Baghdad leadership, a critical reform that led to the martyrdom of Ali and his sons. Significant too - given the usual claims for the uniform character of Islam - is what we find within the Sufi movement that was so strong in India and appeals to western seekers after a new spirituality. This is the Sufi emphasis on a transcendent *interiority*, that often views with critical eye the more common Islamic emphasis on 'believing' the true doctrine and 'doing' the right deeds. Inner change within traditions, in other words, is an essential part of being religious. Again, this means that, for all the conservative tendencies also typical of religion, the self-identity of religious people is well able to change its character during the course of their life-experience.

Rarely reckoned with by phenomenological accounts of religion is the extent to which external factors - cultural, social, economic, ecological, political - have impinged on the development of religions historically, and the extent to which engagement with such external life has led to inner change. Secular historians may, of course, go to the other extreme and disallowing any possible *sui generis* dynamic within a religious tradition, reduce all to an historically identifiable cause-effect process. Everything is explicable by factors other than those professed by believers. The reality is that the inner dynamic of religious traditions has made an incomparable impact on 'external' histories, directing it in ways that only the peculiar phenomenon of religion has been able to. The process of change in other words is interactional, never one-way. This means we have to see the 'social dimension' of religion as two-directional: there is life within the sacred community, and there is engagement with wider society. Here we have further reason for emphasising that religious identities can be quite complex.

(iii) There is, as we saw, an inherently *symbolist* character to all our ways of being religious. No doubt this can also be said of all that we call culture, but it is pre-eminently so of that most intensely focussed of cultural forms identifiable as 'religion'. No doubt this symbolist way of being religious is more obviously so when speaking of ritual and myth, or in a highly and overtly iconic religion like Hinduism. But what of those faiths such as orthodox Judaism, Islam, extremist Protestants, or Sikhs, that in worship and doctrine so stress the incomparable character of God that all worship by means of images is abhorred? They too in fact usually recognise - precisely because of God's otherness - that conceptual images are inevitable.

In other words, we know that 'otherness' of God only through the mediation of some kind of imagery, albeit the imagery of divine self-revelation, as argued by the 20th century transcendentalist theologian Karl Barth, whose writings made such an impact of both Protestant and Catholic thinking. Or this may be by way of divine grace effecting a wonderful 'mediated immediacy', to use the words of another Protestant, John Baillie. Some of the most sophisticated debate at this metaphysical level took place within medieval Islam, and was then taken up by Christian philosophers like the great Thomas Aquinas, in his *analogia entis,* or analogy of being. There are, too, significant insights concerning the issue of transcendence-immanence, or mediacy-immediacy, in the medieval debates within Hindu philosophy, as we see in a moment.

Religious people - and not only those with a more literalist attitude - are usually not overjoyed at hearing the well-loved focal-points of their faith referred to as 'symbolic', certainly not as 'mere symbols'. Few like to hear of central elements in their faith - Christ perhaps, or the Guru Granth (Holy Book of the Sikhs), even 'God' - spoken of as just a pointer to some higher reality beyond, especially if that 'reality' is allowed no corresponding reality in the 'objective' world, as argued by Don Cupit and other extremist neo-Kantian theologians. Faith usually sees things with more naive realism, which is not the same as literalism, the kind of literal approach encouraged, paradoxically, by way of the demands for objectivity earlier forms of modern science expected. Faith-realism gladly retains its mythic/symbolic dimension - as does more recent science as it happens, especially seen in the cosmologies of modern physics.

The fierce debate within Hinduism between the realism of the rigorous, more 'religiously' minded theists and the more elusive transcendentalism of the non-dualists who sat much more lightly to tradition, raises very similar issues. Sankara and the long line of those propounding non-dual Reality were happy to use 'as-though' language: what *seems* to be is not what *really is*. Even the divine embodiments in the saving Avatars are merely 'as though' embodiments. Indeed, all our mythic and verbal imagery, they argued, has to be of this kind according to the non-dualist. No words or concepts, even if from the sacred Word, are able to do more than point towards rather than penetrate the mystery of the one Reality beyond all that seems differentiated. A very different view was held by Ramanuja, Madhva and all those theistic Vedantins committed to the reality both of divine revelations concerning the Other as well as to the distinct personal being of the Other, however mysterious that otherness, and however 'inseparable' our and the world's being from the being of that Other. They found it blasphemous to think of sacred Word, and its concepts, as mere indirect pointers, solely symbols of what is beyond, unable to put us in touch directly with that Other.

So then, the symbols and images essential to faith are interpreted very differently, and the way we interpret that symbolism is crucial, both to the meaning of faith itself and to the self-identity shaped by that faith. Indeed, it could well be argued that the dynamic role of symbols, especially as they function within faith-communities, is more potent than any other dimension of religion in creating and continually re-sharpening people's sense of identity. Having said this, though, it is clear that symbols do not function in isolation from mythic story, ritual performance, and doctrinal interpretation, three of Smart's 'dimensions'.

(iv) Then, too, at no point does religion function without some degree of *aesthetic* expression (again, a point that Whaling makes in his reworking of Smart's analysis). Symbols clearly have a major role in religion's aesthetic life, but when people experience the sacred as overwhelmingly beautiful, we have a cultural dimension that seems to merit separate consideration. Nor is a sense of beauty confined only to the so-called 'higher' religions and their *hautes cultures*. Central to primal religious forms too we find body-adornment, dance-movements, musical rhythms, art-forms, mandala-like patterns. Indeed, aesthetic expression is never completely absent even in its most artifice-free puritanical forms, when there is vigorous rejection of imagery, music and dancing, profane ornamentation, ostensibly indeed rejection of all the culture of the larger community, or when inner experience is made all-important over outer form.

Thus the passionate devotional (*bhakti*) movements in India sweeping the whole continent during different periods at least from the fifth to the eighteenth centuries, while pouring scorn on the wiles of the world, produced India's greatest vernacular poetry, strikingly similar to the massive outpouring of hymns by the rather puritanical Charles Wesley, spiritual poet of Britain's evangelical counter-cultural awakening in the eighteenth century, whose work we noted three verses earlier. Or we might think of the unsurpassably beautiful mosques built by a religious tradition that ostensibly rejects the use of imagery to portray the divine; or the deeply moving music and dance of those most other-worldly of Muslims, the Sufis; or the splendidly realistic art of the Ajanta Buddhist monks meditating in their dark caves in Western India on the follies and delusory ways of the world. There is even a minimalist beauty in the silently seated circle of Quaker Friends, or the long-practised postures of the world-renouncing Hindu Yogi seeking the silent world within, beyond all name and form. Again, very differing forms of this aesthetic dimension have their differing roles in the shaping of distinctive religion-based identities.

(2) The Central Role of a *Sacred Focus*

As the culmination of the defining dimensions of religion, we now move to the *sacred Object,* or *sacred Focus.* It is this that takes the pivotal role, the integrating point of *transcendence* within the immense and complex range of phenomena that makes up each religious tradition. Here we have, in other words, the essential counterpart of Smart's 'experiential' dimension, or that which ultimately is to be 'experienced'.

Few will have difficulties in identifying the central Focus of Islam: Allah, the all-merciful and all-beneficent One, in whose all-powerful will lies our peace. All beliefs and prayers and faithful actions spring from that one Centre. Confusion - for the non-Muslim - might arise from the absolutist role of the Qur'an and the immutable authority of the sacred tradition based on this infallibly divine revelation. Is there, the critic might ask - as may be asked of all traditions in which scriptural infallibility is so dominant - is there a compromising of the role of the living God as the central Focus of faith? Do Revealer and Revelation as sources of authority become confused? This quibble, though, will carry little weight for Muslim believers, or indeed for many looking at Islam from the perspective of other literalist forms of scripture-centred faith. Unquestioning acceptance of the revelation as infallibly given by the Source of all truth, for the believer seems merely to simplify the central role of God. In Islam, as in Sikh faith in the Formless One, there is little doubt concerning what is the sacred Object. Allah, 'The God', the Great One (*akbar*)of the ninety nine beautiful names, has no rival for that central integrating role

What, though, of less clearly monotheistic traditions? It is not only in modern Hinduism that we hear talk of the one God within, behind, beyond his many manifestations. The way this is now expressed may be different from earlier Hindu faith. Oft-quoted is that very ancient text from the Rig Veda's first book: 'They call him Indra, Mitra, Varuna, Agni....To what is one, sages give many a title.'

So, for that substantial if greatly diversified section of Hindus, the Vaishnavas, for example - in spite of the many names used in prayer and the many forms imagined - it is their one God (named and envisioned variously as Vishnu, Narayana, the Three-strider, Rama, Krishna, etc) who is at the heart of faith and experience. For Saiva Hindus, it is the 'Great God', Siva. That there will probably be dynamic linkage in each case with a female form of deity that is inseparably bound up with the dance of life and the powers of earth, maybe even identified as Earth-Goddess, at least in main-stream sectarian life, does not lessen the ultimacy of the Great One at the centre.

Not that these faiths are to be understood exactly in terms of the monotheisms of Islam or Protestant Christianity. Mutiplicity too is crucial to Hindu tradition. Large numbers of Hindus believe they have the option to choose their 'desired god', the one fitting to the inclinations of their spiritual nature. While Protestants and Islamists may not recognise this as 'monotheism', the fact is that central to huge segments of Hindu faith is an integrating divine Focus. Only when the more instrumentalist and perhaps even manipulative aims of Tantrism take over is the Focus weakened and other life-goals, other sacred powers, become primary.

Certainly in the Vedantic ('end of Vedas') tradition that emerged with the reflective, contemplative discipline begun in the Upanishads, it is the all-encompassing, all-pervading, all-knowing 'Great One', mostly called *Brahman* (but also Person, Self, etc) who is this 'sacred Focus'. But then, for reflective *theistic* Hindus, that more impersonal Brahman becomes intensely personal. Thus, for Vaishnavas, Vishnu is equally all-encompassing and all-pervasive, is indeed the supreme Brahman, with Siva having a similar place in reflective Saivism. While it is true that many Hindus do not identify themselves permanently with any particular deity, or with his/her sect, nevertheless a sense of the unitive Sacred Power within all life - whether 'many-formed', or 'formless' - is undeniably central to any who consciously identify themselves as people of 'Hindu' faith. A 'Hindu' *political* identity may well find a very different point of integration.

In Buddhist traditions, while the gods are too weak to warrant a central role, all three great streams of Buddhism - Theravada (the doctrine of the elders), Mahayana (the great vehicle), Vajrayana (the thunderbolt or immediately powerful vehicle) - place the Buddha in one form or another at the centre of meditation and even of devotion. In his cosmicised form in the Great Vehicle, and when a soteriology of grace emerges, it is the Buddha who is an ultimate and transcendent Focus for all experience. In the Doctrine of the Elders, the person of the Buddha at first seems to be but part of the Way as its guide. It is the inner goal of *nirvana* - a transcendent state of 'ego-extinction' - that takes the place of final Focus. Yet, the identity of the Buddha is always more than just an initiating, perhaps highly venerated teacher. In seeking to enter into the Buddha's experience, to follow the same liberating path as that which he pioneered, the *person of the Buddha* clearly takes a decisive role. It is not, however, that of 'God', or one of the gods. For they too are still constrained by the dynamics of *karma*.

Christianity, with its trinitarian faith, does not complicate its understanding of a 'central Focus' as much as those far more wide-ranging ways of Hindus. From a Muslim viewpoint, though, Christian faith shows confusion in what should be the sacred, incomparable, indivisible simplicity of Godhead. How can there be worship of the One God, runs traditional polemic, when Christ, and Mary (the third 'person' of the Trinity identified by Islamic tradition) have equal place? For all their deep respect for Jesus, Muslims see Christian expressions of the divinity of Christ as committing the fatal sin of *shirk* - putting that which is mortal on a level with God. The Identity of God is compromised. Even within Christianity there has been deep and sometimes violent division concerning the relation of Christ to God. Nevertheless, the great confessions of faith throughout Christian history make it clear that the one God - whatever misleading language may be used to describe the God-likeness of Christ - is the all-creating, all-commanding, all-encompassing Centre of things.

How far, then, in the widespread world of religions, does this broad analysis of an invariable integrating Centre for religious faith - a transcending Identity - hold? Obviously it applies most easily in the case of monotheistic or other well systematised, more centralised faiths such. But in principle all major faiths can be included. In less obvious ways, there are what might be called integrating foci even in the world's primal indigenous traditions too - the great Spirit, Mana-power, or some dominant embodiment of a pervasive sacred Power, such as the Totem, the divine Chief, the heroic Ancestor.

Two sociologists of religion have been especially influential:

(a) If the totemic thesis of *Emile Durkheim*, one of the great sociological gurus quite early in the twentieth century, is correct, we have another reason for thinking that primal traditions too have their central Focus, and for seeing that Focus as central to a community's self-identity (Durkheim 1915). The most 'elementary' form of primal societies, argued Durkheim very effectively (building on the pioneering fieldwork of others), is based on the totem - animal, bird, tree, natural objects such as ant-hill (though Durkheim thought this a later adoption, probably based on an incident in the life of an honoured ancestor), even thunder, lightning, mist and suchlike phenomena. Through these totemic forms the social group finds its character, its power, its skills, its essential being and in turn they represent the essential being of the group. It is the totem that gives a clan its name, its identity, that differentiates it from other groups. The identity between totem - symbolic of that which is most sacred - and the basic social group is such that, as Durkheim put it, 'The god of the clan, the totemic principle,(is) nothing else than the clan itself...' Society identifies its own inner life as the embodiment of the Sacred; yet, it is the Sacred by which it lives. In many totemic cultures the bond between social group and sacred totem is intensified by sacramental feasting on that life which is normally taboo.

The theory is persuasive, but however central to primal life the totemic form may be, there are various other styles of primal religious life, other primal phenomena that have to be reckoned with. There is for example the felt potency of ancestors and hero-figures, there are the spirits of revered virgins and other power-laden women, there is the sacred Power pervading all life, but focussed in particular objects. Durkheim's theory, then, is now dated in various ways. Yet his work is still seminally important for sociological understanding of how primal patterns persist in new forms, and in particular the ways in which the sense of the Sacred shapes human self-identity.

(b) In some ways this is even more true of that other sociologist of religion, Max Weber, whose influence was felt from the earlier part of the twentieth century onwards. For Weber traced clear continuities between a religious culture's grounding vision, including its key doctrines, and the self-identity that prompted its way of life generally, including its social attitudes, its economic and political practices. Hence his view that there are systemic connections between

Protestant Christianity's de-sacralising faith and the emergence of a modern secularist worldview, between the 'Protestant work-ethic', and the capitalist economy of today (Weber 1930). I return to the question of Protestant faith as the ground of a secularist worldview in the later chapter on 'secularisation'.

The danger in tracing connections between what we might describe as religious (especially doctrinal/experiential) cause and cultural (especially political/economic/ethical) effect is that the process tends to become over-simplified, with a neglect of other nuancing factors to be traced in the concerned history. Connections between grounding religious belief-systems and wider cultural life-styles *can* be made however. Distinctive self-identities *are* significantly shaped by what religious people identify as the Supreme, and so by their vision of the world integrated around that sense of focal Being, that which for them embodies supreme value and truth. There is little doubt that monotheistic faiths do tend to lead to a more universalising life-attitude. 'My/our one sovereign God is in reality God of all the earth. The truth this one God has revealed is surely universal truth.'

Non-monotheists will find this problematic enough; but we might take an even more explicitly negative cause-effect example. No Christian can easily ignore the connection often made within the modern ecological movement between the de-sacralising of nature seemingly innate to Judeo-Christian monotheism and the industrial technological revolution of modern times in which Nature is seen as the objectifiable and subservient instrument of human exploitation. Lynn White was one of the first to argue, in an influential essay in 1965, that Christianity had to carry a heavy burden of guilt for modern technology's destruction of eco-systems. That it was the secular theorists of the Enlightenment, in particular the English political philosopher and empiricist, Francis Bacon (1561-1626), and the French philosopher of science, Rene Descartes (1596-1650), rather than biblical exegetes or theologians who expressed such an aggressive attitude to Nature in more vigorously systematic form, weakens the argument somewhat. But there is little doubt that a strand of Judeo-Christian-Muslim faith does show a markedly different attitude towards nature, and regarding the human relationship to nature, than we find in most traditional and Eastern religion. The dominant sense of self-identity implied here, rooted in a distinctive way of identifying God, a sense of self-identity that sees our relationship to nature and to other human groups in distinctive ways, is a crucial factor in this process.

(3) Dimensions that Shape Identities

Can we, then, attempt an analysis of religious identities based on these more explicitly inner religious dynamics? Given the wide-ranging character of religious faith and practice, it is hardly surprising to find divergent types of religious *identity* also. Though we can hardly claim that distinctive religious identities correspond directly to the 'dimensions', there is a significant degree of fit. They certainly account for prominent ways in religious people's sense of who they are and how they identify themselves.

(i) There are religious people whose consciousness is dominated by the *mythic* dimension of their faith more than by any other aspect of it; they live in the world of the sacred stories, the heroes of these stories who have become their well-loved friends. Their self-identity is based largely on a consciousness shaped by their 'listening' *(sravana),* as Indian tradition so often emphasises. But there is also 'seeing' *(darsana* and other cognates), by way both of the countless images encapsulating mythic moments and various dramatic presentations of the stories of Rama and Krishna especially. Through faith's imagination the sacred stories transport the listeners and watchers into new worlds. In Buddhism there is a similar role for the Jataka-stories that recount the Buddha's experiences in various 'births', as the name implies. Thus, the Victorian Christian children's hymn, 'Tell me the stories of Jesus...', echoes a theme in many faith-traditions. It was interesting to see the socialist, pacifist and publicly influential Methodist preacher, the Revd Dr Lord Donald Soper, on his 90th birthday celebration which was televised by the BBC, choosing this hymn as one of those summing up his faith.

In the Bhagavata Purana (especially book 10, sections 29-30), for example, and other key sources of Krishna devotion, not only is there the retelling of stories of Krishna as infant, youthful cowherd, mountain-lifter, flute-playing lover, demon-destroyer and suchlike; his postures and actions are re-enacted and his wandering footsteps retraced. Again, in Islam such imitative story-telling does not hold centre-stage religiously in this way. Yet it is there, and potently so. All the incidents in the life of Muhammad and how he responded to them are all-important in the Muslim's life, for the believer is to conform to that great example. And for Shi'as there is the self-denying example of Ali and his sons, celebrated annually as a dramatic public procession recalling their tragic martyrdom. This story clearly makes a great imaginative and emotional impact on the community as a whole. In the Sikh community too there is a potent role for stories (in Sikh tradition often pictured, though outside the worship place, in the Gurdwara) of the ten Gurus, especially those who were martyrs in their religious history, including those of recent struggles for a Sikh homeland, Kalisthan.

In these less prolifically 'mythic' traditions, imaginative stories provide a powerful impetus in other ways too. The willing self-sacrifices made in such conflicts as that between Israel and the Palestinians, or in the self-destructive violence of September 11, are in part because these young men's imagination has been stirred by the story of the paradise to come. And in communities with a strong sense of victimhood - Serbian people for instance - the mythically reworked memories of former heroes, martyrs to their cause, form a stirring motivation for their own commitment to valorous and sacrificial deeds. In general, this theme of heroic sacrifice is one of the most common in a religious community's story-telling, and forms a crucial component in the shaping of self-identity.

(ii) Or, the self-identity of many religious people is perhaps most directly dependent on and regularly renewed by *ritual*. For 'ritual' does not just entail the performance of sacred acts out there, disengaged from the performers. The believer is drawn into the inner microcosmic world of ritual, becomes part of its undergirding sacral structures. Of all world religions it is the Brahmanic Hindu 'world' that traditionally is probably the most ritualist. Indeed, for well over two millennia there was even a supporting philosophy of ritual (Purva-Mimamsa, or the 'Previous Exegesis') that virtually dispensed with a distinct sacred Being or any mythic power other than that within the ritual itself. It is not the gods who ensure the blessings aimed for when some sacred act is performed. Within that act there is, argued the Ritualists, an unseen potency that of itself effects what is hoped for. Providing, that is, the sacred act is performed by the appointed priestly body in the way prescribed by the Vedas and interpreted correctly by the Exegetes.

Ritual, in other words, ensures the continuation of a sacral world in which the mysterious power of the *brahman* is under the control of a priestly Brahmanic body. This is, of course, far from the whole Vedic story. Very different interpretations of that mysterious *brahman*-power emerged. Yet, 'Brahmanism' is a strand of Hinduism making very clear just how closely entwined is ritual with wider ranging sacral worlds of faith. In the practice of Hinduism popularly too, it becomes impossible, for instance, to disentangle ritual from accompanying myth. Each temple and sacred place, perhaps a place of pilgrimage where ritual is believed to be most potent, has its mythic story, often called the 'greatness' (*mahatmya*) of that sacred place, itself seen as the centre of a sacral cosmos. Again, we should not forget the way such faith in ritual has been ridiculed by more radical believers such as Kabir, Tukaram and many others.

Identifying oneself closely with the performance of a special religious tradition is certainly one important basis for religious people's sense of identity. Many look to some initiatory rite, or to related symbols that they bear, as proof of their religious identity, marking them off from those who do not share the life of that tradition. Circumcision in infancy and *Bar mitzvah* arround puberty are decisive marks of belonging within Judaism. Baptism and confirmation are corresponding rites in Christianity, though there are considerable denominational differences concerning both timing and objective significance. During a particularly alarming struggle with the devil concerning his own self-identity, Martin Luther is said to have thrown an inkpot at the evil one, shouting 'Be off with you, I am baptised. I do not belong to you' (Or words to that effect). More commonly in Christian tradition, it is sharing regularly in the 'sacred feast' of the Eucharist/Mass/Qurbana/Lord's Supper through which there is a sense of 'communion' with Christ, a sharing in his identity, that the most decisive sense of being peculiarly Christian is established.

Or, within many traditions, the making of pilgrimage to a sacred place gives those on the journey a new sense of orientation, a sharpened sense of self-identity, and a closer sense of kinship with the community of fellow-pilgrims. In Islam all five great religious duties (*din*), often called 'pillars' of faith, are 'obligatory' and powerfully confirm Muslim self-identity: Reciting the essence of Muslim faith in the oneness of Allah and the essential role of the Prophet, known as the *kalima*; saying daily prayers (preceded by the required ablutions), with repeated acknowledgement of the greatness of Allah; observing the month-long fast of Ramdhan; giving alms systematically to the needy. It is, though, especially in the fifth duty, making pilgrimage (*hajj*) to Mecca, that the Muslim's sense of special identity, shared by millions from across the globe, reaches its emotionally binding climax. Obviously the detailed symbolism and imagery that relate so closely to ritual have their own potency in creating identity.

(iii) *Doctrines* too, whether in official credal formulations or in more general belief-systems, clearly shape religious identities and create strongly felt loyalties. We have just seen how being a Muslim really comes to life with the reciting of the *Kalima*, the Muslim confession of faith in the oneness of Allah and the prophetic mission of Muhammad. These credal words are whispered into the ear of the new-born infant child and are central to what is taught later and recited right up to the moment of death. The 'faith' (*iman*), though, often finds more expanded formulation. Two such statements of faith are: 'I believe in God, his name and attributes, and I accept all his commandments'(i.e. 'I am a Muslim'). Or, 'I believe in God, his angels, his prophets; in the last day, the predestination by the most high God of good and evil, and in the resurrection after death'. The Qur'an's chapter 112, though a mere 4 verses, is regarded as equal to a third of the whole sacred book, because it main point is the indissolvable unity of God:

> Say - He, Allah, is one. Allah is eternal.
> He begets not, nor is he begotten: and none is like him.

A substantial part of Islamic theology deals with the problem of God's unity, and just how his nature and his attributes (life, knowledge, power, will, hearing, seeing, speech) inter-relate. Doctrinal issues, then, have been paramount in Muslim reflection on the meaning of faith, even though matters of conduct and even jurisprudence (the demands of *shariah*) have been far more publicly prominent of late. For it is especially *doctrine* that delineates the divine identity, by which the believer's identity is so crucially shaped.

The frequent contention that Indian and Eastern religions show little interest in particular belief-systems shows a lamentably one-sided understanding of Hindu and Buddhist traditions. True, doctrine has never held the overtly dominant position we find either in fourth and fifth century Christian dedication to credal clarity, or in sixteenth and seventeenth century Protestant struggles for purity of faith in their endless confessionalism. There was, of course, a constraining political correctness about all this too. The East has never been quite so concerned about ortho-doxy as 'correct doctrine' in that way. Yet, 'right belief' is there at the centre of Buddhist discipline. The systematic learning and debating together this 'right belief' is essential to monastic life in the Tibetan tradition. It is fascinating to watch monks engaging together in ritualised debate about faith-issues as part of their monastic discipline. Belief, in other words, is essential in the shaping of at least some forms of Buddhist identity.

More developed doctrine dominates in the theological guidance given by the great Hindu teachers in India's theistic *bhakti* tradition. Harsh words are used (especially by Madhva) against those who do not believe, for example, the sovereignty and loving personhood of God, the dependence of the soul upon God, or the reality of difference between that which is other-determined (*para-tantra*) bound and that which is free (*sva-tantra*). These are taken to be ultimate items of faith. For them, in other words, the meaning of sacred story, act, community, *dharma*, was in each case determined by the right kind of belief in God. That was the essentially required 'knowledge' (*jnana*) which they saw as of the very highest reflective form of true religion. In this way distinctive doctrine was a significant part of what determined the distinctive identity of the serious theists. Even antagonisms that arose between sects and communities had a large slice of belief-difference in them. The two Vaishnava sub-sects of the 'northern' monkey-way and the 'southern' cat-way owe their conflict - the more bitter for being such close family members - as much to differing ways of interpreting divine grace and seventeen other well-listed doctrines as they do to their somewhat differing symbols (e.g. the sectarian nasal line, indicating the Goddess, that extends an inch lower for the 'southerners'), or to their differing sociological histories (the 'northerners' tend to be more Brahmanic). Belief-systems do count in the shaping of ultimate identities, even in Eastern religions.

(iv) Other religious people find the *ethical* compulsions of their faith most important to their sense of self-identity. Christians perhaps recall the words of Jesus that it is 'by their fruits you shall know them', and his insistence that (in Jewish Torah) love of neighbour is linked irretrievably with love of God; the will is as important as heart and mind in loving God. This ethical emphasis - sometimes as an anti-mystical attitude - is a dominant strand in Reformed Protestantism, expressed in wide-ranging forms: Kant's identifying of the 'moral imperative' as the essential mark of the religious spirit; Kierkegaard's existentialist commitment of the will, and contemporary liberationism's radical maxim that the will's action is prior to reflection; the strongly ethical emphasis of the Society of Quaker Friends.

Not that *Catholic* faith and spirituality has lacked this moral strand. From fifth century Augustine, through the great system of Thomas Aquinas (13th century) to the present Pope John Paul, the moral struggle called for by the human race in general and Christian believers in particular is right at the centre. Jesuit 'casuistry' may be the object of slight ridicule by some, but the order's 'moral philosophy/ theology' has in fact been crucial in the development of modern Christian ethics.

But beyond Christian ethical concern we could think of the highly moralistic way of China's

Confucianists, or indeed the strongly ethical early stages in the Buddha's Noble Eightfold Way and the new identity aimed for thereby, or a similarly strong emphasis on right action (work hard, treat widows justly, feed our wandering teachers, and so on) in the new identity called for by the twelfth century South Indian, Basava, in his reformed Saivism. That it was the socio-economic context of his time (and so his quite radical rejection of growing Brahmin dominance) and subsequent history that eventually turned his Lingayat community into just a new caste with mainly political goals, in one sense further underlines his emphasis on doing as necessary to being. This can, though, too easily obscure the strongly God-focussed point of his message that we noted earlier.

It is probably futile to speculate on the impact invasive Islam made on such medieval Hindu reformers seeking a change from the dominance of a Brahmanic ethic with its structured hierarchy of purity and pollution. Basava may well have found sufficient resources for his liberating way within other non-Brahmanic Indian tradition. What is undeniable is the Muslim claim to provide a new basis for the coherence of society. Brahmanic *dharma* too makes inclusive ethical demands. And for the serious Brahmanic theists exactly at that time, *dharma* was not an autonomously given way of life; it was to be conformed to in order 'to be pleasing to the Lord (of all karmic action)', as Ramanuja put it. In Islam, however, there is far greater clarity regarding the integration of faith in God and action in life. The ethical dimension, the will to translate faith into a precisely defined way of life, is unmissable. *Jihad*, more usually translated 'holy war', actually refers first of all to this 'struggle' to ensure that the believer's life, and life around the believer, conforms to the revealed will of Allah. *Iman* and *din*, doctrine and deed, belong together, just as did *kerugma* and *didache*, or doctrinal preaching and ethical teaching, in the Christian apostolic way of seeing things.

(v) Others feel the most potent sense of belonging only when caught up in the fellowship, the *social* dimension, of their religious community. This sense of belonging may well be experienced within their group as over against other socially identifying and differentiating ways of life, whether openly 'profane' or claiming a sacredness of their own. Again, the claim for equality and cohesiveness within their religious group is seen by Muslims, as by Sikhs, as their great strength. It is, though, sad but salutary that no religious community in India - Christian, Muslim, Sikh - has been able fully to transcend the pressures of caste and its discriminations in actual social or even ecclesial relationships. There are, of course, moments in the life of all these faith-communities when differences of ethnic background and social status seem forgotten, moments that can become momentous in their impact. We have already noted how the pilgrimage to Macca expresses very dramatically to Muslims their togetherness with all fellow-believers, to whatever sect, ethnic group or nationality they belong. In North India, the sacred places and ecstatic corporate spirituality initiated by Muslim Sufi saints, such as Nizamuddin, even today are effective in breaking down historical communalist historical distinctions - especially those creating the Hindu-Muslim divide.

Even if external cultural pressures make wider social integration difficult, it is a matter of great significance when a communalist-free social identity is an integral part of faith, at least a hoped-for goal of faith. The prominent symbolism of the *langar*, or common meal, in the Sikh tradition, can be taken at face value as indicating that social togetherness was intended to be intrinsic to Sikh faith-identity. It was directly in defiance of Brahmanic views of cooking and eating separately according to caste distinctions that led Guru Amar Das (Sikh leader from 1552-74) to institute the *langar*, which no doubt had been informally part of Guru Nanak's practice too. When the Mughal emperor Akbar came to visit Amar Das, mainly to discover how Sikhs worship, it is said the emperor was told he first had to sit along with ordinary devotees for the common meal: '*Pelhe pangat, piche sangat*', 'First eating, then worship together'.

As we might expect, Basava's 'Hero-Saiva' (Lingayat) community in South India, especially in the early centuries of this movement, placed almost unparalleled emphasis on the need to meet together regularly in closely binding fellowship. They had their 'Hall of Experience' that was to be such a place of meeting and sharing. More unexpectedly, even from those love-drowned devotees of other less ethically oriented theistic sects within Hindu religious life, for all the emphasis on passionate and personal union with their Lover-God, we often hear equally ecstatic claims that being part of the community of God-lovers is their greatest joy. Even the self-identity of these outstanding individualists seems dependent upon this horizontal dimension of faith.

Tensions are invariably present in this dimension of all faiths however. First, there is often a differentiating, a contrasting, of who they are now with what they once were, or it may be a contrasting of the fellowship now enjoyed with that of some other religious way. While this negative over-againstness is perhaps a necessary part of the process of shaping the God-lover's self-identity, far more dominant and pervasive is the consciousness of the intimate otherness of God.

Then, analysis of faith's social dimension must also take account of the felt-reality of power and authority within religion's *institutional* life. It is, of course, not only in the formal institutions that authority is embodied and power exercised. Here we might list priests, bishops, archdeacons, abbots, imams, sheiks, acharyas, swamijis, and suchlike figures of formally appointed and institutionalised authority. But there is also the authoritative role of more charismatically anointed figures such as gurus, shamans, prophets, preachers, healers, sants/saints, ecstatics. This is not to say that the more institutionalised figures cannot have charisma, or that gurus and preachers are not institutionally recognised, or are not an authoritative and necessary functional part of a tradition. We do find here, though, both a different form of sacred power and a different manner of its being channelled. Submission to the charismatic figure, and thus a sense of togetherness, is usually far more intense than to an impersonal institution. In the end, though, the sense of identity created within those linked with the more institution-based power and authority is not appreciably different from that created by submission to less institution-based power-figures. In both cases the willingness to submerge the individual ego in whatever is expected by the concerned Authority will be similar. For the guru-figure becomes the embodiment of sacred Authority, even if this is temporary and dependent on the disciple's maturing into more complete enlightenment and inner liberation. Clearly there is room for potential tension here too.

Thirdly, there is the faith-community's interaction with wider human communities, another potential cause of tension at this social level that we take up later.

Seeing religious identities in terms of these different dimensions of religious life, then, does help to some degree in probing further into the inner character of the self-identity of people of faith. Most of them, though, only take us so far in understanding the inner dynamics of our ultimate identities in relation to religious life. It is, rather, especially in how we perceive and identity with the transcendent Focus, the Object of faith, that we probe most fully the nature of faith-based human identities. *In religious life, then, that with which we identify as the high point of religious experience is that which most powerfully and ultimately shapes our self-identity.* This thesis obviously will need to be teased out further.

In any case, it is clear that it is not only the 'doctrinal dimension', or more specifically the 'theologian' (to use the Christian term for one who reflects more systematically on the significance of a tradition's faith in a central Focus) who will give great weight to the central Focus of things religious. For not only is it this experiential, visionary part of a religion's life that most powerfully shapes that religion's self-identity. It is its Focus-related dimension too which forms the integrating centre for a tradition's complex of myths, rituals, symbols, sacred priests, holy prophets, fellowship of saints, scriptures, singing, dancing, ethical codes - the list can be made endless. Politicians may just be able to get by without 'the vision thing'; religious studies that neglect it, dealing only perhaps with the impact of social dynamics or political events, thereby vitiate their entire enterprise, for they miss the essential point. It is equally misguided to account for religion solely in terms of its Focus, as will some theologians of the faith, for this visionary dimension is always rooted in - both impressed by and expressed through - those other 'dimensions' of our traditions.

Chapter 4
Diversely Identifying with the Transcendent

(1) Levels of Faith-Engagement

Sacred story, faith's ritual acts, doctrinal systems, community life, ethical values - all play their part in configuring a faith-based identity. It is, though, when we look at religious identity in terms of what Ninian Smart called faith's *experiential* dimension that we find the most clear clues as to how faith-based identities emerge, as well as how they diverge. This means: (a) seeing things in terms of the differing *experiential levels* at which people engage within their religious tradition; (b) looking at the distinctive experiences people have of what is *ultimate* in that life; and, controversially, (c) even evaluating the *authenticity* of how such distinct visions are interpreted within their traditions.

Let me take up (c) first, and rather briefly, though it is a point with which many will disagree. Peace-loving people urging interfaith dialogue will disagree. Postmodernists claiming that any interpretation is merely relative truth will disagree. Objections would also be heard from phenomenologists of religion, who speak of 'bracketting' faith if our descriptions of others is truly to represent the subject's actual religious experience. At the other extreme hardline historians of religion demand more systematic methodological rigour in their concern to avoid 'theological' interpretation and achieve detached objectivity. From all quarters, it seems, we are expected not to allow our particular faith-preferences to determine the way we speak of the faith of others. And in many human and intellectual contexts this is surely quite right.

Religious communities themselves, though, are very much concerned with the subjective dimension of their religious life, and usually have ways of evaluating the authenticity of interpretations within their tradition. They may well not have clear norms and methods for approving orthodoxy and excluding heresy in quite the way monotheistic faiths have tended to, Christian tradition especially.

More existentially critical is the effect for great good and for great ill differing faith-interpretations have on the life of others. So, although any thought of judging the truth or rightness or legitimacy of the way people interpret their tradition will seem anathema to many, we clearly cannot merely ignore the way human life has been affected by the direction religious interpretation takes. And there is a sense in which even at the comparative and descriptive level the study of the sources of visionary insight and their historical interpretations will inevitably lead to some sort of evaluation - a point made with some sophistication by Ninian Smart in his early (1958) *Reasons and Faiths.* Given a modicum of historical imagination and spiritual sensitivity, certain ways of interpreting the significance of the Buddha, or Christ, or the Prophet will surely be more historically and spiritually authentic than others - as people within those traditions also claim.

And a more ethically and existentially pressing point. It is a harsh fact of our interacting histories that some forms of faith-interpretation are *dangerously damaging* to human well-being. The identities they shape may be not just a threat to others (sometimes no bad thing), but may be based on the intention to do evil to any but those encircled within that faith. Yet, crucial to any evaluating of such interpretations is the question of who interprets the interpretation, and from what perspective any such evaluation is made. If judgement of right and wrong, good and evil, are made solely from a position of power, talk of 'authentic interpretation' becomes ludicrous. In other words critical judgement in matters of faith raises mammoth difficulties; but in the end such critical judgement cannot be avoided. The key surely is the stimulation of self-critical evaluation.

Secondly, then, religions invariably function at a number of differing levels - the point stressed so eloquently by Wilfred Cantwell Smith. Their adherents not only share in the life of faith in differing ways, they also share that faith at *differing levels of commitment.* All religious traditions, though, make the assumption that some of their number are more faith-full than are others, more in touch with the sacred power at the heart of faith. Their self-identity is seen as more authentically shaped by those realities of faith. In part this reflects the differing forms of interaction that take place between the internal life of the tradition and that which is external to those essential dimensions (story/act/belief/community) forming the matrix of religious consciousness. In most traditions, though, there are those for whom faith's realities are so inclusive that there is nothing

119

'external' to their religious consciousness. The God-life has become all-embracing.

On the one hand, then, in all traditions we find talk of some kind of dualisms - often proving the basis on which faith-identities are formed. Even all-encompassing *dharma* - the right ordering of things - in Hinduism has to be protected by a struggle against *a-dharma*. Or to move to a 'higher' mode of Hindu religious consciousness, there has to be a kind of 'otherness' at one level even for the radical non-dualist vision of *advaita* for that unitive vision to carry any meaning. But the dualisms may not be ultimate. Indeed, in all religions - not only advaitic Hinduism - we find devotees also moving into a sense of inclusiveness that may well transcend the more common polarities, even in faiths usually considered quite dualist. Christ is 'All', or the One in whom 'all things hold together' (as the letter to the Colossians puts it); Allah is so great that nothing is beyond his controlling will, even his empowering presence; the sacred Power of the 'tribal' may pervade and animate every living thing as well as the objects manifesting this Power in special ways; and the Hindu opponents of non-dualist *advaita* could be enraptured by the all-embracing vision of Rama, or Krishna, who in the Gita's 'vision of (Krishna as) the universe' declares (X.20-22, 41):

> I am the self in the heart of all living things;
> I am their beginning, middle and end...
> Among lights I am the radiant sun...
> Among senses I am the mind...
> This whole universe I hold with but one fragment (of my being).

Kabir's transcending of Muslim and Hindu orthodoxies was linked both with a surprising *nirguna* view of God as 'beyond characterisation' (though his is far from a formal advaitic worldview), as well as with a sense of God's pervading and integrating of all life. In other words, in so many religious traditions, there seems to be no part of life that escapes the divine.

Any differentiating of the 'religious' or 'sacred' and the 'secular', then, could be accused of making a typically modern western life-dichotomy. From my personal faith-perspective I find it impossible to conceive of any spheres of life that have somehow lost touch altogether with the throbbing heart of God by whom we all 'live and move and have our being' (to quote the Apostle Paul quoting a 'pagan'!)- however much that faith also compels a critical view of how most of us live and move and have our being. Some form of divine 'universalism' is surely inescapable for faith. The fact of our pluralistic world has to be reckoned with though, which means at one level accepting the 'reality' of a secularist world and the many secular identities that become shaped by this view of things. Perhaps this is getting rather close to the two-level view of things adopted by Mahayana Buddhism and, through one of their schools, by the most famous *advaitin*, Sankara in the eighth century. There is a transcendental and ultimately real world open to those who see things *paramarthika*, and there is the empirically real, everyday worldview of those who live at the *vyavaharika* level. Our everyday way of dividing 'sacred' and 'secular' is somewhat different from this, but there are similarities.

In any case, distinctions along these lines are of great import in relation to questions of identity. If we allow in any sense that there are legitimate, even necessary human identities that are not directly or consciously 'religious', but from a secular point of view are undeniably there, how are these two forms of identity to relate to each other? Another way of putting this is to ask: How does faith in its highest form relate to culture? Even if it is the case that to separate religious and secular life as moderns do is the creation of western Christians, the Hindu too may well experience a degree of tension between living out the *dharma*, sacred culture though it may be, and what the tradition clearly regards as the highest form of faith, that is *moksha*, or liberation from all socio-cultural ties.

Both the Buddha and Mahavira (the Great-Hero of Jainism), as also quite early fathers in Christianity, worked out two levels of sharing in the Way: monks took the great vows and experienced the highest blessings, lay people were blessed at a less exalted level. Similarly the Sikh tradition distinguishes those who become 'lions' in the faith, and those who share that faith at a less committed level. Islam does not in principle make any such distinction, as a number of Protestant Christian bodies also do not. Yet, they certainly allow special roles and a special authority to those - imams, ayatollahs, preachers, pastors - believed to mediate greater insight into what it means to be 'Muslim' or 'Christian'. Both even have those specially revered as 'saints', literally the 'sacred/holy ones', whose words, perhaps healing touch, and certainly whose presence is seen as a blessing. For the more ecstatic Sufi stream of Islam such saints become an even greater source of healing and blessing after death. That orthodoxy condemns such special forms of charisma merely confirms the multi-level reality.

In various ways, then, all religious communities acknowledge the presence of those with a greater share of faith's charisma, those more advanced in spiritual gifts, those for whom faith has more fully ordered life than is the case with other believers, those for whom the ways of the world ('unenlightened', 'unfaithful', 'disobedient',' secular', 'impure', 'sinful', 'evil','demonic') have been more fully transformed by the ways of faith, than the reverse.

The experience of faith's *ecstasy* is another way of expressing this. Engagement with the Transcendent, however perceived, incurs some form of 'standing outside' of that ego-centred, power-dominated life that those most highly regarded in our religious traditions see as an enemy against which we are to struggle. Are we here talking, then, of levels of *alienation* (from the 'world') that correspond to levels of alignment to the central Object of religious devotion? Is it the case that the more we love God (as the theist would put it) the more we will hate the world? And according to Jesus in his response to the question, 'What comes first in the Jewish Torah?' such love is the ultimate aim of religion, we might say the most important goal of human life. The fact that Jesus immediately links God-love with neighbourly love, and elsewhere with love of enemies too, hardly suggests that 'hate' of the world is the corollary of love of God. The teaching of Jesus in other contexts, however, especially concerning loyalty to his new way, does explicitly call for a kind of 'hating' of objects of lesser loyalty, even family members and the loyalties they command. There is to be 'denial' of anything that proves a rival to one's affections.

Nor is there difficulty in finding in most other faith-traditions similar radical contrasting of the commitment compelled by the Object of faith and all lesser loyalties. It is not only John Bunyan's *Pilgrim's Progress* and such puritan Christian writings that give lengthy descriptions of the obstacles in 'normal' life to reaching the highest levels of faith and commitment. Most traditions do the same. Buddhist and Jaina spiritual treatises, for example, list such obstacles to the supreme goal with systematic precision. The role of 'renouncing' in almost all formal Hindu traditions has already been noted. Much of the highly popular *bhakti* poetry also regularly warns fiercely against the seductive wiles of the world. The 'hero' in all these traditions is the one whose struggles result in victory over all obstacles.

In other words, *a self-identity that is based on the in-breaking of some transcendent insight may well involve a relativising, perhaps even a breaking away from, other identities and lesser loyalties.* The degree to which this happens will depend on just how closely integrated any such identity/loyalty is to the Focus of faith. Usually, though, moving into this higher level of faith entails a certain kind of 'alienation' from a 'world' perceived as in some way at enmity with faith's 'world'. But alienation can be viewed in contrasting ways. Religious people themselves will most likely put it this way: Is it not the world of those without faith's insight that is in reality 'alienated', that is both based on and in turn induces a 'false consciousness' in those deluded by that world? That this world can certainly seduce and captivate the unwary is equally part of much religious belief. However, I leave further discussion of the meaning of alienation to a later section, when I discuss the sociological theory of religion suggested by Peter Berger. My main point here is that our religious identities are shaped by the level at which we are committed to and engage with the central Object of faith.

Thirdly, religious identities are also shaped by the differing ways faith perceives its central Object, that which embodies ultimate worth. Ninian Smart, in his 1964-5 Teape lectures, *The Yogi and the Devotee,* pointed to a bi-polar typology, at least for the supreme Being of Hindu tradition, but equally found in Christian and Muslim experience. There is the pure Consciousness sought by the contemplative, undifferentiably one with the inner self's true being, the impersonal One beyond all qualification. And there is the Highest Person the worshipper turns to, to be adored, loved, served because of the wonderful qualities ascribable to that supreme Person. The former is the inner transcendence experienced by the mystic; the latter is the numinous Other, that which both fascinates and fills with awe, described by Rudolf Otto in his classic but rather one-sided *Idea of the Holy.* Each is in fact able to include the other strand in its overall spirituality, and both are there in abundance in Hindu (and Christian too) textual sources and traditions. One will be given ultimacy, and will then include the other as a lower-level strand in the belief-system.

Many reforming Hindu interpreters of the past century and a half or so - Swami Vivekananda and Sarvepalli Radhakrishnan were the most prolific exponents - have taught that all spiritual paths are valid, but in reality it is the pure consciousness of the contemplative that is the ultimate goal. *Bhakti*, or faith in a personal God, though ultimate to the believer, is seen as a less advanced level of spirituality. But this, say such 'neo-Hindus', does not break the continuum of Hindu religious experience, as each person is to be devoted to that experience of the Ultimate for which he or she is fitted. If we are to speak of reality in any final sense, though, it is invariably said that we need to move beyond all those categories that describe any difference between soul and God, or we might say between self-identity and Self-Identity. Ultimately there is only the One. Mystics in other traditions too - including Christian and Muslim - have pointed in similar ways to the Oneness beyond our differentiating experiences.

And a significant stream of twentieth century Christian theologians - from Paul Tillich to John Hick and Gordon Kaufman, for example - echoing the Kantian distinction between the phenomenal and the noumenal, in different ways urge people of faith to look for the ultimately true God beyond the 'God' we have been conditioned to know. Reforming Hindu understanding of that ultimate Identity, however, points more typically to the ultimate God *within* all as the culminating vision of the many levels of understanding found in the varied experience of Hindus.

How, then, does this perception of the many levels at which the Ultimate is to be experienced, though leading up to withinness, affect the character of religious self-identity? We might think - and is so argued by modern Hindus - that one immediate consequence of this position, in terms of self-identity, is a less exclusive attitude towards others. That ultimate Self which we call 'God', '*Atman*', '*Brahman*', and by many other names, pervades all, is within every creature. To revere and serve the God-embodying creature without any discrimination is to revere and serve God.

Such a worldview has, of course, not been absent in a longer Hindu history; but it is among reforming Hindus of the past century and a half that it has been the basis of a far greater number of effective agencies of social service. The Ramakrishna Mission, set up by Swami Vivekananda after his successful appearance at the world Parliament of Religions in Chicago in 1893, is one outstanding example. Another is the reform and service-oriented movement among the 'low-caste' Iruvalas of Kerala, led by one of their number, Narayana Guru, who very consciously and rather surprisingly based his social action on an advaitic worldview. In the late 1960s and early 1970s I was (as local representative for an Agency for Social Action) personally involved - providing foodstuffs, clothing, and medicines - in a Hindu initiated service project called Jiva-karunya-sangha, or the Society for Compassion to (All) Living Beings, among leprosy sufferers in another part of South India, the Godavari delta of Andhra Pradesh. 'God is present within everyone', was a frequent booster-saying voiced by Hindu co-workers struggling to cope perhaps with the stench of pus-filled foot ulcers.

This Hindu vision of the Ultimate *can*, in other words, be a basis for *identifying oneself with* those more usually thought of as far from one's own community, even a self-identifying with those that one strand of tradition sees as cursed either by bad *karma* or by God. The term '*dharma*', though, includes all those charitable acts by which the suffering of others, though karmically just, is alleviated.

In Buddhism, with its equally great emphasis on the power of *karma*, as well as on acts of charity, there is also another basis for 'great compassion', making it seem to fit more easily into life as a whole. The Buddha himself, the Focus of meditation and devotion, is held to be the personal embodiment of this highly valued quality on the path to Nirvana. At times 'God' takes a similar role in Hindu faith.

It is difficult, though, to escape the conclusion that when - as in a rigorously *advaitic* worldview (and we must not forget the many nuances possible within a broadly 'non-dualist' position) - the central Object of faith is to be experienced as ultimately beyond personal qualities such as compassion and the social concerns this will normally entail. But, when 'God' can only be contemplated in silent mystery if one is to be identified with that Being in any ultimate sense, is it not more likely that the self-identity of the one contemplating will be less committed to any social body and the relationality this involves? Self-identity then will more probably be marked by a sense of aloof detachment. *Passion* of any kind, which surely has to include compassion, is at odds with the detachment called for. But religious faith comes up so often with strange paradoxes and anomalies, and people like Narayana Guru make it clear that there is nothing inevitable about such a link.

There is a strand of the *Gita* which describes the mature Yogi, the ideal person who continues to act in the world but has no attachment to the consequences of that action. Events, actions, duties, relationships - necessary but not ultimately significant - all go on at the level of ever-restless Nature, while the true Self remains unmoved. That, though, need not be taken as the last word of the Gita on the matter of self-identity. For there is also a thorough-going theistic strand too in this complex text. So, what serious theistic interpreters call the 'last word' of the Gita (18.66-8) speaks of the mystery of God's very personal love. And while the devotee is to 'give up all (faith in the good consequences ensuing from) acts of *dharma*', what will prove truly liberating for the devotee is that 'I love you well'. And the one who so speaks is the God who embodies himself on earth (really embodies himself say the theistic interpreters) in order to defeat evil *a-dharma* and uphold good *dharma*, the Creator who always works for the 'well-being' of the whole world, all living creatures. Now, the outcome of this *could* be a life-stance very different from one of aloof detachment.

I have been referring to this strand of the Gita, and those interpreters within Hinduism who have given ultimate weight to this strand, as 'theistic'. Four aspects of that tradition, though, need to be looked at further in arriving at a representative view, or views, of how self-identities within a Hindu theistic framework are modified.

First, the role of *karma* and the karmic cycle of action, the 'fruits' of action and the life-identities determined by this process. At any point in the cycle action may be taken that in part is able to counter previous actions and their fruits, and so makes possible a new life-identity. This means the process is not thoroughly deterministic, in spite of the tendency for more traditionalist people to interpret it so: 'You have been born in low-caste ignominy because of something you did in a past life'. Or, when faced by a personal tragedy, 'What great sin did I commit in the past that this fate has come upon me?'

The more choice-based, change-oriented ways of modernity, though, have brought changes of interpretation of the ways of *karma*. Some studies conclude that the doctrine now fails to hold a key place in Hindu consciousness. And for the serious theist, there is the crucial role of the all-powerful, all-pervading God who initiates and controls the ways of this inescapable law of moral cause and effect. Such a God is able to break the karmic chain and liberate those who believe his grace to be their only hope, even if it is through the karmic process itself that God normally works out his lordly control of the universe.

It has to be confessed, though, that there is an element of ambiguity here in the outworking of karmic law and divine grace - impinging on the believer's sense of identity - similar to the ambiguity in Christian faith between Law and Gospel, or between divine 'wrath' and divine love, between justice and mercy. But, again, where is religious faith without paradox and seeming ambiguity?

Secondly, a self-identity based on absolute devotion to the 'Highest Person', for the God-lovers of Hinduism often means abhorrence of 'the world' in a rather special way. For this form of theism is not that of the rigid monotheist who finds talk of all-pervading divine immanence a threat to faith in God's transcendent otherness. In fact these polarities, expressed in terms of *saulabhya* and *paratva*, or close accessibility and otherness, are key binary categories in the foremost school of *bhakti* theology. God is the 'inmost Self of all' and the universe is his 'inseparably related body' according to this theology of Visishta-advaita ('non-duality whose character is determined by innate distinction'). We have here an understanding of God's relationship with the universe that is clearly one of *pan-en-theism*. Not only is God within all things, but all things are held, though mysteriously, within the being of God. Or as the Gita puts it (VII.7-12):

> On Me this universe is strung
> Like clustered pearls upon a thread...
> Pure fragrance in the earth am I, flame's onset in the fire,
> ...the primal seed in all contingent beings...
> But I am not in them, they are in Me.

With such a vision of God and world inter-penetrating (note they are not mutually inter-dependent though), self-identity based on a

God-identity that is exclusively focussed can still entail an inescapably inclusive relationship with all creaturely life. In any case, we can confidently conclude that religion's most important 'dimension' in the shaping of self-identity - personal and corporate consciousness of who and what we are - is that central Focus of faith with which believers engage in a variety of 'identifying' ways.

(2) Religious Experience as 'Alienation'?

A seriously religious experience of the world has, however, been equally seriously assumed to be one of 'alienation'. When Karl Marx described religion as the 'opiate of the people', he actually intended it almost as a compliment. The working classes are so alienated from the realities even of the industrial productive process by which their life is enslaved, so robbed of its fruits, at least their pain is dulled by the 'comforts of religion'. This too, though, for him was of a piece with the 'false consciousness' created by the capitalist system. Indian historians with more hardline Marxist leanings, such as D.D.Kosambi, have accounted for bhakti movements in a similar way. Peter Berger, one of the leading sociologists of religion in the second half of the twentieth century, have further developed this theme that religious identities are necessarily forms of alienated consciousness (Berger 1969). Here is what he wrote:

> Human beings...project their meanings into the universe around them....The 'objectivity' of religious meanings is *produced* objectivity, that is, religious meanings are objectivated projections . It follows that, insofar as these meanings imply an overwhelming sense of otherness, they may be described as *alienated projections.*

Berger sees this 'alienating power' as the reason for religion's effective role in combating disorder and in creating orderly patterns of life. Both the sacred beings on the basis of which the world is then ordered are given what believers find a convincing aura of objective reality. 'The human nomos becomes a divine cosmos'. But the 'historical part of religion in the world-building and world-maintaining enterprises of man is in large measure due to the alienating power inherent in religion'. Sociologically, then, this sense of the reality of our sacred worlds, which includes how we see and structure the world on the basis of our religious belief, is the result merely of alienated and to that extent 'false' consciousness,

consciousness that is not in tune with the way things empirically, actually are in the world.

It must be said that Berger does not allow sociology to speak about the 'ultimate' status of divine beings. Nor does he go on to equate religion as such with alienation. He retains a transmuted form of faith himself. Empirically, though, our gods and all our higher identities - certainly all religiously based 'lower' identities, are thoroughly 'alien', however useful they may have been for fighting chaos and anomie.

It is the Gita's great vision of Krishna in wonderfully transfigured cosmic form that Berger points to as a clear example of alienated consciousness (along with brief mention of the Hebrew prophet Isaiah's vision in the temple). He does allow that there are what he calls 'more "sophisticated" developments in religion' in which 'this terror of the alien mystery in the sacred is modified, mellowed, brought closer to man in a variety of mediations'. Yet, unless we 'retain an awareness of the otherness continuing as the hidden essence underneath the more "graceful" or "gentler" forms', we cannot grasp the real character of such religious vision.

Elsewhere Berger, rightly I believe, has emphasised the need for religion to retain this sense that a transcendent dimension does break through immanentally, the need not to be swept away by the levelling of a secularist perspective. This position does seem highly paradoxical, though, in view of his own sociological reductionism, his account of religion as a process of alienation and mystification

Berger also goes on to argue that in certain forms of religious faith there is 'the possibility of *de-alienation itself being religiously legitimated,*' along with its 'tendency to legitimate alienation' (Berger 1969: 96) Here he notes what we have already picked up: religion can radically *relativise* all institutional life. He points to the role of *maya* in the Hindu Upanishads, mysticism generally, and the radical monotheism of prophetic biblical religion as examples of this relativising possibility. Only 'the biblical tradition of the confrontation of the social order with the majesty of the transcendent God' (very Barthian and Niebhurian this) is taken to qualify seriously as a religious position leading to 'de-alienation', in which established sacral structures are so relativised that they can be challenged prophetically. Their status is 'debunked'. *Maya* and mysticism, on the other hand, like the non-terrible aspect of Krishna, are seen as 'sophisticated' developments, not really endemic to religious life generally.

The fact is, though, that when Berger refers to these dimensions of Hindu religion as 'sophistications' he is seriously mistaken. Rudolph Otto's normative account of the Holy impinges too strongly here. In Krishna-*bhakti* it is ludicrously distorting to see Krishna's terrifying otherness as the most typical, or even the most significant aspect of Krishna's character. Of course the transcendence is very significant; the great vision in the Gita does have a climactic position there. And in any Krishna scripture or cult, without being seen as the Other, Krishna would not be worshipped. But the dimensions of gracefulness, enchantment, seductiveness, passionate love, the mystery of nearness and separation, forgiving mercy, the stories of his mischevous infancy, his adventurous youthfulness, his heroic manliness are all far more prominent - outside the Gita at least - than the awesome terror in that 'otherness'.

Indeed, it is essentially the erotic passion that most seriously challenges the institutional status quo, in the form of normative, dharmic married relationships, as the most famous *bhakti* scripture, Bhagavad Purana, discusses quite openly. Here too the mystery of *maya*, far from being peripheral, is a key theme in Hindu religious life, and certainly does serve (as Berger says, 1979: 97) to relativise the social order from the perspective of the ultimate vision of things. But precisely what *maya* means in the Bhagavata, or in the Gita, or in the Upanishad (Svetasvatara) that Berger quotes, calls for much more nuanced interpretation than simply calling the empirical and social world 'an illusion'. This is merely one interpretation of what is intended by the term *maya*. That it always questions the usually perceived identity of the empirical and social worlds, that these worlds have an illusory dimension, is another matter. How we read and translate the text here is everything.

The quality of 'otherness' seen by believers in Jesus or the Buddha could be questioned in a similar way. It is not the Transfiguration, or even glorious visions of the Resurrection, that for many Christians at various periods have most transformingly impinged on their consciousness - though the whole story is indelibly coloured with this aspect of Christ's otherness, and certainly the image of *Christus Victor* has been prominent in one form or another in Christian history

(Aulen 1953). But it is the stories of healing, of evil powers overcome, of liberating teaching, of forgiving grace, of being freely accepted, of love unto death, of atoning blood, of saving presence that have been most central in Christian perception of the identity of Jesus.

All this does assume, of course, a sense of sin, identifying oneself as an unworthy sinner alienated from God, from what is good. Critics such as Sarvepalli Radhakrishnan - Spalding Professor at Oxford, prolific apologist for Hindu thought, President of the Republic of India - have accused Christian faith of being obsessed with sin. But the contrast he made with Hindu faith is blinkered. There too, in the great *bhakti* movements, most of the saints at some point bewail their unworthiness, their impure state, the contrast between themselves and their God. During periods of great Christian devotion too, the starting point was invariably an overwhelming sense of alienation. Yet, the experience of divine majesty is far from central, as it is not in the grounding texts either. Even in the resurrection narratives, it is the sense of a mysteriously elusive risen Christ that predominates - even if along with fearful awe. Certainly in the God-consciousness of Jesus (as far as the texts allow us to penetrate this consciousness) it is not awesome divine power that is foremost, but a sense of paternal accessibility, the immediate sign of which is the power to heal and forgive. Even the kingly righteousness so prominent in Jesus' teaching - calling for a corresponding new identity in the people of the kingdom - is more about forgiveness and new beginnings than about numinous terror. Rudolf Otto's account of the essence of religious faith as a numinous that is *tremendum* yet *fascinans* is too dominant.

In spite of Berger's very one-sided account of the otherness in religious faith (echoing a dominant strand in twentieth century post-liberal Protestant accounts of religion generally), it is a fact that in our religious histories there have been various forms of 'alienation'. Perhaps chief among them is the humanly dangerous form of religious sacralisation where the institutional forms, the mythically created sacral, ecclesial and social worlds are imbued not only with objective but with ultimate reality, so that the necessary dialectic, the lived dynamic between vision and corporate life - social, ethical, political - is lost, the status quo becomes fixed, institutional life is not to be questioned, and corporate life is alienated from the reality of lived human experience. And Berger himself has written of the loss of dialectic (1979: 93). This is religious fundamentalism with a vengeance. It is this which is 'false consciousness'.

(3) God & World: Further Bi-polar Identities

Any emphasis on an inter-penetrating 'dialectic' clearly cannot avoid ambiguity in analysing the dynamics of religious faith.

(a) In *Hindu tradition*, for example, there is a further complication in another undergirding cosmic theory. It is that vision of things which makes a clear categorial divide between Nature and Selfhood, or *Prakrti* and *Purusha*. This is the worldview, widely pervasive for some three millennnia in Indian religious thought (very strong in the Gita), that the creative process is made up of two intermingling realms, linked by the sensory process: one is the realm of restlessly changing objects, the other that of ever-conscious but unchanging subjects. Both - in any theistic form of this theory of Samkhya - are dependent on God's creating and controlling, but Nature is essentially a seducer and deluder, pictured as a dancer on creation's stage, deliberately enticing into helpless slavery the self that looks on her bewitching movements. Yet, selves can be *set free to become like the supreme Self*, especially through meditation on the perfections of that Self. Classical Yoga, then, has this provisional dualism as its undergirding metaphysics.

Whatever these 'complicating' beliefs that we find to be part of the Hindu theistic world, there is still room within that faith-world for *the God-lover also to be a world-server, for self-identity not always to imply that the world of the senses* per se *is to be renounced*. It is, then, misleading to assume, as critics often have, that 'Hinduism' has no concern with transforming the world, only with being passively resigned to whatever fate is ours while here in this birth, and with escaping the illusory traps of materiality (Madan 1987). As we have just seen, there certainly are deeply embedded strands of Hindu tradition that *can* lead to passive resignation, but it is far from the only form of Hindu faith.

(b) In the *Judeo-Christian-Muslim* traditions too there is no lack of such an attitude, though differently articulated. In Islam there is the popular notion of *kismet*, the belief that everything to be is predestined, already 'written on the forehead'. Clearly this can potentially undermine the will to act. But it can equally lead to total commitment to the task in hand, for it is what must be done.

The preordaining of divine purpose is strong too in forms of Christianity. Augustine's fifth century teaching on the all-determining omnipotence of God in human activity was countered by the synergism (the collaboration of divine grace and human effort) of the English monk Pelagius. The Reformed Protestant Calvin's (16th century) similar emphasis on predestination was countered by the Dutch theologian Arminius, for whom God's sovereign will is not incompatible with human freewill. By accepting this interpretation of human choice within a framework of divine sovereignty (as many Hindu theologians did too) there was far greater scope for the inclusivenss of 18th-19th century evangelical movements. The oft-repeated slogan was, 'All are welcome into the arms of grace'. In other forms of Christian faith, though, apocalyptic destruction of the world may be linked with an attitude of resignation. All is doomed anyway, so why struggle to change things, even if souls otherwise lost can still be saved? Or the opposite, equally disastrous, attitude may follow: by provoking the mutual destruction of alien peoples we are hastening the apocalyptic destruction prophesied by divine revelation. Some contemporary critics believe it is just such a sinister worldview that inspires key foreign policy advisors of the present Bush regime.

(c) Dominant, though, in Christianity, and in a differing way in Islam too, is the view that the world is to be *transformed* in a healing way, and that acting to bring it into conformity with that divine purpose is an essential part of the believer's very self-identity. This is the dominant basis of their commitment to world mission - at least at key periods in Christian history. In the Buddhist self-identity, too, in spite of the dominant emphasis on *self*-transformation, there has often been commitment to a mission of compassionate service, and - as in other faiths - spreading the teaching of the one through whom the truth was revealed. We noted earlier that Hindu service-projects may be based on the faith that God is present in all.

In some cases, though, we see a more dynamic view of faith's impact on the world. Towards the end of chapter one above, we saw an impassioned outburst from that God-drowned Tamil Alvar, Nammalvar, asserting that 'life's curse is gone, hell's agony destroyed...the power of the dark age eclipsed.' Now, 'the beloved of the Lord...uproot disease, hatred, poverty, pain.'

Here faith perceives a new age dawning, people everywhere are touched by God's grace, and ecstatic devotees sharing in this transforming process. It is the passionate Krishna-bhakti movement in the tradition of the 16th century God-lover Chaitanya, more recently expounded so successfully to western devotees by A.C.Bhaktivedanta Swami Prabhupada in the Hare Krishna movement, that most clearly expresses the kind of religious identity embodied in this worldview. Devotion to Krishna is enthusiastically believed to be a way of world-transformation.

(d) A further strand in Hindu theistic experience draws us at first back again to the *antithesis of God and world*. Passion for God has no doubt been expressed more forcefully in the devotional poetry of Hindu India than anywhere else in human religious history. In the South the singing lovers of Vishnu were called 'the drowned ones' (*alvars*), love-drowned. Siva-lovers were faith-'leaders', 'heroes'of faith. In both, sexual passion is paradigmatic both for the soul's longing for God and for the Lord's relating to his Lady. Sexual passion is transmuted into spiritual passion. Yet, in stanza after stanza, especially by those devoted to Siva, we find feelings of abhorrence at the wiles of the world and the flesh. Women, and the delights the love of women can offer, are seen as especially potent sources of seduction from single-minded faith in God. The paradoxes of devotional eroticism in Hindu *bhakti* have been brought out astutely by Friedhelm Hardy, especially in his *Religious Culture of India*.

It is fascinating to think that Augustine and Jerome and other Christian Fathers were, in the Mediterranean world, similarly engaging in their heroic struggles against the flesh and the dangerous delights of sexuality in particular, at more or less the same period as these South Indian love-drowned saints began their songs of God-passion. In the Christian tradition, however, while spiritual and liturgical devotion in the East kept its links with such erotic ground-texts as The Song of Solomon, and the dialectic remained, in the West generally the anti-flesh pole in the dialectic dominated. Deep tensions are found in Islamic tradition too. There is a certain open earthiness about sexual life. Yet, the Prophet in Arabia in the same period as the God-drowned of South India were at their peak, warns frequently of the dangers of faith in God being weakened by the attractions of womanly charms. Sexual life as such is good, but in society sexual relations are charged with dangers.

The story of sex in our religions, in other words, is complex. Within Hindu theistic faith there is generally also a more positive attitude towards the *delights of sensory life* to be seen in the lovers of Vishnu, in his Krishna-embodiment especially. Indeed, the love of women, dancing with women, being enchanting to and attracted by women is, as we saw, made the central model for God-love, much to the scandalised horror of those not part of that bewitched circle. (The Bhagavata Purana even has to defend Krishna's dalliance with the cowgirls infatuated by him, largely on the grounds that because Krishna is God he is not subject to the usual rules). Descriptions of passion for God are as erotically phrased as any poems of passion between earthly lovers.

But Bible-believers too should not forget the delicate eroticism of that Hebraic scripture, the Song of Solomon, usually interpreted as an allegory of the soul's love for God. A similar phenomenon occurs even within Islam: Sufi songs of love. While certainly not as erotic, even sexually explicit, as Krishna-directed songs like Jayadeva's Gita-Govinda, these Sufi songs too, both by men and women, express their longing for God in ways similar to poetic longing for an earthly lover. The Christian evangelical Charles Wesley in the eighteenth century, was quite a puritan. Yet, echoing Christian medieval devotion as much as his Methodist fervour, he writes longingly of Jesus as 'Lover of my soul' to whose 'bosom' he longs to fly, to lie there in love's ecstasy. He often speaks of 'pining', 'languishing' for 'closer communion....hid in thy breast', in imagery at times so like that of the *viraha* (separation)-*bhakti* of Indian devotion (that we look at again in a moment). Ecstatic and erotic experience can be close in this love-based religion, in spite of the emphasis on ascetic self-denial that is often part of the path to ecstasy.

(e) Then, too, in so many forms of religion - primal shamanism, the way of the Buddha and of Jesus, Sufi devotion to the Pirs - *healing* and a new wholeness of life are linked closely with the experience of ec-stasy, 'standing outside' oneself. Here too, any contradiction between God-life and earth-life is resolved.

(f) Yet another form of this 'resolving' is the way in which the whole *earth and the many delights of earth's life* become - very prominently so in the ecstatic poetry of the Vaishnava 'drowned ones' - *signs of God's presence, channels of the vision of God*, both for agonised mourning over the loss of the Divine Lover and blissfully sensing his presence, whether hidden or manifest. The Tamil poet Nammalvar ('Our drowned one') from time to time took on the persona of a love-sick girl infatuated by Krishna. She feels her Lover has left her, yet she is poignantly aware of his hidden presence at every point where Nature touches her. So she 'caresses the earth' as though this is her Lover; she 'points to the red sun' and 'the radiant moon'; she 'feels the cool wind'; she 'smells the Tulasi flowers'; she 'wonders at a standing mountain'; she delights in being 'drenched by the pouring rain'; she 'hugs a tender calf'; she 'watches the arising of darkly heavy clouds'. And each part of Nature, sensually experienced, brings her parted Lover vividly to mind (Tiru-vaimoli *passim*). Many of these images are typical of the way in which reference to Krishna is made within his tradition. Clearly here, as in a number of other forms of Hindu *bhakti*, God and earth are far from incompatibles.

(g) And so we return to our starting point: the *distinctive character of faith-shaped identity*, often leading to a distinctive social identity, results from the *particular character of faith's central Object*. The variations are found even within the one tradition in the case of Vishnu-devotion. Rama and Krishna, usually interpreted as Avatars or 'Descents' of Vishnu, eventually prove, in interpretation and experience, to be very different characters. Not even a common name guarantees a common Focus. The Krishna we find in the Gita, with his primary concern for the right ordering of *dharma* in society and on earth generally (in spite of Krishna's 'last word' about *dharma* we noted earlier), is very like the character of the ideal king of *dharma*, Rama. In many ways both great epics - the Mahabharata (in which the Gita is found) and the Ramayana - are undergirded by a *dharma*-oriented Brahmanic worldview. The Krishna found in both vernacular poetry and in later Sanskritic Purana (Hardy 1983) is a far less *dharma*-bound figure. At the level of social life, and in its formal ordering, the Krishna-devotee will usually be quite ready to submit to the requirements of *dharma*. But the transcending vision of the seductive flute-player, dancing ferociously on the head of the monster-serpent he has just slain, dancing with erotic abandon with the cow-girls, was a convention-liberated God. And that even more compulsive dancer, Nataraj Siva, is even less bound by the usual restraints of Brahmanic *dharma*.

In both traditions, then, a taming, domesticating, *'brahmanising'* process takes place, and the constraints of social *dharma* assert themselves for the devotees of these two great Gods of Hinduism. In fact, within the stream of Vaishnavism most dominant especially in the South, i.e. the followers of Ramanuja, it was not long before the status of Krishna in the community diminished, and Rama became the more dominant Focus. Krishna's seductive dancing was too dangerous for a community that culturally was becoming increasingly Brahmin-dominated.

(h) Again, within both Christianity and Islam a similar re-directing of divine identities takes place. As Christian faith spread in the Mediterranean world, the growing understanding of faith and worship as a sharing in the convention-defiant dance of Jesus, was condemned by council after council in early Christian centuries, until it was all but suppressed as 'Gnostic excess'. And in Islam, the Sufi experience of finding transcendent Allah within the heart, with rhythm, music, dance as the way by which such realisation is attained, was equally abhorrent to traditional authority. No wonder one of the earliest suppressive acts of the Taliban in recent years was to ban Sufi activity in Afghanistan, the heartland of Sufism in many ways. And one of the earliest cultural changes when the Taliban were overthrown was the re-emergence of Sufi music. In Islam too there is this bi-polar perception of the ultimate Focus of faith.

Typical Bi-Polar Patterns of Faith

In this typical bipolar pattern involving two views of faith's Focus, then, there may be a corresponding tension between *ecstasy* and *conformism*, in one of which there is a religious identity based on, or giving importance to, social norms, the other being an identity that moves beyond, may be indifferent to, perhaps even flouts given social norms. At this point the yogic renouncer aiming to calm all passion and the ecstatic for whom God-passion is of the essence show a similar attitude to normative social identities. Neither find their ultimate self-identity in what either the world or even the conformists of their own tradition expect as a proper human role in society. Even when either the God-impassioned or the passion-calmers come to find a basis for self-identity in a new community - a community of monks, *sanyasis*, *bhaktas*, or ecstatics - it is not hitherto normative society that now shapes their understanding of who they are, what they are to be, where they belong. Life among the fellowship of saints or the brotherhood of fellow-monks determines what they are to be and how they are to live.

So, then, one crucial point to note again within this bi-polar patterning: there is often diverging interpretation or experience of the same basic sacred figure - Brahman as Person and as impersonal Absolute; Krishna as restorer of order and as order-defying seducer; Christ as law-giver (a second Moses) and as deviant dancer; Islamic institutional submission to Allah whose sovereign will is made known in the Shari'ah, and Allah to be experienced within the heart of the whirling dervisher. In all these polarities of religious experience we see how deeply dialectic, how full of 'coinciding opposites' (*coincidentia oppositorum*), faith is. John Carman, whose work has primarily been on Ramanuja and the Sri Vaishnava tradition, has explored this aspect of religious life with great competence (Carman 1994).

Perhaps the sacred figure allowing more room for divergence than any other is that of Siva. Even in the earliest sources - Rudra-Siva of the Rig-Veda - Healing Helper and Howling Destroyer are two dominant but contradictory identities ascribed to Siva. Then there were the ascetic and the erotic aspects of his nature, symbolised by yogic pose and matted dreadlocks on the one hand, and (sometimes erect) phallic *linga* on the other. Or there is the contrast between Siva as Nila-kantha, the 'blue-throated' drinker of poison intended for his devotees, and the one who drinks from a skull as he inhabits his death-filled cremation grounds. Most startling of these polarities is Siva's unpredictable violence (shown towards some who thwart him) as against the unparallelled grace experienced by a number of his devotees. Both sides of Siva's character emerge in his dance. It can be gently *lasya* and liberating, or it can be ferociously *tandava* and destructive, even destructive of all creation.

Violent Imagery Again

Fiercely destructive violence in religious imagery is, as we saw earlier, in no way confined to Siva's character. Few religious traditions do not have their violent side. Even the banding together of world-renouncing *sanyasis* and taking up arms to defend their faith and its followers is not restricted in Indian tradition to Saivas. In the (Vaishnava-related) Ramanandi sect closely associated with violence-torn Ayodhya in North India, for example, the function of the naked Nagas within the community was similarly militant (van der Veer1997). The gentle character of the Buddha would not seem set to produce violent imagery. There was, of course, the enraged elephant sent by a jealous uncle, but instead of trampling on the Buddha it knelt in peaceful homage. Yet, in Himalayan Buddhist Thangkas - pictures used as a focus for meditation - the figure of the Buddha is often surrounded by the most violent imagery, and he is even embraced by a ferociously sexual female partner, to whom in some 'left-handed' traditions he responds with obvious physical vigour, though his face remains utterly serene. No doubt there is some effective proto-Freudian psychology at work here in the liberative techniques of this Vajrayana (thunderbolt) Tibetan Buddhism.

My point here is not simply that violence erupts in unexpected places when religion is concerned. It is rather the contradictory interpretations possible on the basis of the same faith-image. To one who finds the suffering and death of Jesus a revelation both of the heart of God as well as of the self-denying love expected of a Jesus-follower as made explicit in his teaching, it is almost beyond belief that there are Christians who have taken this same image as a call to violent slaughter of all 'enemies'. No doubt the title 'Christus Victor' (Gustaf Aulen's work with this title is a classic account) with which later theology interpreted the death of Jesus (and there were numerous interpreting theories) was intended to refer to spiritual powers, the demonic powers that disrupt the soul-body life of humans especially, with which Jesus did battle in his healing acts. *Healing Wings* (Lott 1995) interprets these healings as being 'for human wholeness'. But his own call to 'take up the cross' was, within three centuries, to become a rallying call for those taking a crusading stance against enemy peoples and their religions, blatantly contradicting the clear and explicit teaching of Jesus concerning the life of love for enemies expected of those following him.

When we look at the Judeo-Christian tradition as a whole, there is a strange mixture of the violent and the pacific. In Isaiah there is that beautiful picture of the 'peaceable kingdom', so beloved of Quaker Friends, that speaks of the time when the lamb will lie down with the lion and there shall be no more war, 'no harm or hurt in all my holy mountain'. Yet, it is set within passages speaking of horrendous violence against the enemies of God's people. Nor do the Christian Gospels speak only of self-denial and love. When Jesus weeps over Jerusalem, before being cruelly crucified outside its holy walls, there is a hint of the apocalyptic visions of its destruction - regretted with

139

such deep feeling - that find fuller expression elsewhere. Violence in religious visions of the future, violence with reference to unbelievers, violence done in the name of faith - all are widespread in our varied histories.

It would be good if one could say that at least in a tradition in which non-violence to life (*jiva-ahimsa*) is absolutised, as in Jainism, the 'conqueror' (i.e. 'Jina') aims solely for a victory that is spiritual. Yet even here, when linked closely with ruling powers, as for example in medieval Karnataka in South India, the community's life was not free from temporal conquest, with its accompanying political pressures and compromises, and even violence. It has to be said, though, that history records far greater acts of violence against the Jaina monks, as when we read that some 6000 were done away with by the Vaishnava-favouring regime of the time. The reference may possibly be to conquest through public debate, very frequently engaged in then, the outcome of which decided the future group identity of whole communities of religious tradition.

Even so, there is no denying how pervasive is violence in religious histories, and therefore potentially so in *interpretations of the focal Identity of faith and so of the religious identities we then take on*. And because it is reflected even in central symbols of faith, central terms of faith - the Saiva trident, the Vaishnava discus, the war-chariot, the crossed swords of the Sikh, the victorious 'soldier of Christ', sacred *jihad* ('struggle'), and many more - the key to the role of violence in any faith-tradition, and in the religious identities emerging from these, is dependent on one crucial factor: how a tradition is *interpreted at a time of critical change*. For there are also strong strands urging mercy, love, compassion in all the sources of our faith-traditions. Which means, then, that just as response to Power is crucial in shaping the basic character of the originating vision in each religion, so response to the historical forces by which our contexts change is decisive. So much depends upon just how the symbols, the imagery, the key terms, even the central sacred Figures, are projected and articulated at times of crisis. The role of interpreters in the shaping of our religious identities, and how they relate to wider human identities - the institutions of political power in particular - are factors of immense import.

Chapter 5
'The Clash of Civilisations'

A quite recent account of the nature of our corporate identities, and how human communities relate to each other, an anlysis that has made a major impact on leading western perceptions of global relationships, is Samuel Huntington's *The Clash of Civilisations and the Remaking of World Order* (1997). Huntington is a professor of political science at Harvard. Political gurus such as the influential Henry Kissinger and Zbigniew Brzezinski claimed it will 'revolutionise our understanding of international affairs'. Even before 9/11 it had struck a deeply resonant note among thinking conservatives, and fierce debate globally. The original essay has been translated into more than 30 languages.

Huntington's hard-edged but sophisticated political realism posits *self-interest*, and the acquiring of *power*, the power to promote self-interest, as the primary dynamic on which nations and civilisations are and indeed should be based. Yet, his position does take us further than the naked assertion of selfish power. He refers to himself as a 'child of Niebuhr', attracted by the 'compelling combination of morality and practical realism' that informed this mid-20th century Protestant theologian's thinking and writing. (See Robert D. Kaplan, 'Looking the World in the Eye', *The Atlantic*, Dec 2001).

For Niebuhr the demands of justice had to shape any valid Christian expression of love, and the wishful thinking of liberal Christian love could only lead to a dangerous impotence. Love was not the principle on which societies and the hard facts of politics could be based. The realities of the world, including the struggle for power and the hard facts of evil, have to be faced with harder eyes. This made necessary the dialectic - an interpenetrating dualism - of both Augustine and Luther's two realms - the realm in which God holds sway and the realm of 'this fallen world' - that Niebuhr sees as implicit in radical monotheism.

Huntington, then, writes within the framework of what is at key points the worldview of a certain form of Protestant faith. An even more recent book of Huntington's, *Who Are We? America's Great Debate*, is even more explicitly pro-Protestant, arguing that just as

American self-identity has been grounded in a Protestant ethno-cultural core. so must America's future, if there is to be a coherent identity. Cosmopolitan multi-culturalism can, he believes, lead only to disintegration, especially in view of the rapidly growing numbers of inadequately assimilated immigrant Latin-Americans. That so many convert to evangelical and pentecostal faith does not help this process, as Huntington sees it.

Unlike Niebuhr, Huntington - in his *Clash of Civilisations*, eschews cultural *universalism*, the assumption that what we see as the highest values can be introduced to others. He is unexpectedly critical in particular of western unwillingness to accept *diversity*, the essential differences between cultures. He rejects the widely held notion that 'people throughout the world should embrace Western values, institutions, and culture because they embody the highest, most enlightened, most liberal, most rational, most modern, and most civilised thinking of humankind'. This 'particularly American belief....suffers three problems: it is false; it is immoral; and it is dangerous' (1996: 310). For such universalism to be a reality is in the context of the military-backed spread of imperialist power across the globe. To make the hegemonic belief that 'our' values should be 'their' values a reality calls for globalising agression, which implicitly denies those very values - self-determination and democracy. Universalism and imperialism belong together in mutual interdependence.

What may seem strangely like a postcolonial critique with its postmodernist relativism is actually a much older conservatism, a kind of civilisational *apartheid*. Each civilisation has its own forms of cultural life. Even western democracy is unique to western Christian culture and cannot be fitted into the corporate life of other cultures. This rules out *unilaterist intervention* into the life of other civilisations, especially with the idea of reshaping others into our own image, as a regular way of trying to extend power. Rather, various levels of *mediation* and *cooperation* are essential to the process by which distinct civilisations are to maintain their separate being.

Clearly this view of global relations is very pertinent today. America may now be the only global superpower. But, argues Huntington, with the end of the bipolar situation that existed before the fall of the Soviet empire, if America now acts as though the world is *unipolar*, inevitably it will be seen as an arrogant rogue superpower that could well provoke coalitions into resistant reaction. The 9/11 apocalypse (after Huntington's book) led the Bush administration, in the name of 'war against terrorism', into pre-emptive military intervention and 'regime change' in any Muslim country perceived as in some way supporting terrorist activity and therefore a threat to American self-interest. There was for some time the dark promise of more such pre-emptive actions against other 'rogue states', against a widespread 'axis of evil', the clear intent being to reshape a whole civilisation, even a 'new world order' by these 'shock and awe' tactics.

Huntington's argument can certainly be seen as providing a basis for some kind of concerted effort, including military force, to fight the global threat of 'terrorism'. An attack by coalition forces on perceived al-Qaida camps in Afghanistan would be legitimate in this view of things, though not necessarily to the total and massively violent overthrow of the Taliban regime. And the almost unilateral attack on Iraq can only have disastrous effects according to this political realism. Even within such a conservative perspective on our civilisations, it is surely far from serving the self-interest of either America or western Christian civilisation.

At the opposite end of the spectrum of political historians, the socialist Eric Hobsbawm interestingly finds recent American belief in its absolute and invulnerable military power, and its view of the world as unipolar - a view that is leading potentially and very dangerously to inclusive global self-extension - to be the first such case in human history, though not a role that many American people actually want, and in any case one its economy cannot sustain *(Guardian*, 14 June 2003, 'America's Imperial Delusion').

Human cultural identities, argues Huntington, are essentially 'civilisational identities'. 'A civilisation is a culture writ large' (*op. cit.* p.41). The boundaries may not be precise, but they are decisive, shaping the 'patterns of cohesion, disintegration, and conflict' in the modern world, as they ever have (p.20). He divides global life into eight major long-standing 'civilisations': Sinic, Japanese, Hindu, Islamic, Orthodox, Western, Latin America, African (though he has some doubt about the cultural cohesion and civilisational resourcefulness of Africa). Within the overarching civilisation to which a person belongs there may be a number of other lesser cultures and lesser identities; but the integrating *civilisation* provides the 'broadest possible cultural entity', the 'broadest level of identity' to be experienced as a human (p.43). It is this divide that creates the age-old 'us' and 'them' way of seeing the world. The Muslim division between 'Dar al-Islam' (house of Islamic peace) and 'Dar al-Harb' (house of conflict and war) is the epitome of the 'us-them' worldview.

It is *religion*, claims Huntington, that is 'a central defining characteristic of civilisations' (*op. cit.* p.47). He quotes Christopher Dawson: 'The great religions are the foundations on which the great civilisations rest'. Cultures emerging from Hinduism, Confucianism, Christianity and Islam directly undergird several of the eight primary civilisations Huntington identifies. And Buddhism is an important component in China and Japan, though is not seen as directly creating their civilisations. Each civilisation, therefore, is said to embody distinct forms of life-vision and core-values, that diverge discernibly and crucially from those of other civilisations. Through the centuries any civilisation can go through striking evolutionary changes, especially times of conflict that may lead to seeing itself as a universally valid state, but will then - in part because of its false belief in its own absoluteness - move on eventually to decay and disintegration.

The boundaries between these eight civilisations make for mutual exclusion. So, to interact culturally with one another, or be mutually absorbent, according to Huntington is just not viable. Any such inter-mixing will inevitably weaken not only the distinct identity each has, but also its necessary power-base. It is a serious political and cultural mistake, therefore, to advocate either *multiculturalism* - the idea that the preserving of distinct cultures should be encouraged within a 'civilisation' - or *unipolarism*. A degree of uniformity is essential to integration - a well-rehearsed conservative principle. It is only by western Christian civilisation asserting and strengthening its distinctive identity that it will recover its lost strength. A strong sense of civilisational identity is itself empowering. At the same time, other civilisations should be left to affirm their peculiar identities. Again, this idea of live and let live has obviously been thrown overboard by the present Washington regime with its aim to set up a 'new world order' based on an aggressively neo-liberal capitalist democracy even in the thoroughly Muslim cultural ethos of the Middle East.

Huntington, though, is strangely reluctant to acknowledge both the pervasiveness and the ideological character of the globalising process now taking place, a process that so alarms many non-westerners. Globally there is a 'modernising' process, but this does not mean 'westernising', argues Huntington. He sees the changes to modernity as mostly neutral, when in reality they are irrevocably locked into a very distinct strand of secular western culture and capitalist ideology, and thereby are perceived by non-westerners as undermining many of their cultural values, values that Huntington himself argues are so distinctive to these different civilisations.

Huntington at least recognises the potent role of *religion* - though understood in terms of quasi-political culture - in global affairs. It must also be said that the book includes a huge amount of global historical data, even if carefully selected and often strained to fit his thesis. His writing is 'noisy with the sounds of sawing and stretching as the facts are forced into a bed that has been prepared for them', was what one critic wrote of an earlier book. Even if there is much that reads convincingly, the rightwing political assumptions soon become clear, and his 'civilisations' appear as little more than competing power-groups.

Clearly, with religion given such a prominent civilisational place, we cannot say that the inner dynamics of faith have *no* place in his understanding. But the process by which faith shapes civilisation is seen in a very limited way. There is little nuancing of religion's ways. Certainly there is far too little weight given to the actual diversity found within any one of the 'civilisations' he identifies, and within their undergirding religions. Even the struggle between strikingly antagonistic worldviews within the 'Christian West' seems to have no place. While he writes freely of continual changes taking place within cultural histories (hard to deny anyway), there seems to be no role for the positive value-changes within a 'civilisation' resulting from the impact of interaction with others: the impact, for example, of Islamic life on European medieval thought; the African and Indian impact on the twentieth century's revolution in music and other cultural styles, more recently in the widespread accepting of New

Age values, even if these should still be seen as counter-cultural rather than mainstream; the interpenetration of Muslim and Hindu cultural life in India over the centuries. Openness to outside influence in this way can only lead to inner weakness and decay.

And most notably, there is no recognition of those streams within religious traditions that are intrinsically *counter-cultural*, serving not to harden existing community identities, but to question and redirect them by reference to some transcendent Focus beyond those identities. Religious faith and therefore religious loyalties are not all to do with self-interest, at least not in any recognisable sense of seeing to one's own interests. They have often, in fact, been exactly the opposite in any recognisable worldly-wise sense.

The group identities based on a common faith invariably *do* empower, and may well be engaged in a life-or-death struggle for the power to give expression to that common faith. Power is at the centre of faith, too, in the sense we noted earlier in Gerardus van der Leeuw's key idea that religion is to do with the way in which ultimate Power is perceived and responded to. But certainly faith itself is not essentially about the acquiring of power politically. Huntington may be correct in assuming that civilisations are concerned primarily with the increase or diminishment of *power;* their political flourishing and decaying is essential to their life. But when it is then assumed that each civilisation is based on a religious tradition, a more subtle faith-power linkage has to be made; in particular, the driving compulsions of religion have to be differently understood, and power itself has to be far more nuanced.

There are even questions to be raised about the dynamics of contemporary global history. Although the externals of imperial histories are recalled, Huntington gives little weight to the crucial fact that so many of the world's extremist and 'fundamentalist' identities are the direct or indirect product of previous, sometimes quite recent, Western actions in relation to these other civilisations. Colonial histories throw up other consequences too no doubt, perhaps not all of which are bad. But the reaction-chain of that history is inescapable.

And there is another reality that is overlooked. Huntington clearly sees Islam as a global 'problem'. Nearly all his most serious 'flaw-lines', the clash-points between the world's peoples, involve Muslims.

They just do not seem able to accommodate themselves to others in their difference. Much of his analysis is put forward as hardnosed description: this is how things are all over the globe. The description itself, though, conveys more judgemental presciption. No one can claim that Huntington is not self-critical. He is highly critical of western 'universalist' assumptions for instance, as we saw. He also recognises the inevitability, even the right, of Muslims to react angrily to western intrusion, violent or otherwise. There is, though, far too little critical awareness of just how widespread are the hegemonising global tentacles of strands within western 'civilisation'. The element of *justifiable resistance* in that fractious Muslim world is not given enough weight, however un-justified may be the forms of terrorist resistance adopted by extremists. And again it has to be said that the 'worlds' Huntington finds in conflict are far too easily identified. Our inner struggles call for far more nuanced analysis.

Along with the simplistic global divisions Huntington makes, then, there is an unreal *separatism* that ignores - as most analysis from both extreme right and left does - the tangled histories that have brought us where we now are. The civilisational *apartheid* that Huntington in effect advocates emerges as such most clearly in the guiding principles he urges for preserving Western civilisation (1996: 311-12). There is to be greater political, economic and military integration of North America and European states, including non-Orthodox states from the previous USSR. Any Muslim states, however - Turkey, Bosnia, for example - are to be excluded, for Islam is far too prone to 'fundamentalist extremism'. Latin America is to be further westernised and thus brought into closer alignment with Europe-America. The military power of Islamic states and China is to be restrained. Japan's drift from the West towards China must be slowed.

Western technological and military superiority over other civilisations must be maintained, though Western intervention in the affairs of other civilisations should be avoided, as 'the single most dangerous source of instability and potential global conflict in a multi-civilisational world'. The nakedly imperialist intervention in the past of Western nations on Islamic and other regions is clearly acknowledged, but strangely not the continuing impact of this historical legacy particularly on Islamic consciousness. Islamic identity is described as 'consciousness without cohesion', again

147

showing clearly that political and military power alone is seen as significant. Nor is there overt recognition of the intrusive power - cultural and ideological as much as economic - of America and its Western allies in the life of other 'civilisations' through the globalising process, an intrusion that in various ways continues to be effective in spite of the violent resistance.

Huntington's position, though, for all its simplistic alignments, at least should lead us to see the fearful dangers to 'civilisational stability' posed by such intrusions as on 9/11 and the American-led military interventions in Afghanistan and Iraq by way of response. These events, for many on both sides, pull the world into mythologised conflict between Christian West and international Islam. That western political leaders and most media interpreters have usually been careful, in public rhetoric at least, to differentiate between the perpetrators of that horrific attack and Muslim people generally has done little to lessen the Islamophobia on one side and the conviction that the faith and future of Muslims are under mortal threat.

There are, however, several reasons, all interlinked, why this fails to convince large numbers even of quite 'moderate' Muslims.

Firstly, there was the way the USA and its allies so quickly identified what it called an 'axis of evil' that is almost entirely comprised of Muslim countries. The hardline Islamic regime of the Taliban in Afghanistan was almost immediately destroyed with massive 'shock and awe' air bombardment. Ostensibly the aim was to destroy Osama bin Laden's al-Qaida training bases and other forms of support, though bin Laden himself escaped. The extent and intensity of the attack, and the fact that at least the same number of non-combatant people were killed (some claim three times the number), and that there was little planning, little follow-up support for economic, political and social reconstruction, strongly suggests an act of retaliation for 9/11 and the destruction of radical Islam as the primary motive.

This perception by Muslims (and many others) was confirmed by the US/UK coalition turning quickly to the invasion of Iraq, first - it was claimed - because of its al-Qaida connection, then because such a 'rogue state' possessing weapons of mass destruction is a threat to neighbouring and western countries (weapons initially provided by the same western powers), then finally because Saddam Hussein's regime is despotic and genocidal. Regime-change and/or the removal of the leader was claimed as essential both to world peace and for the emergence of a 'new world order' in the Middle East.

Most Muslims and many non-Muslims found the talk of an al-Qaida connection ludicrous, as Ba'athist 'secularism' was always fiercely condemned by radical Islamists, whether Shi'a or Sunni. Most were unconvinced by the evidence concerning 'weapons of mass destruction'. At the United Nations - in spite of the Ba'athist regime's atrocities - few believed there was no other option but an all-out invasion. Although its standing to some extent was weakened by stories of corruption among personnel handling the oil-for-food arrangement, the United Nations remained the one body with international connections and credibility. Yet its resolutions in the end were humiliatingly dismissed. Pleas for much longer periods of intense political pressure and negotiation made by Muslim and many other countries including Russia, China, France, and Germany, along with all Christian leaders but the Southern Baptist Church of America, were ignored. The new Bush policy of all-out pre-emptive strikes led many to wonder who was to be next on the hit-list.

Muslims, feeling especially vulnerable in the face of this new resolve by the world's most powerful ever military force to introduce a new 'world order' conforming to their own interests, are increasingly driven to respond in faith-terms. To what extent this is a *jihad*, a holy struggle that will be blessed by Allah, and precisely what is meant by *'jihad'*, will be explored later.

Secondly, in the minds of international Islam this military action against two Muslim states (with others being threatened), however crudely tyrannical one regime's interpretation of Islam, or un-Islamic and viciously despotic the other, is directly of a piece with the long-standing and powerful *support of America for the state of Israel's violent oppression of* the largely Muslim (with some Christian) Palestinians. While the many United Nations' resolutions on Israel's actions against Palestine have been ignored with impunity, lack of complete compliance by Iraq - that many see to be in any case much less serious non-compliance - was made the pretext for war. Three months after the invasion of Iraq, seemingly in the face of so much the Bush regime stands for, the new American-led 'roadmap to peace' between Israel and Palestine was for a while seen as a sign of hope by public optimists like UK's Prime Minister Blair, whose profile has been very high throughout all this. Some were surprised that President Bush has gone along with this public commitment to a separate state for Palestine, in view of apocalyptic Christian opposition in the US to any such move. Many more, though, including most Muslims, were deeply sceptical, seeing the usual and expected gap between rhetoric and reality, between words and intentions. If this is the general perception, how much more unlikely that militant Islamic groups in the region will ever accept the American version of what the future there for Israel and Palestine should be. Even moderate Muslims throughout the world, while accepting the need to collaborate with western demands regarding violent extremists ('terrorists'), now find it difficult to resist the contention that there is an anti-Muslim Christian-Israeli conspiracy, determined to weaken global Islam by attacking states in any way resistant.

Thirdly, these massive military attacks are believed merely to be the climax of what was seen as the cruelly deprivatory action against the people of Iraq, led by the United States, in imposing several years of economic *sanctions*. These exacerbated the already dire conditions of many *ordinary Muslims* there already impoverished by a tyrant's self-aggrandisement. And as a result an estimated one million Iraqi children and vulnerable people died. To equal their number, Muslims claim, the World Trade Centre killings would need to occur every day for well over a year. The anger over sanctions, however, is as nothing compared to the upwelling of rage throughout the Muslim world over the recent invasion of Iraq, with the subsequent killing of several thousand non-combatants, and (in late 2004) the growing chaos inevitable in view of the lack of planning for 'reconstruction'. That rage may have been tempered precisely because Muslims globally saw Saddam Hussein's regime as the opposite of good Muslim governance, even if they also held a sneaking respect for his long-standing resistance to western power.

This same regime, however, was for many years massively supported by the West. The US and UK governments were eventually forced to acknowledge that there were in fact no 'weapons of mass destruction' (the amassing of which had been claimed as the primary reason for the invasion), even though the those same western nations had supplied materials for the production of just such chemical and biological weapons. This was then believed to be a ncessary counter to the newly emerging Shi'ah Islamic nation of Iran - in its aggressive Islamic naivete seen as a threat to the stability of the Middle East and so to the safe flow of oil. But this manipulative 'imperialism' is just one of this long list of western actions unlikely to be forgotten by international Islam.

Fourthly, the Islamic world sees quite clearly that the West's primary concern in all its dealings with the Middle East is the fact - not just a geographical accident for believers in the divine Will - of those massive *reserves of oil* to be found in the Islamic crescent. They have long been absolutely crucial to western industry and its consequent affluence, and to America in particular with its huge appetite for oil. As a consequence, during the past 125 years or so state after state in that part of the Muslim world has been treated with belligerent disdain. Both the boundaries and the ruling regime in a number of these states were originally put in place and subsequently kept in place by western military power, usually on the basis of what will ensure the continued flow of sufficiently cheap fuel. Even the Taliban came to power as a result in large part of American action, albeit through Pakistan, not this time because of oil, but in the struggle against the Soviet Union. Again, Muslims see a calculated exploitation of a pawn-like Muslim country. In terms solely of global Islam's view of civilisational clash, there is agreement here with Huntington's analysis.

Fifthly, there is the vigorously promoted consumerist culture of the West, linked indivisibly as it is in Muslim eyes with the West's offensively permissive, dangerously immoral *cultural aggression*. The nauseating pictures that emerged in 2004 showing American soldiers perpetrating all manner of barbaric and even sexually repulsive acts against prisoners at Abu Ghraib prison in Iraq were taken by many Muslims as final confirmation both of the moral decadence of the 'Christian' West and of the aim to humiliate Muslims as a body. Earlier, the *Satanic Verses* affair was seen as but one more instance of the West's cultural war against Islam. Salman Rushdie's assured place among the western cultural elite, not in spite of but because of his Muslim roots, marked him as a treacherous stooge of the anti-Muslim attitudes endemic to this cultural aggression of the West. That, for all his liberal values, he publicly supported the military invasions does not surprise Muslim critics.

All such attacks are seen as part of a grand anti-Muslim conspiracy. Rupert Murdoch is but one media 'moghul'(!) whose aim is to control political attitudes through his many newspapers, magazines and TV channels, and beam down on a global scale satellite programmes peddling western cultural life, obscenely inimical to the cultural values of many of the countries which they aim to saturate. This particular 'sky-war' is seen as just another battle in the conspiracy to weaken and finally destroy Islam. Again, at this perceptual level Huntington's 'clash of civilisations' becomes a reality. Events conspire to draw even thoroughly non-extremist Muslims into a dangerous sense of 'them' and 'us'. Identity boundaries become battle-lines.

Huntington is correct, then, in highlighting the potent impact of religion and religious loyalties on political events and the way communities relate to each other. Do not the majority of the points of community conflict in the world today witness to this all too forcefully, even if the cause-effect sequence needs much more careful disentangling than the superficial linkage so often portrayed in his *Clash of Civilisations*?

To sum up: Huntington misses so much that is crucial to the dynamics. For one thing there is the great divergence *within* religious traditions that Huntington's civilisational conglomerates fail to reckon with. Moreover, *political* ambitions, faith-bereft power-struggles, and certainly *economic* conditions, are often crucial in shaping how religious tradition is appropriated and how religious attitudes are conditioned. In the Balkans, for example, there has been fiercely murderous political expression of differing faith-loyalties - Orthodox Serbs, Catholic Croats and Muslim Bosnians and Albanians increasingly conscious of their global Islamic connections.

The politicisation of religion can result in a potent brew by which even the most peace-seeking of religious practitioners such a Buddhist monks can become intoxicated. Again, these are issues of power and the search for power. What casually observing man-in-the-street, let alone the Buddha himself, would have thought that gentle Buddhist monks in Sri Lanka would vigorously lead anti-Tamil violence, or that the saffron-clad, world-renouncing *sanyasis* of Hindu tradition would be also in the vanguard of the mosque-destroying mobs of Ayodhya, signal for the slaughter of many hundreds of Muslims throughout India? And how can we trace any linkage between viciously violent Christian crusaders - maybe not all medieval - with the clearly declared ways of the Jesus in whose name they kill?

My argument may sound like a call to keep politics out of religion and religion out of politics. In one sense it is, in another it is not. There is, though, an urgent need to be aware of the *power-issues*, and aware of the *distinctive dynamics of political and religious worlds*, even as they interpenetrate so potently. Calls to 'keep religion out of politics' can express genuine concern that the institutions and inner potency of a particular religious tradition have become politically exploited, or that political judgements are being made with the welfare of only one group of the nation's people in mind. 'Identity politics' have taken over. On the other hand, the claim heard with equal frequency that 'religion is a purely private affair' may be made from a secularist perspective that refuses to see either the innate potency of religion in public affairs or the potential for good of religious faith, whatever the attendant dangers. Or such a position may reflect merely a concern to keep moral considerations out of political judgements, especially when market forces, the creation of wealth and the retention of power are seen as the ultimate values in public life.

Even so, when religious identity and political identity become institutionally one, when faith is expressed in the structures of state power, especially in modern state power with its militarist undergirding, we have a dangerous mix, dangerous for religious faith as much as for political style. That 'power corrupts, and absolute power corrupts absolutely' (as the British Liberal Lord Acton quipped) is perhaps especially true of religion based political power. For within a religious worldview Power will necessarily be seen in absolute terms. The danger is that it may then be transposed to and be seen as embodied in a sacralised or theocratic institution.

Theologically, of course, for any radical monotheist such as a Muslim, to identify that absolute power of God with any human institution of state - even an institution claiming divine sanction - would seem to be blasphemous sacrilege, the Muslim sin of *shirk*. Shi'as in particular tend to this position; hence, paradoxically their insistence that the dominant authority lies with clerics, not politicians as such. In any case, a government that sees itself as in power by divine decree, and establishes itself as 'Christian', or 'Muslim', or 'Hindu', or 'Sikh', will face almost impossible ambiguities, and there is a loss of the necessary dialectic between the ultimacy of faith-Identity and all other lesser life-identities. There will then also be an inability to accept the necessary diversities instrinsic to human cultural life.

The American Constitution ostensibly separates secular and religious power. Officially no US government can act as though it were an overtly Christian regime, especially in ways favouring Christians over against others. Yet, the leadership and advisors in the Bush administration are not only closely connected with conservative Christianity. Convincing reports have been made showing key members of that political leadership locked into an alarmingly apocalyptic worldview. This not only sees United States power as God-given precisely in order to unilaterally direct world affairs. It also sees as inescapably pre-destined a massively destructive conflict (Armageddon) taking place very soon now in the Middle East, following which Christ will reign from Jerusalem. This event may include the 'rapture' when true believers are caught up into heaven with Christ in order to be spared this final conflagration. But there is more than one version of this apocalyptic vision, and in political circles it is mostly a covertly held worldview.

Apocalyptic worldviews more typically emerge among communities that are vulnerable to and therefore feel terminally threatened by the power of others: the Jewish people hopelessly exiled in Babylon (modern Iraq), or later faced by the far superior military might of Antiochus Epiphanes the Syrian in the second century BCE, or the imprisoned Christian seer John and his small group of Christians overwhelmed by the might of Rome two generations after Jesus. It was in these oppressed circumstances that the books of Ezekiel, Daniel and Revelation, the present sources of apocalyptic 'dispensationalism' were written (Anderson 1978). In modern America, too, it was among the crushingly poor and disadvantaged of the southern states, people with little reason for hope in 'this present age', that apocalyptic imagery first most forcefully appealed. It takes a more subtle theory to explain why now we find those sharing such great wealth and power still so closely linked with an apocalyptic identity, and the combination is alarming indeed.

However, in spite of the claims of some critics - both secularist and those of more world-affirming faith - it is doubtful if more than a few members of the Bush regime would resort to this apocalyptic imagery to describe their view of the future and boulster their own sense of identity. But the linkage is there. And what is held in common is the fierce conviction that their nation's incomparable power is given by God to bring in a new world order in which America is to hold a specially privileged status. It will be the 'new American century'. Richard Perle (chairman of the Defence Policy Board, an advisory panel to the Pentagon) and others of the inner group openly despise the very concept of a United Nations body whose authority should in any way constrain the United States. Unparallelled power brings with it a sense of unilateralist privilege. When also based on a sense of apocalyptic destiny, a 'clash of civilisations' would seem alarmingly inevitable.

Chapter 6
Globalising Faith-Identities

Clearly there are periods in human history, and in the experience of nations, when a common faith is the focal-point for an intense community loyalty, even able to create a sense of nationhood. This may well be an identity that goes beyond all other loyalties, creating the confidence of being a distinct people. (But we look more closely in later chapters at how nations and nation-states are shaped by and themselves shape religion).

While common *phenomenological* patterning within the shaping of faith-based identities has by now become clear, what is equally unmissable are the distinctive *differences* in the way these patterns work out. Such unpredictable diversity is even found within what is usually taken to be the *same religion*, the same common tradition. 'Hinduism', 'Buddhism', 'Judaism', 'Christianity', are actually all made up of such strongly contrasting ways within these traditions, that even if they do share a common rootage, every generalised statement about their religious life usually has to be rigorously qualified, the variants taken seriously.

Very often these variants within the great religions reflect the *inflow of divergent ethnic and cultural streams* in the course of their incorporating histories. And this may well entail also differing social and economic histories. In other words it is, paradoxically, the globalising, the movements into each other's histories that has already occurred which often accounts for our diversities. Indigenous cultures live on, often in unconscious and imperceptible ways.

Diversity, though, is seen by 'fundamentalists' at any extreme as greatly threatening. Only one identity can be permitted. It is quite possible that any such imposed over-arching religious identity, even if willingly embraced, merely serves to obscure and in time to modify earlier indigenous identities. Yet, those more indigenous ways of seeing things may well, at least for a few generations, remain primary in a people's corporate self-consciousness, determining how they most immediately identify themselves over against others. Preachers seeking to purify the faith from local loyalties and politicians seeking a broader power-base will both call for such an enlarged identity.

Beneath the surface, though, the older identities will remain powerful.

(1) Global Identities for 'World Religions'

This persistence of an older identity is certainly true of many distinctive ethnic groups that have been incorporated into one or other of the greater traditions, or 'world religions': Hinduism, Buddhism, Christianity, Islam. It is not just that there are striking contrasts between, let us say, the Buddhisms of Tibet, Sri Lanka, Japan, between the Christianities of the Highlands of Scotland, the Caribbean Islands, Romania, South-West and North-East India, or between the Islam of West Africa, of Bosnia, of Hyderabad, of Indonesia, or of Saudi Arabia. And obviously there are many more geographical variants that could be listed.

Equally important, even *within each region* are the very diverse forms of these major religions, often with a religious identity shaped by migrant origins. Within the United States alone, for example, there are immense contrasts between the Christianity of Afro-American churches, Hispanic, Italian and Irish Catholics, Lutheran, Episcopalian, Methodist, Congregational and the many semi-conformist churches as well as the more radically non-conformist groups such as Mennonite, Baptist, exclusive Brethren - all originally from Europe. Then, even more significantly, are the huge number of home-grown American churches (the powerful Mormons for example), many of whom are based on an original faith-identity of extreme isolation and exclusiveness. The contrasts make for a 'Christianity' seemingly impossible to bring into a coherent pattern or a single identity. The apocalyptic worldview referred to earlier is worlds away from the faith of great swathes of Christian people globally - from among Catholic, Orthodox, Protestant, Pentecostal communities - whose identity is bound up with greater optimism concerning the world's destiny, greater self-restraint in seeking to work for a transformed world, and a very different understanding of divine power, prophetic vision and the nature of revelation.

Yet, the globalising process within faith-traditions is a reality.

(a) Islam:

Huntington writes of the Muslim world as being characterised by a common 'consciousness without cohesion'. In other words, while there is a sense of being part of the *umma*, the one people of Islam, that common consciousness does not translate into common organs of action. This suggests an impotent identity, and to some extent Huntington is right. Whether such inclusive spiritual identity will continue to lack embodying global organs - including military power - still remains to be seen. It will depend as much on the treatment of Muslims by others as on inherent Islamic faith. In any case, it should not be assumed that the creation of politically and militarily effective organs of power would further the effective establishing of true Islamic faith.

So, inner diversity is as true of Islam as of other faith-traditions. Islam is just not the monolithic entity so often claimed, usually by believer and critic alike. Imam Rashied Omar is far more true to reality - and exhibits great courage - when he highlights this fact of Muslim diversity in a sermon responding to the violent acts of 9/11:

> Islam like Christianity or any other religion is not a monolithic entity. The global Muslim community comprises a number of diverse articulations or understandings of Islam, frequently locked in fierce rivalry in their claim to be the privileged, orthodox and authentic voice of Islam (Website publication: www.culver.org).

This is not to deny the strength and importance of a common Muslim consciousness, the strong sense of *intrinsic oneness* transcending the differences. For this is a common faith-identity far more than just the growing globalist perspective willy nilly pervading the human race. But that globalism is double-edged. In the face of globalist forces, not only does the world-wide Muslim *umma*'s uniting belief in the oneness of Allah enable it to ignore its internal differences. There is now also the clearly identifiable presence of a global power increasingly perceived as a common and dangerous enemy. A common enemy will always both sharpen and broaden a sense of common identity. Thus, the recent invasion of Iraq has united Muslims both inside and far beyond the country. Ironically, too, this invasion ensured that the extremist al-Qaida-related militants became a powerful force in the country (Iraq) where previously they were non-existent in spite of claims to the contrary by the Bush regime..

The US/UK forces had been led to believe that at least all southern Iraqis would welcome them warmly, especially as the Sunni Saddam Hussein had so ruthlessly suppressed the southern Shi'as when (openly encouraged by invading powers) many had rebelled against his regime at the time of the 1991 war. In 2004, however, in the face of a common infidel aggressor with very mixed motives for attacking, no longer did Sunni-Shi'a differences divide so decisively. In fact, contrasting responses from Shi'a Ayatollahs have been crucial. There was damning *fatwa* from one. On the other hand, there has been the quieter piety of Grand Ayatollah Ali al-Sistani, with his policy of 'wait and see how Allah leads'. Ali al-Sistani powerfully embodies the spirit of the revered martyr Ali (focussed at Najaf in southern Iraq). And his persona and policy has been decisive in the Shi'a acceptance of the 'hand-over' of power in June 2004, that many have seen as a cover for continuing US/UK influence in the country. Thus, when resistance to the interim Iraqi authorities on these grounds was mounted at the Nijaf shrine by Moqtada al-Sadr and his militant followers, and when American forces came dangerously close to desecrating the sacred shrine to the holy martyr Ali, it was al-Sistani who was able to lead a great procession of Shi'as to Nijaf and effect a cease-fire. His stance of patient waiting on the 'greatness' of Allah is able to transcend the obvious ambiguities regarding the interim authorities, and he tries to point in hope to a future for genuine Iraqi rule. This spiritual leader remains widely and deeply revered - even beyond the boundaries of the Shi'a community.

Unity of faith, then, *is* an important factor in this crisis. Yet, Sunni-Shi'a mutual rivalries and suspicions remain. And having Islam in common did not bind the non-Arab Kurds in the north - also persecuted because of their wish to break away from Iraq. In western Sudan, too, subsequent to armed rebellion by Black African Fur people, in mid-2004 there were violent attacks on them - burning of villages, rape, enforced migration, and the killing of many - by Arab Sudanese militia, often with the Sudanese government's connivance. Both sides are Muslim. It may be that a distorted picture is being presented by western media, for close to that region also are untapped sources of oil, so greatly needed by western powers just at this time, with oil-prices soaring and economies burgeoning. Cynicism concerning the seeming altruism of western nations is not mere paranoia. Even so, here too a common faith in itself has not been enough to create a well-integrated common national identity.

In Iraq there was also the change of strategy by Saddam Hussein before his overthrow. Though a Sunni himself, he had traced his family genealogy to Ali, the sanctified hero of Shi'as. This ploy may have been far from convincing to Shi'as generally, but it did provide at least an official basis for loyalty, and so for a stronger common Muslim identity. And in the end, in spite of all the ambiguities, it is probably this faith-identity, rather than Arab or Iraqi nationalism, that in Iraq commands the most widespread and binding loyalty, however much nuancing we also have to engage in.

It was certainly not only neighbouring Arabs who were so deeply incensed by the invasion, even if their anger was largely ineffectual. And this rage was in spite of their general dislike of Saddam Hussein's regime. To extremist Islamists such as Osama bin Laden the Ba'athists' 'secular' rule is despicably un-Muslim. Yet, almost throughout the Muslim world, people's sense of identity with their beleaguered fellow-Muslims was powerfully enhanced precisely by an attack from non-Muslim 'imperialists'. Other differences were thereby transcended. Significantly, as the attacks intensified and casualties increased, the Baghdad leadership used more and more the language of extremist Islam, calling for all-out *jihad* against the enemies of Islam, bitterly condemning Muslim leaders for not helping them resist, and speaking of the joys of paradise awaiting those who give their lives for the cause of true Islam. The aim was to create a common resistant identity, transcending all other differences, on the basis of this threat to a common faith from a common enemy. The rhetoric and even the widespread rage deepened a sense of common identity among young men from Syria and elsewhere. So many factors contributed to this common consciousness - focussed as it is in a common faith.

But there were, too, many years of despotic oppression within Iraq, that left many with uncertain loyalties. Even the regime's late religiosity could hardly carry conviction, given the earlier history of persecution of fellow-Muslim Shi'as and Kurds, as well as such anti-Islamic life-style of the leading family - including of course the setting up everywhere of statues to Saddam. In spite of all this, there was a surprising strength of emotional togetherness. The wounded pride in being Iraqi emerged clearly enough, but a common Muslim identity was the stronger overall, with an unexpected unity of Shi'a and Sunni against a common enemy to Islam in spite of Saddam Hussein's grossly self-indulgent style. And the wounding went deep - well beyond the fact of many thousands (up to 100,000 according to a

Lancet report) Iraqi civilians that made up the 'collateral damage'. Militarily, as in Afghanistan, American fire-power so quickly overpowered the ill-equipped resistance that for many it was then largely the common feeling of impotent humiliation that bound together a people with so many innate differences.

(b) **Hinduism & Inclusive Faith-Identities** (see also chapters 14 and 16):

On the issue of both intrinsic diversity and inclusive identity the Hindu community is surely a special case. The process of growth into 'Hinduism' has been a very long and very distinctive process of incorporating such wide-ranging indigenous cults. It has been an 'absorbing' that ensured a relatively relaxed attitude to *diversity* of religious faith and practice. Rivalry and even violence between major Hindu sects is also part of the picture of course. It is complicated too by the social hierarchy of caste, based on each group's functional purity/impurity and the form of power/vulnerability this entails. In matters of faith, although there has been hierarchical grading based on the theoretical primacy of Vedic faith and ritual (controlled by Brahmins), it is mainly within the sects, and the need to maintain the boundaries of their faith-identities, that there has been concern for religious uniformity.

It is even increasingly questioned within postcolonial thinking whether 'Hinduism', as the homogeneous entity now identifiable, is not a relatively recent construct, brought into being by political concerns of diverse kinds, including the constructed identity given ιt by colonial powers and their 'orientalist' interpretations. The sense of belonging to a common *dharmic* identity - even if itself a 'construct' by increasingly powerful Brahmanic influence - was certainly not created *de novo* by European imperialism. What can be said, though, is that from quite early in the 19th century onwards Indian people became increasingly aware of the need for a common self-definition over against western imperialist rule, and that for nationalists such as Dayanand Sarasvati this increasingly included a sense of being Hindu as against Muslim (or Christian, etc).

One direction the 19th century Hindu reforming spirit took was to claim a kind of super-identity, a position transcending the particularities of all our divergent histories and therefore inclusive of all faith-identities. The ecstatic Ramakrishna - taken as guiding light ('Parama-hamsa' or 'heavenly Swan') and the name of Swami Vivekananda's new global mission - believed that by way of enhancing mystic consciousness he had passed through the various experiences of each of the other great religions. In turn he had experienced the nirvanic tranquillity of the Buddha, loving communion with Christ, Muhammad's experience of the majesty of Allah, and so on. Thus, for his disciple Swami Vivekananda the spiritual path arising from this (usually called neo-Vedanta) embodies inclusively all those other religious paths in a kind of superfaith-identity.

Of late, though, even the Hindu community - seen by so many as tolerant and inclusive, able to absorb all manner of deviations and contradictions - has developed more sharply defined self-identity both nationally and globally than ever before. For many Hindus it has been only in situations of religious or cultural *encounter* that this uniting sense of 'Hinduness' is the dominant identity shaping their consciousness of who they are. The more sharper edges of religious self-identity have usually related to a less inclusive grouping - both sectarian and caste - within this more general 'Hinduness'.

External political pressures have obviously loomed large in the creating of this more clearly defined Hindu identity. Yet, this is far from the whole story. Internal religious factors making for a shared consciousness - commonly celebrated festivals, shared places of sacred power and so of pilgrimage, shared deities and doctrines, however nuanced, however much prompted by Brahmanic 'hegemonising intentions', and therefore also undermined by hierarchical divide between the pure and the polluted - all these have also been an inclusive part of Indian cultural life for a long, long time. And this has been the case even if the name 'Hindu' is more recent, and the more globalised Hindu identity, as well as its more intensely nationalist significance today, has been fostered by aggressively nationalist groups such as the Rashtriya Svayam-sevak Sangha (National Volunteer-service Organisation, set up formally in 1942), and its offshoot the Vishva-Hindu-Parishad (World Hindu Council/Association) . For all the inner exclusions, then, a 'Hindu' *religious* identity is a significant reality for many millions of people. It has not merely been a name indicating those who are not Muslim, or not Christian.

Along with other religious traditions, then, Hindus today are more conscious than ever before of belonging to a *globally* significant community identified as 'Hindu', with a cultural identity distinctive from others, from Muslims and Christians in particular. Earlier, the more sharply defined identities were based either on religious sect, or on social sub-community of caste. Regional and linguistic identities have also made for strong cultural differentiation. This new sense of belonging to a worldwide religio-cultural tradition, then, spings both from inherent compulsions to such a wider identity and - more immediately - from compulsions that are, in the boadest sense, *political*. The nationalist factor is prominent.

The aggressively nationalist Vishva Hindu Parishad, or World Hindu Council/Association, is the global organisation most forcefully encouraging this newly cohesive identity. But VHP only flourishes because recent international politico-cultural realities - including the dispersion of huge numbers of Hindus throughout the globe - push Hindus into this more sharply defined all-Hindu self-identity (Hansen & Jaffrelot 1998). Identities of caste, language and sect are still significant, often locally powerful; but the last two decades of the twentieth century saw the Hindu community responding to the pressures of global life as never before.

But there had been precursors to such pressures long before, again contradicting the view that this sharpening of self-identity within the Hindu community was primarily a creation of the British imperialist presence and indigenous reactions to this. There were, too, compulsions for a broader front from India's own imperialisms. In the Vijayanagar Hindu empire, which like previous South Indian Hindu empires was not without power in other parts of South and East Asia with which it traded, we see a growing concern for a more inclusive Hindu religious outlook. Along with the sectarian (Vaishnava) sacral underpinning of the royal dynasties, there was also a more clear expression of a pan-Hindu outlook, though very different from modern religious nationalism. No doubt the incursion of a more unified Muslim front then too was part of the reason for this early move for a greater Hindu inclusiveness.

One of the prominent imperial Gurus, Madhava (not to be confused, as some scholars have, with the more theistically focussed and far less irenical Madhva of Udipi in West Karnataka, advocate of a

'Dvaita' or 'dualist' vision of things, 150 years earlier) - Madhava was born more or less exactly as the Viyajayanagar empire began, and just a decade or so after Muslim forces had looted the great Vaishnava temple of Sri Rangam in Tamil Nadu. Madhava's most famous work is what he entitled *sarva-darsana-samgraha* (a 'summary or holding together of all viewpoints or visions'), and points to the more broadly tolerant Hindu perspective, appropriate to an inclusive empire, able to draw together various particular doctrinal viewpoints and sectarian loyalties.

Perhaps not too much should be made of the novelty of this position. At other periods much earlier than Madhava - both the Gita and Sankara, for instance - there is good reason to see trans-sectarian interpretations of Brahmanic Hinduism worked out to some extent as a response to a politico-religious challenge, in their cases involving the spread of Buddhism. And such a response to political context was not always in terms of tolerant inclusiveness. At times it was the opposite, with militant sectarianism the order of the day. In any case, political context and religious convictions were, as usual, interacting in complex ways.

(c) Christian Ecumenical Dynamics

The natural commonsense response to movements for unity within broad religious traditions is to applaud them. Has there not been far too much sectarian in-fighting? Is not ecumenical effort towards wider unities within our traditions one essential step towards wider peace among humans? For it is certainly one possible consequence of ecumenism within broad-based traditions that they then go on to seek positive relationships with people outside that tradition. Christianity's World Council of Churches began early in the twentieth century as a movement among various leaders of Protestant churches, sometimes against strong opposition from within, a movement for more inclusive Christian unity of faith, worship, community life and action. This led quickly to the inclusion of both Orthodox and then Pentecostal bodies, and in the second half of the century to the growing participation of Rome, and eventually to a conviction by some that ecumenism was bound to include positive relationships with people of other faith-communities.

The dissident Catholic theologian Hans Kung is one of the many ecumenicals who see the movement for closer relations within

Christian faith-communities as leading inexorably to wider inter-faith understanding and togetherness. The summary of his position has become almost a *mantra*: The can be 'no peace among the nations without peace among religions'. And there can be 'no peace among religions without dialogue between religions'. Kung then takes two further steps, leading to the 'global ethic' that was to be accepted substantially by the 1993 Parliament of Religions (the centenary of the 1893 'Parliament' in Chicago at which Swami Vivekananda made such a strong impression). There can, he argues, be 'no dialogue between religions without common ethical standards,. And there can be 'no survival of our planet in justice and peace without a global ethic'. It is at this point that both other-sensitive multi-culturalists and believers strongly grounded in their own tradition will see danger signs. For - in spite of good intentions, and even a quite radical critique of western global ways - Kung's writings reflect inevitably both his Christian theological presuppositions (rightly), and his modern western interpretation of that Christian tradition (more questionable within a 'global' context). Crucial as a 'global' understanding of our ethical stance may be, therefore, this kind of 'global ethic', even with voluntary representatives of other faiths, may not result in the inter-penetrative global stance that is needed.

Within the WCC, the reality has been quite often a painful struggle between those urging wider inter-religious relationships, and those concerned almost exclusively for the inner strength and unity of Christians worldwide. Stanley Samartha (who died in Bangalore in 2001), a South Indian theologian with considerable knowledge of Indian religions, describes in his autobiographical work, *Between Two Cultures: Ecumenical Ministry in a Pluralist World* (1996) something of the struggle he had to engage in as a WCC Secretary (1968-80) concerned primarily with Dialogue with People of Living Faiths and Ideologies (A sub-unit with this title was set up in the 1970s, in large part as a result of Samartha's influence, at the Central Committee's meeting in Addis Ababa). He writes (*op.cit.* p.76):

> ...fears were expressed in my hearing that the train of truth might be in danger of derailment if it went on the dialogue track or, to change the metaphors, that the river Jordan might be polluted by the waters of the Ganges....These were difficult years for me because I was being attacked from two sides: by Christians who felt that dialogue was a betrayal of mission and by neighbours of other

faiths who regarded dialogue as a new tool for mission. Besides creating a spiritual struggle within my own consciousness, this underscored the need to establish dialogue as part of the *ecumenical* ministry of the church in a world that was very different from (the 1930s).

On returning to India in 1981, Samartha had further struggles, this time with the reality of a world that was very different - socially, culturally, politically, and especially ecclesiatically - from that of ecumenical Geneva, and in many ways, too, different from the India he had left only 13 years earlier. The challenges on the one hand of a newly assertive Dalit Christianity, and on the other of militant religious nationalism in the pro-Hindutva movement, were already being felt. The global dimensions of a burgeoning fundamentalist Christian stance were also now more clearly apparent. Samartha was deeply distressed by these newly polarised identities.

On all these fronts, as well as in much mainstream Christian ecclesial life, an appeal for a dialogical approach to other religious communities failed to bear the fruit Samartha was hoping for. Both to the rapidly growing movement for a Dalit-based Christian stance, and to the increasingly hardening evangelicism, talk of 'interfaith dialogue' was largely spurned, either as unrealistic, or even as treacherous compromise. But not entirely so. There is - in lip-service if nothing else - a growing theological recognition even among evangelical Christians that we need at least to know about the faith of others. And among more radical Christians there is, as Samartha puts it, 'the slow, almost reluctant recognition that religions do indeed have "liberative resources", even "messianic movements" within their traditions, and that these need to be critically recovered.'

This 'slow recognition' is part of the growing acceptance in mainstream Christian circles of theology as 'story-telling', as needing to be rooted in people's experience and their ancient corporate memories. But, as Samartha also wrote: 'In India, as in Asia as a whole, there is tension between two concerns: the struggle for a theology of liberation and the search for a theology of religions'. 'Creative tension' between them is eminently desirable, and is certainly a possibility, as Samartha suggests. High-minded exhortation - which as a theologian Samartha tends towards - in itself obviously will not bring about that 'inter-religious dialogue (that) must be an unending process in the global community', so that we 'seek new relationships between different communities of faith for the sake of enhancing the quality of life in the global community' (1996: 83). While at times adopting this rather off-the-ground idealism in the face of global realities, he also attempted an analysis of those realities in a way that leads inexorably to a 'dialogical imperative'.

It is possible, in other words, to be an ecumenist, and be gripped by a vision of a new 'global community', without having as a primary goal the *enlarging and strengthening of one's own religious identity in the world*. (Among many inter-faith writings, see e.g. Cracknell (1986), Coward (1989), Phan (1990), Forward (1995), Selvanayagam (1995)). Yet, it is difficult to imagine that this was not the main agenda of ecumenical mandarins such as the Dutchman Visser 't Hooft, for many years General Secretary of the World Council of Churches, and some of his fellow European ecclesiatics with whom Samartha - by nature a slightly prickly character himself - had to do business there in Geneva. Visser 't Hooft's *No Other Name* makes it very clear how sharply defined was his own sense of Christian identity and how doctrinally precise and exclusive its basis. Apart from such authority figures, however, there has always been an evangelical-ecumenical divide within the WCC. We have to note too that many conservative evangelicals have refused to be part of any such inclusive body, regarding its faith-basis as hopelessly compromised. They formed their own international evangelical alliance, openly opposed to key points in the stance of WCC.

A later chapter (on Indian-Christian faith) raises the question of a primal cultural grounding underlying Christian faith in India that is innately disposed to a more 'fundamentalist' stance. I leave that discussion to later. Here I merely note that there are others who would argue the opposite: are not the innate attitudes of Indian Christians more disposed to a pluralism that accepts the different forms of the faith of others more easily than is the case in the West? Is there perhaps special significance in the crucial role of those numerous WCC officers and representatives from South India and Sri Lanka (among them Paulus Mar Gregorius, M.M.Thomas, Russell Chandran, Wesley Ariarajah, Christopher Duraisingh, Thomas Thangaraj, Aruna Gnanadason, Israel Selvanayagam, and of course especially Stanley Samartha at that crucial point of WCC history) in pushing for an ecumenism that includes not only the whole human race in general - as the word *oikou-mene* implies ('inhabiting the house') - but includes the world communities of faith in particular?

Whatever innate differences there may be East and West, or South and North, during the first half of the twentieth century European Christians passed through a series of traumatic experiences that forced deep changes in their worldview. In the Christian ecumenical movement it is not difficult to see the impetus provided by that series of devastating crises in European political life. No doubt there are nineteenth century precursors of ecumenism too.

Some, though, see the most potent origins of the twentieth century's ecumenical movement as lying in the great missionary conference of 1910 at Edinburgh. Edinburgh 1910 can be said to have celebrated, even if unintentionally, both the past glory and the coming demise of the Empire. The triumphalist slogan raised by the American John R. Mott (an international YMCA secretary and mission-ideologue) rang out loud and clear: 'The whole world for Christ in our generation'. But so did the plea of South Indian V. S. Azaraiah (later 'Bishop Azariah of Dornakal') that western missionaries cease their patronising ways in the world. To paraphrase his appeal: 'You spoke with the tongues of angels, you gave your bodies to be burnt; now we need your love.'

So, an event prior to the terrible European war of 1914-18 made its mark on ecumenism. But more important is the fact that this international Christian body, the World Council of Churches, was set up and new forms of 'global community' worked for during a period exactly corresponding to the diminishing power of European global empires and their gradual withdrawal from direct political control of their colonies, as well as coinciding with the rapid growth of international socialist and - violently opposed - fascist national movements. The Christians of Europe had seen only too starkly what nationalist division can lead to.

Looking at this phenomenon from the other side, the growth of Christian ecumenical union within India was almost exactly co-terminous with India's nationalist movement. The formation of the united Church of South India took place in 1947, the same year as the declaration of India's independence. It should be noted that the first meeting - Tranquebar 1919 - in which the vision of a united body of Christians was proposed was made up almost entirely of Indian Christians with a strong sense of the need for the Indian church to move, along with the nation, beyond the foreign leadership to which it was then still subjected. Neither of the only two non-nationals at the Tranquebar meeting were ecclesiastical dignitories, but well-respected *bhakti*-style preachers.

In the context of political and international factors affecting Christian ecumenism, we can also note that a number of those churches becoming part of the united churches (Church of South India in 1947, Church of North India in the early 1970s)- e.g. the American Lutheran and American Methodist churches - held back from such wider national union mainly because of their international connection and, it has to be said, their fear that funding support from their particular western denominational bodies would be less. Other churches - certainly Catholic, Orthodox, Pentecostal - not part of these union schemes, remain separate because their ethos is more clearly distinctive and their ecclesial attitude tends to be exclusive. It could well be argued that the Baptist churches in South India held back (from the 1947 Union in the South, though not from the later Union in the North) because of very distinct views on the faith-process. But this argument carries little weight in the case of either the American Methodist Church, or the Lutheran Churches with their mission links with both USA and Europe. Other support-factors were dominant in the shaping of identities here, for their ethos, ecclesial structure and theology do not seem in themselves distinctive enough to keep these churches permanently separate. The Lutherans, for example, when preliminary talks were initiated, had little difficulty in finding common doctrinal ground with the Church of South India. Even the CSI episcopal structure could hardly be a barrier, as in some Lutheran European churches bishops continued to be part of their tradition (as they are in American Methodism, though functioning rather differently).

There are those, of course, who would argue that the ethos and identity of *every* religious body with a specific history is distinctive, and that ecumenical union projects invariably entail the incorporating of those with less power into those with more. The process of ecumenical reconciliation is in reality, such critics might say, a process of enfeebling accommodation and probably of hegemonic domination. Given that religions necessarily interact in some way with political movements, this will always be one of the 'dangers' of religious loyalty we will need to look at: when the potential dynamic of religious identity is manipulated and exploited - whether in overt or hidden ways - to serve political power.

Such religious politicising is frequently found in nationalist movements. The nation-state as we know it may be a relatively recent political institution. Yet, it is clear that earlier imperialisms - in their promise of a *pax romanica* or a *pax brittanica* (perhaps distant precursors of ecumenism, certainly similar to recent forms of globalisation) were equally prone to make use of and thereby modify the character of religious tradition. Two random examples are Constantine's fourth century christianising of the Roman empire, or the rather different trans-sectarian aims in the fourteenth to sixteenth centuries (just before the Mughal empires dominated the sub-continent) that characterised the Vijayanagar empire. This medieval Hindu empire was based in southern India but extending to the whole of Southeast Asia and Indonesia. In Constantine's Christendom, the concept of the 'one, holy and catholic (in the sense of inclusive, ecumenical, global) church', with a commonly accepted credal orthodoxy, was introduced, with the powerful 'encouragement' of the emperor. Rome aimed at a common liturgy too - not happy with the considerable regional diversity in ways of Christian worship that had developed in the first few centuries of Christian history. But in eastern Christianity greater divergence remained, for example in such third century indigenous worship as that of Jacobite Syrian, paradoxically preserved by Christians in south-west India. Rome too eventually came to accept the reality of regional diversity in worship, and in 1987 endorsed the legitimately distinctive character of three liturgies in India, derived from the complex histories of 'Malabar' and its Syriac tradition fused later with Latin liturgy.

So, then, political aspirations, and cultural life generally, impinge on religious identities in a variety of ways. An interpenetrating of some kind is inescapable.

(2) A New Inter-Faith Consciousness?

What we must not ignore, though, is the *faith-dimension* in that interactive process. In all these religious traditions there are also factors *within* faith, perhaps well hidden within faith, that make for the various forms of growing inclusiveness we have noted.

Ecumenicity is not forced upon faiths solely by politics or changing global cultural or economic life. Within Hindu, Christian, Muslim and other traditions there are, in differing ways, innate thrusts towards new forms of togetherness, along with the very opposite - the potential to exclude the non-conforming other. Dividing walls are both torn down and built up - to use imagery well-known to biblical readers. While the new walled enclosures will primarily be for fellow-believers, there are widespread instances too of the capacity of faith - Hindu, Buddhist, Christian, Muslim, Sikh - to move in more inclusive directions.

Indeed, scholars such as Harvard's Wilfred Cantwell Smith have argued that to be fully religious today is to be *inter-religious*. In *Towards a World Theology* (1981: 4) Smith outlined with his usual skilful enthusiasm a new 'world theology' on the basis of the historical fact of a rapidly growing new global human consciousness. There is even a 'unity of humankind's religious history', though Smith carefully differentiated this from any idea of the the more vague 'unity of all religions'. It is historical (and theological) interconnectedness that he argued for. Each religion has to be 'understood only in terms of a context of which the other forms a part' (p.5). There is a 'global continuum' of our religious histories, a process of mutual interaction that has made us what we now are. Mostly this was an unconscious process of responding to and incorporating elements of the vision of others. Smith then took his argument further. All religious people now are caught up inescapably in at least the possibility of a new 'corporate critical self-consciousness' (pp.50-55, 59ff). Perhaps Smith's idealist vision of identity-dynamics is as much a consequence of the increasingly rapid process of globalisation as it is based on the innate dynamics of religious faith. But we look critically at this globalising process in a later chapter.

Was Wilfred Cantwell Smith correct? Is being able to respond to and even in some sense to incorporate aspects of the faith of others one inescapable strand of being a believer in our world today? This surely sees the reality in too positive a light. It is a fact that no faith in today's world can continue without reference of any kind to the faith of others. This is part of faith's inescapable interpenetration with modernity and its relativisms. 'Theologically', too, we can see that intrinsic to faith's commitment to an Identity transcending all lesser social and conceptual identities, there could be a thrust towards incorporation and inclusiveness. And yet, a great question-mark is raised by any talk of 'inter-penetration'. For, there is the historical reality of the obscene *global asymmetry* of political, economic and therefore also of cultural power. The playing-field in interfaith dialogue is far from even.

It is this imbalance in the worlds people of differing faiths inhabit that make dialogical inclusiveness almost impossible. When people of a sharply defined faith-identity see a call to soften those sharp edges as a threat to what is essential to that identity, their fears are all too real. One possible consequence of moving into a world of multiple identities is not just the weakening of a well-defined sense of who we are. There is too the paradoxical danger of an alienated and vacuous condition in which it is all too easy to accept some new totalitarian identity, or the re-interpretation of an old identity that is fiercely exclusive of others. From simple clarity of faith fierce 'fundamentalist' exclusion of all others is then born. Here, though, we should not immediately think only of old 'fundamentalist' or new 'cultist' religious identities. There are strands in a secularist view of the world of others that are equally 'exclusive', equally 'dangerous' distortions of the world of others. And in turn such hardline secularism helps to create, by way of alarmed reaction, sharper and more excluding identities within faith communities. Religious people are not the only 'fundamentalists'. That the growing *internationalising* of our faith-consciousness has resulted religiously in growing global *separateness* of religions, rather than in a growing inter-faith consciousness, is due in large part to dogmatic secularist faith.

(3) Inclusion, Exclusion, & Pluralist Fluidity in Global Faiths

Globalised faith-identities, then, do not merely take two forms: one *inclusive* enough to see itself even in terms of a single human self-consciousness; the other a faith-identity which is inclusive of all fellow-religionists, but *exclusive* of others in any primary sense. Both these are clearly found in our global religious consciousness. But there is a third globalising of faith, more distinctly *pluralist* in form. Many people of faith, though consciously grounded in one distinctive faith, are able increasingly to see all people of faith, perhaps even all humans, as in some sense *fellow-pilgrims*. It was

Alan Race who first formulated in a systematic way the categories exclusive, inclusive and pluralist as typical stances towards other faiths (Race 1983). As is usual with typologies, these three terms do not exclude each other entirely, as Martin Forward among others has pointed out.

Generally, post-Vatican II Catholic theology, when engaging positively with other faiths, has tended towards an inclusivist position. Christ is assumed to be an enlightening presence within all and somehow 'includes' them within his cosmic being. Hence titles such as Raimundo Panikkar's *The Unknown Christ of Hinduism* in the 1960s. The subtle nuancing of Panikkar's position should not be missed, or the further modifying and elaborating found in his later writings. Some have called this inclusivism a 'Christo-monism', though Panikkar's was worked out within the paradox of a monism that also tries to incorporate radical pluralism. Hindus, too, are able to make the same (paradoxical) universal claims for Krishna or for Rama. It is on a more widely theo-monist basis that 'liberal' Protestants such as John Hick have been similarly *inclusivist*. That - in his *Myth of Christian Uniqueness* (1988) Hick (jointly with Catholic Paul Knitter) has also argued for a pluralist stance shows the inadequacy of these three popular categories.

The 'process' Methodist theologian John Cobb, as well as Paul Knitter and Stanley Samartha, on the basis of a theo-centric position, have in different ways developed a *pluralist* stance towards other faiths (Swidler 1990). Both the Catholic theologian, Gavin D'Costa, and Baptist theologian, Mark Heim, are among those who have responded with a critique of pluralism. The title of D'Costa's book - *Christian Uniqueness Reconsidered: the Myth of a Pluralist Theology of Religions* (1990) - in itself indicates that this is a riposte to Hick's rather bland assumptions about the essential oneness of all faith. Mark Heim (1996) makes the serious point that the pluralist insistence on allowing each faith uncritically to be itself holds an intrinsic contradiction. How can we argue both that we should merely accept all our differences as relative and also that all universalist claims are anathema? For, one of those differences is that some faiths make univeralist claims. And the divergent nature of each faith's goals in any case should be given the serious status they clearly intend. O.V.Jathanna's critique of 'Religious Pluralism' (1999), applauds this point of Heim's in particular, yet goes on to argue that differing faith-claims cannot remain at this 'phenomenological' level. Divergent faith makes encounter inevitable. Jathanna's closely argued analysis makes rewarding reading.

While, however, there are numerous and serious tensions and ambiguities in all inter-faith relationships, such complexities in no way invalidate the innate thrust towards such faith-with-faith engaging in many forms, some of which have still to be explored.

Muslim Pluralism?

Among Christians, then, wide-ranging positions are possible, some clearly offering more scope than others for engaging dialogically with differing faith-experience. What, though, within the world of Islam? Few would regard Muslims within today's increasingly polarised global situation as 'pluralists'. Traditionally they have referred to all non-Muslims as 'infidels', those without (true) faith. Yet, one important strand of Muhammad's view of Christians and Jews (as against the animistic polytheism he was primarily rejecting) identified them as, like his own believers, 'people of the book' (*ahl al-kitab*). They were respected as people with faith in God based on a scripture witnessing to countless prophets of the past whose revelations are also to revered. In fact, the Arabic phrase for these other believers can be translated 'people of an earlier revelation' (Armstrong 2003 (2000): 9-10). The Qur'anic text runs:

> Do not argue with the followers of earlier revelation other than in a most kindly manner - unless it be such of them as are bent on evil-doing. And say: 'We believe in that which has been bestowed from on high upon us, as well as that which has been bestowed upon you. For our God and your God is one and the same, and it is upon Him that we (all) surrender ourselves (i.e. are 'Muslims').

Later conflicts put paid to that initial respect and sense of mutuality. But the point here is that even in seventh century Arabia, seeing other kinds of believers both in a pluralist way and as sharing something of a common faith-identity was not impossible. When the faith of others is seen as very different - in its content and its consequences, its Object and its objectives - very strong feelings of animosity have also been aroused, as is all too obvious from religious histories.

But along with this there has always been the opposite response: the willingness to recognise and rejoice in the faith of others as sufficient to be the basis for a faith-kinship. The Buddhist emperor Ashoka (third century BCE) and the Muslim emperor Akbar are but two among many with this broader vision of 'faith'. In their case no doubt political compromise too was an important factor. But the seeds of a pluralist tolerance, even of inter-faith mutuality, within the Muslim tradition have led - in the right kind of encouraging circumstances - numerous Muslims in our time to take a critically important role in inter-faith projects. For example, Samartha spoke highly of the positive dialogical stance of Hassan Askari in WCC discussions.

Even among nineteenth century Christian missionaries - especially in India - there were those who stood resolutely against the almost overwhelming tide of anti-heathen animosities, and were able to find much in Hindu, Sikh and Muslim faith they found attractive, as the researches of Geoffrey Oddie, Kenneth Cracknell, Julius Lipner, Eric Sharpe and others have made clear. And in the second half of the twentieth century there was an increasing counter-stream of writings exploring the varied ways in which faith-sharing cuts across all traditional boundaries and the identities they create. Such boundary crossing may well be confined to a minority - but it is highly significant.

Faith-Grounds for a Common Humanity?

We can note two forms of this broader faith-identity, especially if seen in terms of response to the powerful secularist ideologies of modern times. That all people of faith must draw together in common resistance to secularist attacks is one possible motive. Another very different response, though, is when people of faith accept one of the key themes of the secularist - that is, recognising our *common humanity* as a transcending bond - but at the same time seeing a faith-dimension, variously manifest, as essential to this humanness. Here people of faith too accept the reality of some form of growing global consciousness.

Invariably, people of faith, however much certain humanist values may have touched them, will find other grounds too for a 'one-world', 'one-humanity' perspective. These will be grounds they believe to be *implicit to their faith*. Jews/Christians/Muslims will speak of the one Creator of all life and therefore the one divine value on and purpose in all life. Imam Omar Rashied, for example, in the post-9/11 sermon referred to above, quotes the Qur'an:

> O humankind! We have created you male and female,
> and fashioned you into nations and tribes,
> so that you may come to know each other
> (not to revile, subjugate or slaughter each other
> but to reach out to each other with understanding and
> compassion)....

Christians will insist too that Christ's ministering to all, ignoring the usual discriminations, brings in a newly inclusive divine dynamic (e.g. 'The kingdom of God is for all'). Hindus - more mission-minded of late - will tend to speak of the one eternal selfhood innate to all life, and the one 'order' (*dharma*) of things, within the eternal and inclusive law of which all life is inter-meshed. Buddhists might refer to the inclusive way of the Buddha and his 'compassion for all creatures'.

Inescapable, though, is the historical reality of the many and sharp differences among faith-identities. And these are differing ways of belief and of behaviour *within* our great religious traditions as much as *between* them, differences that create their peculiar points of self-identity. The ignoring of such inner divergence by believers is a naive imagining probably innate to all faith-communities. Even the need for people of faith to live distinctively, and therefore in *some* ways even separate from others because of their faith, is a necessary part of religious life.

When, though, there is a very deliberate strategy by politically conscious leaders belonging to the community to create a more sharply defined identity for calculated institutional purposes - perhaps the enhancing of community power - we surely have a more dangerously distorting form of imagining. This is akin to the deliberate creating of a 'false consciousness'. Its insistence on global uniformity then entails not just being 'alienated' from the realities of our human existence. It alienates others too in ways that may not be intrinsic to faith as such. When the globalising of faith is this kind of political strategy, it is far more than just an innocently idealist way of interpreting the absolutes of faith. It may well then entail a deliberate dominating of others by one interpretation of the tradition, and this can so easily become a broader hegemonic political takeover.

And it is, unfortunately, all too easy to be led into this simplistic, diversity-denying, communalist way of viewing and interpreting the world, seeing broad, pluralistically structured traditions in terms of uniform religious cultures, even as 'civilisations' that are mutually exclusive, mutually threatening. If it is the case that, with Huntington and others, when we speak of 'Christianity', 'Islam', 'Hinduism', 'Judaism' we can only speak in terms of politically motivated and constructed, even if culturally grounded, 'civilisations', we see both the weakness of failing to give adequate place to faith-factors that are not purely political, and also the reality of these great faith-conglomerates having deep involvement with political realities. The naivete of faith can become blind to such hard realities.

The Dialectic of Faith & Contextual Realities

The more *inclusive* form of faith-identity found in the other two types mentioned above also poses problems for faith. My argument earlier was that analysis of religious life solely in terms of political or social or even cultural dynamics is a reductionism which inevitably distorts the reality of religion and in particular the inner life of faith. Now we have to reckon again with the *dialectic* in which religious faith is always and inevitably caught up. Faith and culture, faith and social environment, faith and wider human community, even faith and power - in spite of the mortal dangers of power to faith - these and many other forms of faith's outworking are a necessary part of the dynamics of religion in the life of the world. Christian social ethicist, Max Stackhouse of Princeton, taking a Weberian view of socio-religious dynamics, writes of the need to 'integrate our lives in, through, by means of and in terms of the necessities of wealth, power, potency, creativity, and piety that are part of our inner possibilities' as well as being 'the inner fabric of every viable society' (2000: 44). That complex process is inescapable. The question is, though, how far even Stackhouse has sufficiently recognised the inbalances of 'wealth, power, potency', and therefore the need to counter these disparities.

When, therefore, we seek to answer the question, What is it that shapes most forcefully the way people's religious identity takes shape? - so often the immediate and most obvious response will need to be in terms of historical and political factors, seemingly external, but in time powerfully internalised. It is such contextual pressures that often forge those hard-edged boundaries by which people have come to identify themselves. On the one hand, faith will need to question these assumed identities, for they may innately contradict essentials of faith. At the same time it may well become necessary to accept positive elements from these external sources of identity. For it is that contextual life, interacting with faith, that provides valuable new dimensions of life, that perhaps draws out liberating potential somehow obscured to believers by earlier cultural masks.

Just one example may be mentioned - the role of women within religious traditions. In both Buddhist and Christian faiths, the initiating sources describing the new liberated consciousness of the Buddha and Jesus reveal impressive potential, inherent compulsions, even an inner logic, for breaking free from the patriarchal culture that was dominant. (Other traditions could be listed here too - perhaps *bhakti*-Hindu, Sikh and even Sufi Muslim faith - but would make the issue even more complex). It almost comes as a surprise to find in both Buddhism and Christianity how quickly women were at best given a lower order within monastic communities, but in common society most often a subservient domestic role. There were, of course, exceptions.

Generally, though, women remained not just dependent but slightly lower-order humans, often seen as sources of temptation to men. The Buddha is shown as reluctant even to permit an order of nuns, Jesus appointed only men as apostles, and Christian women in the great Roman and Orthodox traditions were never reckoned worthy to become fully priests, even though within Catholic women's orders the abbess might function as though a priest. Cultural tradition surely 'quenched the spirit', stifled the new consciousness of what constitutes a faith-identity in both these movements - if the originating vision was to prevail. Is there not, therefore, good reason for faith to find within the largely secular movement for women's liberation resources for the *liberation of faith's* outworking in the form of new women's roles both in society and within religious institutions - a new self-identity for women of faith? And certainly in many Christian circles this is precisely what has happened, with an insistently critical movement even within the Catholic church.

The issue is more complicated though. Women's liberation is so closely linked with western secularism and its permissive sexuality that quite often even 'modern' women within male-dominated religious communities such as Islam deliberately adopt the outward symbolism of the hidden, silent woman - either the head-scarf or the all-covering *hijab (or burkah)*. For them, their acceptance of what seems to others an inhibition to women's freedom has become a symbol of their resistance to western secularist values, a sign of a kind of counter-liberation.

Global Sectarian Fluidity

To return to the globalising of religions and conclude this part of the discussion. It is a fact that many older sectarian and denominational identities have become quite weak. Within western Christianity and Hindu society alike, loyalty to sects and subsects - Anglicans, Congregationals, Lutherans, Presbyterians, Methodists, or the various subsects of the Vaishnavas, Saivas and Saktas - these sectarian identities often no longer stir the same fires of group loyalty they once did. Being inclusively 'Christian' and 'Hindu' has usually come to mean much more. Forms of ecumenical consciousness are a reality.

Yet, there are struggles *within* these major faith-families that are still often more significant than conflicts with other such families. Indeed, there is usually far more common ground in terms of life-values and even of basic beliefs, certainly of spirituality, between, let us say, a Sufi Muslim and a Vaishnava Hindu, than between the Sufi and a hardline Muslim, either Sunni or Shi'a. There may be more common ground between an Advaitic Hindu and a Christian whose faith craves for a mystical dimension, than between the latter and a hardline Protestant. There are certain kinds of 'fundamentalists' in every tradition who, in spite of their usual confrontational attitude towards other faiths, may well share a worldview quite at variance with the less literal-minded interpreters of their own tradition. Hindus, Buddhists, Jews, Christians, Sikhs and others whose faith gladly accepts the need to include values from a humanist/modernist worldview probably have more in common in the way they see the world and their faith's role in it than they do with those hardline literalist interpreters of their faiths. Shared symbol-systems have often served, in times of social and political crisis, to draw the wider community together.

In the modern world, in other words, the self-identity of religious people is rarely experienced only in one form and at one level. There

179

is an all-important new *fluidity of identities*. Yet, the faith-factor must never be ignored nor underestimated. Changing contexts and changing conditions may change also the boundaries of our faith-identities, but the faith-factor remains crucial. A Vaishnava Hindu may move between identities shaped by originating Sri Vaisnava tradition, a later loyalty emerging from sub-sectarian difference, community differences based on caste, and the more recent Hindu identity based on national culture. An Afghani Muslim may move between identities shaped perhaps by belonging to a regional group with its powerful chief, the sense of being Pashtun, a Sunni as against a Shia identity, and the universalised Muslim identity. Political circumstances determine which identity is dominant at any given time. They also determine just how intensely any one identity is felt, how sharply it takes shape. In Bosnia, for example, Muslim consciousness had little difficulty in relating to non-Muslims in terms of a shared socio-cultural and political identity. Following that dark period of aggression by other groups against them, including 'ethnic cleansing', but equally in response to growing global Muslim consciousness of its distinctiveness and fears of an anti-Muslim conspiracy, Bosnian Muslim consciousness became more exclusive, more political, more globalist.(Huntington 1993). The faith-factor itself, however differently experienced and expressed, remains highly significant.

(4) A Common Text for a Common Identity?

One of the grounding factors in universalising movements has been the *central role of a sacred book* in the concerned tradition (Coward 1988). The emergence of a broad consensus within mainstream Christianity regarding the findings of biblical scholarly exegesis is often claimed as an important impetus for the modern ecumenical movement. Yet, here too, very different conclusions can in fact be arrived at. In the first place we have already noted the conservatives within and as a rival to WCC, diverging precisely on the basis of what is perceived as greater fidelity to biblical teaching. But on this issue the more ecumenically minded can also vigorously argue for their own fidelity to revealed truth.

The division, though, is not solely on these grounds. At least three perspectives can be distinguished, all claiming to be biblically based, even if their primary texts and their hermeneutical procedures differ. So we are not including here such liberal modernisers as may sit very lightly to any form of authority for their sacred book. There are then: (a) conservative evangelicals (that could be further divided into on one side Pentecostal/charismatic and on the other those with greater emphasis on non-charismatic, doctrinal orthodoxy - more typical of e.g. Lutherans);

(b) radical liberationists, grounding their social action in the biblical story; and

(c) inclusive ecumenicals, with faith based on more broad-ranging biblical exegesis.

A simpler *bi-polar* division of these three would be along the lines of those who are exclusive and those who are inclusive of the wider human community. And in terms of self-identity these are important categories indeed. Vis-a-vis scripture, the debate concerns the engagement between the believer's reading of the sacred book and the believer's life in the wider world. In broad terms it is the engagement between faith and culture, faith-community and human community. And this may be either in relation to other faith-traditions, or indeed to the wider scope of human culture. Grounding in a sacred book will necessarily entail some kind of critical perspective vis-a-vis the 'world', but the believer's response to events and trends in the wider world is certainly not one solely of negative rejection. There is far more often a dialectic of interaction that is both negative and positive, critical and affirming.

The differing emphasis here is crucial though. We find that some kinds of 'evangelicals' and 'liberationists' belong essentially together, both seeing the givens of human cultural systems with radically critical eyes. For, both radical liberationists and conservative evangelicals describe opposing forces in the world as 'demonic'. Liberationists will be more critical of the systemic 'structures' - social, economic, political - that hold the world in their grip. Evangelicals are more critical of 'spiritual powers'. Some focus more piously on personal and family mores. Others are not averse to the compromises involved in working for political power, as for example with the close linkage of extreme conservative evangelicals and rightwing Republicanism in the United States.

On the other hand, one of the most damning indictments of recent American global policy that I have read was written by an Indian resident in America who holds office in a global evangelical organisation. Ostensibly based on the authority of the same Bible, and the New Testament writings in particular, Christians in America (as everywhere) are worlds apart from each other in their views on going to war against Iraq, or against any other Muslim country perceived as in some way a threat to American interests. Previous US president Jimmy Carter, a devout Baptist lay teacher himself, has argued that the attack on Iraq cannot be called 'just' on any of the usual grounds by which Christians have traditionally claimed, as a last option, a 'just war'. He has noted the serious divide between virtually all mainstream church leaders in the States and those of (his own?) Southern Baptist church, and expressed his alarm at the dangerous 'eschatological' ideas the latter are locked into as a key part of their biblical exegesis, apocalyptic ideas that we looked at in an earlier chapter.

The Crucial Role of the Gita

This inclusive/exclusive, way of seeing different religious attitudes and identities, has wider validity than just concerning Christianity. It could, for example, equally be applied to Hindu self-identities based on that 'Gospel of Hinduism' the Bhagavad Gita. While it can be argued that Hindu self-identity will never be so thoroughly book-grounded as with Judaism, Christianity, Islam and Sikhism, since the nineteenth century the Gita has increasingly been seen in a similar way. It is believed to provide the essential grounding for a burgeoning Hindu self-identity. There is something of an intrinsic problem here, in that the Gita is a Krishna-related book, whereas it is Ram(a) who is the Focus of much Hindu faith in the North of India, the central base of Hindutva.

Traditional Brahmanic Hindu religion has, of course, a much wider scriptural basis than either the Gita or the Ramayana. It claimed to be grounded in the vast sacred traditions embodied in ancient Vedas and later Sastras, sources of sacred knowledge and sacred law. Then, from at least the first century, sectarian communities within that hierarchically overarching society that emerged as 'Hinduism' each had their own special books, their Agamas and Puranas - records of esoteric myth, ritual, and doctrinal tradition - whose authority was binding to them. The Krishna-lovers of North and East India, for example, took the Bhagavata Purana, probably inspired by impulses from the South, to be the supreme source of spiritual potency (Hardy 1983).

But, for the emerging 'Hindu' consciousness of the nineteenth and twentieth centuries, an integrating base-scripture was seen in the inclusiveness of the Bhagavad Gita. The Gita no doubt was a very popular book within certain more reflective sections of Indian society long before that. Even by the first century CE it had already become one of the three necessary foundations for Vedantic reflection - along with the Upanishads and the Vedanta Sutra (or Brahma Sutra, 'sutra' referring to the 555 brief aphorisms linked together like a garland, i.e. a 'sutra'). To a large extent, though, it was the several centuries of encounter with Islam and Christianity - religions self-consciously 'of the book' - which gradually led to modern Hinduism seeking its grounding in a single text. Or one can argue, as convinced Hindus may well do, that it is the Gita's inclusive range, as recapitulating all that came before, yet retaining its own instrinsic authority, that accounts for its role in creating a more cohesive, more universally inclusive Hindu identity.

The main point I intend here is that even though grounding faith in a sacred book has been a potent factor in creating a wider, perhaps internationalist sense of identity within the great faith-communities, consciousness of being a people of the one book does not in itself guarantee a united worldview or a single faith-based identity. For one thing, it depends which strand within the sacred book is made the hermeneutical key, which part interprets the whole. One believing reader will focus on the spiritual equanimity of which the Gita speaks, the sense-yoking of its Yoga (note the common origin of 'yoga' and 'yoke'). Another, as did Lokamanya Tilak, the late nineteenth century nationalist, will find the greatest authority in the Gita's call to committed action.

Others, like Gandhi in his non-violent resistance to the imperialist presence, found most resonance in passages bidding us act without concern for the benefits of our action. There is historic irony of a tragic kind here, in that Nathuram Godse, the killer of the Mahatma, was deeply influenced by Lokamanya Tilak's reading of the Gita. A similarly militarist reading of the Gita lay behind an internet declaration in 2004 by one claiming to be a Vishva Hindu Parishad leader in UK: the loyal Hindu must, like Godse, be ready to do away with any, like Gandhi, who stand in the way of the elimination of the Muslim threat to Hindu identity.

Others turn to the many passages in the Gita urging loving devotion to God. Yet others find security in what is quite a conservative attitude towards the status quo of social and ethical life: the different classes of society, different types of people, rooted as they are in the way things are ordered by Nature; so, 'do not fight against Nature', only fight for maintaining the *dharma* of what must be by the eternal ordering of things. And there is in the Gita much more too, in spite of its being a relatively short work of eighteen chapters. Hindu proponents argue that this inclusiveness is precisely the strength both of Hindu tradition in general and the Gita in particular. Our response is to be whatever we are capable of, what our inner nature is fitted for.

In any case, responses to this grounding text have often been impelled by particular contexts. Even the Gita itself, and the message of Krishna therein, is set within the particular dilemma faced on a battlefield, a *kshetra,* when a leading warrior loses his will to fight. This parallels the crisis faced by those charged by tradition with protecting Brahmanic *dharma* but deeply attracted by the call to monkish renunciation, and to a new 'noble' *dharma*, given by their fellow-warrior/prince (*kshatriya*), Gautama Buddha. In particular, the great emperor Ashoka, perhaps a century or two before the Gita was written, was seen to have been convinced by the Buddha's Way, and turned his back on the violent ways of war, though he did not himself become a monk. Here too, then, we have to reckon with the *political and cultural milieu*, the arena or *kshetra* within which hermeneutical and other forms of religious drama are enacted. There is a *political* as well as theological and spiritual basis to the Gita, as to every scripture in some way. The significance of the Gita, then, as with other scriptures, depends on how the vision of the world it inspires is able to transcend and enable transformation of the politically entangled world of which the believer is part.

(5) Responding to Context: Islam's Interpreting Method

The political dimension, then, is crucial to the recently increased consciousness within many different religious traditions that they belong not only to a very distinctive community, but to a community that has either national or international dimensions. The engagement - the 'dialectic' referred to elsewhere - is inevitable and not sinister or evil in itself. Yet, even when faith reacts fiercely against political ambition, its priorities and emphases are thereby changed. Certainly when religion beds down with political power and ambition, the necessary dialectic is lost and faith's character is compromised.

This holds true from the Emperor Constântine's fourth century vision of the triumphalist unifying of the empires of East and West under the banner of the Cross, through eleventh century European Christian identifying of 'cross-taking' with crusading passion, to the marriage of Gospel religion in 'middle America' with the fervently capitalist politics of the Right; from the eye-gouching rage of politically motivated Saivas (forcing the Vaishnava Ramanuja to flee to Mysore), to the aligning of a number of Sri Lankan Buddhist monks with the anti-Tamil politics of pro-Sinhala parties. To link commitment to Jesus with either the securing of Mammon or the slaying of Jews and Muslims, or the way of the Buddha with ethnic violence, might seem ludicrously anachronistic, but is what can and does happen when a community's life and the interpretation of its faith is determined primarily by factors other than its life-transforming core vision. Lesser identities become absolute, and threats to those subordinate identities become the demonised enemy.

And what of Islam, with the goal its very name points to - 'peaceful (peace-giving?) submission' to the will and the way of Allah as revealed through the Prophet? In principle every possible life-contingency is covered; the true Way has been made plain in all its detail. Inherent to such a view of historical revelation - and this applies equally to orthodox Judaism and fundamentalist Christianity - is the problem of how one particular culture can be the vehicle for revealing how life is to be in all its detail in all cultures and at all times. Transposing analogically - intrinsic to Islamic hermeneutics - calls for very great interpretive skills. But in the process of moving into worlds very different from seventh and eighth century Arabia, another quite opposite kind of problem emerges. The pressures of the historical process, political pressures, pressures of conquest and power, and the desire to sustain the status of power, have inevitably left a massive mark, however strong the intent to retain an original purity of character, and Qur'anic rectitude that remains untouched by circumstances.

From the earliest days of Islam - including the events surrounding the martyrdom of Ali and then his son Husain (cause of the Shia-

Sunni divide: Armstrong 2002) - Muslims have struggled with the question of just how and by whom the *ummah*, the Muslim community, is to be ruled, and just how that rule links with other ruling powers and their contrasting cultural styles. Internally, still there is little that more vigorously exercises global Islam than the issue of the one universal Caliphate (*khalifah*), especially how the power of that Deputy (of the Prophet; in time the Envoy of Allah) relates to other national and secular powers. Many Muslims believe royal dynasties in Islam (especially if largely set in place by foreign imperial powers) and military regimes are corrupt and certainly are to be subordinate either to the power of the one true Khalifa or to the agreed Quranic decisions of those appropriately trained in interpretive skills. The tensions within the traditional Muslim chain of Power (Allah-Prophet-Caliph-King) shaping Muslim identity are probably as pressing today as they have ever been.

And within this struggle there is the issue of how Islam is to respond to non-Arabic cultures. The character of Islam as envisioned by the Prophet was deeply affected, and quite inevitably so, by the transition from the simplicity of that relatively small Arab community of believers in Medinah and Mecca to the more complex, more self-indulgent and power-driven life of the society and leadership found just a few years later in Baghdad. Persian opulence made a powerful impact. Later, Indian culture - as well as the contrasts of imported Moghul tradition there - introduced new compulsions, though within forms of Hindu devotion Muslim Sufi spirituality in particular found a fertile ground for fruitful growth (Madan 1998). These challenges to Quranic fidelity are most severe in the transition to a context in which great empires or modern states and their cities are to be under the rule of the *shari'ah,* with its interpreters and administrators. Whether or not 'power corrupts and absolute power corrupts absolutely', power certainly does change personal and institutional character, even given the belief that absolute power belongs only to God, and that those who submit to that power are to be Envoys of the Prophet and therefore of Allah too.

But the dilemma for many Muslims in the modern world is precisely because the degree of interaction of faith with changing contexts can be so rigorously limited by Islamic tradition, especially as interpreted by the currently dominant extremists in that tradition. In what ways must modernisation be resisted? The 'submitting' inherent to 'Islam' entails the faith that how we are to be and behave is precisely and authoritatively laid out in original Qur'anic revelation and complementary Hadithic traditions. The words and acts of the Prophet living in the cultural particularities of sixth and seventh century Arabia, yet seen as the instrument of the one God's perfect will for all humanity, is central to that revelatory Word.

The outworking of this Word in differing contexts brings in two further accepted principles of interpretation. There is the unanimous agreement (*ijma*) of recognised Islamic interpreters, representing the consensus of the whole Muslim community - and the opinion of the first four Khalifas and Imams is essential here. And there is the principle of reasoning by analogy (*qiyas*): in a similar situation what did the Prophet or his Companions do? The detailed rule of life resulting from these four 'roots' or 'foundations' has created the *shari'ah* that prescribes precisely what human behaviour is to be. In exceptional circumstances the believer is to act from personal conviction, based of course on the infallible 'foundations'. Islamic life can be far from merely a legal system of objectively given laws, and Muslim identity merely a rigid conforming to a pattern given from seventh century Arabia. Yet, when the imposing of the *shari'ah* given in that specific context is the legislative instrument of power - especially in today's kind of nation state - and becomes the primary mark of Islamicness, Muslim identity is in danger of being robbed of the dynamic interplay of life and Qur'anic faith that many Muslims themselves desire, and recognise as the way religious faith is to work (Askari 1977).

Throughout the history of Islam, from seventh century Arabia, then moving through large parts of Asia, north and east Africa, the fringes of Europe, and now as a global movement, cultural and political contexts have impinged on the ways in which the divine rule has been implemented. At times this has made for a more pragmatic and perhaps irenic policy. But the ruthlessly violent ways of extremist 'Islamists' too is often directly in response to prior oppression, alienation and a sense of threat to their very identity as loyal Muslims. So, there are differing ways of understanding 'loyal Muslim'. However idiosyncratic for his times the sixteenth century Indian emperor Akbar's interpretation may seem, there is no reason to doubt that he believed he acted as a good Muslim ruler in directly countering the violently oppressive style of most Mughal rule, in encouraging dialogue between Muslims and Hindus (and Christians), and thereby aiming to bring about social and cultural change. Akbar's irenic ways were not merely a quirky aberration, insignificant to Muslim history.

In the striking case of Akbar, as much as with the emergence of today's militant Islam from Hamas to al-Qaida, and certainly the Taliban, we have to reckon both with the impact of historical context and with hidden potencies *within* Islam. As within all our religious traditions, there is the potential fire for the configuring of violent identities, and there is the potential to compel to dialogue and wider human integration. Akbar and many devout Muslims in our presently troubled world have been committed to this latter way. It may well have been his political assessment of what he felt was needed for his times that motivated Akbar as much as did his religious convictions. But religious responses to what are politically compelled contexts, even if by those whose primary concern is politics rather than religion, in turn become of crucial importance in any analysis of these identity-dynamics.

Part II :
Crisis-Points For Global Identities

Introduction

In parts two and three of this book I want to reflect on a number of specific crisis-points in the changing identities of our time, especially as they interlock with religious faith. The first group of 'crises' has very obvious global scope, even when confirmatory examples are from the Subcontinent. The other focuses mainly on critical points in India's experience, religious and social. Not only do these crises of identity mean that this is a pivotal category for India's self-understanding. A number of them also give us a broader understanding of the impact of religious faith on the shaping of human self-identity than is the case with any other region of the world. In part this is because of the rich range of religious life and tradition in India, both local and classical, vernacular and Vedic. In part it is because of the strong flow of secularist streams of influence, culturally and intellectually, that has also become part of India's tradition. Not that these divergent influences have been integrated into anything like a coherent new self-identity, or even form a smoothly working multi-culturalism, as we shall see.

Globally, the identities of religious people are caught between two extremes. Postmodernist relativism on the other hand (and by speaking of 'post-' rather than just 'late-' modernist as earlier, I indicate the more radical position), questions any form of the absolutist claims innate to religious faith. Telling our stories to try to make sense of things, and so 'creating an identity', is a fair enough concept. But that is all there is by way of truth, argue radical postmodernists. Truth can never be more than our own very limited perception of it. We should not then try to enhance that story with any kind of ultimate cognitive reality. Yet that is precisely what religious people do in one form or another. Many are also able to adopt pragmatically a form of pluralism - because of the innate mystery of the Ultimate they believe in - allowing at least a kind of co-existent ultimacy to faiths seemingly quite distinct from their

189

own. Even this is undermined by a fullblown postmodernist relativism, where visions of cognitive ultimacy contradict what is innate to a view of truth that can never be capitalized as Truth; truth must always remain provisional. As we shall see, there are certain similarities between a postmodernist stance and a key strand of Hindu spiritual tradition. And in any case, people of faith today, of many traditions, find they have willy nilly been touched by this relativising strand in modernity.

At the other extreme is the absolutizing of positions, polarized fundamentalist positions that in each case finds any vision but its own to be dangerous falsehood, any identity but its own a demonic threat. Few liberal idealists of the past two centuries would have believed it possible that early in the third millennium such hardening of worldviews and heightening of identity-boundaries would be on the increase. Yet, this is the reality. In the next but one chapter I attempt an analysis of 'Fundamentalism'. But first we look at its apparent opposite - modern secularism.

Chapter 7
Secularist Faith

Westernisation and its secularist worldview are intrinsic to the globalising process. This means that the crisis of identity experienced in so many parts of the world today is caused in part by *the secularising effect of modernity*. A key factor in the alarming phenomenon of extremist 'fundamentalism' is said by many social analysts (see next chapter) to be its *reactive* character. It is a response to what is believed to be a fearful threat: the faith-destroying tide of a secularist re-viewing and re-configuring of our world.

Indians in the Independence era have mostly used the term 'secular' merely to refer to a form of democratic government in which no particular religion, or religious community, is given a dominant role. Here the Indian Constitution itself seems to be a good illustrative point of reference, where the followers of all religions are given equal freedom to 'profess, practice and propagate' their religion. We should note, though, that there was at the time of framing that Constitution, and has been often since, fierce debate about whether the third of these freedoms is necessary or desirable. It was at the insistence of the Christian representatives among the framers of the Constitution that it was finally included.

In any case, the policy insisted on at the time by Gandhi, Nehru, Ambedkar, Prasad and most of those who had taken leading roles in the Independence movement, was very soon the basis for consciously differentiating between Indian nationhood, Indian selfhood, and the form of Islamic regime for which Pakistan was soon to opt. The new India, even though comprised of a considerable majority of Hindus, was intended to provide a hospitable home to all the religions within its boundaries.

Toleration was the keyword; and often this was argued on the grounds that Hinduism is essentially a tolerant religion. The neo-Hinduism of interpreters such as Swami Vivekananda had put it thus: the 'crown of Hinduism', indeed the crown of all religious experience, is Vedanta, which teaches that all paths lead to the same goal - oneness with the supreme Self. Therefore all paths are equally valid. In that it is Hindu Vedanta which is then said most effectively to teach this climactic truth, we can see why other faith-positions may find such lofty superiority irritating.

However, cultural critics such as Ashis Nandy (in various essays during the 1980s) and India's leading sociologist of religion, T.N.Madan, have pointed to a dimension of the post-Independence discourse of 'secularism' that goes far beyond the lofty inclusiveness of Vedanta and the more specific promises of the Constitution. Because of the seductions of secularism, to be 'secularist' is innately more than just being tolerant and treating all religious traditions equally (Madan 1992: Introduction and 394-412, 'Secularism in its Place'). This critique of Madan's is clearly far removed from the primarily anti-Muslim, anti-missionary polemics of Arun Shourie, a key polemicist for the right-wing nationalist Hindutva movement in recent years (1997). No doubt Shourie makes some valid points arguing for greater weight to be given to Hindu tradition in his form of 'secular agenda'. Swami Vivekananda's late nineteenth century fulminations - in some cases well justified - against missionary distortions of Hindu practices are presented as somehow a more genuinely secular worldview.

A brief look at the theoretical springs of Madan's analysis helps us understand his thinking. In a page of frontispiece texts prefacing his collection of essays *Religion in India*, Madan quotes very aptly both Emile Durkheim and Max Weber. There is Durkheim's thesis that in religion we have to do with 'fundamental categories of thought' and so, conversely, that basic to our social institutions are hidden religious dynamics. In turn this means that deeply embedded elements of religion will 'survive all the particular symbols in which religious thought has successfully enveloped itself'. Religion 'seems destined to transform itself (rather) than disappear'. This is then juxtaposed alongside Weber's conclusion (in *The Protestant Ethic and the Spirit of Capitalism*, published in 1930, fifteen years after Durkeim's *The Elementary Forms of the Religious Life*, in 1915) that the powerful march of secularism and so the 'disenchantment of the world' (Friedrich Schiller's phrase) was irreversible. 'Modern man' is 'unable to give religious ideas a significance for culture and national character' which, Weber believed, 'they deserve'.

In this way both Durkheim and Weber foresaw the inevitable decline of traditional institutional forms of religion, as has in fact taken place in much of the western world. But while Durkheim saw the society-structuring role of religion as innate to our humanness, for Weber what is innate is the ability of humans to construct their religious and social worlds. Within this process, though, the power of deeply embedded tradition from the past has its impact on what we construct socially in the present. Thus, for example, Protestant religious belief leads to capitalist socio-economic practice. But Weber, with sad pessimism, could see no other future for religion than its 'replacement by progressive rationalization and the decline of mystery, magic and ritual'. What is to come will be like a 'polar night of icy darkness and hardness' (Madan 1992: 9).

Both these seminal theorists in the sociology of religion, along with other more recent scholars such as Peter Berger, have clearly made an impact on Madan's analysis of India's socio-religious situation today and the critical dilemma that characterises that situation. Yet he quite rightly highlights the fact that in India, far from being enfeebled by the impact of modernity, anyone can see that at a popular level religion flourishes ever more vigorously. With greater mobility today it is doubtful if there have ever been so many pilgrims to the great Kumbha Mela in the North or to other popular sacred places such Lord Venkateshvara's Tirupati in Andhra Pradesh, Murugan's Palani in Tamil Nadu, Ayyappa's Sabari Malai in Kerala, and countless more. With ease of publishing have there ever been so many scriptures and other religious writings available in all India's major languages? With massive growth of the middle-classes, huge numbers of new temples are being built. With increased search for a spirituality that is more esoteric than temple ritual provides, and with more international travel, the popularity of 'God-men and gurus' continually grows.

And now, with the increased politicisation of religion - a specific form of 'identity-politics' - the Hindutva card has, at least until the shock election results of 2004, been paying rich dividends. Nationalist religion may not deepen genuine faith, but it certainly intensifies awareness of religious externals. In short, the growing secularist and diminishing religious attitudes of Europe have not been seen in India. Exactly the same is true in large parts of Asia, in Africa and certainly in all countries where Islam is dominant.

Secularism as an ideology clearly involves rejection of both the authority of sacral institutions and the sacred status of earthly authorities. But it is not just 'the will of the people', or democratic authority, that is placed on the throne. Nor is it even scientific rationality as such, though claims for this will often be made. Enthroned rather is a worldview born in a particular kind of western capitalist-industrialist context, and the will of what, at least in an Eastern context, is a quite small minority of people. Naturally, political systems take different forms, whether East, South or even West of Suez. But ideologically paramount is what can be either a callous disregard (whether by Marxist or Fascist) of the individual in the perceived interests of the greater good, or it is liberal modernism's great theoretical emphasis on individual choice and personal satisfaction, an emphasis that in cruder forms of modern secularism leaves little room for social duty.

More than this, though, innate to a secularist worldview is not just the fine aim that all religions are to be treated equally. Usually too there is the assumption that they are to be privatised and so marginalised. Perhaps the most significant characteristic of this worldview is its rejection of religion as a potential source, in relation to human society as a whole, of either truth or authority. Thus fullblown secularism overlaps with a hardline humanist position which sees all faith-positions as at best irrelevant and at worst dangerous superstition that should certainly not, even indirectly, be allowed to influence social policy or ethical judgement. Religion should not be part of public debate, not party to the public domain.

The discourse of a number of modernising leaders in India, Nehru in particular, reveals a way of thinking that is essentially 'secularist'. In part this is the legacy of the Western imperialist presence. In spite of his critical words about western values, and certainly about the imperialist project, Nehru and the great majority of those who went through the colonisers' educational system, were deeply influenced by western liberal attitudes, though with greatly differing levels of 'Indianness' or Indian values being retained. Along with the typical blend of elitism and democratic values imbibed through the British system, of course, there was the free flow of critical insights from *socialist* sources. This meant that English-speaking interpreters within India's intelligentsia, especially the powerfully articulate left-wing ideologues among them, have been deeply imbued with secularist assumptions in which the religious dimensions of our humanness are not only ignored; in ways sometimes hidden, those religious dimensions are contradicted. True, there have been many

Indian Marxists who have not been overtly anti-religious, as was clearly seen in the Marxist governments of Kerala and West Bengal. For a number of the more articulate westernised intellectuals in modern India, however, religious realities not only count for little, they are seen as dangerously anti-human.

Madan argues that the adopted secularism just did not fit the realities of India, any more than for the rest of South Asia. Secularism, he wrote (1992: 395):

> ....is impossible as a credo of life because the majority of the people of South Asia are in their own eyes active adherents of some religious faith. It is impracticable as a basis for state action either because Buddhism and Islam have been declared state or state-protected religions or because the stance of religious neutrality or equidistance is difficult to maintain since religious minorities do not share the majority's view of what this entails for the state. And it is impotent as a blueprint for the future because, by its very nature, it is incapable of countering religious fundamentalism and fanaticism.

A hundred examples could be given of accounts of Indian life where religious realities have either been ignored completely, or where this all-pervasive religious dimension has not been incorporated effectively into political, social and intellectual language, where God-talk has been alienated from power-talk. It is probably unfair to compare Leela Gandhi's *Postcolonial Theory* with Gauri Viswanathan's *Outside the Fold: Conversion, Modernity and Belief,* both published in 1998, for their aims are different. Leela Gandhi's is not directly an account of Indian culture: as its title implies, it concerns East-West interpretive discourse. Many aspects of this dialectic are discussed with great insight and clarity. Yet, when so much of India's interaction with the West, both in the past and now, hinges on religious and religio-cultural issues, should there be virtually no reference to such an inclusive life-dimension? There is page after page concerning M.K.Gandhi, for example. Yet nothing about the religio-cultural roots of his ethics. The sole reference to 'religion' (p.104) is a quote from Benedict Anderson to the effect that the birth of nationalism and the nation-state in the West came at the time of the death of religion. The 'nation' filled the void left by religion's demise. And with no further reference to religion, we are left assuming that religion's demise has been globally total. No doubt the postcolonialists are in something of a bind here. In their concern to refute the religiousness of the East that western Orientalists 'invented', they play down that religiousness altogether, so playing into the hands of western secularism. Visvanathan's book, on the other hand, recognises so very clearly the pervasive dynamic of explicitly religious factors.

The secularist thinking underlying Indian policy has meant that the great majority of Indian people, whose ways of experiencing life are inextricably bound up with religious faith, have found themselves alienated at various levels of national life and its ideology. At least for some this was specifically the felt lack of an integrated Hindu identity. Among Muslims, Sikhs and Christians, on the other hand, distinctive identities seemed to be burgeoning. And so among the Hindu majority a dangerous vacuum was created. At a local and certainly at a personal level, leaders in political and commercial life often quite extravagently showed their orientation to the symbols of Hindu tradition. But this world of symbols was not reflected in public debate, in social, political and intellectual analysis and vision for the future. The 'scientific temper' was held to exclude, even to be opposed to, religious worldviews. The result was - quietly, even imperceptibly among the unpoliticised Hindu faithful, but overtly, even raucously, with the more militant - there was a growing sense of need for a more clearly defined, more nationally integrated self-identity. When the opportunity came to align themselves with a cultural-political project claiming a basis in Hindu tradition and in openly Hindu symbolism, they eagerly embraced it.

As Madan puts it: '...it is the marginalization of religious faith, which is what secularization is, that permits the perversion of religion' (*op.cit.* 396). Hindus' largely submerged sense of *alienation* - ideological alienation at least - within their own homeland led to the embracing of a mythology which compels them to alienate, even demonise, the 'other'. All this was fertile ground for a Hindutva programme which at its most extreme has included the most appalling violence against Muslims - especially in Gujarat - and to a less extent against Christians in some places. That there are here issues of power and commerce, of land reform and of the rising aspirations of Dalits and tribal people, in no way softens the hard fact of *religious identity* being a key factor. But, as we have seen, there are deeply embedded strands of many religious traditions in which such a polarising attitude either already prevails or is potentially present. It is, though, not invariably and necessarily so. Crucial to the process are the particular response religious faith makes to times of crisis and the particular interpretation of the tradition made by empowered teachers.

There is posed here a *dilemma* that secularists, and quite often from the other side religious people too, perceive as of huge proportions. How on earth is it possible to incorporate into a pluralist national life this religious dimension, with its distinctive beliefs about how things should be and with its particular loyalties, without being discriminatory against others, minority groups in particular? Is it possible to combine both a *pluralist national identity* and a *particularist religious identity*, especially if the religion concerned seems to regard accommodation and compromise as disloyalty to faith?

And we can broaden the question further: Is it possible to be committed both to such modernity as is surely necessary to a successful nation's life today and at the same time also to the traditions of a particular faith-position? Indeed, can faith creatively incorporate important insights from the secularists, even to the enhancing of faith? Does a traditional sacralist worldview perhaps need certain leavening, redirecting influences from the secularist movement? At least, in a country of diverse faiths and cultures - even if one of them forms a substantial majority - is there not the need for a national policy involving the promotion neither of the absolutes of faith over the pragmatic adjustments of rationality, nor the specific requirements of any one community over the life of others?

Several forms of response can be made to this seeming dilemma.

Firstly, there are the hidden limits, already noted, to the freedom and inclusiveness claimed by full-blown secularism. Its invariable claim to be pluralist, open to all religious groups and discriminating against none, misleads precisely to the extent that a fully secularist perspective dominates. The conditions for partnership are too often impossibly loaded against a faith-view for those not sharing that secularist view of things. 'Secularism is the dream of a minority which wants to shape the majority in its own image, which wants to impose its will upon history but lacks the power to do so under a democratically organized polity', is the rather startling way in which Madan puts it, when thinking of secularism in an Asian context. He even defines it as 'a phantom concept', a 'social myth' which attempts to form a 'cover over the failure of (the) minority to separate politics from religion in the society in which its members live'. For the people of Asia 'religion establishes their place in society and bestows meaning on their life, more than any other social or cultural factor' (1992: 395). It is, therefore, both 'moral arrogance and political folly' to foist a secular ideology on to such people.

Secondly, there is the response that in principle we must welcome any critical perspective with regard to the modern nation-state (so much a creation of the secularist West) and its absolutes. Why should we assume that our modern secular 'democratic' states, with the values and life-styles they have engendered, are the final pattern for human community? Modern democratic theory may give us insights that are absolutely essential to human community and its governance; but do we not need far more rigorous forms of critique of the glaring weaknesses of democracy in present practice? This applies to Europe and the US as much as to the 'failure' of democracy in Africa and Asia. What, for example, do representatives of the Bush regime intent on 'reconstructing' Iraq - for a short while at least, after themselves violently deconstructing it - actually mean when they insist on setting up a new 'democratic' regime there and elsewhere throughout the Middle East?

In any case, Western universalist assumptions need to be questioned, and at least within some religious traditions there are prime resources for this. Of course, when religious absolutes are used instead to intensify and legitimate the absolute demands of the state and its organs of power (as against the human good, the wellbeing of society), or to absolutise the political institutions of a particular faith-tradition and its sacral forms, we have a serious problem indeed. (I look at the dangers of nationalist and religious identities being locked together too closely in chapters 9 and 14).

Thirdly, then, we need to think more in terms of how a religious commitment and its community loyalties can, alongside other ideologies and other religious commitments perhaps, be part of a modern pluralist society. There is the plain fact that, along with the tragic memories of inter-religious animosity and violence - keeping pace with inter-ethnic and inter-national warring - there have been many instances of the very regimes accepting the authority of one or other religion having made room in varying degrees for other traditions. The survival of ancient Christian communities within Muslim rule in the Middle East and Africa - Egypt, Iraq and Iran for example - witnesses to this longstanding coexistence, whatever the tensions may have been. Or the reverse: Islam has been well able to adapt to minority status, and has even accepted a degree of 'secularist' adjustment.

The Shia community in both Iraq and Iran is not the minority. Yet, in the unexpected words of Karen Armstrong (in 'Faith and Freedom', *The Guardian* 8 May 2003; see also her *Islam: A Short History* 2001) that community's attitude in Iraq is essentially one of 'religiously motivated secularism' - a startling contradiction of most people's assumptions about all forms of Islam. Underlying this Shia potential for 'secular' nationalism is their longstanding suspicion of all political rule - the result of their experience of autocratic injustice from ruling caliphs, and the 'tragic fate of all the Shia imams'. Their transcendent belief in a just and egalitarian society led them to believe that it is 'impossible to integrate the religious imperative with the grim world of politics'. Even in Iran, where the Ayatollah-run regime established by Khomeini broke with 'centuries of sacred Shia tradition', 25 years after the revolution there is a remarkable struggle for forms of true democracy and pluralism, even if unlike those in the West. Even Khomeini came to recognise the inevitability, and therefore the need for, a gap between politicians and religious authorities. The chief intellectual of Iran's Shia-dominated world sees a mix of three identities in a typical Iranian person: Shia, Persian and western, and not even the last can be merely eradicated. Probably Armstrong exaggerates the 'secularist' element, and the 'privatising of faith' within Shia tradition. But the facts are strikingly at odds with general assumptions concerning Iran and Shia faith.

Accepting 'pluralism' in some form has usually been a pragmatic response to unavoidable circumstances. But this in no way lessens the significance of our histories of religious accommodation. For one thing, whatever extremists may claim about making no concessions to context, *interaction with contextual realities* in some way is the only possible course for people of faith. Obviously this does not mean that religious faith will always opt for being conformist rather than transformist in relation to wider society. It is rather a question of how the process is seen, and so of how interaction is to take place.

Fourthly, each religious tradition itself is usually in reality pluralist. And so there will be divergent responses to the fact of a pluralist context. Some will argue that any kind of accommodation to the secular world and its values is the death of faith, that faith-identity must not be compromised in any way. Others will recognise that *for the sake of faith itself* the tradition has to engage interactively with the challenges of whatever secular context faith finds itself in. At least some will likely have been led to find intrinsic faith-reasons, resources within their faith-position, for becoming friends of the infidels; others will have found grounds for those 'others' being demonised. Even within these differing responses, context has been all-important. Revelatory texts themselves show us contrasting ways of relating to others, and here too context has been crucial. Interpretation of these authoritative sources by exegetes and preachers, Imams and Acharyas, Gurus and Lamas, then becomes equally crucial.

Here are further examples, from the two traditions - Christianity and Islam - usually seen as most confrontatory. We find Jesus at one point saying: 'He who is not with me is against me', and in another context what looks like the reverse: 'He who is not against you is on your side' (Luke 11.23; 9.50). In places, belonging to the ancient 'people of God' seems an important identity. Elsewhere that identity stands for little; those who are outside the usual boundaries are identified both as people of notable faith and as those among whom God is at work in a special way. Then, on the relation of 'secular' and 'sacred' authority, there was the oft-quoted word of Jesus on the question of whether faith-loyalty rules out tax-paying and therefore collaborating with an alien occupying power. We are to 'give to Caesar what belongs to Caesar and to God what belongs to God' (Mark 12:17); elsewhere the appointed regional semi-King is denigrated as 'that fox Herod'. 'My kingdom is not of this world' (John 18:36) has to be taken along with the many words and acts suggesting that the claims of the divine realm very much intrude into the life of this world (e.g. Luke 11:20 - the healings Jesus does are said to be signs that 'the divine realm as come among you').

Or there is from one context the apostolic injunction to submit to Roman secular authority, for we should not resist what is by 'divine institution'. Rather we are to pray for all who have 'sovereign high office', that 'we may lead a tranquil and quiet life' (Romans 13:1-2; 1 Timothy 2:1-2). In other more critical contexts of persecution by these authorities, Rome is described as 'Babylon', an image for an oppressively evil regime (1 Peter 5:13), a designation apocalyptically and dramatically elaborated in the enigmatic Revelation of John, sent from his island imprisonment. Some passages suggest an exclusive rejection of anything but the name and the lordship of Christ; others make it clear that God has been at work in other prophets 'at different times and in different places' (Hebrews 1:1). Or, that 'God has no favourites' - those who do right, of whatever race or religion, will enjoy God's glory (Romans 2:11). And this in the most determinedly doctrinal of apostolic epistles. There is, too, Paul's speech to Athenian sophists (Acts 17 22-34) when he concedes that all of us 'live and move and have our being' in God, as is witnessed to by their own religious tradition.

Later Christian history too is replete with instances of contrasting responses to the fact of other faiths. A striking example is the difference between Pope Gregory VII in 1076 and Pope Urban II less than twenty years later. One appeals to the Muslim ruler of what is now Algeria that they must show each other neighbourly love, just as they believe in and love one God. The other initiated the First Crusade against Muslims, beginning two centuries of vicious violence against Muslims and Jews that - for all the misguided 'heroism' and self-sacrifice also part of this crusading period - left an indelible trauma on Muslim and Jewish consciousness.

Further Islamic Pluralism

Equally striking divergence is to be found on the Muslim side at different periods of Muslim history. As with Christian sources, Islamic revelatory sources too provide contrasting guidance on how Muslims are to treat people of other faiths. In the Qur'an 2:62 Muhammad is very positive about 'Believers, Jews, Christians....whoever believes in God and the last day, and does what is right'. All 'will have their reward from their Lord'. Probably this reflects the earlier situation when the Prophet still hoped for collaboration from the Jews of Madina. In various other instances too, all who are 'people of the book' (or 'of a previous revelation') are urged to join in the Prophet's mission of restoring the original purity of faith that was theirs.

That they did not support the Prophet - the Jewish community especially - obviously led to a changed attitude. 'Believers! Do not take the Jews and Christians as your allies: they are allies only of each other. Whoever among you becomes a friend to them is one of them. God does not guide unrighteous people' (Qur'an 5:51). Even so, as Martin Forward points out in his chapter on 'Muhammad and Other World Faiths' (1997: 56), 'by and large, Muslims have acted honourably towards Jews who lived in their territories' (see whole chapter). While there is dangerous animosity between the two communities in many parts of the globe at present, this 'should not obscure what has often been a mutually profitable history of relations between Jews and Muslims'. Certainly, Muslim treatment of Jews, as a minority even if sometimes commercially prominent group, has mostly been much more humane than can be said of Christian treatment of them during the Middle Ages.

Forward also points out three further pertinent matters. (a) There is the ambivalence in the Qur'an concerning what is meant by 'Islam'. For instance: 'There is no god but he, the almighty, the wise. The true religion with God is Islam' (3.18). In this and other cases is it the wider sense of a proper response to God of 'submission' (Islam) that is intended, an attitude of heart and life that in principle possible - as other texts imply - to any person of genuine faith? Or does 'Islam' here, and elsewhere, carry the narrower meaning of becoming part of the Islamic tradition as embodied in the community established by Muhammad? Is it a specific community identity that is intended? A number of Muslim interpreters do not wish to set this more confining kind if boundary to the meaning of 'Islam'. And immediately this opens the door to at least a form of pluralism (pp. 57-8).

(b) Then there is the issue of what *jihad* means. 'Holy war' is how this Qur'anic term is invariably understood by non-Muslims, and more often than not by extremist Muslims too, even making this their justification for going to war against another Muslim country they have serious disagreement with. Yet, for many Muslims the word primarily means that struggle required of any believer both within the self and in the world if faith is to govern life. This may entail a violent struggle for God against ways that are contrary to God's revealed way. But often such 'holy war' is regarded as the 'lesser *jihad*'. Yusuf Ali, in his translation of and commentary on the Qur'an, writes about a verse (9.20) suggesting that the self's struggle to be true to God has 'higher rank with God':

> Jihad...may require fighting in God's cause, as a form of self-sacrifice. But its essence consists in (1) a true and sincere Faith, which fixes its gaze on God, (so) that all selfish or worldly motives seem paltry and fade away, and (2) an earnest and ceaseless activity, involving the sacrifice (if need be) of life, person or property, in the service of God. Mere brutal fighting is opposed to the whole spirit of Jihad....(quoted by Forward p.60).

The final sentence here echoes another word of Muhammad's: 'Struggle in the cause of God against those who fight you, but do not be aggressors, for God does not like aggressors' (2:190). The believer is left with little doubt that the killing of those who oppress the weak ('for oppression is worse than slaughter') and who are aggressive against those who conform to God's ways sometimes becomes unavoidable. But such violent resistance, as well as the struggle to bring others to 'submission', is to be tempered with the memory that God is 'forgiving and merciful'.

(c) Thirdly, Muslim history has been greatly influenced by the twin concepts - reflecting contrasting contexts - of *dar al-Islam* (or 'house of Islam', i.e. a situation of Islamic rule) and *dar al-harb* (or 'house of war', i.e. when Muslims are a 'struggling' minority). Does this imply that Muslims can never feel entirely at home, never feel their identity is not threatened, unless they are within a context where Islamic *shari'ah* law is in force? Much Muslim writing on this issue does suggest this. But such feelings of threat when apart from the supportive sanctuary of a believing community, or even when still separate from the glorious company of saints in heaven, is not atypical of other religious traditions too. The sense that there is to be a continual struggle, not only within one's self, but against ways of life that contradict the just and peace-giving ways of God, is found not only in Islam. The question here is precisely how that sense of alienation is experienced and how the 'struggle' is expressed, especially in relation to the enchanting power of secularism in the modern world.

In comparing the claims of a 'secular' basis for religious faiths to co-exist and the attitudes to such pluralism shown by particular communities of faith, the test comes when one faith-community has attained the power to rule others. History generally provides us more with examples of those who, in the name of their faith, after struggling against what they saw as the oppressive ways of others, became themselves perhaps even more oppressive when able to wield power. But this has not always been so.

At least two remarkable exceptions can be mentioned again: the Indian convert to Buddhism, Ashoka in the third century BC, and the Muslim ruler Akbar of the Mughul empire in the sixth century CE. Especially significant was their recognition of the right to an equal place for the numerous communities of faith within the land they ruled. No doubt it is what we might expect of a Buddhist ruler - identities being deemed so provisional within Buddhist tradition. Which makes the violence and unjust discrimination against Tamils demanded by extremist Sinhala nationalist monks in Sri Lanka all the more bewildering. In Akbar's case, it is the openness to other religious viewpoints that is unexpected. He was an outstandingly inclusive Muslim ruler, given the violently oppressive rule enforced by most of the Mughul emperors. In Akbar and Ashoka, then, we have a pluralist understanding of the empire's identity and of the identities of faith-communities within this. Political expediency, a calculating of what would best help the life of the empire along, obviously plays a large part in their eirenic rule. But in neither case was it solely a matter of strategic calculation.

We have noted elsewhere how Hindu governance of wide-ranging communities within a single political body at times aimed for the inclusion of others than the concerned dynasty's own sectarian allegiance. As for imperial rule by Christians - we have the contrast between the refusal of the British colonisers in India up to the first part of the eighteenth century even to allow in Christian missionaries, for fear of disturbing the status quo and the relative balance of things, thus making control more difficult. On the other hand there was the fierce insistence by the Portuguese colonisers of Goa 300 years earlier that local Hindus should be forcibly converted or be exiled from the colony. Perhaps this difference merely reflects the changing attitudes to the sacred and how the sacred relates to the secular found in Europe during those centuries, and especially a differing view of this sacred-secular relationship between the Catholics of the South and the Protestants of the North.

The Protestant Source of Secularism?

Finally, there is the question of whether a secularist attitude to things owes quite as much to Protestant influence as is assumed by those scholars who accept Weber's contention on this. T.N.Madan, for example, arguing that 'secularism' just does not fit into Asian life, says that the privatising of religious life and the separation of the sacred from the secular, is only possible to 'Protestant Christianity' (1992: 395).

The one-time Catholic nun, Karen Armstrong, in her highly regarded *Battle for God* (2000), describes the essentially secularist worldview of the Protestant Reformers even more forcefully. And it must be said that the exuberant vigour of her historical and contemporary interpretation makes for what must be among the most gripping and in many ways (in spite of my caveats below) most persuasive writing on religious history in our time. She describes first (pp.64-67) the crisis facing the Reformers, and the personal *angst*, even despair, they experienced, as a result of the epoch-making changes taking place throughout Europe. This led them to lay great stress on the absolute sovereignty of God and the impotence as well as the corrupt sinfulness of humans. Their religious world had to be re-created to meet the crisis of faith, especially that posed by the new role for reason and for human autonomy in relation both to nature and to the authority of ecclesial institutions.

One response was that scripture (as against tradition) and the faith of the individual (as against the magisterium of the church, especially its embodiment in Rome) took on an infinitely enhanced role. '...the old symbolic understanding of religion was beginning to break down'. In that earlier spirituality 'a symbol partook of the reality of the divine; men and women experienced the sacred in earthly objects; the symbol and the sacred were thus inseparable' (p.65) For medieval Christians this sense of the immanence and accessibility of the sacred was especially strong with the relics of the saints and the eucharistic bread and wine. In the case of the latter, the presence of the sacred was even dangerously potent for common people.

By contrast, claims Armstrong, in the minds of the Protestants sacred relics were blasphemous 'idols', the sacred elements in the

Eucharist were 'mere symbols'. Instead of seeing religion as *mythologia*, its mythic character was seen as rigid logic, with sacred scripture being 'read literally for information it imparted', i.e. about the world. Because this was 'silent, solitary reading' based on individual faith, religious truth was 'increasingly subjective', with believers being set free from 'traditional ways of interpretation and from the supervision of the religious experts'. Moreover, at least in Luther's view, reason - as against faith - was vehemently rejected. 'In pushing reason out of the religious sphere, Luther was one of the first Europeans to secularize it' (p.66)

Poor Luther is further castigated:

> Because, for Luther, God was utterly mysterious and hidden, the world was empty of the divine. Luther's Deus Absconditus could not be discovered either in human institutions or in physical reality....God had begun to retreat from the world, which now had *no religious significance at all* (my italics). Luther also secularised politics. Because mundane reality was utterly opposed to the spiritual, church and state must operate independently, each respecting the other's proper sphere of activity.

To respond adequately to this summary account of Luther's teaching would take a major essay in itself. Armstrong is in some ways quite accurate here. The crisis Luther faced did lead him to set up new boundaries for both church and state, and therefore new distinctions between them. His doctrine of the two 'realms' or 'orders', one the realm of faith, the other that of the world and history, made much more radical Augustine's dialectical relation, over a thousand years earlier, between the City of God and the kingdoms of this earth. There is even greater emphasis upon the corrupt state of human nature and human rationality. There is unrelenting emphasis upon the 'hidden' character of God, and so upon God's self-revealing. Like Immanuel Kant (a Lutheran!) two centuries later - and the Hindu theologian, Ramanuja, more than four centuries earlier as it happens - here is an epistemology claiming that God 'in himself' cannot be known by human inference based on what is shown of God in creation. In Kantian language, the *noumenon* has to be distinguished from the *phenomenon*. For Luther, it is finally only in that most 'hidden' revealing, the 'veils' of weakness and self-effacing seen in the incarnation, suffering and death of the Mediator, that God is truly, savingly known.

There is, though (argued John Baillie with his usual persuasive elegance) a 'mediated immediacy' implied in this process, a concept that I have applied also to Ramanuja's epistemological faith-talk. But such an exclusive identifying of Christ as the one focus of faith meant leaving out other aspects of Christian tradition (the wider range of divine activity implied in the Trinity for instance) (Cf Baillie 1963:189-96) as well as the more obvious ruling out of any openness to other forms of knowing, such as other worlds of faith. And the closed systems of the Barthians (in spite of his later talk of a 'divine conscursus' in the human) and Brunnerians in twentieth century Christian theology was a child of this Reformation exclusiveness. The 'dialectic' so central to their thought was distortingly one-sided. The decisive role of Jesus as Mediator in Christian faith *can* be of a far more dynamically 'open' kind.

Similarly with Luther's idea of the fixed 'orders', in which for example the oppressed serfs were to accept their appointed place, cease from rebelling against the overlords under whom God has placed them, and rejoice in the Christian faith that provides them their hope of heaven. When they did resist, Luther invoked the power of the state to 'put them in their place'. This rules out any interacting of religion and society, faith and culture, and so the transforming role for faith in the life of the world. Conformity to established order was Luther's way for the faithful (except when this established order was the powerful position of Rome, both religious and secular). Many have pointed out the dangers of such a position (Cf for example Reinhold Niebuhr). In later Lutheranism this strand appears as extreme pietism, for which the boundaries of faith are inner feelings alone, and otherworldliness in the heart is all. Some commentators have even seen a connection between this limiting view of faith and the lack of sufficient resistance to the rise of fascism in the 1930s. Others, like Armstrong, have pointed out the dangerous implications of the extent to which Protestants have often held that human nature is so completely corrupt, that (for many) nothing remains of the divine image within the human. What emerged from this was a 'secularization of politics....as a new way of being religious' (2000: 67).

Here, though - as Armstrong is well aware - we again have to reckon with the *diversity within* the Protestant movement, taking note too of those more radical ('sectarian', 'anabaptist', etc) movements, equally prompted by faith, against which Luther railed so fiercely. Armstrong rightly points out that the other most famous Protestant leader, John Calvin, differed considerably from Luther for instance on the question of Christian engagement in the life of society, even in scientific study of the natural world. Indeed, all work was, for Calvin, a high vocation, and so 'helped to baptise the emergent capitalist work ethic' (*ibid.*).

On one important point, though, Armstrong misleads. It is just not true that Luther, any more than Calvin or other Reformers, held that 'the physical world....now had no religious significance at all', that 'the world was empty of the divine' (*op.cit.* 66). True, God is 'hidden'; but there is the mystery here that the God who is still the 'God of all the earth', reveals himself 'in, with and under' the veils of creation that also hide his being. Even if the dialectic here leaves Luther's position open to extremisms in both directions, it is a position vis-a-vis the life of the world that is very different from full-blown secularism.

Lutheran theologian Paul Santmire, in a systematic and perceptive account of Christian attitudes to the natural world, also reads Luther very differently from Armstrong (Santmire 1985: 219):

> Luther often speaks powerfully of the immanence of God in nature, of the Creator's dynamic presence 'in, with, and under' all the creatures of the natural world....the Creator (is) 'with all creatures, flowing and pouring into them, filling all things....The world is full of God and He fills all, but without His being encompassed and surrounded by it...'

There is no doubt that the Reformation period marks a hugely significant transition point in European history. It was from this point onwards that the modern de-sacralisation of the world and dividing of sacred and secular in the West increasingly emerged. For a long time there were still many in the western world who were to find their primary identity in their religious belief and religious belonging. It was that identity which still provided them with 'meaning for life' and at least indirectly with 'their place in society', to use Madan's criteria. Yet, increasingly that religious realm was to be distinguished from their world of education, science, commerce, culture and politics. Was this, though, the result of their religious assumptions? If so, why is it precisely the most 'Protestant' forms of Christianity today that are most *resistant* to secularizing influences?

Or is it rather the case that Protestant distinguishing between sacred and secular was their religious response to the seemingly autonomous and unstoppable rise of a secularising tide that gradually submerged so much of western Europe? Protestants, with their prophetic rejection of the sacral structures dominating European life up to that point, were then better placed to make their diverse responses, to work out new ways of seeing the sacred in the secular and the worldly forms of the sacred. There were even mid-twentieth theologians who were to try to speak only in 'secular' terms, though with little success in the eyes of either infidels or faithful. No doubt many western Christians (for the boundaries between Protestant and Catholic in Europe on this issue were increasingly to disappear in the twentieth century) were to lose altogether a sense of the world's enchanting character, thus fulfilling Weber's pessimistic view of the future.

But many - in line with Durkheim's thesis that the sacred will somehow find new forms in human experience of the world - in diverse ways discovered divine dimensions to what unbelievers see only in secular terms. For liberationists, the divine realm and sacred worth has been found in the struggle to bring freedom to the oppressed. For those in newly independent countries in Asia, Africa, Central America and the Caribbean, commitment to 'sharing in nation-building' (the favoured expression in the 1960s of P.D.Devanandan and M.M.Thomas of India's Christian Institute for the Study of Society and Religion) was seen as a sacred task. For eco-believers, there are again sacred dimensions to the creative process inherent in nature. For feminist believers, the female body has again come to reveal sacred power. For certain forms of evangelical faith, the very humanity, the suffering vulnerability, of their divine Mediator is taken as inclusive of all humanity, so that every human takes on sacred worth. What we have here, though, is a new way of seeing the world of the sacred and its absolute claims, even its impingement upon the 'secular'.

Then, there are those Protestants who, seeing the changes imposed by the secularising process as a critical threat to faith, are as fiercely resistant in their 'fundamentalism' as are the most extreme Muslims.

There is no simple dichotomy of the dimensions of sacred and secular in modern Christian faith - Protestant or Catholic - even if ways of understanding the interpenetration of these two dimensions of life are so many. It would not be difficult, indeed, to find equally divergent ways of relating faith in the 'sacred' with life in the 'secular' world in many other religious traditions today. That Protestantism has been a potent vehicle of the secularising process does not mean it is either instrinsically or uniquely secularised. What has been true is that forms of Protestantism were more rapidly and more deeply influenced by, and in turn themselves influenced, the secularising process than any other religious tradition. Protestant identity, though, is far from that of a hardline secularist.

Chapter 8
Fundamentalist Reaction

No one can hope to examine systematically and cross-culturally issues relating to fundamentalism without reference to the five-volume *Fundamentalism Project* (1991-95), sponsored by the American Academy of Arts and Sciences, Chicago. From the outset it was inevitable that the Project would find a *definition* of 'fundamentalism' problematic, especially as the term has been used by the secular media to include almost any religious and cultural activity claiming an authority that a secular perspective questions.

The term 'fundamentalism' was originally a self-appellation. It was first used early in the twentieth century by a group of American Protestant leaders determined to resist what they saw as the threats of modern science and trends within Christianity to accommodate a more secular way of life. These conservative leaders called for uncompromising commitment to what they saw as the biblical fundamentals of their faith (Marty & Appleby 1995: 403). This 'no compromise' attitude was further expressed in and strengthened by the 'monkey debate' a little later between creationists and evolutionists, especially in the southern states of America, that resulted in a famous court case concerning what can be taught in schools. It would obviously be misleading, though, to apply the term 'fundamentalist' to those in any religion committed to certain fundamentals of faith. When this becomes rigidly literalist resistance to any but a particular traditional interpretation of those fundamentals, any but the norms set by a particular period within the tradition, we are clearly closer to a more valid use of the term. As we shall see, though, we are still left with one or two intrinsic definitional problems.

The Fundamentalist Project: Defining Characteristics
The Fundamentalism Project concluded from its comparative cross-cultural research that there are nine characteristics of the phenomenon we can properly refer to as 'fundamentalist' (*op.cit.* chapter 16). And these are found within a very wide range of religious traditions, in each case naturally taking on a distinctive form and style dependent on the distinctive character of the concerned religious

tradition, as well as the peculiar context within which the 'fundamentalist' response is made. Shi'ite Islam (or Sunni in its distinctive way) manifests these nine characteristics in forms that are different from militant Hinduism; Sri Lankan Buddhism is different from Hasidic Judaism in New York; Protestant 'fundamentalism' tends to differ from Catholic, and so on. But it is always in part the particular context too, the circumstances of the time - political tensions, cultural histories, social and economic disparities, emergent personalities - that help to account for dissimilarities.

So, what are fundamentalism's nine defining characteristics?

Firstly, there is a common *reaction against* the marginalising and relativising of what are seen as the fundaments of religion. Defensive postures are adopted in response to the threats felt from the secularising process of modernity, a process which is seen to erode and weaken the role of religion in society. Efforts may be made to gain control of the organs of state, political power being seen as a means either to re-sacralising or de-secularising essential elements of corporate life, or perhaps mainly to gain a position of power over the 'enemy'. The Christian 'silent majority' right-wing in the United States, Islamic movements from Bosnia to Indonesia, Khalistani Sikhs in the Punjab, Hindutva in wider India, the Hasidim in Israel, Protestant Unionist preachers in Northern Ireland, nationalist Buddhist monks in Sri Lanka - all share this strategic goal of gaining control of the state. An equally intense concern of many Islamic extremist movements is to resist the growing control of crucial areas of life and belief by western neo-colonialism and its all-pervasive secularism.

(Note: the Fundamentalism Project differentiates movements that are fundamentalist proper and those that 'fundamentalistlike' (*op.cit.* 419):

> Whereas fundamentalist movements are most at home in a religiocultural enclave, but find themselves drawn into politics as a result of their religious beliefs, fundamentalistlike movements tend to reverse the process. That is, they reach for religious justifications, tactics, and organizational patterns in order to mount the most effective opposition possible, based on ethnicity, community, and religion. These movements include the Ulster Protestants, South Indian Christians, Hindu RSS, Sinhala Buddhists, and the Kach

movement in Israel. The militance and reactivity of these movements is not primarily toward (against?) modernization and secularization but tends to be an affirmation of ethnonational-identity in the face of threatening ethnonational minorities, or preemptive ethnonational majorities.

I find no problem in making some sort of differentiation. But the dissimilarities between almost every one of the instances given as examples make for a very strange common grouping.)

The 'enemy' will not always be the secularist world itself. It can as well be what is seen as a compromised, corrupted form of the fundamentalists' own originating institution. Often, then, the enemy is the established religion that the fundamentalist believes has become a traitor to true faith and therefore is even more dangerous than the unbelieving secular state.

Secondly, fundamentalism is *selective* in a number of ways. Particular themes from the tradition are made all-important, others played down or interpreted in the light of what has been chosen as hermeneutically central. In Christian movements apocalyptic prophecies of dramatic global change, especially if seen to point to the imminent return of Christ, texts making clear the supremacy of Christ over all other authorities - along with the expectation that the whole world will be made subject to Christ, and those texts emphasising the need for the chosen ones to be separate, are commonly selected themes. Shi'ah Muslims give a central place to the role of Imams and learned jurists in directing their country's affairs at every level.

This selective attitude can also be seen in reactions to the 'enemy'. Engagement with secularising modernity will overtly be one of resistance and opposition to secular values and to the changes these have brought in. Yet, fundamentalists will at the same time use selected aspects of this modernising process - perhaps technological skills developed in modernity, or modern communication and management techniques - insofar as these seem to further the aims of their sacral world. (Some social analysts see fundamentalism as the secularist mindset dressed up in religious garb). Even features of an 'enemy' religious tradition may be adopted: so we find proponents of Hindutva taking over Christian and Muslim missioning strategies, and even some of their theological emphases. At the same time, fundamentalist oppositional stance will be focussed on particular issues, such as abortion in the United States, the tourist trade in Egypt, conversion in India.

Thirdly, fundamentalists invariably hold a *dualist* worldview. The Fundamentalism Project's description of this, though, is surely questionable:

> Reality is considered to be uncompromisingly divided into light, which is identified with the world of the spirit and of the good, and darkness, which is identified with matter and evil. Ultimately, light will triumph over darkness. For fundamentalist movements the world outside is contaminated, sinful, doomed; the world inside is a pure and redeemed 'remnant'(p. 406).

There is no need to question the deep-rooted dualism of fundamentalists. But it is doubtful if across the board they link the *material* world with that which is dark and doomed. Their sacral world is not one in which the spiritual is opposed to the material, even if this may be so in some cases. Opposition to materialism in its modern consumerist form is a different issue, and this is very much a concern for some fundamentalists, as for many people of faith. Others, though, have made material success, and profitable alignment with capitalist ideology, the hallmark of true faith: an important strand of both South Indian and American rightwing Christian fundamentalism for example, and a number of those supporting the Hindutva movement in India.

Fourthly, *the sources of authority within the tradition are seen as absolute and inerrant.* 'The Torah, the Talmud, the Halakha, the Qu'ran, the Shari'a, the Bible, and the Granth Sahib are....true and accurate in all particulars.' They are not to be subject to 'the canons of critical rationality' (p.407) The Vedas do not appear in this list for some reason. On the question of scriptural authority, Eastern religious traditions do differ from 'Abrahamic'. Authority in matters of spiritual insight is also invested in gurus, swamis, acharyas, sants, gifted bhikkus, lamas and suchlike charismatic figures. It is true that for millennia there has been in key Indian traditions a belief in the eternal and *infallible* character of 'that which is heard' *(sruti),* the sacred Vedic text. But because the interpreters of scripture are themselves mediators of divine truth, and because the 'truth' is not so clearly seen as a set of cognitive beliefs, the authority of the text as such is diffused in various ways. Even so, since the impact of Islam and the West on Indian life there has been increasing evidence of a more literalist view of scriptural authority. It is not uncommon, for example, to hear claims that the Vedas many ages ago provided information about modern scientific 'discoveries' in fields such as nuclear physics or cosmological theory. Modern Hindu thinking, then, as other faith-traditions can easily become 'fundamentalist'.

Fifthly, *millennialist and messianic faith in a miraculous culmination to history* is, in various forms, usually typical of fundamentalist movements everywhere. The almost universal myth that the forces of light will overcome the forces of darkness is believed to be working out in a *particular* history. While messianism may be especially characteristic of the Protestant fundamentalist's worldview, there is also the Hidden Imam who is to come out of hiding for the true Muslim, Hindu hopes for Lord Rama's sacred Rajya on earth, and even among the monks of Sri Lanka expectations of a purely Buddhist kingdom. The Fundamentalist Project concludes that Eastern militant movements are less likely to have clearly messianic saviour-figures. The Avatars of Hindu tradition, though, were surely in essence just that - mythic 'Descents' who came to 'destroy those who are evil and save those who are good', to remove *adharmic* disorder and set up *dharmic* order. And the last of the usually listed Avatars, *Kalki*, is 'one still to come (in the final age)'. Militant movements within Hinduism, such as Sivaji's in the seventeenth century, have been led by messiah-like figures. So there is no reason to assume that this phenomenon will invariably be absent from Eastern religious movements, even if the undergirding view of history is different. A cyclic historical process can also produce moments of great crisis.

Sixthly, there is belief in the special status of the *inner group of the faithful, the chosen, the pure*. The various fundamentalist manifestations of this phenomenon of living as an 'enclave' in the world are examined in detail in a fine essay entitled 'The Enclave Culture', by Jewish sociologist Emmanuel Sivan (*op.cit.* 11-70). It is very clear that this sense of belonging to an exclusive inner group contributes very strongly to the creating of an identity sharply differentiated from and resisting influences from those outside; outsiders become demonised as alien others.

Seventhly - consequent to the sense of belonging to the chosen - one way of ensuring the purity of the 'enclave' is to set up *sharp boundaries* between those within and those without, between the faithful and the infidels, the pure and the impure. For ultra-orthodox *haredi* Jews, as for the traditional Brahmin, such marking off is one of differing forms of literal spatial observance. The *haredi* walk from home to the sacred place on the sacred day must not be more than the prescribed distance; the sacred Brahmin (in earlier tradition) must not allow anyone polluted to come within the prescribed distance around his body, itself seen as a sacred temple. More usually, the separation is maintained by the boundaries set up by ways of life, ways of speech, what is permitted to be seen or read. Holiness is the required boundary.

Eighthly, fundamentalist organisations are typified by the *extraordinary authority of the charismatic leader.* Usually there will not be a traditional hierarchy, with priestly or inherited gradations of status. The emphasis may well be on the equality of all who belong to the movement. But the authority of the person who has emerged as having special gifts of scriptural exposition, or public preaching, or organisational flair, or personal magnetism and persuasive power, will often be absolute. This leaves little room for critical reflection on the movement's life and direction. The resulting tensions mean there is an underlying institutional fragility, and breakaway fragmentation is not uncommon.

Ninthly, there are *elaborate behavioural requirements* to be observed by those within the movement. Distinctive music, dress, hair-styles, ways of eating and drinking, rules of relations of the sexes, the discipline of children - all these not only act as boundary-markers; they 'create a powerful affective dimension, an imitative, conforming dimension' (*op.cit.* 408).

To sum up, it can be said that all nine of the above are in fact further expressions of the basic impulse of the first - 'reactivity'. Fundamentalist movements are 'by definition militant, mobilized, defensive reactions to modernity' (p. 409).

In spite of this Project's undeniably great importance as a resource for understanding the dynamics of militant religious movements, there are a few further critical points to be made. Some are matters of detail, such as whether it is helpful to term the Hindutva movement 'ethno-...', or whether South Indian Christian fishermen's movements can be dubbed 'fundamentalist' (See chapter 15 below, on Indian-Christian forms of faith).

There are three perhaps more weighty questions though. (a) One has to do with how proper it is for such a major descriptive work (more than a million words) of what primarily concerns religious phenomena to be so dependent on the historical analyses of sociology/anthropology? Clearly there are key elements in these movements that are interpreted more incisively by the descriptive skills provided by this discipline than by any other. Even so, distinctively *religious* dimensions, peculiarly *faith* perspectives, can hardly be fully evoked and explored within the constraints of these necessarily humanist disciplines. Religious behaviour no doubt is still *human* behaviour, and therefore in its form as behaviour, accessible to the anthropological historian. But it is a peculiar kind of human behaviour. And we have to ask if all the potent inner compulsions of religious people will best be drawn out by disciplines which necessarily regard all human compulsions as of equal significance.

It would have been intriguing to see if, for instance, phenomenological or even comparative theological analysis had brought out insights overlooked by the socio-anthropology of modern historical method. In a number of places the Project writers (T.N.Madan for example) clearly imply that the secularist materialism against which fundamentalists react is in some way intrinsically problematic, a provocation making some kind of reaction by seriously religious people inevitable. Yet, it is precisely within the limiting parameters of secularist Enlightenment thinking that the essays are written. There is, no doubt, by many writers a concern that religion should not be 'explained' as though from some more elevated perspective. Just one example: Daniel Levine refers critically to the dismissive assumption that 'religious belief (is) epiphenomenal' (*op.cit.* 165). Yet the 'anthropological' analysis is itself made within the constraints of that secular world. The Sacred Object of the believer is not, and cannot be, seen as the key to understanding. There is surely an intrinsic dilemma here. (I explore this methodological issue in other writings: e.g. 1987: *passim*).

(b) Further, how valid is the defining assumption that *only as a response to modernity* is such fundamentalism possible, when there are many cases of similar beliefs and actions to be found in a variety of our much earlier religious histories? That the extremist forms of militant religion in recent times are indeed a reaction to what is seen as the militancy of secularism is undeniable. That modern secularism makes inevitable the intensity and even some of the distinctive features of recent extremist religion is also likely. And of course the term 'fundamentalism' itself is of recent origin. But to make modernity the definitive context for any phenomenon that is to be called 'fundamentalism' is hardly convincing. How is the self-identity of, let us say, a modern Christian or Muslim fundamentalist categorically different from the self-identity of Christians and Muslims fighting in the medieval crusades? Or, how is the self-identity of a fiercely militant RSS Hindu essentially different from that of a medieval Saiva or a Ramanandi militant Naga/Sadhu/Yogi intent on protecting his tradition and its institutions? The nature of the perceived 'enemy' necessarily shapes features of those identities: secularist, materialist faith is very different from eleventh century religious faith. Nor does the character of religious faiths themselves, or their ways of relating to political power, stand still. But it is difficult to see just why, if we are to use the term 'fundamentalist' at all, it should only be for movements that are in reaction to secularist modernity.

(c) A third critical point closely relates to the above, but pushes the argument in the other direction. Has the 'fundamentalist' umbrella become to wide? For, are not the nine defining features listed above not equally typical - very often at least - of religion *per se*, not merely of 'fundamentalism'?

A lively essay by Robert Frykenberg (1994: 591-616), introducing the section on South Asian movements, lists somewhat different categories as fundamentalism's defining features. And his eight categories too seem equally applicable, not just to 'fundamentalism', but to a very wide range of religious traditions, even if very differently experienced and expressed in different contexts.

(i) There is a set of beliefs, 'the Truth', found in sacred text, a sense of final truth whose role is definitive and authoritative. (ii) There is the charismatic person, 'the Messenger', variously known as Guru, Prophet, Preacher, Leader, Enlightened One, mediator of the authoritative word, the truth of things. (iii) There is the sacred

Community of the faithful, radically set apart from those outside marked by darkness and impurity. (iv) There is the Destiny, a future of blessedness and perfect peace. At this point, though, it has to be said that in many religious traditions such 'blessedness' is not by way of world-transformation, but as an inner transcendent state of being, or as the life of heaven hereafter. But quietism too can surely be 'fundamentalist' in terms of the other defining features? (v) There is a sense of Evil, dangerous forces that corrupt the good, either from without or from within, forces against which the faithful must be vigilant and must fight vigorously. (vi) Then, as part of the strategy for overcoming evil, transforming conversion is needed from that way which is false and evil to that which is true and good, a change 'in identity and personality, changes in ideology and institutional identification...', a 'reorientation' of life (p. 595). (vii & viii) The final two defining features Frykenberg lists are 'Revivalism', or movements to restore vitality to the tradition, and 'Separatism', in which there is an attitude of 'alienation toward the outside world' and even toward those within who are thought to have 'abandoned, betrayed, or compromised the Truth' (p. 596).

Illuminating as this essay may be, there is not one of these defining features that, albeit in differing form and intensity, is not to be found typically within a wide range of religious traditions through the ages. Not that there is any doubt concerning the dangerous forms and intensity of 'fundamentalism' found globally as part of today's resurgence of religious, ethnic, nationalist identities. Nor is there any doubt that the exercise of *power* globally in our times - economic, cultural, military - and the global institutions by which that power is exercised, make a crucial impact on the shaping of these identities. Militant forms of religious life usually emerge in reaction to the threat posed by the dominance of other systems. In recent times, aggressive modern secularism has been seen as just such a potent threat.

However, the marks of 'fundamentalism' that have been identified above have always been latent within our religious traditions. Exclusivist dangers as well as liberating energies are all potentially present.

Chapter 9
Imagining the Nation Religiously

Then there is the question of *nationalist* movements and the distinctive identities they forge. Lumping them together with all ethnic movements as 'ethnonationalist' (as, for instance, Walker Connor does:1994) on the grounds that both 'nation' and 'ethnos' 'connote a group of people who believe they are ancestrally related' (p.xi), is not helpful. It may be etymologically correct, but hardly makes for historical or conceptual clarity. Both 'nation/national' and 'ethnos/ethnic' have acquired particular meanings, and we shall consider them in separate chapters.

Adrian Hastings (1997) mounted a spirited and impressively well-documented attack, from what some find an over-traditionalist position, on those historians and political theorists who of late have given such great weight to the inventive 'imagining' of both the character and indeed the very existence of the nation as 'nation'.

Hastings aimed to counter in particular the arguments of the 'modernists' - Elie Kedourie (in *Nationalism*, 1960), Ernest Gellner (in *Nations and Nationalism,* 1983), Benedict Anderson (in *Imagined Communities*, 1983), John Breuilly (*Nationalism and the State*, 1993), and especially Eric Hobsbawm (*Nations and Nationalism since 1780,* 1990). For them the nation-state is essentially a post-medieval, post-industrial phenomenon, the product of *modern* conditions. The state of the world - in both senses - and our consciousness of it are unprecedented. As Hobsbawm puts it: 'The basic characteristic of the modern nation and everything connected with it is its modernity' (p.14).

In part their idea of the essence of nationhood arises from an indifference to the role of traditional culture and religious faith in that process, for these have been overtaken and mostly, these writers assume, made obsolete by modernity. Prior to the late 18th century those factors that have created nationalism and the modern nation were mostly unknown. For example, Benedict finds the secret of the universal breakthrough to new nation-based forms of human community in the American War of Independence (ended 1783). This created a new 'horizontal' consciousness, a new national spirit and democratic policy, and the throwing off of older 'vertical' authorities. The French Revolution (began 1789) quickly followed, and played its part in creating what is today understood as the 'nation'. Yet it is said to be thoroughly 'Eurocentrist' to see the origins of the modern nation-state in Europe (Hastings, 1997: 191).

Gellner and Hobsbawm on the other hand - led by a more Marxist perspective - see European capitalist and industrial systems as the creators of the nationalist spirit and thereby the modern nation-state. As an account of modern European nationalist imperialisms, and of more recent American neo-imperialism, the valuable insights of a Marxist analysis are obvious to the reflective spirit, however low Marxist stock may be just now in global affairs. As an account of nationalist movements as such, though, Hobsbawm's explanation creates an equally obvious problem. It is not always in regions where industrial life has been the motor of change, either in Europe or globally, that the eruption of nationalism has been most vigorous. Serbia, Chechnya, Palestine, many African and Asian nations, provide very varied examples not only of nationalist movements, but of the setting up of typical nationa-states too. Except in a very induNrect way, they can hardly be said to have arisen out of the pressures of industrial development and a capitalist system. And if Anderson's claim that loss of power by dynastic and religious systems be taken as a primary factor, then America - driven by capitalist forces well enough - can hardly be taken as the originating paradigm. Links with royal dynasties may have been broken, and Christian institutional religion disestablished, but the power both of religious worldviews (Christian and Jewish) and even non-royal family position (e.g. the Kennedys, the Bushes) in American life is very great indeed.

It is always possible to counter such objections by saying that only within modernity and its compulsions does the fully developed nation-state emerge. Or that (as Anderson argues) there has been globally a great deal of 'pirating' of the modern western model of the nation-state, by new governments for whom it does not innately fit. Many such have sprung out of the European imperialist legacy, creating nation-states throughout the Middle East, Africa, Asia, Central America out of territories carved out by the need first for exploitation of resources and then for administration of a region - however artificial may have been that territory as an innately integrated nation or political body.

Indeed, the greater the lack of inner cohesion the better, if 'divide and rule' was in fact the colonisers' policy. Iraq, created by the British in the 1920s out of three separate regions of the previous Ottoman empire is an obvious case in point. The very fact that Kurds, Sunnis and Shias were far from natural comrades-in-arms, that force from outside would be needed to keep them together, was quite openly spoken of as a good basis for maintaining control if they were cobbled together into one political entity. Even so, these unnaturally invented countries in many cases developed their own common aspirations, their common rejection of alien rule, their common struggle to become a 'nation' - often able to refer back to a golden age of togetherness long ago.

In spite of the many years of despotism experienced under Saddam Hussein, there clearly was - as we have already noted - a strong nationalist feeling of common 'Iraqi-hood' among great numbers in that country, in addition to their sense of being mostly Muslim and perhaps three quarters Arab in common. There was, too, the great power of Babylon of ancient times. It still remains to be seen just what their future as a nation-state will be following the invasion, 'reconstruction', and appointing of an interim 'Iraqi' government by America and the coalition forces, along with the humiliatingly limited role the invading powers have allowed the United Nations in this nation-rebuilding process. Religious, even sectarian, loyalties and the identities they shape, will certainly continue to play a dominant role.

As we noted earlier, even Saddam Hussain, in spite of his essentially secularist stance, despite too his ruthless murder of many thousands of Shias and their leaders whenever they showed resistance to his attempts to gain absolute power, had eventually to reckon with the powerful loyalties faith inspires. His grand buildings for them, though, could hardly serve to mollify Shia feelings and gain their approval. In post-Saddam, post-occupation reconstruction of Iraq, as the 'shock and awe' faded, and as the political goals of all concerned parties become more focussed, there has been increasing resistance to the foreign occupation - an attitude of resistance innate to Shias - as well as anti-western militancy from Sunni-inspired sources. How these potencies can be welded into an integrated national identity of the newly 'liberated' is hugely problematic. Similar kinds of questions can be asked of other nations recently 'liberated' by outside military power. Afghanistan, for example, with its endemic tribal rather than sectarian divisions, far from being in any sense now an integrated nation-state, with a cohesive self-identity, in spite of having been militarily nursed to the point of democratic-style elections, seems perhaps more than ever chaotic and dis-integrated, more ruled by local warlords.

Hastings: Religion's Role in Nationhood

At this point we might note Hastings' efforts to re-establish the *role of religion* in our understanding of the shaping of a nation's identity. He quotes Stalin's derisive query in response to mention of the power of Catholicism: 'The Pope: how many divisions has he got?' The irony was that Stalin's empire began to fall apart just at the point when the resistance of Catholic Poland - Pope John Paul's country - made continued identity with the USSR impossible. Nationalist Ireland and Serbia, are quoted as further instances of 'the defiant power of a nationalism grounded in religious identity' (1997:185).

It is, though, claims Hastings, a strange paradox that it is the biblical story of the Hebrew people's self-identity, beginning with Abraham - father of three world faiths - that provides the 'true proto-nation'. It has been such a powerful paradigm in the consciousness especially of Christian nations, and even of the Jewish people, in spite of their loss of territorial nationality for two millennia. That Abrahamic faith may take unexpected forms, but it runs deep indeed.

Taking examples mostly from medieval Europe, Hastings lists six notable ways in which religion shapes the identity of peoples (*op.cit.* 188-97):

(1) It gives formative shape and sacral status their sense of their origins, defining who they are in distinction to the nations they confront.

(2) Thus, any threats to their national identity are mythologised, deepening the sense of 'us' and 'them'.

(3) The 'clergy', or sacred faith-figures, especially those functioning locally, as they both represent and interpret the community's special faith-identity, take a leading role in 'affirmation of nationhood'. In medieval England 'village priests (the lower clergy) ensured that the articulation of a nation was shared by every class'.

(4) Religious faith has encouraged vernacular literature, thus 'stabilising a conscious sense of national identity' (p.193). Here Hastings directly contradicts Anderson's claim that only when the influence of religion and their sacred languages declined was nationalism possible. 'Christianity never had a sacred language' (p.194), for again and again it was eager to translate the original into other regional languages - Syriac, Armenian, Coptic, Ethiopian, Latin (the 'vulgar' language), Slavonic, and then all the vernaculars of western Europe. 'Neither Hebrew, Greek nor Latin had any special claim on its loyalty....sacred texts remained equally sacred in translation'. Clearly, Hastings does not give quite enough weight to institutional jealousy at certain periods in wanting to keep the sacred texts in the language of power, and even at times the *people's* reluctance to accept translation for fear of the text losing sacred potency. But in general he is right, especially in the powerful role of that sacred text in creating community identity.

(5) The Bible became a 'mirror through which to imagine and create a Christian nation....(in particular) the Old Testament provided a detailed picture of what a God-centred nation would look like'. It inspired, too, 'belief in divine predilection for a particular people' (p.195). True, mission fields provide ample instances of whole peoples taking on an identity as the 'new Israel' (the Mizo and Naga people in Northeast India for example - see next chapter). And even when a minority group, Christians have believed themselves to be a special 'remnant' among the faithless, just as biblical post-exilic Israel thought of its calling and its special destiny.

(6) The development of national/state churches led by religious leaders who were separate from the state ('primarily within the Orthodox tradition...(and) Protestantism') is a final important development that reflects the biblical tensive relationship between monarch and faith-leaders. 'Total ecclesiastical autonomy of a national church is one of the strongest and most enduring factors in the encouragement of nationalism', for it makes contemporary a sense of being both the one people of the Old Testament and the one ecclesial body of the New (p.196). Tragically, the more powerful a European nation's sense of being God's chosen, the greater seemed to be the urge to 'eliminate the first chosen nation, the Jews, from the face of the earth' (p.198). Hastings, then, makes a strong case for the potent role of biblical faith in the developing, for better or

worse, national identities in subsequent centuries leading up to modern Europe.

Another key factor is just how *ethnic* identity relates to national identity. In general while Hastings sees greater continuity, Hobsbawm and others distinguish sharply. And for the '(post)modernists' ethnicity is essentially good, nationalism bad. Again, Hastings will not denigrate nationalism *per se*, especially if ethnic roots still provide nurturing sap - even a pluralist fusion of differing ethnic identities, as in most modern states.

Then there is the struggle for a more inclusive *inter-nationalism*, or the *trans*-nationalism, perhaps as the highest possible form of the State, for which in their different ways international socialists, certain kinds of Muslims, Christians and especially globalising capitalists will all aim. Indeed, a strong case has been by political theorists such as Philip Bobbitt - from a rather conservative stance - that already in modernity there is a fatal weakening of the nation-state's sovereignty, as global forces take over. In his BBC Reith lecture in early 2003 Rowan Williams, then recently made Archbishop of Canterbury, took this as the undergirding assumption to his re-assesment of the role of religious faith today. It is, he claimed, precisely the loss of national sovereignty and the loss of this mooring of people's self-identity that now gives religious faith added urgency as a resource for providing a focus for a sense of self-integration.

Nations and nationalism, then, are in reality created by many different causes and are configured in many different ways. Roots and fruits are manifold. Even when the form of nationhood and its outward trappings may seem very similar, the compelling inner dynamics may have little in common. State power, for example, may call itself 'democratic', but can carry very different meanings even in the rhetoric used by different agents of the most powerful guardian of 'democratic freedoms', the United States, whose Constitution affirms that state rule is to be 'of the people, for the people, by the people'. Many critics have pointed out the self-contradiction of American state actions post-9/11 against those - almost always Muslims - suspected of terrorist connections, actions that blatantly deny democratic rights to those suspects, yet claiming to be for the sake of protecting democracy's freedoms. Whether authoritarian or liberal in tradition, will not the state invariably, in the face of perceived threats to its security and sovereignty, in the end claim these as having priority over its 'democratic freedom', even if in the name of protecting that freedom?

And all too often within liberal democracy 'our democratic freedoms' *can* merely mean the freedom of those with the will to power and the privilege of capital to indulge their greed and - put crudely, for the process is ugly - make as much money and stuff themselves at the feeding trough as fully as possible. Power, of course, is not only a matter of wealth and consumerist greed. Knowledge, charisma, even sacred status still carry great weight. Yet, the link between power and money becomes ever closer, and the 'fat-cat' phenomenon is an increasing obscenity within 'liberal democracy' claiming to be 'for the people....' But that power-money link is also far from unknown in the 'democracy' claimed by more authoritarian regimes. The configuration of our nation-states is complex; any rhetorical slogan can mean many different things.

With his more traditionalist imagining of history, Hastings allowed far more weight than the 'modernists' to the *continuities* of history. In fact, it has to be said that he seemed unwilling to reckon sufficiently with the newness of modernity. Too much weight is given to ancient, biblical and medieval talk about 'nations', not enough to their very different perceptions of what 'nationhood' entailed. In particular, the distinctive 'imagined constructions' consequent to industrialising, imperialising and globalising the world are underplayed.

Hastings does, though, have a strong point in arguing for the hidden potencies of *religious culture* and the *literacy* by which this was transmitted. In Europe and the States this meant the impact of the *bible* as - especially from the 15th century onwards - through vernacular translations and then mass printing its message increasingly shaped the way people thought of themselves and their world. The bible and its stories shaped their identities. Again, Hastings does not allow sufficient weight to the differing ecclesial traditions within which that biblical worldview was set and through which it was so often perceived. Nor to the loss of its impact through the secularising process - ironically hastened through that faith-stream, Protestant, which valued most highly the biblical message (see chapter 7 above on Secularisation). This does not mean, though, that the cultural continuities stretching from the medieval to the modern world are insignificant, that our present imagining of nationhood has no organic links with earlier history.

Ethno-Nationalism?

While we cannot assume that the nationalist spirit is always *ethno-*nationalist, the issue of *race* and nationalism cannot be ignored. The most ardent nationalists have all too often been ardent and often utterly ruthless racists. Germany's Nazi period and South Africa's apartheid policy in differing ways are clear example. No doubt the question of 'race' and racial identity confuses the issue, especially because of the grossly distorting theories of race and racial differences invented to boulster White supremacy in White-Black relations, and Aryan supremacy especially in Aryan-Semitic relations.

But when it comes to distorting theories of the identity of the 'other' invented by white people, there is no end to the racially dehumanising images used, especially by post-Enlightenment Europeans as, in their quest for new resources with which to feed their growing economic needs, they conquered and decimated the tribes of the Americas, of Africa, of Asia, of the Middle East, of Australia. In subjecting and exploiting the *ethne* - the peoples of the earth - European imperialist compulsions also inevitably created racially humiliating identities for their subject people, images reflecting their own view of themselves as masters of the earth.

The dominating and decimating of other groups, even demonising their identity as a way of boulstering the status of one's own group-identity, has been part of human history of all time. European industrial, technological and military superiority, though, meant that the mastering had never before been so globally expansive and, eventually (especially if we include the Soviet empire and the aftermath of its fall), ideologically effective. In such a context, therefore, the inventing of humiliating identities for others - imperialist racism - too was never more systemic and potent.

Historian Niall Ferguson has recently come to prominence for his popularly presented defence of *Empire* (the title of a recent book) - in terms of what he perceives as immediate and eventual benefits both to subject and ruling peoples. To the colonised, he argues, came the blessings of the rule of law, the English language, incorruptible administration, free trade, the abolition of slavery, the implanting of Christian civilisation, the spread of technology and hugely improved communications and mobility. And all this paved the way for the present great boon of globalisation. The fact is, though, great question marks, even exclamation marks, can be put after each of these 'benefits'. The positively *evil* aspects of the imperial process are played down or ignored completely. Not least was the accompanying racism. Given the constant denigrating of the subjugated peoples, counter-racist hatred and accompanying rhetoric was inevitable. Yet, the forces unleashed by this imperialist process did go on to create national and global identities capable of transcending all the previous demonising.

Politically, it is clear that 'nation' and 'ethnos' do interlock, vigorously and violently. For it is when an ethnic group, convinced of their distinctive cultural self-identity, struggle for political independence, probably with the aim of having their own national life and institutions independent of the presently established Nation (or at least a greater measure of autonomy within the Nation), that we have a contributing reason for most of the violent insurgent movements of recent times. Equally a 'reason', of course, is the resistance to such independence by the established Nation. Again, it is not possible to distinguish these struggles for cultural self-identity from political struggles for power, and from control of the institutions of power. But, as noted above, 'power' does take many forms and is not solely to do with the crude exercise of political muscle.

Crisis for Minorities in India's Nationhood

It is obviously not only in the Indian context that the question is raised of *how religious identity can dangerously relate to national identity*. But in India this potential linkage has become a key factor in the present debate. India's religious nationalists presume that loyalty to a religion whose roots are outside India fatally weakens loyalty to the Indian nation. I was not aware of just how deeply felt this mistrust is until, while preparing these lectures, I was part of an informal discussion about Hindu-Christian relations in India between seven or eight British Hindus and an equal number of Christian representatives. Muslims and Christians in India, the Hindu representatives in that meeting vehemently argued, can never be truly nationalist. Their primary loyalty has to be to their religion and therefore to its foreign rootage. There seemed little difference in opinion on this issue within members of the Hindu group between those who were from the more fiercely nationalist Visva Hindu

Parishad and the more evangelically pious Hari Krishna devotees. The North-Eastern States with a large proportion of Christians, and Kashmir with its largely Muslim population ('incited by Pakistan'), were cited as examples.

The Sikh struggle for an all-Sikh independent nation of Khalistan was not mentioned, presumably because Sikhism is a home-grown religious movement. Indeed, it is claimed as 'Hindu' by a certain kind of Hindu nationalist, in spite of Sikh believers furiously rejecting such a claim. In all these cases, though - over 'Khalistan', Kashmir and various states in the North-East - India's military forces have had to engage in fierce struggles to prevent States seceding from the Union, and so formally renouncing Indian identity. *Identities formed by alien religions* are the cause, it was argued, of this un-Indianness, and so the loyalties of Indian Christians and Indian Muslims will always be suspect. My defence of the strongly nationalist commitment of Indian Christians to their country, based on more than forty years of close relationship with a very wide range of friendships in South India, was robust.

But the same issue is debated fiercely *within* Islam and Christianity. As they reflect on how religious faith relates to national loyalty, Muslims may well not agree with each other. Iran, Iraq, Saudi Arabia, Pakistan, Egypt, Turkey all have markedly differing views on nationalism, the nation, the state and their identity as Muslims. Christians certainly do not always agree with each other. In both communities there are those who emphasise the inclusiveness of faith - meaning that every area of life, including national life, is to express faith and its absolute claims - and there are those who emphasise the inwardness of faith, or that the vertical takes precedence over the horizontal. Other ideological loyalties are also part of this debate in recent years. The naive faith of Karl Marx that the universal comradeship of the liberated proletariat would be far stronger than divisive national loyalties has been shown to have a very patchy historical basis.

What of religious loyalties, though? Even in its infancy the Christian Church was accused of being seditionary, of lacking loyalty to Rome right in the heart of this great imperial power. The word of Jesus about giving appropriately to both God and Caesar (Mark 12:17 and other Gospels) was obviously an answer both to Roman and Christian doubts on this question (no doubt debated in generations after Jesus too). It was the question of who Christians ultimately belong to. Augustine's doctrine of the two realms, echoed by Luther again at a crucial moment of Christian self-identity, was a continuation of this debate: how does the kingdom of God relate to the kingdoms of this earth? Absolute loyalties can only be commanded by God, however necessary to human identity the role of the State may be, and however interactive these two identities. The tensive relationship between faith, with its originating sources, and culture, with its localising and contextual compulsions, is of a similarly dialectical kind.

To return to my recent Hindu-Christian group discussion of the relationship of the two communities in India. My protestation of true nationalist loyalty among Indian Christians, as well as pointing to the writings of Christian scholars that show great respect for Hindu faith, was not helped by the claims of a strongly evangelical Indian Christian in the group. He argued that the loyalty of a true 'biblical Christian' to Jesus is so complete that a Jesus-follower will inevitably antagonise all others, whether Hindu, Muslim or western secularist. There is, too, no lack of texts able to confirm this openly avowed exclusiveness, even if there are also more inclusive texts also. It was, in fact, no bad thing that the exclusivist was there in the discussion; for this does represent a not infrequent position in the Christian faith-spectrum. And realism is everything if dialogue is to be fruitful. So, we are left with the fact that just as religious loyalties, and the character of religious identities, range widely, so does the extent to which people with religious faith identify with the national community and its goals.

A Hindu nationalist such as Arun Shourie has no doubt at all as to where ultimate loyalties lie. He acknowledges the fact of many kinds of group identities, but there is only one ultimately binding identity (1997: 46):

> Every individual is also a member of a family, a religious order, a class, he is the resident of a locality, a region in that State. And often the issues of which he is seized pertain to one of these identities. But....his primary identity....is as the member of a nation-State....When the issue is joined his commitment to the interest of the nation-State must over-ride all other interests.

The emphasis in this book on the necessary 'dialectic' of an inter-relational process may seem hopelessly ambiguous to either Hindu nationalist or Christian conservative evangelical. Yet, it is not the likely ambiguity within this spectrum of religion-state relationship that is dangerous. Far more dangerous is the loss of the relational process - on either side. Certainly when there is a fiercely held religious nationalism, religious loyalty becomes identical with national consciousness. The myths, symbols and passions of religious tradition are then exploited for political ends perhaps bearing *little relationship to the intended goals of the concerned faith*. For one thing, these passions are not easily controllable. After watching the demolition of the Babri Mosque in Ayodhya in 1992, L.K.Advani and A.B.Vajpayee, having encouraged the march of the saffron armies up to that point, professed deep alarm at the way politico-religious passion suddenly became violently out of control.

The Nation & Inner-Group Identities

There is also the fact that 'nationalism' and the call to nationalist loyalty will always be tied up with group loyalties that are narrower than the 'nation'. The literal meaning of *natio* implies those *born* there. But religious tradition, political affiliation, or some other conformity as well as ethnic origin, can often be the basis for exclusion from the nation's organs of power. In the British-Irish context 'nationalism' and 'loyalism' have been in fierce conflict, each side boulstered by the divergent religious grounding associated with Irishness and Englishness. So, Catholics fought against Protestants, and the long-held animosities still lead to deep suspicions. And there is 'nationalist' feeling on both sides, even if only those fighting for a united Ireland have been called 'nationalist'. For those fighting to preserve another identity and its privileges, there is a very different 'nationalism', one that is by tradition intensely loyal to the British monarch, a monarch linked closely with the non-Catholic national religion, as well as being the apex of a powerful establishment prominent in the nation's affairs.

Throughout Europe it has not just been the loss of power and prestige by princes or monarchs, but other far wider-ranging changes - the crash of Communist governments among them - that have led to that angst-ridden question high on many national agendas: 'What is our national identity now?' In western Europe the crisis is linked with an astonishing loss of power and influence on the part of established and formal religion. In eastern Europe and Russia the equally astonishing recent crash of Communist governments has suddenly brought new power to the Orthodox churches and a surge in affiliation to counter-cultural, non-establishment churches such as Baptist and Pentecostalist. National identities, in other words, have an erratic relationship with religion.

For Britain, a number of European nations and now Russia, the crisis has in part been brought about by the fall of their empires. For the United States the fall of the 'evil empire', as they saw the Soviet Union, has itself led to such an unchallenged sense of global power - economic, cultural, military - as to form a new and very serious global threat. Uncritical religious belief and affiliation in America are still remarkably resilient and too often serve to boulster and legitimate a sense of global destiny. Nationally this can express itself in either political (not economic) withdrawal and isolation from the international scene, or to a trans-nationalism in which the nation's military and economic power is used to force its will globally. Post 9/11 the Bush regime, for a while at least, seemed intent on enforcing a 'new American century', to use the slogan under which a key neo-conservative planning group set out its plans for global supremacy.

Such enforcing of national will globally at present seems to be in tune with a wide swathe of feeling in 'middle-America', with its still strong forms of conservative Christianity. In more liberal sections of American society there is a very different kind of Christian commitment. Among a newly influential strand in American culture we even find Eastern spirituality making significant inroads. The attacks of September 11 did bring a crisis of national identity as people nation-wide asked, 'But why do they hate us so much?' There was, though, no weakening of national coherence and confidence, even though hidden within academic faculties and other more self-critical organs of national life there has been great doubt regarding America's international policy.

A Narrowing Nationalism

To return to the question of the narrowing of the nationalist viewpoint. It is all too common for the 'nation', even in these inclusive days, to be defined in terms that immediately exclude - perhaps in subtle ways - some groups that are in fact part of the living, working, contributing body of that nation. Or these people are reduced to second-class citizenship. Myths picture a nation with a glorious past and a yet more glorious future. Stories of a 'pure' nation are recounted to go on shaping a common identity, today perhaps reinforced films of national war-heroes. Rituals - involving flags, military posturing, perhaps even sporting prowess - will be used both to sharpen the sense that national identity has absolute sway over all other identities, and to separate out those groups whose histories tie them also to other identities, or are themselves identified by militant nationals as 'alien'. Then there may well be various sorts of 'cleansing' the nation of its impurities, usually ethnic 'impurities', from Hitler's gas chambers for Jews, to calls by British and European nationalist parties today to 'send back the Blacks and Pakis'. I write this chapter in the week that nearly one third of those voting in the primary presidential elections in France opted for an openly anti-immigrant fascist candidate. It is not surprising that critical commentators in India regarded calls by some leading Hindu nationalists that - as part of a policy to cleanse the sacred soil of mother-India of her impurities - Indian Muslims and Christians who do not declare themselves to be 'Hindu' must be expelled from the country, is similar to the Nazi cleansing programmes of the 1930s and 1940s.

The other possibility is that militant nationalists will also, consciously or not, overtly or not, be promoting the strength - socially, economically, politically - of a particular class or community within the 'nation'. The 'nation' in other words can be the invention of an elite minority. Claims have been made, for example, that the Hindutva programme, though identifying the selfhood of the Indian nation in the ostensibly broad terms of 'Hindu cultural values', and making membership of the movement casteless, does nevertheless promote the interests of people in the upper-middle castes, the professional and business communities, with the traditional Brahmin leadership as its spearhead throughout the Sangh Parivar network. In any case, this analysis argues, not only do the weaker communities remain weak, it is precisely to resist their uprising that the movement flourishes. What is patently true about India's Hindutva movement is that being fundamentally conservative, little is attempted by way of radical socio-economic reform. Traditional structures continue to dominate.

On the other hand it is also clear that nationalist movements, like religion, do have the potential to empower those previously disempowered, and to draw together disparate segments of a nation's

233

communal life, perhaps even while seeking to sift out 'alien' elements. Such new togetherness and empowerment for communities who see their status as threatened is precisely the secret of the success of such nationalisms. As long as the 'enemy within', the perceived 'alien', is the primary target, there is little hope that nationalism of this kind can in reality create a fully inclusive 'nation' and break down endemic structures of oppression. Prospects for India under a Hindutva programme do not look promising.

For all his accepting that patriotic feelings of love and loyalty to one's nation can be a fine thing, Hastings fully recognised the *evils* of full-blown nationalism. Its evil, he contends, lies in its denying 'both the divisibility of sovereignty and the reality of a plurality of loyalties and identities within a healthy world' (1997: 182). The 'pressures of modern government, imposing uniformity in area after area of life, are inherently destructive of many of the particularities which constitute a recognisable ethnic culture.' Only if we move on to a *multi-ethnic state*, making for 'new ethnic-based nationalisms' will that 'healthy world' be possible.

We should not assume, then, that the *only* form of 'nationalism' is one of the militantly 'cleansing' kind. No doubt some form of 'purifying' is almost inevitable - as, for example, with the anti-imperialist movements sweeping the world in the twentieth century, of which India's resolve to rid their country of the British was a remarkable instance. Especially among oppressed peoples, to be moved by deeply held feelings of love and loyalty, a form of *bhakti*, for the cultural and national traditions that have made them what they are, shaped their core self-identity - in spite of invaders' attempts to weaken, even destroy, that identity - is not just natural, it is an empowering sentiment rightly encouraged by nationalists. When nationalist feeling coincides with the natural claims of ethnic identity, and especially if it is reinforced by a commonly held religious identity, then an even stronger sense of *inclusive identity within the community of the 'nation'* will very naturally follow.

But confusing questions arise: there is the 'othering' involved in this heightened sense of nationalism - does it need an enemy to survive? There is the fear of wider togetherness, xenophobia and the fear of embracing and inter-national human community, with all the pluralism of life this calls for, that such nation-bound identities are likely to engender. There is the clamour for cultural uniformity, and denial of plurality. So there is too the danger that one form of religion will be promoted, perhaps nationally re-invented and brought to dominance, with that religion and the power of its symbols exploited merely to strengthen the State and its claims. For what cultural life has greater mythic potency than religious tradition in creating sharply defined identities?

Nationalism Inherently Religious?

This leads, finally, to the question raised among students of religion as to whether nationalism itself is inherently religious. As Ninian Smart made clear (1996: chapter 6 on 'The Social Dimension') nearly all the typical dimensions of *religious* life are also part of the way we saw nationalism expressing itself. There are *rituals* on great national occasions with dramatically choreographed parades and military music, there are flags and other emblems of state. There are national *myths* glorifying the history of the nation, perhaps intensifying sentiments of glory achieved through suffering. At such occasions there may well be overwhelming feelings of belonging to a *community* set apart from others in the human race, of being in touch with a *world-transcending* destiny. The willingness to deny oneself and even give up life for the sake of the nation is even characteristic of those not especially fervent in their nationalism. Even when it has to be artificially invented (Nazi cultural underpinning was merely one such), nationalists will want to feel a strong sense of the special cultural ethos of the people to whom they belong, marking them as different from, usually superior to, 'others'. Conserving this distinct way of life and its values is seen as a paramount duty. And so many of these typical ways of being nationalist are also typical of the religious life.

Nationalism, in other words, is very close to religion in its form and scope. Yet the limitations of the nationalist spirit make it necessary to draw a line between the two. It can be 'religious', yes. But it is a very limited expression of being religious, often an aberrative and distorting way of being religious. For in radical nationalism it is the power and sovereignty of the State - embodied in its leadership - that is in the end made absolute, and within all religions there are counter-dynamics to this that cannot allow the State to be absolute. The sovereignty of the State is neither absolute nor indivisible. Even if its authority has necessarily to be accepted as very great, its limits too are in the end very clear. Not to accept those limits - as religious faith invariably insists, is to be seduced from core-factors in faith, seduced by the attractions of a different kind of power than that set forth by faith. So, the dangers of nationalist religion, or 'religious nationalism' - as some historians of religion like Mark Juergensmeyer (1996) refer to the Hindutva movement - are equalled by the dangers apparent within religious institutions when those religions allow their institutional forms, and the leadership embodied in them, to be identified with absolute power and absolute truth. T.N.Madan (1998: 273) is surely correct in affirming that '...religion itself is devalued when it becomes (a means to)...the acquisition of power'.

Chapter 10
Faith in a Common Ethnicity

Nationalist and ethnic loyalties, then, overlap - and interpenetrate with religion - in crucial ways. Yet, ethnicity is distinct from statehood, certainly as found in the nationalism of the modern state. So, here we have another area of changing self-perception involving crisis and conflict: *the growing and empowering sense of social and cultural self-identity among ethnic groups regarding themselves as distinct, not innately part of the dominant community.*

Both in Afghanistan and Iraq 'tribal' loyalty and inter-tribal rivalry have been key components in the internal complexities, manipulated by invading forces as so often in imperialist dealings with the people they 'sub-alterned'. In creating the nations of Afghanistan and Iraq, while the British were thus bringing divided 'tribes' into new combinations, they were fully intent on manipulating the tribal tensions thus involved in maintaining their control. Recently, in Afghanistan, Pashtun identity was an important factor even in the Talibanising process. More obvious still was Saddam Hussein's dependence on the absolute loyalty of his own Tikrit clan in maintaining ruthless dominance of the Iraqi people. Tribal and clan identities were not the only cohesive factors. Both a sense of being Iraqi (that is a national identity) and a sense of being Muslim (that is an Islamic religious identity) also locked people into feelings of a shared destiny in the face of adversity - both the oppression of the Saddam regime and the humiliating impotence felt as a result of the US/UK invasion.

In the Sudan, while the main conflict earlier was between strict Islamists in the North and Christians in the South, what has come to prominence in 2004 is the inter-Muslim conflict - involving competing claims on natural resources and differing nationalist loyalties - between Arab militia (the dreaded *janjaweed,* backed by the Sudanese government) and Black Africans. As in most such conflicts, what has directly contributed to the violence has been the free flow of modern arms, usually from ·unscrupulous outsiders, and the arbitrary boundaries marking modern nation-states resulting from earlier imperial control. Natural ethnic and even geographical boundaries had little to do with imperialist nation-making, and the consequences have been tragic. Nor, in their condemnation of Sudan, are the motives of world powers entirely clear.

Tragic tensions too, both ethnic and religious - between Serbs, Croats, Bosnian and Kosovo Muslims - have led to tragically violent conflict in the Balkans. The larger nation-state of Yugoslavia, created again more by outside ideological coercion than by indigenous compulsion, and kept intact for several years under the iron hand of Marshall Tito, has disintegrated, and deep inner tensions are still felt in some regions.

Ethnic Identities in India

In this chapter, however, I intend to confine the discussion to *ethnic identities in India*, and that too the north-eastern region. We could debate endlessly what descriptive term to use here. 'Tribal' is most usual. But this term, and generic appellations such as 'animist', 'primitive' and so on, are found demeaning by the more ideologically aware in these groups. So I will largely avoid them. Nearly all the suggested alternatives, though, are problematic for one reason or another: 'indigenous', 'traditional', 'primal/primordial', or India's Sanskrit-derived terms, *'adivasi'* (first inhabitants), *'vanavasi'* (forest people), *'girijan'* (hill people). I will mostly, therefore, use the term 'ethnic', though even this is often felt by the peoples concerned to convey prejudice, and means using clumsy expressions such as 'resurgent ethnic groups' and the like. In some contexts reverting to 'tribal' will be inevitable. An advantage of using the term 'ethnic' is its wider range of meaning. And this movement for an 'empowering sense of cultural self-identity' is global, wider than would be meant if we spoke of 'tribal resurgence'.

The range of ethnicity in India certainly surprises people. Occasionally foreign tourists are surprised to find they are not allowed to visit certain wildlife sanctuaries in regions of Assam or the hilly North, such as Arunachal or Manas. 'Tribal insurgency' is likely to be given as the reason. And even if mention is also made of India's ethnic groups being stirred up by a 'foreign hand', non-Indians still remain surprised, for there is rarely recognition outside India of either how widespread (461 'scheduled tribes' is one semi-official count) or how greatly diverse are the Subcontinent's 'unassimilated' ethnic communities. Certainly there is little knowledge of how marked by ferment, by change and by resistance to the changes worked out by others, is this Indian ethnic life.

The official classification of 'tribals' within India is rather crude and shows the 'blatant prejudice of the dominant people' (Jaganath Pathy in 'The Idea of Tribe and the Indian Scene', Chaudhuri 1992: 49). Official lists of criteria have included: animism, primitiveness, being carnivorous in food habits, living naked or seminaked, being fond of drinking and dance. Unofficially there may well even be mention of 'dislike of work', being 'fickle and childlike', or some such degradingly pejorative term. Not only do such descriptions reveal the contempt with which the dominant community usually perceives 'tribals'. They are defining criteria that miss the mark completely with at least 90% of those listed as 'tribals'. So statistics themselves are not very accurate. But in the 2001 census around 84 million people were classified as 'tribal'. Almost half are found in the central region; nearly 30% are in the western region; 12% are in the North East, with the remaining smaller numbers being in the South and the Islands of Andamans and Nicobar.

There is, then, a very large number and great diversity of distinctive ethnic communities in India. Their distinctive histories give us special insight into the contrasting ways in which they are 'Indian'. They respond very differently to attempts to incorporate them into a wider cultural self-identity, whether these are attempts to 'modernise', to 'Hinduise', or to re-form their identity by way of religions such as Christian, Buddhist or Muslim. The great efforts made to Indianize or perhaps Hinduize have met with hugely varied response - anything from fierce resistance to enthusiastic collaboration. In any case, this complex process of interaction between traditional ethnic worlds and worlds from outside that seek in differing ways to change them means that many 'ethnic groups' are now in a process of transition. 'Tribes in transition' is one way of classifying these changing communities. (As Beteille in *A Tribe in Transition*, 1987).

The issue of Dalit liberation and their new consciousness is taken up in part III. While there are some clear points of convergence, it would be a mistake to link Dalit liberation too closely with the new ethnic consciousness explored in this section. Both, though, at their resistant edges do have an increasingly strong sense of identity as people to be differentiated from 'Hinduism'. Both have developed a consciousness of having been socially, economically, politically oppressed by the dominant communities. Both, to very differing degrees and with differing results, have found their symbolic world impinged on by the mythic worlds of classical Hinduism.

Sanskritising Tribal Identities

When it comes to the Hindu tradition's epic-stories (Maha-bharata and Ramayana) and their hero-characters there is little doubt that often it is from India's distinctive ethnic cultures themselves that the heroes have come, not from Vedic or Sanskritic sources. Even Dalit identity, traumatised in ways almost 'pathological' by caste mis-shaping - as some of their own leaders have contended - has not always been forced to give itself an entirely negative self-image as a result of the re-mythologising impact of Epic and Puranic traditions. Panchama Vaishnavas in Andhra, for example, claimed a sacral role that transcended the profaning impurity loaded on Dalit identity by the dictates of caste.

In general, though, it is the less remote 'tribal' communities that have found their identity given more of a positive re-shaping by the bardic stories of the Epics. In fact they are not far wide of the mark who say that many of the perhaps 2,378 caste communities of India were once ethnically distinct 'tribal' communities that became incorporated into the Brahmanic dharmic system, in the process being Hinduised and Sanskritised. Many such communities long ago made the transition from 'tribe' to 'caste'. Others remain distinct enough still to be identified as 'tribal', even some who have been relatively 'Sanskritised'. In Assam, for instance, Sankaradeva's Vaishnava mission some five centuries ago was highly successful in the sense of partially Sanskritising the many ethnic peoples of the Brahmaputra plains and foothills; a number of them are still identified as 'tribal'. Relatively few, though, of the peoples of the more remote hill states have been touched by such explicitly classical Hindu traditions and taken on explicitly Hindu names. And it is when people identify themselves by the names of divine figures from a wider cultural world that people's own self-identity begins to be redefined, and the sense of who they are is re-shaped.

The Epics themselves, then, reflect the long history of interaction between Brahmanic and other ethnic worlds, and how very disparate peoples became incorporated into dharmic society. Hanuman, the great leader of the monkey people, is but one of the characters drawn into the story of the *dharma*-king, Rama. Krishna, the dark-hued hero from pastoral people, is but one of the non-Vedic hero-figures who eventually becomes crucial to the Mahabharata's story. Yet, there is the irony that unlike the Dalit communities, the self-identities of the majority of India's peoples still referred to as 'tribals' have not been so indelibly stamped by the impact of Brahmanic *dharma*. Their identity as 'tribals' is precisely because they have not been dharmically assimilated. Not having been 'assimilated in(to) the main body of the people' is even seen by the Indian Government's Backward Classes Commission as a mark of being classed as 'tribal' (Lalsangkima 1998: 52).

When ethnic communities, therefore, who may be geographically as well as culturally far removed from that dharmic world, are referred to (especially by Hindu nationalists) as 'Hindus', it is little more than ideological polemic. The new Dalit consciousness argues along the same lines when Dalits are identified as 'Hindus'. In the course of India's long and complex history many ethnic groups have acquiesced in becoming part of the wider dharmic world of Hindus, maybe quite willingly deciding to be identified as 'Hindu', even gladly claiming this wider identity as an essential enlarging and enhancing of who they feel themselves to be, so that this Hindu-linked identity becomes an essential part of their emerging new consciousness. To critical historical analysis this is Brahmanic 'hegemony'. To more traditional interpretation it is a sign of Hinduism's all-embracing assimilative tolerance, Hindu culture's ability to provide mutual interdependence for a vast range of differing groups.

Christian Conversion in the North-east

There is another crucial, controversial political and religious fact today relating to a number of ethnic groups, as well as to a significant proportion of Dalit communities. The dynamics of recent history has led to their opting for a consciously *non-Hindu identity,* as the way to respond to the crisis that modernity poses in one form or another for all ethnic cultures. Clearly this was not a new identity that was politically imposed: the British colonial powers, with individual exceptions no doubt, were in general alarmed by changes in the status quo. For a long period, in fact, there was rigorous opposition to 'natives' becoming Christian. Converts to Christianity were not allowed to serve as sepoys for example. And (as Richard Eaton has pointed out in relation to Nagaland) 'Nagas as a whole converted most dramatically only after the dismantling of the colonial state and the expulsion of foreign missionaries by the newly independent government of India' (Longchar 1999: 1-29). The census of 1991 shows a *five-fold increase* in the number of Christians in the North East compared to 1951, immediately after Independence (See too Downs in Robinson & Clarke 2003: 391).

In spite of the fact that among the Nagas and probably many other ethnically distinct peoples conversions occurred at a much faster rate in areas and among groups where there were very few or no foreign missionaries (the Sema Nagas for instance), the charge of missionary 'inducements' being the reason for such changes of identity is not so easily dealt with. Even though few missionaries offered direct and deliberate 'inducements'('If you convert, we will give you the following material benefits...'), the anomalies in their converting role cannot be easily ignored. As representing the imperialist western power in Asia, the very presence of foreign missionaries in an indirect way acted as an 'inducement'. Primarily, though, it was precisely the felt need for a new identity that effected such a change.

Frederick Downs, another historian who has written with considerable authority about those peoples of the North East of India who converted to Christianity, has concluded that *identity* is the key interpretive category for understanding the far-reaching changes of some recent histories there. To summarise briefly, his argument is that the incursion into the North-East by the British administrative power in the 19th century traumatised the 'tribal' groups directly affected by the new politico-economic regime. They faced a crisis of identity. This was further deepened by the transfer of power in 1947 to the new Indian government, whose central leaders and local agents were regarded with even more suspicion than the British.

Ethnic groups such as Mizo and Naga people may now seem to be marked by quite a strong sense of common identity. Previously, though, there was not only a lack of connectedness due to wide dispersement in remote hill regions, with just the village unit, or perhaps clan relationship, providing the only strong sense of identity. Sub-groups within these major communities were deeply divided.

Animosities between villages could be very fierce indeed, raiding other villages seen as a group duty. Often there was not even the bond of a commonly understood language to hold them together. Whatever may have been the originating rootage, even people of the same ethnic grouping frequently had to communicate through gestures and signs. But this lack of general cohesiveness should not blind us to the easily aroused sense of belonging together over against any 'outsider', especially any outside rule, as exemplified by the various armed resistance movements against the British incursion and setting up of colonial rule - the Khasi Wars of 1829-33, the Jaintia Rebellion of 1860-62, the Khonoma Uprising of 1878, the Kuki Rebellion of 1919-20 and the Jadagong Cult rebellion ten years later (Downs 387 in Robinson & Clarke. Downs also lists a clear summary of the 'traumatic' changes the British administration brought, p.388).

It was initially the impact of this alien colonial process that made for a renewed sense of common origins. Yet, that process also broke down locally binding traditions, even when the Administration did not intend this. The result was that some new sense of common identity became vital and inevitable. At this critical point it was what was believed to be offered by newness innate to Christianity's belief-system, including in particular the 'modernising' educational system the missions were given reponsibility for, that provided just such a common new bond, a unifying self-identity. In effect, then, the new faith not only strengthened a common sense of identity. In some ways it actually created the powerful sense of being a common people that has emerged especially among the various groups of Mizos and Nagas.

Richard Eaton (*ibid*.) has convincingly added a further dimension to this identity-shaping process. In a Weber-like way, he links the process of being drawn into an enlarged *macrocosmic* world with the indigenous theologies and cosmologies of the Naga peoples in particular, depending to some extent on Horton's thesis regarding African experience. This new macrocosmic experience brought a new significance for the higher deities. For the powerful Christian God, Creator of heaven and earth, of which they now heard, was seen by Ao and Sema Nagas as corresponding with their indigenous high gods, Tsungren and Alhou. The complications in missionaries' translating of such a God for Angamis is an interesting, even amusing sidelight in the process, but this is not the place to go into details.

In general, then, the God who was to become the focus of their worship, and the basis of their new identity, was not a wholly alien Being. Continuities were there, including no doubt corresponding facets of the perceived saving work of Christ, though Eaton suggests nothing along these lines. Others, by way of contrast - in the case for instance of the role of the cock in the mythic tradition of the Kashis of the North East - have seen significant points of continuity with the role of Christ in Christian interpretation.

North-Eastern Indigenous Christian Identity

Whatever the continuities, this process of change, and especially the change in religious faith and worldview, did throw up considerable tension between modernity and tradition within the Christianised ethnic groups. To some extent this has reflected tensions between indigenous self-identity and the new 'Christian' identity missionaries believed to be required. There have recently been a number of important critical studies of this issue particularly by Mizo Christian scholars. We might note for example K.Thanzauva's *Theological Basis for Social Transformation...in the Context of Mizoram* (1993), Mangkhosat Kipgen's *Christianity and Mizo Culture* (1997), and Lalsangkima Pachuau's *Ethnic Identity and Christianity in Northeast India* (2003). Each approaches the subject somewhat differently, with perspectives in differing degrees indebted to historical, missiological (with a social-anthropological emphasis) and theological disciplines. Of the numerous specific points of tension between indigenous tradition and the new identity, I will focus only on that of *the role of drum and dance*. This touches indigenous life at several related points. For, drum and dance were closely linked with shamanic healing, possession by spirit(s), and events relating to the seasons of nature, as well as being a crucial means to community togetherness and cultic worship.

As L.Pachuau's is the most recent work, we will refer largely to that. It is clear that a number of the early missionaries to the area (especially Welsh Presbyterians arriving late in the nineteenth century in the north of Mizoram, with some Baptists in the south) were committed to the quite radical principle of 'the creation of independent and indigenous churches' (Pachuau 1998: 131) To them this meant the 'three-fold indigenous principle' of self-support, self-propagation and self-government. Allowing Mizos to be self-governing, though, was a step the missionaries found quite difficult to take. For this meant indigenous people making decisions about what, in traditional indigenous practices, was appropriate and what not appropriate for Mizo Christians. However, once Mizos themselves had been well grounded in the Welsh missionary version of proper faith and practice, a few of their own leaders sometimes proved as opposed to key traditions from the Mizos' past as the Welsh were.

Here we should not exaggerate the discontinuity that was expected. There clearly was a genuine desire to keep a strong sense of Mizo identity among their new Christians. And the Welsh feeling for self-identity as well as for what constitutes good religion has usually been very different from the more staid and formal English attitude. The place of song and bardic poetry is also very different. Indeed, one missionary wrote in the late 1930s of how differently a 'mystic Celt' and an English Christian are likely to see the outbreaks of ecstasy there (Kipgen 308). Even so, missionary fears of their Mizo Christians reverting to tribal 'demonism' and its 'grossly immoral practices' rarely abated. There were, however, so very few missionaries that, in spite of their greatly respected status, their control was always going to be stretched. And one or two were remarkably aware of the need for cultural continuity.

From 1905 to the 1930s there was a series of extraordinary outbreaks of corporate ecstasy in the hills of the Northeast, referred to as 'revivals', in that they are strikingly similar - with clear differences too - to the phenomena experienced in the Welsh evangelical revivals, the last of which occurred in 1904-5. In the course of these community experiences, cultural forms previously quite vigorously suppressed by most mainstream Christian leaders - missionary or Mizo - erupted spontaneously and uncheckably. Various forms of ecstatic dance and other bodily movements, accompanied by the insistent rhythm of the old Mizo drum, as well as a wide range of vocal sounds and indigenous singing, were the most common forms of expression at these times.

Puma-songs were one special form of singing that re-emerged. Its origins are obscure, but the infectious impact was great, such was the emotive, dance-inducing, and often triumphalist style of the *Puma* verses, that included much hypnotic repetition as with all the singing during these periods of ecstasy. These ecstatic phenomena lasted for days and even weeks. In traditional Mizo culture (as with all such 'ethnic' community events) alcohol was drunk freely as part of the way of breaking through normal inhibitions. Naturally, church leaders issued a total ban on drinking, as well as on the *Puma* songs. And even the missionary strictures on the drum and various forms of dance were accepted, at least in the main centres, for some time. Yet, even among the missionaries, there were a few (the Welshman E.L.Mendus for example) who recognised that the strength of the Mizo church was deeply indebted to those ecstatic movements. Others - and not only missionaries - described any aspects of these movements characterised by uncontrolled spiritual abandon as 'the work of Satan', or 'a resurgence of heathenism', even as a movement to 'stop people from becoming Christian' (Pachuau p.162).

The tension within the Mizo community obviously could not easily be resolved. A number of ecstatics formed their own groups, usually committed to a more radical inclusion of traditional cultural forms. Interestingly, even Pentecostal opinion at first seemed to be that most of this ecstasy was 'devilish'. Later, though, quite a number of those for whom the ecstatic experience was of the essence of being Christian turned away from mainstream churches and became Pentecostalist. One group of a triumphalist spirit believed the Mizo people were the new Israel, chosen to reveal God's ways to the whole region and far beyond. In the year 2000 I heard even the Chief Minister of Mizoram State publicly voicing this vision of Mizos' national and Asian role.

For a while the compromise agreed on in mainstream Christian circles was that as long as indigenous traditions such as the old seasonal festivals were merely being 'commemorated', they could be allowed as celebrative performance. In other words they were part of Mizo history, and to that extent part of prior identity. But such practices - according to the official church position - must not be seen as an essential, integral part of present Mizo-Christian self-identity. They are not to be part of actual worship. On the other hand, the drum, an indigenous style of singing and music, and even on occasion dance, have to a large extent become acceptable - though still not in all cases as part of normal 'sacred' church worship.

But, the deeper resonance of the drum, the hidden power of dance and song within Mizo consciousness, can hardly be confined to some non-sacred corners. Mizo self-identity in its unconscious depths is still deeply bound up with all that was happening during those ecstatic movements, even if their particular form was conditioned by the crisis of the times. While modernity and conformity may well have won a number of battles in the struggle with the less controllable dimensions of tradition, to retain tradition solely in commemorative form is not only artificial, it just cannot be held in captivity there. But analogous struggles can be seen in most 'ethnic' communities in the Northeast and elsewhere throughout ethnic Christianity, including Africa and South America..

Other recent writings (e.g. Longchar 1995, Longchar & Vashum 1998) by Christians of the North East and Eastern tribal regions of India, reflecting on their tribal identity and the implications of this for an authentic tribal theology, give great emphasis to their relationship to their *land*. The spirit-powers by which many daily activities, and therefore significant dimensions of self-identity, are determined, are bound up with all the natural phenomena that make up their environment, their territory. As Nirmal Minz puts it: '...we live in a world of spirits. Land defines our personhood. Reciprocity and the concept of nature as our relative, make us...' (Longchar & Vashum 1998: 5). A.Wati Longchar stresses the significance of the important Spirit Lijaba, meaning 'One who enters', both as the home-enterer and earth-enterer, and so home-dweller and earth-dweller. This is a prominent Ao Naga name for the supreme Being (*op.cit.* 27-33). 'The land is not mere space; it is a place that gives identity to the community. It owns people. Without land there is no personhood, no identity....Tribal people dance and sing with the land itself (herself)'.

K.Thanzauva (1995), reflecting on the theological meaning of Mizo tradition, speaks of 'a community model of God-self-world relationship' (which is remarkably akin - though Thanzauva makes no such comparison - to that 'primordial' vision of reality articulated by Vaishnava and, to a less extent, Saiva theistic Hindus, using a triadic God-self-nature model in which God is the Inner Controller). God is envisioned as 'bodying forth', as the mother does, which means that the land, territory, space, is integral to the Mizo concept of their history, their selfhood, and this is contrasted with dominant western attitudes.

No doubt there is in some of these writings a degree of romantising, perhaps a superimposing of globally burgeoning indigeneity and the growing ecological concensus on how humans should relate to earth's life. But their pointers are important. We return in a later section to the implications of ecological vision for human self-identity.

The North-East's Political Struggles

How, then, do these inner struggles, seen in the course of changing religious and cultural identities, relate to the more violent *political* struggles of recent years in the Northeast? Militant Indian nationalists are convinced that there is a clear causal line between the widespread Christianising under British rule and the violent tribal insurgency movements, beginning from around 1960, aimed at seceding from India and the Union. A Christian-based identity, say Hindu nationalists, is inevitably alienated from an Indian national identity. As a general principle it is rather easy to show that this is not only a false assumption, but is itself a cause of alienation and disaffection. It was certainly the already alienated and disaffected condition of Dalit communities that led so many to become Christian. Was this also the case with these other communities whose ethnic self-identity was so clearly distinctive from that of the pan-Indian national body?

As we have seen, that strong sense of being part of a wider ethnic community - especially in the case of the new Mizo and Naga self-identity - was itself deeply indebted to both the initial impact of British colonialism and then to the Christianising process, especially the educational work. The sense of being Mizo and Naga actually emerged far more strongly and more inclusively than before. But there was now also a sense of being *Christian*. Both dimensions of the new identities contributed to the increased feelings of antagonism in relation to 'pan-Indic' people, who were seen as very different from their own ethnic community. The ever more militant Hindutva denunciations of the Christian communities within India have merely served to intensify feelings of alienation, though ever-increasing amounts of central monetary aid to border states has ensured sufficient political loyalty to avoid rupture from the Union.

Asoso Yonuo, a Naga, wrote in 1974 that it was their fear of 'losing their identity' in the face of growing moves towards a 'Hindu rule' that led the Naga National Council to take a more separatist stance. Not merely regional autonomy of some sort, but a 'sovereign Nagaland state' then became their demand. It was not only what they saw as the growing Hinduisation of India's politics. A growing number of leaders of Northeastern regions, perhaps Nagas in particular, experienced what they felt to be humiliating treatment on the part of 'converted Hindus and Muslims in Assam and Manipur who regarded them as 'untouchables'...', mainly because it was their custom to eat both beef and pork. So there were real as well as imagined animosities, which were 'skilfully nurtured and manipulated' (Pachuau p. 223) by the secessionist leaders. A 'politics of identity' became inevitable. As Pachuau puts it: 'The people's self-understanding of their Christian identity became a pervading factor in their socio-political self-definition', a self-definition that grew out of 'the interaction between Christianity and the old traditions. With this new sense of identity shaped significantly by their new religion, the new society faced a wider new world of politics.' And it was, as we noted earlier, during this post-Independence period, with foreign missionaries withdrawn, that conversion to Christianity has taken place at a more rapid pace than ever before.

It has to be stated, though, that the mainstream churches 'were never officially involved' in the moves for seceding from the Union, and regularly spoke out against the use of violence as a political strategy. A number of ecstatic 'prophets', on the other hand, spoke out fiercely in favour of separation as a truly Christian state. And many of the leaders of the insurgency groups were strongly committed Christians, and saw their Christian identity as a reason for breaking from the Delhi rulers. While the more conciliatory stance and statements of the official churches, especially in Mizoram, evoked the anger and often disaffection of those fighting and dying for separation, it did mean that the churches remained in a position to mediate. Soon after the violent insurrection in 1966, the church officials at the time were forcibly persuaded by the Mizo National Front to sign a declaration stating their rejection of the 'Indian Government of idol worshippers', and their acceptance of 'the Government of Mizoram which is a Christian government...' It was not long, though, before the President of the Front, when meeting with the Christian Peace Mission Commitee, promised that such force would not be used again against church leaders (Pachuau p. 225).

In general, then, we see points of ambiguity on the part of the Christian communities concerning their national identity. Their ethnic and religious differences are very clear. And in view of what they see as demeaning acts done against them by Indians from alien ethnic and religious communities, their allegiance to what they see as Hindu India is tested by serious doubts regarding such an identity for themselves. But this is very far from saying that political loyalty to the Union is not possible. In practice the acceptance of some sense of being 'Indian' is very likely indeed.

I close this section by noting how significant it is that Dalits and tribal peoples are seen very clearly by aggressive missionaries, whether Christian, Hindu or Muslim, as well as by liberationists of broader vision, as comprising a decisive frontier area where there is a battle for the soul of India, or the struggle for a more justly treated body of the oppressed. It is not merely their 'vulnerability' and therefore the ease of access that accounts for this. Rather, it is the fact that in terms of their self-identity, their sense of how they relate to wider worlds, they are still very much at the crossroads. For some groups that 'wider world' is wholly threatening to their sense of identity; for others it offers new possibilities of enhanced self-identity. In any case, it is on this frontier - though not the North-East but in 'tribal' areas of Gujarat, Bihar and Orissa - that most of the violent acts against Christian 'missionaries' and their converts have taken place in the recent past. Some of this violence may be genuinely indigenous resistance from tribal tradition; some is clearly manufactured by outside forces.

Chapter 11
Resisting the New Globalist Identity

Fundamentalism is not the only form of reaction to modernity. New-agers, deep-greens, and many in the very mixed *anti-globalist* movement, are all part of the resistance. As critics of the 'neo-liberal' (neo-conservative!) global stance increasingly taken in recent times, new internationalists, radical economists, NGO local activists, urban social workers, postcolonialists, multiculturalists, remnant socialists and many others have also to be included in the opposition. It is, though, not the change necessary to the modernising process as such that is resisted. What is opposed is the highjacking of that process by the powerful forces of the Right, to the extent that it is now difficult to disentangle modernisation and capitalist globalisation.

Cultural & Consumerist Imperialism
The issue is well put in a penetrating essay by Joe Arun (Fernando 2002: 242). While global connections deepen 'a sense of the interdependent character of human society', the way they have in fact developed 'creates a conflict between the global market and peoples' cultures, often leading to the domination of the powerful over the powerless'. And what must not be lost sight of is that 'the globalisation process is fundamentally a cultural process'. It is a process in which 'people restructure their institutions, reimagine their finitudes, and reconstruct meanings for their lives'. Arun rightly refers to the writing of such critics as John Tomlinson (1999), as well as to Anthony Giddens (whose approach we have already looked at in some detail). Like Giddens, but with a more critical perspective, Tomlinson contends that 'globalisation lies at the heart of modern culture; cultural practices lie at the heart of globalisation' (1999: 1), and the ensuing 'capitalist monoculture' is a powerfully insidious 'cultural imperialism'. (Gert Ruppell also provides an astute critique of the globalising process in 'Liberation of Humanity? What Kind of Challenge is Globalism?'; followed by a similarly critical analysis by I.Mohan Razu, 'Globalisation and Under-Development as Two Sides of the Same Coin: 'Development as if Subalterns do not matter', in G. Robinson (ed.), 2000. *Challenges and Responses*, Bangalore: ATC).

251

Max Stackhouse, in general less pessimistically critical of the globalising process, is more explicit than most ethicists and cultural critics in pointing explicitly to the *religious* dimension of our corporate life. His central argument is that 'political, economic and cultural values' are always 'nested in moral and religiously-held perspectives' (2002: 6) . This position is more fully worked out in the essay by Scott Thomas, on 'The Global Resurgence of Religion and the Changing Character of International Politics', in the collection to which Stackhouse writes his introduction. Those political theorists, claims Thomas, who once took for granted that religion and all its influences must be 'privatised, marginalised, or confined to an isolated sphere by the state', have been compelled by the global resurgence of religion to acknowledge 'the global role of religion and its inevitable social and cultural pluralism...' Thus, 'a new approach to international order is required' (*Op.cit.*111).

In spite of the compulsion – stimulated by religious as much as by humanist faith – to hope for 'one world', optimistic belief (with certain reservations no doubt) in the 'transformational' effect of the globalising process (Stackhouse 2002: p.3) is problematic. Again, religion itself poses counter-forces here. In particular, at the heart of this globalising process there is the rampant consumerism of our times, an accelerating sense of need to consume more, to possess more, and so to exploit more fully the earth's resources. In affluent societies, people's sense of who they are, their self-identity, becomes more and more dependent on the goods they consume. And the world's impoverished continue to be denied even a subsistence share of what is produced from earth's resources. The gulf widens, a gulf created by greed, by that self-indulgence identified by so many forms of religious faith as one of the main obstacles to spiritual growth. In globalist terms, then, faith that speaks of ego-restraint, that offers a ground for self-identity that counters self-indulgence, is as great a human need as ever.

Ironically, at the heart of today's global struggles is one faith-oriented power-group in the West (based in the oil-lands of Texas, with their commercial institutions) locked in ferocious battle with an extremist group in the Islamic world. Both, then, stand in reaction to key strands of modernity. Yet, one vigorously seeks to encourage and exploit globalisation, and consumerist life-values one fears. The other - also close to the ground-resources (literally) fuelling the world's expanionist life-style - vigorously resists consumerist and globalising institutions that it sees as evil products of western modernity.

What is 'Modernity'?

What, though, are other key characteristics of 'modernity'? Is not one of them an almost boundless range of viewpoints on the world and its meaning - i.e. pluralism – overtly at least? Yet, certain typical ways of thinking do stand out, even dominate, and have been subject to vigorous criticism from one or other counter-perspective. Within 'modernity' we noted, for example, the ultimate value given – again, ostensibly - to *individual* identity. As the thinker who 'inaugurated the discourse of modernity'- to quote the radical social critic Habermas - Hegel pointed to subjective freedom, the right to criticism of all tradition, each person's responsibility for their own actions, and the ability to know one's own identity without reference to given roles grounded in religion, as comprising the very 'dialectic of enlightenment'.

If 'dialectic' entails a constant countering of opposites ('thesis' faced by 'antithesis' were Hegel's terms) and the irony of inner contradiction (moving on to a provisional resolving in 'synthesis' as Hegel saw it), then we certainly have an abundance of that in modernity. For all the huge emphasis on 'freedom of choice', in reality, as we noted earlier, many of the institutions of modern life allow less and less significance to the individual. With the huge power acquired by modern corporations and the military might flaunted when felt desirable by governments so clearly interlocked with these powerful commercial conglomerates, our most influential institutions and their orbitting bodies make talk of 'individual choice' laughable. With the market (providing seductive goodies) and the military (proving who has real muscle) as our great gods, how can there possibly be the dialectic between personal self-identity and corporate self-identity necessary for true humanness as well as basic to religion?

Religious faith - and even from time to time liberal critics - will no doubt speak of these dilemmas in very different ways. In all the great world religions, even in differing ways and with divergent emphases, overcoming the *other-destructive lusts* of ego, pride, greed, and suchlike inclinations of our 'lower' nature, are central in pointing

253

the path to the *summum bonum*, whatever is envisioned as this most desirable goal of life. Self-denial, conforming to life's ultimate Goal, acceptance of an ultimate Power, an ethic involving com-passion in some way - again, all worked out in varied forms - are at the heart of faith's understanding of what it is to be truly human.

Also seen as a typical part of a 'modern' worldview has been the virtual absolutising of rationalism, the 'scientific spirit' and its detached objectivity? And it is but a small step to the equally pervasive belief in the earth-mastering power of technology. Much of the challenge to return to a more holistic view of reality has come from the eco-feminist movement, that sees an atomistic, objectifying approach to knowledge, with its emphasis on 'mastering', as essentially masculine. But I leave further questions of sexual identity to the next chapter.

The Globalism of Religious Mission?

Huge questions of self-identity are raised by the innate dynamics of globalisation. In a 'globalised world', even the missioning activity of religious bodies can be perceived as of a piece with the negative dynamics of globalisation. The Hindutva movement, for example, sees Christian missioning and conversion as having a direct and organic link with the globalising goals pursued by western nations - and their trans-national corporations.

It is, of course, not only Hindus who see things this way. Islam too may have its effective missioning strategy, also seen as threatening by Hindus. But Muslim people generally are gripped by the same conviction, not entirely without basis, that the Christian West is intent on shaping the world in its own image, and aims to destroy Islam as part of this plan. It is not only by means of their grossly more powerful military resources (with Pakistan at present as the only Muslim nation with nuclear weapons) that Christendom is seen as intending to overpower Islam. Following up their humiliatingly easy defeats of two Muslim nations, Muslims found it alarming to hear it reported that evangelists such as Billy Graham's son and his missionary troops were poised ready to move in after the marines have 'shocked and awed' Iraq into a disorientated state of readiness to submit to a new faith. Insistence that the mission's aims were not to proselytise but to minister to human need did little to change Muslim perceptions. Christian mission was once again too closely connected with both military and commercial invasion, as post-war Iraq offered hugely lucrative contracts to privileged companies, with the powerful group closely related to Vice-President Cheney first in the queue.

The fact is that many supporters of global faith-missioning do see their work as being on a par with economic globalisation. They may be critical of many aspects of that globalising culture (just as many missionaries in 19th century India were very critical of various attitudes of colonial and commercial compatriots). And it is precisely in the nature and degree of Christian critical perceptions that a possible case for any such global missioning lies (cf. Stackhouse 2000). Unless we take an isolationist position of complete withdrawal from global affairs, and leave everyone to their own devices (impossible at this juncture in world history anyway), it is rightly argued that among the many voices - all voices of faith in one form or another - heard speaking on behalf of the world's marginalised, and speaking words of hope, a suitably sensitive Christian input is one that should not, indeed cannot, be made mute. Yet, there is much ambiguity here. For, there is an eliding, a converging of globalist movements that makes it impossible wholly to differentiate the global missioning of Christian evangelists and the global missioning of corporate executives. And very naturally this is perceived as a threat to those whose cultural identity is shaped in other ways.

At the same time, Islam too is thoroughly internationalist, though often anti-globalist in the modern sense. Serious Muslims believe - as do Christians of any evangelical hue - that its message not only has worldwide significance, but in some sense has revelatory authority for everyone. It is an identity committed to furthering Islamic religious, cultural and political influence across the globe. There is an internationalist spirit inherent in most forms of Islam, as in Christianity - and in Buddhist faith in a less assertive form. For all the inner tensions between Shias and Sunnis, between Arabs and non-Arabs, tensions deriving from other national and tribal loyalties, and between militants and moderates, Islamic identity is increasingly a global identity. Yet it is also an identity in part shaped by its sense of being a victim, threatened by the power of western (often identified as 'Christian') globalising influence and military might.

255

While radical forms of both Christian and Muslim faith oppose each other's globalist outreach, resistance to what is more usually identified as 'globalisation' is far more clear in Islam. It is ironically significant, though, that so much of the oil which is the life-blood of the burgeoning consumerism at the heart of globalisation lies beneath Muslim soil - and, for all recent protestations to the contrary, has been a key cause of western ('Christian') moves to exploit Arab peoples particularly since the combustion engine began firing. Essential to radical Islamic globalising, then, is the paradox of its vigorous resistance to western globalisation. We must, however, not lose sight of the great divide among Muslims between militants and moderates regarding the means by which Islamic ends are to be realised. Terrorist methods are as abhorrent to the great majority of Muslims globally as they are to the great majority of Christians and Hindus, though for all three terrorist tactics by the *state* can so easily pass unnoticed.

In any case, to see the rampant globalising process of today as of a piece with the colonial process of yesterday is far from fanciful. In some ways, no doubt, the tentacles of influence that stretch out from the various economic-cultural outposts of the new imperialists, being more insidious, touch people's lives more compellingly than did the foreign rulers of the past, as critical economists such as Will Hutton (2002) argue. The new imperialism can never be as directly oppressive and humiliatingly threatening to self-identity as was militarily backed foreign rule. But the symbols of those new global powers are felt by many people in Muslim countries, in India and all over the world as a threat to their being, their historically shaped, culturally distinct humanness.

The activists in India who attack Macdonalds, lurid cinema posters, terminator seed distributors, the Babri Masjid, or Christian mission centres, may have differing ideologies. One strand in the newly aggressive Hindutva identity, though, is a very distinct expression of anti-globalisation. Another strand - found within India and even more where the Hindu diaspora flourishes so successfully - is quite happy to exploit to the full the financial gains to be made from global capitalism. The anti-imperialist resentment of western power, however, is a common factor, even if fear of global Islam and Christian missioning may be an even more potent strand within Hindutva's support. Muslims or Christians in India or anywhere else may be equally convinced of the dangers to local economies, local cultures, local identities by the expansion of western globalising influence, with its all-embracing economic or cultural tentacles. But uniting in common resistance is clearly difficult.

The accelerating process of globalisation, then, is seen from many different perspectives as dangerously threatening to local communities. Leave aside the loss of cultural integrity. Can anyone, even key officers of the World Trade Organisation, not be moved to tears by the fact that from 1997 to 2003 there were 20,000 suicides by small farmers in India (Andhra Pradesh and Karnataka especially) due as much to globalist agricultural policies as to greedy local money-lenders?

Crucial Role of USA in Contemporary Crisis

The economic power of the USA is crucial in this ever-quickening process of globalisation. The extent to which the present regime rejects the concept of controls by a United Nations body may show us how far it is still isolationist, wanting to be free from internationalist constraints, yet dependent upon its global role for its wealth. But it may also show how far it intends to transcend that collaborative institution through its unilateralist globalising power and influence - how far it intends to be a new form of imperialist power. Recent military action in oil-rich Iraq, accompanied by astoundingly belligerent rhetoric from key advisors to the US President, but with no credible United Nations' mandate, confirms the worst fears of those who have spoken of the 'neo-imperialism' of the new millennium (see e.g. an essay by the relatively conservative Michael Ignatieff, in *Prospect* February 2003; but cp. Hutton 2002: 182ff).

Richard Perle, for example, Chairman of the US defence policy board and on an advisory panel to the Pentagon, writes that far from the United Nations being the organ by which a 'new world order' can emerge, this will only happen by weakening and bypassing that body, by 'coalitions of the willing', those who have the power and the will, taking preemptive military action against any territory believed to be supporting 'fanatical terror' as a weapon against 'liberal civilisation' (*The Spectator,* March 2003). Making the same point in a different way, James Woolsey, who was CIA Director from 1993-

95, and the Pentagon's choice to head the postwar Iraqi ministry of information, in writes: '....this is a war to extend democracy to those parts of the Arab and Muslim world that threaten the liberal civilisation we worked to build and defend throughout the 20th century....Clearly the terror war is never going to go away until we change the face of the Middle East' (*Tribune Media Services International*, April 2003).

The role of Europe's nations in creating through recent centuries our present polarised world leaves it even more culpable than the United States. Blair (Britain), Berlusconi (Italy), and very few other European leaders apart, in Europe generally - as in America too let it be said - very large numbers of people still believe the manner in which war was waged against Iraq was politically, legally, morally, humanly wrong. Some, moreover, would question exactly what ideologues like Perle and Woolsey mean when they speak of 'democracy' and 'liberal civilisation'. The rhetoric often sounds quite grand. In reality, though, these are terms heavily loaded with the values of a very rightwing capitalist culture, with its hegemonic political style and economic system that, in its consumerist violence is seen by anti-globalisers as the ultimate threat to the world's wellbeing.

Even so, the basic notion underlying Woolsey's words - the need to engage in changing traditional worlds that are so unlike our own - is deeply embedded in a powerful strand within the western worldview, largely held as a self-evident truth. UK Prime Minister Blair's understanding of his global role may be based on a political idealism much softer-edged than that of the ideologues of his US partners in coalition military action. It is nevertheless tinged with messianic intent, based on the absolute conviction that 'strong' western nations must go out and change for the better all those situations where they see indigenous problems. Our way is *the Way* for the world. It is our inescapable duty to make sure that others share the great benefits of that way. We are to make the world in our own image. Blair's is a typical 'missionary' stance towards the world. Though within missioning circles (not only Christian, but Buddhist, Hindu, Muslim even) there are those of us who have a very different vision of their true missionary task.

Ambivalance of Mission (of any Faith)

For, talk of a 'new internationalism', or of a new human consciousness with global dimensions, is not necessarily driven by the hegemonic motives of the old imperialism. Is it always misguided to see signs of hope for our human destiny in instances of a new togetherness for peoples previously alienated from each other by seemingly unbridgeable cultural differences? Is it innately impossible for the local and the global to interpenetrate each other in such creative ways that each is enhanced? Must that which is experienced as liberating locally never be taken as universally true?

These are issues not only at the centre of postmodernist debate, with postmodernism's acceptance of cultural, ideological and even cognitive relativism. The relativist debate is central too for people of religious conviction. For inherent to religious vision is the sense of its carrying absolute truth, of its being an absolute reality. And, given the right conditions, this moves on to faith in its universal validity.

This has certainly been the case with Hindu, Buddhist and Jain belief-systems, as well as with Christian and Muslim. In spite of the frequent contention, it is just not historically true that global mission is inherently restricted to Christians and Muslims. Even when a religious community's sense of identity is closely linked with a particular geographical centre, as is the Muslim's with Macca, global identities can be implicit within this orientation. Mission - as an innate compulsion both to share a distinctive vision of things and to act in ways believed to change beneficially the lives of others - was inherent to Buddhism even in the life of the Buddha himself. Hindu identities have been generally less dynamic, more oriented to sacred-place and sacred-person, with less freedom to move beyond the set boundaries prescribing and circumscribing that identity. So it was only when other factors, such as trade, education, and political requirements, made such mobility necessary that a more globally universalising outlook developed. Within India, of course, from the earliest times 'universalising' tendencies are clear - in the 'Brahmanisation' throughout India of local cults and communities for example.

A New Human Self-Consciousness?

In an earlier section we noted how Wilfred Cantwell Smith, late Professor and Director at Harvard's Centre for the Study of World

Religions, contended that a new interpenetrating human self-consciousness, hence a new faith-consciousness, has now dawned. Smith made this point in the context of a radical critique of a 'scientific' quest for 'objective' knowledge, whether knowledge of religion or of any other aspect of human life. But his enthusiastic account of our new 'corporate critical self-consciousness' has a strongly idealist basis. Visionaries among us may, or may not, long to agree with him. Such an account, though, has to reckon with the historical reality that any such global changes to human consciousness have been brought about largely through modernity's science and technology that is the engine of the industrial, commercial and communications' revolution of recent centuries. And it was western imperial and economic power that made these changes global in scope.

Let me not be accused of equating such an account of human history with the 'end of history' thesis of Francis Fukuyama, who argues that the socialist-capitalist struggle is over, and that we have now all become part of the one great liberal capitalist world. Fukuyama badly miscalculated the negative effects of the fall of the Soviet empire and of the rise of American superpower dominance. But from the perspective of most non-western nations and their varied forms of resurgent religious consciousness, these changes have reduced them to a seemingly permanent subaltern status. We ignore at our peril this downside of any new human global consciousness there may be. For we then ignore the feelings impelling widespread anti-western, anti-globalising, often religiously expressed, resistance movements.

Even anti-globalising resistance to the pressures for globalisation creates its own global consciousness. And though the western search for new markets and for new economic resources initiated this greater global interaction of such diverse peoples, the movement is far from one-way, especially as a result of the dispersion of people from East to West, from South to North, and the new ease of communication and mobility worldwide. Perhaps it was precisely this that Smith was pointing to. There is even a new global sense among peoples of widely scattered *tribal* communities that they are the inheritors of a common primal vision, distinctively located no doubt, a common vision that a modern ecologically destructive world is sorely in need of. That all these pressures to see things globally has made an immense impact on religious people's sense of identity is very obvious. All this, too, could be seen as lending credence to Huntington's thesis, that we looked at in some detail in chapter five, on the 'clash of civilisations' in terms largely of globally expressed religious identities. His nuance-less politicising of the process still remains a serious flaw, as well as the separatist ideology undergirding it.

Chapter 12
Eco-Identities, Sex-Based Identities

(I) Eco-Identities

Evolutionary Grounding

Charles Darwin, theorist of the evolutionary process, is deservedly one of the great heroes of modernity. He is also seen - by fundamentalists and often by secularists alike - as the great enemy of creationist faith. This is yet another mistaken identity. The 'Origin of Species' is far from being an explanation of ultimate origins - or of ultimate destinies. It is to be taken merely as a description of a basic life-principle, highly complex and of supreme importance, in that great mystery which is the creative process: creation is evolutionary in form, and evolutionary theory points out key principles by which creativity proceeds. Some aspects of that process - collaborative sharing, the aesthetic dimension, the crucial role for maternal caring - are no doubt underplayed, often ignored, and the needed gene-perpetuating aggression in that process even glorified by those seeking to justify elitist dominance on evolutionary grounds. Creation is characterised not only by 'survival of the fittest' brutalities. Nature is not only 'red in tooth and claw' as depicted even by pre-Darwinians such as Thomas Hobbes.

In general, though, the 'evolution of species' can no longer be viewed as 'just a theory'. It describes biological and zoological realities. Creationist faith has to incorporate these facts, if it is truly to be faith in the reality of creation and its Creator. Obviously, religious faith that gives little or no place to creatorship (though it may have its own strongly held idea of creatureliness) does not have quite the same problem with evolution, as Buddhist and certain kinds of Vedantic writers in differing ways are quick to point out (Gosling 2001).

The ecological movement of more recent times - the belief in the interlocked interdependence of all creatures, all bio-systems - is based foursquare on evolutionary theory. That cosmic life has evolved over a huge passage of time is now a central strand in a modern worldview and is the basis for strikingly inclusive forms of human identity. Humans related biologically to their antecedent life-forms. Yet, a cosmically inclusive eco-identity for our humanness is still not dominant in a typical modern worldview.

Paradox in Eco-Vision

So, there is a paradox here. This eco-vision has become the basis for questioning other key strands of modernity, or at least of 'established' Enlightenment-grounded modernity - its basis in rationalism, the supremacy of the cerebral, scientific objectivity, the technological engineering, the exploiting of natural resources, our medical atomism, our military expertise, our anthropo-centrism, and much more that is endemic to being modern. Perhaps the most effective challenge to these fundamentals of the modern worldview has been the burgeoning counter-conviction of recent decades that to be *eco-centred* is essential to being human, to being truly biological creatures. For the sake of our humanness, our whole human outlook, our ethical values as well as religious beliefs are to become more bio-centric, less anthropo-centric (Hessel & Ruether 2000:377). Quite often it has been to pre-scientific primal and folk tradition, though enhanced by insights from modern knowledge of the world's bio-systems, that eco-exponents turn.

One outstanding such critic of modern science/technology, its irreversible link with 'patriarchal' political control and western colonial capitalism, and the effects of this on Indian farmers, is the Indian eco-activist Vandana Shiva. Her impressive critique, though seeking to reclaim folk and primal tradition, derives in part from those empirical principles claimed as the basis of the modern science that she, and other eco-visionaries, attack with such vigour. On the other hand, Vandana Shiva's eco-feminism. Indebted to Indian women's traditions, diverges sharply from much western feminism (See e.g. her *Staying Alive: Women, Ecology and Survival in India*, 1988; also, with Marie Mies, *Ecofeminism,* Zed books, London 1993).

Journals such as the *The Ecologist*, edited by two generations of Goldsmiths, and no small numbers of books, though arguing largely within the accepted paradigm of modern science, have disseminated the essential principles of this eco-vision. Similarly, writings such as those of Fritjof Capra (the *Tao of Physics* 1975, *The Turning Point* 1982, *Uncommon Wisdom* 1988, *The Web of Life* 1996, etc) have proved highly effective at a popular level in undermining naive faith in what had become the established wisdom of modern science. And along with this, bookshops everywhere have been stocked with amazing numbers of less reason-based, more intuitive new-age-style writings for whom key themes of modern science are clearly anathema. The rapidly increasing forms of 'alternative medicine' are far from the only counter-cultural movement in the West turning its back on key strands of modernity.

The Eco-Movement's Anti-Globalism

There is, for example, the more militant anti-globalist movement that makes its presence felt especially at times when the wealthy and powerful nations meet to work out their global trading strategies. The primary reason for protest may well be the obscenely unjust trading systems within which third-world farmers and producers have to struggle. In spite of the claims made for the great benefits of globalising all economies, the gulf between the world's rich and poor just widens and deepens. Anti-globalists such as Vandana Shiva place the responsibility for the many suicides among India's farmers in recent years firmly on the heads of a globalism that has destroyed both local economies and viable indigenous practices, including species-diversity. It is surely a lack of moral awareness to be indifference to, not to protest about, such destructiveness. Yet, antiglobalist demonstrators are vilified by the establishment as dangerous 'terrorists' to be crushed ruthlessly.

Anti-globalist protest, then, has as one of its sometimes far too vague reasons, the destructive results of many modern engineering and agricultural practices to our world's habitat. For all the magical seductions of modernity, no one seriously reflecting on how humans have been (mis)managing the natural world can ignore the fact of global warming, the rising sea levels, the destruction of thousands of life-species, the poisoning of others on which humans depend, massive flooding in some regions, deadly drought or raging fires in others. And even the renewed vigour of a variety of drug-resistant bacteria and viral diseases.

It can hardly be argued that our massive ecological crisis is entirely caused by market-driven capitalism, for the industries of the Soviet Union satellites continued to be crudely polluting long after those in non-communist countries were forced to clean up their output. Even so, the driving goal of quick profitability has been, and still continues to be, a major threat to earth's health. And fuelling those economies with vast amounts of oil, burning that oil as the primary energy-source (25% of the world's total by America, with a mere 5% of the world's population) also points to the principal global problem. Global warming may not be entirely the result of the startling rise in our burning of such fossil-fuels. But, that it is a major factor can only be denied by those who refuse to face the evidence. To change direction now seems to pose too great a challenge to the self-identity both of those caught up in a consumerist culture with its expected affluence and especially of those who personally profit from and are empowered by present energy-systems. Yet, without some form of quite radical change, sacrificial change to the way affluent societies have come to see themselves, it is difficult to envisage any future for modern civilisations.

Even the modest attempts - little more than gestures in effect - at Rio and especially Kyoto in the last few years of the twentieth century to respond to the growing global ecological crisis were thwarted by the short-term economic self-interest of the world's most powerful capitalist nation. And it was the consumerist self-indulgence of that economic system which has been the major force in producing the ecological crisis in the first place, even if the run-down industries of the Soviet empire's communist regimes and the hunger for cash in previously forest-rich third-world countries have also contributed to that crisis. The rapidly increased exploitation in Asia and elsewhere of forests and other natural resources by colonial powers, Britain especially, in order to feed soaring national and imperial needs, cannot but be seen as another major historical cause (e.g. Gadgil and Guha 1993 and 1995).

Resistance has at times sprung up from the reflection of sophisticated culturalists too. For example, the deep workings of *landscape* within human consciousness, as the cradle within which now hidden layers of our identities were initially nurtured, have become central to an important cultural insight - even at the level of popular TV presentation (Schama 1995). What is affirmed is the creative role of imagination in shaping human interaction with the particular natural world we inhabit. Not only does nurturing environment shape how we see ourselves and those sacred powers in which we believe. At the same time there is what the human spirit has made imaginatively of seasons, rivers, seas, mountains, deserts, forests and the many beasts and birds inhabiting them along with the human race. Imagination too is essential to the shaping of how we have come 'to see ourselves and where we belong'. In this way our landscape becomes an inner reality, an in-scape. Simon Schama's free-flowing *Landscape & Memory* (1995) and Evan Eisenberg's similarly imaginative *The Ecology of Eden* (1998) - both with Judaism as their background - explore with equal verve but differing insights this theme of landscape and human consciousness, as also do the reflections of Indian artists such as Jyoti Sahi (Sahi 1986).

Eco-Metaphysics & Gaia Theory

Metaphysics, or cosmological vision, is far from irrelevant here. Sometimes in our speaking - East and West - about the process which relates mind and matter, inner and outer life, consciousness and landscape, imagining subject so dominates imagined object that there seems little other created givenness but consciousness itself and what that inner life produces. The subject-object 'inseparable relationship' can thus be fatally lost. This stress on 'inseparability', with loss of neither Subject nor object, is central to the vision of of the eleventh century Vaishnava Vedantin, Ramanuja, protesting against such loss of any final reality other than the inner self that he believed was taught by extreme non-dualist Vedanta. The Oxbridge limerick caricaturing extreme European idealist thought of the nineteenth century is rarely quoted these days:

> There was a young man who said
> God must find it remarkably odd
> That the sycamore tree simply ceases to be
> When there's nobody else in the quad!

Far more common of late has been new forms of ancient pantheism, such as is implied in the recent Gaia theory of the planetary biologist James Lovecock (who had worked for NASA in its project to find life on Mars) (Lovelock 1979). Gaia was the earth goddess in the Greek pantheon, equivalent to Bhu-devi of Hindu tradition. This Gaia-based late-modern cosmic view gives the fullest possible weight to the inter-relatedness of earth's life. The complex web of life-forms that is the eco-system here becomes a super-organism. Not only is all life intricately inter-related within her. She is also in the end indestructible. Humans may have the power to change the course of earth's life, but not to destroy that life. Nuclear war may eliminate *human* life, but could never destroy *all* life. The notion of the ozone layer as 'earth's fragile shield', claims Lovelock, is a mistaken myth insofar as it is not earth herself that is dependent on such a shield. It is only some of her creatures, humans included. It is not earth's life as such that is vulnerable to disruptive human intervention. In the end Earth will adapt and will live on.

Others, such as Bill McKibben, in *The End of Nature* (1990) rightly see greater inter-penetration of human and earth-life. Human action has left 'an indelible imprint everywhere'. Yet, McKibben's main concern is to show the dangers of human hubris and the belief in unlimited human control, such as was apparent in another book entitled *Gaia*, the theme of which is hinted at in its sub-title, *An Atlas of Planetary Management*.

Clearly there are serious theological questions for all our faith-traditions here. The return to Gaia-faith, or to a perspective that sees cosmic life holistically and human life as participant within this, is either ignored or seen as a threat by far too many traditional theologians. How is God the Creator able to share a faith-world with Gaia? At this point the worldview of most Hindu believers, and in differing ways Buddhists too - for whom talk of a Creator has always been problematic - is not so radically challenged. It is monotheists who have to make the more serious faith-shifts, as indeed a significant number have, women especially. Rosemary Radford Ruether's *Gaia and God* (1992), or Anne Primavesi's *Sacred Gaia* (2000), are examples of the attempt to make a paradigm shift. Significantly, though, Ruether leaves out reference to various aspects of Lovelock's view of the cosmos - that humans are impotent to destroy earth's life, for instance.

Earth-Human Dualism?

In general, monotheist faith-exponents under the spell of the post-Enlightenment worldview, even those with a clear concern to relate differently to the environment, still tend to see things in a fundamentally dualist way. An earth-human dualism is not intrinsic to monotheistic faith. Yet, such is the pull of the cultural worlds built up around Judeo-Christianity, that *earth's value* is still seen primarily in terms of *human value*. Earth is the environment for humans to work out the destiny of their choice, even if an environment to which somehow humans are to relate with a little

267

less destructive aggression. Our alienated state is not only the starting point, but a continuing assumption.

An example is found in the collection of essays edited by David Hallman, *Ecotheology: Voices from South and North* (1994). Some of these essays are among the most ecologically sensitive ever written by Christian faith-exponents. Yet, few seem able to see human life basically as inescapably part of Nature herself. An exception is the essay by Samuel Rayan, who, significantly, moves between the cultural worlds of Indian faith-talk, biblical insights and the common life of a Christian monastic order, along with his deeply felt commitment to social justice

At a basic cultural and ethical level, then, Gaia-talk obviously raises the serious issue of just how important human life is in relation to earth's life and other life-species. The anthropo-centric view of the Enlightenment, and so of Judeo-Christian attitudes, that ultimately humans are all-important is vigorously challenged from many quarters. Late-modern vegetarian movements throughout the western world have their springs in the radical respect for life - the 'non-injury to life' *(jiva-ahimsa)* - so deeply embedded in Indian religious tradition, and given such prominence by Mahatma Gandhi (in turn influenced by the Jaina and Vaishnava traditions of his home region in Northwest India).

There are deep-green activists who give others the impression that they regard animal life, or

'nature' in the abstract, as of greater worth than human life. Certainly in the debate about laboratory experiments on animals, or vivisection, this is the standard assumption of pro-vivesectionists. 'What is of greater value, human life or the life of mice?' Those opposing the practice argue that alternative methods of experimentation are just not sufficiently explored. Now, when millions of people in the Ganga delta region are made homeless by flooding (loss of tree-cover? soil-erosion?), when it is probable that within a very short time the Maldives will disappear under the sea (global warming perhaps by 11C degrees within 40 years?), as but two of countless eco-crises, what scientists do with artificially-bred white mice hardly seems the most pressing eco-problem facing the human race.

Yet, passions run high on just such issues. Whichever side we may support in lesser debates, the polarising of human identity in relation to earth's life is literally a matter of life or death - for the life of our own race as well as for that of a myriad other species. It is precisely in believing their cause to be a matter of life or death that Pro-Life campaigners can become extreme in their protests, usually on the basis of their faith in the unique and sacred status of each human life at whatever stage. That the abhortion of foetal life (in some cultures female foetus especially) is carried out too casually on the global scene is hardly deniable, however intensely any denial of such action also raises issues of both personal choice and social well-being. Similarly, the new possibilities for bio-genetic engineering, stem-cell research and cloning of animal and human species raise hugely challenging questions, faith-based as much as purely ethical. Unless, as a minimum, there is a sense within the scientific community of the *mystery* of life, there seems little chance of authentic human attuning with the life of earth wherein lies our health.

There are two seemingly distinct stances to be taken up here. We are lost unless there is both an earth-sharing and an earth-caring. To be aware of and live as co-participants within earth's life is as crucial as to live and act as responsible 'stewards' of earth's life and its mysteries. When we declare our human self-identity - 'We are human' - unless we include in such a self-defining both that we are more earth-children than earth-lords, fellow-creatures with all creation more than co-creators, we will continue to move on the road to self-annihilation and earth-despoilation if not earth-destruction. Humans all too obviously have the technological power to *intervene* and even *re-direct* earth's life. We do not have the freedom to *contravene* that life in ways that we all too clearly have done already. These are deeply faith-based issues, further aspects of which are taken up in the second part of this chapter (Porritt & White 1988; Gosling 2001).

(II) Sexuality and Eco-Feminist Insight

Marked by more limited focus and often even more political intent is the *eco-feminist* movement, into which we are naturally led by Gaia-talk. Eco-feminism not only asserts female gender as a basis for a powerful new feminist identity, and the liberating of the female from the age-old oppression of male patriarchal systems. It also finds that new identity in an empowering sense of *togetherness with the body of earth's life,* which may be wounded by male aggression, but can never be vanquished, such is that body's creative potency. It is this *eco-perspective* that we now look at more closely.

First, a word about gender and sexuality as defining categories for self-identity. These two are often used with distinct meanings: sex is more biological, gender derives from culture. I do not in this chapter want to make this kind of clear distinction, though in some contexts such a difference of approach is valid. Usually the two are closely intertwined. Nor is there anything new about defining oneself in terms of a gender-role that is also very sexual. 'I am a man, and therefore being a heroic hunter and virile lover define my being', affirms a certain kind of traditionalist. Or, 'I am a woman and therefore bear and nurture children, cook and care for planting, harvesting and home-life.' In a number of Indian languages the wife is the *bharya*, the 'one who bears'; and the husband is *bharta*, he who 'causes to bear'. These ancient self-definitions can be decisive for consciousness.

Women in Faith-Traditions
Even though women's assigned roles in age-old tribal and folk tradition included the passing on of religious wisdom and household ritual, later cultures largely confined priestly power to men. Prophetic voices too, in earlier societies may well more often have been female, outbursts critical of some local injustice spoken while possessed of the spirit. Yet the critical public voices in dominant accounts of our histories have usually been male, as in that extraordinary phenomenon of human and religious history, the Hebrew prophets. In this and in many other major traditions, though, we can find women's voices of protest hidden beneath the surface. Thus, for all the frequent criticism of Judeo-Christian cultures as anti-women, persistent probing of scriptures and traditions by feminists still intent on finding resources for the life and faith of women has uncovered powerful witnesses. Vedic and Epic traditions too have yielded far more material elevating the role of women as sources of power than many thought likely. And what Muslim will not be aware of the crucial role of Khadijah in Muhammad's prophetic vocation, or that of Rabi'a in Sufi history.

In other words, it has not been faith as such, but its cultural and institutional embodying, that have led to the dominating of women.

Christian faith, in the apostle Paul's words, affirms that 'there is neither male nor female'. Yet, in the same apostle's culture-formed ecclesial life the female is enjoined to public silence. While some would call this hypocrisy, it in fact illustrates just how vigorously faith has to struggle for cultural embodiment. Its counter-cultural implications are rarely easy to work out in practice. No doubt similar instances could be culled from many other religious contexts.

As we now move on into the third millennium, in spite of the sexual revolution that has shaken modernity, the power of women and their roles as institutional leaders within all our religions, are still greatly limited, in some cases even proscribed altogether. Femaleness is all too often a bar to power. This contrasts with the premier public roles, powerfully exercised, even in some 'traditional' cultures, by at least a few key women in politics and increasingly in business. But it is the fact of women becoming wage-earners almost worldwide, and being able to control conception, that has effected the most far-reaching transformation of women's identity. That they are usually paid less than men for doing the same work, and so denied full empowerment, is an anomaly that must surely soon be set right. That men in some modern societies already speak with some bewilderment of their own dis-empowerment itself bears witness to just how unjustly ordered our societies were.

There are more serious contradictions to the claim that in secular worlds women can now control their own bodies. For one thing, the huge number of abortions West and East draws in issues of female identity - psychological, socio-biological, ethical, theological - far more complex and critical than is usually made clear in the pro-life versus pro-choice conflict. In some countries, including China and India, aborting a foetus solely because it is female is not uncommon. Far worse, of course, is leaving unwanted female babies to die, a practice not unknown in at least a few societies. Nowhere, though, does secularist contraception and 'choice', provide quite the freedom often claimed. In any case, from the point of view of women's self-identity, however desperate the need to break free from patriarchal control, it is still such a self-diminishing perspective to see life primarily in terms of being free to assert personal sexual control over one's body.

Responding to AIDS & Gay-Identity

Secondly, there is the tragic global fact of the killer-disease, AIDS. During 2002 alone over three million people died from the disease, and by the end of that year nearly forty million were HIV positive. The main mode of transmission globally is sexual intercourse, infected women and the babies they bear far outnumbering gay men, with whom it was once almost exclusively associated in public perception. Nor should we forget the substantial numbers who have contracted the disease from contaminated needles, especially in less affluent countries. The scale of this new epidemic in Africa and Asia is horrifying, yet it is so difficult for the political leaders of these regions openly to ackowledge either the extent of the problem or the need for drastic counter-measures.

There is a clearly religious dimension to counter-AIDS politics. It is almost beyond comprehension that the US government in 2002 refused to ratify action that would have provided effective medication to suffering millions through the United Nations' health mission (WHO), and in 2003 cut off funding for an AIDS programme to refugees in Africa. This was six months after the US president had promised substantial help in fighting AIDS as he toured the continent in some triumph. The fact that the same government makes large grants to those rightwing religion-based organisations, mostly Christian, opposed as much to providing protective contraceptive devices as they are to abortion, leads critics to believe that there is a punitive policy in force against those bodies advocating more 'realist' responses. The US government accepts the stance of those religious groups who preach that personal abstinence alone is the legitimate means for fighting AIDS, whatever the social, cultural and economic conditions making a response based on this moral principle alone highly impracticable for the immediate future. Clearly this placing of assumed moral principle - even when claimed as divinely ordained - in an absolute and non-negotiable position over the pragmatic alleviation of suffering itself raises a huge moral question-mark, especially for faith.

It is the world-wide Anglican Church that has, in 2003, made most obvious the split within its ranks on the gay issue - more specifically, whether a gay person (for almost all Anglican provinces this still means a male) can be consecrated as bishop. This gay issue has almost become the identifying benchmark of what conservative evangelicals regard as genuinely Christian faith. Rallying traditional African and Asian cultural morality to strengthen evangelical ranks - though usually in the name of true 'biblical' teaching - has not been difficult, as it is from Africa especially that the most vitriolic condemnation of gay people has been heard. The link with both facts and fantasy relating to the AIDS disease is obvious.

Yet, it is only in part AIDS-fears that lie behind the sudden surge of anti-gay feeling, in spite of the presence within clergy ranks for centuries of large numbers of gay men. The polarisation also results from the growing acceptance within modernity of openly gay practice - again, seen by traditionalists as one more sign of the rampant growth of God-less secularisation. The same reversion to moral certitudes of the past, especially on sexual issues such as celibacy among the clergy, is typified too in the rejection by Pope John Paul of so many of the reforming moves initiated by his predecessor, Pope John. That practising gay men and women fellow-Christians are also so often manifestly and deeply committed to faith and to various forms of effective ministry, and claim absolute acceptance by Christ, makes their condemnation by other believers hugely problematic for the Christian church.

Exploiting the Female Body

Thirdly, there is in western globalist culture the exploiting of the female body as a means to marketing all manner of products. The multi-billion fashion and cosmetics industry, the artificial enhancing and gratuitous flaunting of the female body, the casual sexual relations expected in western films and TV - presented with a minimum of imagination and seen by some as mainly intended to gratify male expectations - are but part of this modern exploiting of the female body. Some feminists now argue that at every point, even these various forms of selling the female body as sex-object, women are asserting their power. Their sisters who disagree surely have the greater insight. When female identity is allowed to be so closely bound up with the sexuality of our consumerist culture, the boundaries of that identity will be more and more determined by others and by their desires. Sexualized identities of this kind are thoroughly artificial marketting constructs, and potentially very dehumanizing.

And yet, for all its anomalies, this 'sexual revolution' has made a great impact on female self-identity, and there surely have been liberating victories. The perceived 'enemy', though, in this battle for female freedom has not merely been male resistance. So often, in the West especially, it is religious tradition that is automatically seen as anti-women. And as we have seen, our religions are undeniably bound up very closely with cultural mores that have for millennia been the basis for how people have viewed their sexuality. The absolute commitments of religious faith *can* become the basis for an absolutist moral stance that ignores its human consequences. But also clear are the numerous ways in which faith has led to unexpectedly positive perspectives on our sexuality.

Complex Sexuality in Faiths

If we dig a little deeper, to what extent have sexual attitudes been of a piece with wider faith-perceptions of earth and earthiness? In popular perception the usual division regarding both sex and earth between Judeo/Christian/Muslim puritanism and the less inhibited attitudes of Primalist/Hindu/Buddhist (or some forms of Buddhism) naturalism does have some factual basis, institutionally at least. As ever, though, such groupings miss the diversities. Latin Christians, for instance, are not generally known for their inhibitions. And the sexual attitudes of large numbers of Protestant Christians in the second half of the twentieth century seem to have inherited little of older hangups.

In fact, at the centre of Islamic condemnation of western 'Christian' culture is that 'degenerate' flaunting of female sexuality they encounter in the West. Muslims (Sikhs and Hindus too) living there feel under constant threat of their young people being contaminated by this sexual permissiveness. To see this permissiveness as integral to being Christian, is clearly mistaken, for Christians from more conservative cultures such as India's, are equally alarmed by western permissiveness. To see it as integral to western capitalist consumerism is far more accurate, though the cultural story can hardly be subsumed entirely under economics. Things are more complex.

Neither are there, for example, uniform 'Hindu' attitudes to sex. No doubt the Muslim incursion into India, beginning a millennium ago, as well as earlier puritanical movements such as Jainism, and then the Victorian inhibitions of the British, with their condemnations of Hindu sexual explicitness as 'unspeakably obscene', 'morally repugnant' and so on - all made an impact on Hindu attitudes. The growing 19th century view of all dancers as crudely promiscuous 'nautch-girls' (from the Sanskrit *natya*) resulted from Victorian British puritanism. In general - as can be seen from both scripture and iconography (such as the famous imagery at Khajuraho) - earlier Hindu tradition was usually far more relaxed at least about public exhibiting of the female form and the powerful role of sexual relations in human culture and the shaping of human identities. Is not erotic/aesthetic *kama* one of the four great goals of human life? Is there not a sophisticated science of love-making in the Kama-sutra?

Hindu Sexual Ambivalence

Yet, it was precisely the *potency of sex* at the deepest workings of the psyche that entailed a much more complex Hindu view of sexual identities than is often acknowledged. Even issues of same-sex relationships and transvestism are not as clearly outlawed as formal statements imply. Tensions of unbearable intensity related to sex can be seen in great swathes of Hindu tradition - mythic, iconic, sectarian, social. The ancient paradoxical imagery of Siva (O'Flaherty 1973) both as lonely ascetic and as rampantly erect, seed-ejecting phallus cannot be completely ignored, even if openly phallic imagery has little place in the more important Siva-bhakti poetry and teaching in movements of the past two millennia. The contrasting images of Krishna as Gopi-lover and as restorer of *dharma* and its established norms may be less mythically intense, but do present anomalies.

The esoteric Tantric (linked with Raja-yoga) tradition that came to influence so much of Hinduism, and Buddhism too, may well have had its rather modern-seeming therapeutic role as integrator of *soma-psyche*, of body and soul. Other forms of Tantra express more extreme crises of psychological and sexual identity. Attaining a new identity by relating in various ways to a virgin placed at the centre of the circle, partaking of the five things (including sexual congress) that were usually means of bondage and destruction, and suchlike esoteric practices, indicate something of the felt tension regarding sex and sexual identities. Tantric Buddhism, with the meditational Tanka hangings depicting the Bodhisattva as in continual sexual congress with the embodiment of fleshly temptation

- yet remaining ever detached and tranquil - reveals the same potential tension, albeit to be transcended in nirvanic equanimity.

Or, there is the way in which Tamil bhakti poetry and mythic material show women as such a potent threat to male spiritual wellbeing, even though often it is by taking on a feminine persona that devotees become true lovers of God (Hardy 1983). In modern Indian society, too, no one can miss the ambivalence regarding sex (Chaudhuri 1996). Sexuality itself is far from hidden. Yet, those working to combat AIDS in the East, for example, speak of the fatal silence concerning pertinent sexual issues. Or, we could take the Mahatma's 'experiments' in his relations with young female assistants as another very different but almost archetypal example of this ambivalence. As we saw above, within classical Hindu sources too, in spite of the robust projecting of sexuality and sexual roles, there is also ambiguous renunciation of all sexual identities. A *kama*-transcending level of being and self-identity is typical of important deities too, even when at one level their story is also very sensuous.

Gender roles and sexual identities in Hindu tradition, then, are not simply a matter of 'be yourself', 'don't fight nature' (the advice given to the hero of the Gita). In fact, this advice is based on the need to be true to one's *dharma*-given identity. But from the other side, neither are the identities expected of believers in Judeo-Christian and Muslim religious life merely those of de-sexed God-followers. Sexuality is to be constrained, disciplined, and eventually transcended. It can never be the principal strand of human identity. Yet, it is essential to the God-given scheme of things, even to be enjoyed to the full. That a much more ambiguous attitude than this has regularly crept in is hardly surprising, given both the powerful emotions sexuality stirs and the intensity of the religious person's desire for goals extending beyond that sexuality.

New Eco-Sensitivities

Then there are the wider issues of ecological feminism. Overlap can be seen between eco-feminism and that other indefinably amorphous movement of our times, New Age-ism. In this latter way of seeing things, however, there is often explicit reference to Indian and other Eastern belief-systems. *Karma, avatar, nirvana, yoga, guru,* etc are terms all sprinkled freely in New Age vocabulary - evidence perhaps of the new 'hybridity' of which postcolonialists speak. But new-ageist attitudes, overlapping with postmodernist ways of critique at various points, have now spread for beyond the California ex-hippy, guru-led scene. They are now so much part of new westernism that the cross-cultural connection may not appear at all on the surface.

Indeed, in the West conscious reference might as well be made to more ancient European cultural traditions, such as Celtic and Nordic. The recent highly popular stories of Tolkien and Philip Pullman draw dramatically on such long-hidden cultural roots, though Pullman's mythology includes a little modern Quantum theory, as well as being almost polemically anti-theist and anti-church. Even without reference to rootage, it is not uncommon, and not only in science fiction, to find an eco-psychic or cosmo-psychic view of things: seeing the whole cosmos as an extension of inner psyche, or inner consciousness as of a piece with the forces creating our outer worlds. This micro-macrocosmic way of looking at ourselves is precisely the basis of that ancient Indian practice of Yoga, now widely practised in the West, though there usually stripped of its more esoteric Tantric associations.

Central to all these post-modernist, eco-feminist, new ageist movements is - as we saw in the chapter on Globalisation - a vigorous, if often vaguely expressed, rejection of the basic assumption of the modern scientific worldview. Far from vague in his critical response to the ramifications of this worldview has been that of holistic writers such as Fritjof Capra, referred to earlier in this chapter. The fatal flaw is seen to be the attitude underlying modern science which assumes that the human mind can and should *transcend nature*, and thereby control it, even aggressively mastering it for human uses. It was on this basis of the dichotomy of mind and nature that there has been such a burgeoning of human technological skills able to exploit the natural world. West and East, though, increasing numbers of people have pointed to another far-reaching consequence of our world-conquering 'modernity' and its technology: a long and deeply damaging process of alienation from the natural world.

Francis Bacon, early in the European Enlightenment, may have been one of the first to throw off traditional views of a sacral world around us, and use language of violence to describe how Nature is to be 'whipped into submission'. But it was Descartes, early in the

17th century, who provided modern Europe with a metaphysical basis for the new rationalist worldview. He it was who provided us with that famous aphorism: 'I think, therefore I am'. It is not our feeling, our moral capacity, our creating of mythic worlds, our corporate relationality, and certainly not our corporeality, that identifies what is of the essence of being human. The highest form of human identity is to be understood essentially by our ability to think abstractly. To live intellectually as those superior to all that belongs to the natural world is the way to ensure that we are masters of nature (Ruether 1992: 194-7).

Eco-feminists see this way of understanding the universe, this wanting to master the world, as essentially masculine. And it is not coincidental that the vocabulary of this philosophy of science identifies the thinker as masculine - the 'master' etc - and nature as feminine. In describing the process both of acquiring scientific knowledge and of using that knowledge for technological purposes of human advancement, imagery of quite shocking violence is used. Francis Bacon's language for this process suggests rape as part of the paradigm the scientist is to keep in mind!

Creation in Christian Thought

However inextricably 'Christian civilization' has become bound up with the destruction of much of the natural world, this is far from the imagery of the original Judeo-Christian account of creation. All nature is said to be from God and valued by God. Yet, the key role of humans is equally clear. Two original stories coalesce in the first two chapters of Genesis. The first story-teller is clearly reshaping Babylonian material, giving new emphases, and five key points emerge. (i) It is from God alone, 'in the beginning', that all creaturely life derives, and by whom chaos gives way to order. (ii) It is the powerful, purposeful Word, the trans-material self-articulation of the one God that brings about this creative process. (iii) Creaturely life is, in the purpose of this Creator God, essentially and originally 'good' (several times repeated). (iv) Human life is seen as the crown, the climax of this creative process. And (v) humans bear the 'image and likeness' of the Creator in a special way, and are therefore commissioned to exercise a deputed lordly role over earth, representing God in so far as they act in tune with the creative purpose. In passing, we might note that this Genesis story tells us humans were expected originally to be vegetarian! And two further significant points emerge from the second and probably earlier creation story. Humans are made literally from earth, animated by divine breath, and they are to 'care for', 'tend', 'husband' the garden-like habitat in which they are placed (see my 'Changing Eco-Perspectives in India', in Muthunayagom 2000: 153-172).

Other relevant biblical themes include the story of a solemn covenant of peace with humans and 'with every living creature' that God makes (in Genesis 9) following the destruction by massive flooding, here too making use of Babylonian mythic material. It is just prior to this that humans are given freedom to eat meat, and therefore to become a cause of 'dread' to all other creatures. But the divine promise is given - the rainbow being a token of this - that the earth will not be cursed again, as in the flood, because of human evil. Then, too, there are numerous psalms expressing divine delight in and care for creation, as well as gratitude for the blessings bestowed on human life through creation (e.g.Psalms 65, 67, 72, 104 etc). The prophetic books in places describe the harmonious *shalom* promised for all creation (e.g. Isaiah 11). Up to this point we have what might be called an 'Adamic' account of the human place within creation, Adam being central to creation narrative in Jewish, Christian and Muslim tradition. In the Christian New Testament the healing, feeding and storm-calming stories told about Jesus further suggest the restoring of creation that is part of messianic promise. Then Apostolic passages speak of the liberation of all creation (e.g. Romans 8), of all cosmic life being created through Christ and cohering together because of Christ (Colossians 1), and of the renewing of the divine image in humanity both in the person of and through identification with this cosmic saviour.

I have at least two reasons for giving this fairly full account of a Christian Adamic understanding of creation. (a) In the first place, any sense of human identity in relation to nature based on such narratives should hardly be able to collaborate easily with an identity which sees unremittingly rapacious mastering and exploiting of nature as its proper role. At some point in the identity-shaping process, an alien perspective became dominant in western culture, and even theological interpretation too often accommodated too comfortably with that dominant view. The critical dimension of a faith-culture dialectic was lost.

(b) A second reason is that for the modern deep-green eco-critic the Judeo-Christian Genesis vision itself is woefully inadequate ecologically. In essence it is also part of Qur'anic accounts of creation. It is, goes the attack, both ludicrous and abhorrent to think of Nature as dependent upon the purpose of a personal God, especially one depicted in male terms, and of humans as the 'crown' of creation, or as 'stewards' of creation, who bear crucial responsibility for earth's destiny. Such anthropo-centrism, even homo-centrism, is anathema to radical greens. And the specifically Christian notion that the Christ-event has a necessary instrumental role in realising this divine purpose seems even more objectionable to the swelling tide of opinion that is much more at ease with a Gaia view of Earth. Earth - say the Gaiaists - has powerful, self-sustaining life of her own, within which humans, capable of much that may be either destructive or constructive, are to find their lesser earth-dependent identity.

Western & Indian Eco-Views Compared

Whatever weight we give to originating mythic tradition, there are other factors to be

reckoned with that in any case have obscured and distorted that originating vision. There has been the sense of a fall from innocence and grace, and, especially in the Christian worldview, the conviction of deeply ingrained sinfulness, escape from which is now the highest human goal. This soteriological dualism took a new and in many ways fatal direction in the instrumentalist dualism of the technology of recent centuries. Earth and her powers are there to be exploited in whatever ways are useful to human 'development', and even more crucial, that are deemed likely to prove commercially profitable. For, our modern capitalist economy, with its dangerously unjust inequalities of distribution of wealth, has been inextricably linked with modern engineering exploits. And as we noted above, those 'fathers' of modern science, Bacon and Descartes, provided the undergirding philosophy for a sense of human identity in which both the divinely given value and the mysterious enchantments of Nature are forever lost. Nature's one great value is to be of use to humans and their unending 'development'.

Compare this imagery with that of most classical Indian traditions and the differences are obvious. Yet, it is not so much the originating Judeo-Christian-Muslim earth-vision, but the attitudes of those early philosophers of science, with their distorted reinterpreting of Judeo-Christian imagery, that seems to contrast so strongly with key images in the symbolic sacral world of classical India. What, for example, can be less like this paradigm of mastery and rape than the Saiva image of the 'Lord of the universe', Siva, dancing together in ecstatic bliss with 'Lady Energy', Sakti, a sacred name that also encompasses all nature? By their dance together as one they mysteriously bring all worlds into being. Or Krishna, even more seductive in his flute-playing dance, and famous for his love both of the milkmaids and for their cattle, lifting up the peak of the sacred mountain in order to provide safe refuge for all the creatures threatened by excessive rain? Idyllic pastoral scenes fill his life narratives.

We cannot, though, here make an absolute contrast with classical Indian thinking. For Siva's dance is as much about wild destruction, reducing all things to ashes, as it is about beneficent creation. And there are, in the Saiva tradition itself, mythic accounts of the dance in which Siva actually does rape creation's agent, Sakti. Krishna, too, at times wreaks havoc both with women and with nature; his collaboration with Agni's burning down of the Khandava forest, and playfully preventing any wildlife from escaping the sacrifice-like fire, is an instance of the anomaly and paradox characteristic of almost all our religious traditions. Moreover, in the Samkhya worldview that undergirds much of India's classical cultural life, again the contrast is sharply drawn between male-gendered thinking Selfhood (*Purusha*)and female-gendered unthinking Nature (*Prakriti*). And here it is only Nature that is depicted as a dancer, a dancer who seductively unveils herself and in so doing bewitches Selfhood, causing the creative process to emanate spontaneously out of the resulting entanglement. In other words, neither the creative process nor the role of the female are without ambiguity in Indian symbolism and their belief-systems. Religious traditions are rarely without their points of paradox, so that we left with no absolute contrast between Eastern and Judeo-Christian-Muslim worldviews.

Having said this, we do have to take seriously the frequent claim by the ecologically sensitive, East and West, that it is to Hindu, Buddhist and Jaina traditions we are to look for eco-visionary resources for modern living. To repeat my point above: Basic to an eco-sensitive view of things is the need *to see our humanness as of a piece with and participant in nature. Human identity is to include earth's identity*. I am seriously at risk of over-simplifying here, but there is little doubt that a major thrust of the Hindu traditions - Vedic and Agamic, Sanskritic and vernacular - has pointed to such a continuum of being, an interconnectedness of all life-forms, including humans. Human life is part of the cosmic life of nature, the ground for which is a pan-en-theistic view that all exists within the Great Being; humans too are embodied within the eternally changing 'body' of God. Belief-systems are, of course, much more nuanced than this within the complex set of traditions that is 'Hinduism'. Ultimate identities involve the recognition of the mysteriously other character of the inner Self, both within each microcosmic life-form as well as all-pervasive in macrocosmic life. The participant character of our being, though, is a basic assumption. And it has often been in some way an *identifying of* and then *identifying with the inner Self of all* that has formed the undergirding strand of this eminently eco-friendly metaphysics, a theme more fully explored in essays published earlier (e.g.Lott:1985, *Indian Culture and Earth-Care (Justice Vasudevamoorthy Memorial Lecture)*, Bangalore: Indian Institute for World Culture).

Two examples to note: there is that traditional morning prayer to be said by all the devout, when they first step on to Mother Earth, asking her forgiveness for such intrusion onto her sacred domain. And there are the prayers in the 'Earth-section' of the fourth Veda (the Atharva), a compilation in which we can assume more indigenous materials have been incorporated. Any digging or ploughing, mining or exploiting earth's treasures, is assumed to be dangerously invasive of the sacred Mother's life.

> Impart to us those vitalising powers
> that come, O Earth, from deep within your body,
> your central point, your navel; purify us wholly.
> The Earth is Mother, I am son of Earth.....

> Whatever I dig up of you, O Earth,
> May you of that have quick replenishment;
> O purifying One, may our thrust never
> reach right to your vital points, your heart.

Then, at a more practical level we find traditions such as Ayurveda systematically exploring the healing resources in herbs, berries, bark, resins and the leaves of trees. The human body itself is assumed to be made up of the same elemental life-forces as are found in all nature. Much has been made by Indian environmentalists - and rightly so - of the ancient and widespread practice of never cutting down the trees and bushes of sacred groves and temple gardens, or of not catching the fish of waters near sacred places.

Perhaps such restraints are merely a taboo-relic that hardly forms an inclusive eco-policy. But it is of a piece with the attitude to cosmic life summed up in the words of Swami Vivekananda, who probably more than anyone redefined what has increasingly come to be accepted by the literate in India as a 'Hindu view of life':

> ...to understand that the idea of separateness (is) erroneous, that there (is) a connection between all those distinct objects....a unity which pervade(s) the whole universe - trees, shrubs, animals, men, devas, even God Himself....In reality, the metaphysical and the physical universe are one, and the name of the One is Brahman. (Quoted by Gosling 38)

Concomitant with a sense of the interweaving of life, is the doctrine made more famous by Gandhi (in more idealist days always called the 'Mahatma'), that as a life-principle we are not to injure or do violence to any life form, we are to practise *jiva-ahimsa*. It is no coincidence that Gandhi, as well as being nurtured by his mother's devout Vaishnavism, with its traditionally non-violent stance, came from a region close to the centre of Jaina faith. In addition to the subtle but deep-reaching influence of the Buddha's way on the Indian corporate psyche, Jainism too accounts for important elements of what was to emerge as that complex entity, Hindu identity. Partly as a result of the now unimaginable ferment of debate and reaction and interaction over at least fifteen centuries from the time of Mahavira in the eighth century BCE, Vedic sacrificial Brahmanism was radically reinterpreted. The details do not concern us here, but we can at least note this central emphasis of the Jains on non-violence to all life, the basis of their rejection of the Vedic sacrificial system. It is not the all-pervasiveness of the divine Self or sacred Brahman that makes non-violence to all things necessary, but the inalienable presence of souls, *jivas*, within all life-forms, even plant-life in less complex soul-form. And to do the slightest violence to any kind of life-form is also to harm one's own soul, to open it to the inflow of karmic particles. The soul's liberation lies in rigorously purifying it of its heavy burden of *karma*.

The rigorous asceticism through which this soteriology was worked out may not seem to have much to do with viable eco-practice. But in Indian religio-cultural history, Jainism, and then even more so Buddhism, made quite an impact. In time this was to become a global impact, though such a term may seem too violent. The Vedic system was based essentially on the principle of desire-satisfying. 'He who desires the blessings of the good life, longevity, heaven, peace all around, should sacrifice'. This paraphrases, a little expansively, a well-known Vedic maxim. And *kama* - desire that is both erotic and aesthetic - remained one of life's four great goals in the Hindu view of life. Neither the Jaina nor the Buddha's way, though, was based on such indulgence or fulfilment of desire. Exactly the opposite. Desire, taught the Buddha, is to be uprooted, for it is the cause of all that suffering, or dis-ease (*duh-kha*), that ultimately typifies all our existence. The naturally urgent human 'thirst' for extending our existence has to be quenched at its source, the fire that burns like fever within us has to be 'extinguished' (*nirvana*). Self-indulgence, the self-fulfilment that has become axiomatic in the modern view of our humanness, is the way to further bondage to the karmic cycle. So the Buddha steered a Middle Way between indulgence and ascetic denial. And in response to the Buddha's impact, the Vedic way too was modified in the Gita's compromise: continue to act, sacrifice in life and in accord with the Vedic way (though without killing animals). But act without desire for the fruits of your actions (*nish-kama-karma*).

So, then, it was in Jainism that the most thorough-going ever regime of desire-restraint, of setting limits to indulgence and consumption, was developed. Those who take the Vows, whether at the lower or higher level, are not only to refrain from injury to any life-form, from any kind of falsehood, and suchlike, they are to set rigorous limits to the amount they acquire, possess, consume, and even the distances they move around. Here is the extreme opposite from a human identity dependent on the amount consumed, and on the range of choice of consumable goods and sensory stimulants, increasingly typical of modern living. In the Buddhist life-paths restraints are also present, but they are far less rigorous, in part because there is no 'soul' to be strenuously purified. The emphasis is much more positively on compassion for all creatures as essential to the uprooting of the arch-enemy 'desire', the growth of inner awareness and the cultivating of the nirvanic life. It is understandable that many eco-sensitive westerners - such as Edward Schumacher of 'Small is Beautiful' fame - have found significant resources for the countering of western eco-destructiveness, for developing an eco-based identity, within Buddhist life-attitudes.

It remains to be seen, though, whether these Eastern cultural visionary resources can help to shape the strong corporate sense of human responsibility, the rigorous economic and ecological policies, the political will sufficient to redirect global life and transform the present earth crisis. Green parties in some countries do seem to be endued with both motive and method. Globally there is a divide - between eco-consumers, determined to keep up their indulgent life-style, and radical eco-conservers critical of the disastrously destructive results of global capitalism. The question of whether or not authentic human identity can ever be other than an eco-based identity is of momentous importance for the world's future.

Part III :
Crisis Points For Indian Identities

Chapter 13
An Ancient Postmodernism?

In a strict sense some of the crisis points in issues of identity that I have been reflecting on may seem to lead us a long way from the instructions of the Revd William Teape when he endowed this lectureship in 1926. His intention was that Christian theology reflect on the significance of the insights of those pivotal ancient Hindu scriptures, the Upanishads. In recent years few Teapers have confined the lectures strictly to these limits. Any treatment of issues of self-identity, however, at least at some points makes it easy to keep to the good Reverend's original intention. For one thing, there are significant parallels between the Upanishadic world and our postmodernist world, and between their respective understanding of self-identity. (I here use 'Postmodern' in the less precise sense that I write of 'late-modernist' in chapter one, following Giddens' usage).

'Postmodern' is, no doubt, an elusively amorphous label for a way of seeing things. Some basic perceptions have already been identified: our worlds of discourse, including the institutions of the modern nation-state and even the received wisdom of modern science, are constructs, not to be absolutized as representing some objectively given reality. Our beliefs can never be more than relatively true, our ethical position never given more than relative value, our ultimacies never more than provisional. Clearly this leaves room for a wide range of nuancing. But is not such a perceptual world in tune with the grounding insights of any religious worldview in which *mystery* is prominent? Certainly increasing numbers of postmoderrised intellectuals in the West have turned to Buddhist and Vedantic ideas, sometimes very seriously, but even more often as filtered through amorphously New Age ways of seeing the world.

Upanishadic Insights

In what ways, then, can the Vedantic worldview that arose in ancient India be thought of as akin to a postmodernist view of things? Vedanta is based on the insights of the Upanishads, those books of 'secrets' concerning the ultimate nature of things - self, cosmos, sacrifice, sacred Brahman and more - revealed to those 'sat down near' (*upa-ni-shad*) an initiating teacher. The Upanishads, usually dated from 900 to 300BCE, are appended as the 'end' of the ancient Vedas.

Seemingly there is a great gulf fixed between the Upanishadic world and where we stand today. Some conclusions differ very clearly from each other. In particular there is the contention of many postmodernists that our selfhood, the identity on the basis of which we see the world, is not some immutably given core, but is rather the product of the powerful mind-shaping structures impinging on us from that world. *All* identities, even those aiming to transcend common group identities, are constructs of the human imagination, all created - even if unconsciously - to further some group's power-aims. Even the 'self' is relative. No absolutes, no universals are possible. While Vedanta would accept such a relativist view of our sensory and intellectual life, including our conditioned perception of our selfhood, the self within in reality transcends all life's changes and instabilities. There is, for Vedanta, an unchanging core of being within the true, eternal self.

Yet the underlying question is strikingly similar: it is precisely this question of what constitutes our normally held sense of *self-identity* - an issue very high indeed on the Upanishadic agenda. We should not over-simplify Upanishadic concerns, but we can rightly summarise as follows: 'Who am I, who are we, really, in the hidden depths of our consciousness? What constitutes our core selfhood, our essential being, beyond all our varied forms of role-play? When all *nama-rupa* (name-form) existence is stripped away, what remains as the immutable basis of being?'

The Postmodernist is likely to say, 'No unchanging core remains. Every cohering point of consciousness is a conditioned construct'. And we are, as we saw, not far at least from the 'elder' Buddhist doctrine of 'non-self'. But while the worldview and liberating way of the Buddha overlap Upanishadic thought at many points, it is not (as neo-Vedantins usually claim) 'essentially at one with the Upanishads'. The immutability of the transcendent Self-beyond-the-ego is an unquestionable given for the Upanishadic seers. Thus, Upanishadic and Postmodernist assumptions regarding core selfhood differ very markedly. Yet, in both traditions (as well as in Buddhist thinking) recognition of many layers of self-deception, and the power of external structures to create these illusory worlds, are central.

Other concerns expressed by the Upanishadic seers seem far removed from such existential *angst*. Foremost among these is the assured claim that it is through internalised consciousness of the *sacred Power (Brahman)* within and beyond all life-powers that the self becomes empowered, becomes immortal. (Of course, for one kind of interpretation - the strict Advaitin - there is in reality no 'becoming', no change from one state of being to another, there is only a realising of what is).

So, these 'secret sayings' are made up of the dialectic between life-probing questions about human identity and cosmically inclusive affirmations about the identity of the 'Great One', *Brahman*. Indeed, what are invariably seen as the key passages of the Upanishads are concerned directly with this question of *the identity of inner selfhood and cosmic selfhood*, of *Atman* and *Brahman*. There was, though, fierce debate among Vedantins on precisely this issue, a debate that should prevent us from making easy assumptions about what is meant by these seminal sayings.

Further Common Patterns

There are other aspects of the Upanishads that have a sort of post-modernist look about them, though again we should not try to push the parallels too far. As the 'end of the Vedas' (i.e.'Veda-anta') the Upanishads raise critical questions about the dominant (Vedic) culture inherited from the past. Not that the institution - the ritual priestly system, undergirded by the notion of Brahmanic purity and sacral power - was rejected in itself, as was the case with Buddhist and Jainist counter-cultures. But the efficacy of remaining locked into and merely performing the roles expected within that established system was vigorously questioned. There was an identity change. Life-goals themselves became different, more internally focussed. Peace, purity, a powerfully auspicious life - all understood largely in corporate terms - and certainly the more personal blessing of immortality, were all still desired. But no longer was the sacrally established community seen as the primary recipient of such transcendent blessings. Awareness of the inner dynamics of life-transformation became all-important, if there was to be liberation. Indeed, all action - with the newly emerged conviction that it is our actions that perpetuate the karmic life-cycle - all action became ambiguous, all social relationship became relativised. And so a new self-identity emerged.

Put differently, the status of the ego was radically revised, as a key point in many of the then new movements - the Jainas, the Buddhists, the self-transcending ways of the various forms of Yoga, the Ajivakas, for example, that were all part of the amazing religious ferment of two and a half millennia ago. Only the 'worldly ones', the Lokayata-vadins were committed to an ego-boosting hedonism that gloried in the gratification of the senses. Even previous to this outburst of inwardly directed struggle (*sramana*) to burn up dangerously misleading egohood, individual ambitions were bounded by community ties. Corporate identities, centres of corporate ego, were strong. Absent, though, in the pre-Upanishadic Vedic spirit, was the unrelenting questioning of the status of ego that emerged at and as 'the end of the Vedas'.

In the case of the Buddha (as the 'Elder Teachers' interpret him) the continuing existence of selfhood in any form was seriously challenged. Liberation lay in the snuffing out of every flame that springs up from ego-led desire, the quenching of all thirst for continuity, for any self-identity other than that based on the new reality of the perfect experience of the Buddha, his Way, his Community. So emerges the central creed of Buddhism: 'I go to the Buddha for refuge (*saranam*); I go to the Dhamma for refuge; I go to the Community of monks (*bikku-sanga*) for refuge'. All dependence on previous institutions, and the identities derived from them, were to be torn up relentlessly by their roots. That is how ultimacy is to be found.

In terms of some of the phenomenological patterns involved, it is not entirely fanciful to see here also parallels with the prophetic movement, and the passionate call to 'turn round' (*shub*) that arose about the same period in ancient Israel. With the Hebrew prophets, though, however much they challenged particular forms of their people's corporate identity, there was no thought of weakening the Israelite sense of corporate identity *per se*. Yet all-important in this prophetic movement was the call to break free from faith in Israel's sacral institutions. The sacrificial cult was not what God really wanted (Amos, Micah, Isaiah); even the Holy Temple, central symbol of Israel's elect and sacral status, could no longer stand as the enduring mark of or the ensuring protection of that identity (Jeremiah); and it is not that corporate sacral identity that matters, for 'the soul that sinneth, it shall die', implying that the identity of the community is to be radically re-constituted, by a 'new covenant' (Ezekiel, Jeremiah). So the parallels are there.

In many ways the parallels are closer in the cases of the Jesus-movement in the first century, the Franciscan movement in thirteenth century Europe, and with at least some aspects of the reformation movement in the 16th century. Admittedly, corporate, institutional and even political identities are still strong. But then, the need for corporate identity of a new kind is equally envisioned by the post-Vedic 'strugglers' for whom the earlier sacral and political insititutions no longer sufficed. The earlier rubric, 'Do what is prescribed within the sacral structures and all will be well, the heaven you desire will be yours', no longer carried weight; inner renewal became paramount. There are identity-breaking parallels too with the *bhakti* movements within Hindu India. But as we shall see even within the Upanishads there were the beginnings of the kind of new directions that *bhakti*-religion called for.

Post-Vedic Search for New Identities

The post-Vedic period, then, was marked by a sustained and intense search for new identities. There is little doubt that it was the impact of indigenous cultures, tribal cultures - far more complex than is often recognised - upon Vedic religion that brought about this self-questioning, and the emerging new perceptions of selfhood. In any case the Upanishadic period was one of deep and wide-ranging religious, cultural and ideological ferment. The two most prominent contestants in this ferment were those who took the way of *brahmanika*, or the Vedic way of sacrifice for corporate well-being, and those of the various more indigenous paths of *sramanika*, or counter-cultural 'struggle, effort'. Mahavira's 'heroic' way of purity through rigorous asceticism, Tantric and Yogic techniques of inner power-enhancement, the Buddha's quenching - through calmly ordered meditation - of the thirst for self and ego-empowerment: these were all differing ways in which this 'struggle' was worked out.

In places the 'skilful means' adopted did overlap. More significant was the common goal, the common 'struggle' for a new identity transcending all earlier identities. The old power-structures were found wanting, the boundaries imposed were found to be too inhibiting, the blessings promised were themselves found to be too binding. In particular, the Brahmanic sacral world was found to lack liberating meaning; *brahman*-power was relocated and reinterpreted. The Buddhist, like the Upanishadic seers, could still speak of 'becoming-*brahman*', but the *dharma* by which this transcendent state of unflickering bliss and inner knowing is attained showed a radically new ethical and meditational path, in which the Buddha himself very soon became the focal point, a key point of 'refuge', along with the new *dharma*-path and the community of those walking this path. And non-Brahmins (along with some *brahman*-controllers too) flocked to walk this path, as well as the 'heroic' paths of Mahavira and of the Yogis and Tantrics. The diversities were richly widespread, and the search for new identities intense. Yes, there are parallels of a sort with our own age.

There is a further parallel, at least with one important strand within that ferment of long ago, a strand that has in fact become almost normative for Indian spirituality. It is what we may call a postmodernist agnosticism in matters of human knowledge. This loss of cognitive realism in the postmodernist world extends even to the highest realms of religious knowledge. So we find most but rather conservative schools of Christian theology arguing along neo-Kantian lines that the 'God' of human discourse can never be more than a human construct. Some even go on to argue that we can never claim any kind of ontological correspondence between our belief-system and objective cosmic realities. Our faith-identity can never be more than that sense of selfhood we arrive at by 'telling the story'. Our individual story may be explored within a larger narrative, but it is narrative alone that creates meaning for our subjecthood. Relativism reigns. (See Introduction to *Concilium* 2000, No.2, 'Creating Identity'). There are no doubt other possible parallels between Upanishadic and Postmodernist thinking.

Diversity Within Upanishads; the Move to Bhakti

Even within the Upanishads we find diversity and movement. In particular there is the move in Focus: we could speak of Brahman as the One that is subtley, indescribably, impersonally hidden *within* all things, but who moves on to become the One gloriously, adorably *beyond* all things. Or (in early Upanishads) the mysteriously hidden Self within all, the 'Inner Controller' (Brhadaranyaka III.7) of whom it is said in a seminal statement (Chandogya VI), 'That (Brahman) thou (seeking soul) art', who moves on to become numinously endowed with all the most wonderful qualities imaginable (as in later Upanishads and culminating in the Bhagavad Gita's 'vision'). But this typification misses the mystery of immanental transcendence, beyondness that is withinness, found throughout the Upanishads. There is, though, a clear if very general change, when we compare earlier and later Upanishads, from more *impersonal* to more *personal* categories. Worship and love, perhaps the wonder of God embodied among us (for the Gita is an Upanishad too), eventually become central, even though still found alongside the impersonal strategies of *yoga*. Within the Gita itself in fact, after earlier chapters exalting first dharmic duty and Vedic sacrifice, followed by the need for that stillness attained through *yoga*, gradually (if we bracket the 'social ethics' of chapters 13-17) we find the intense love and trust expected of *bhakti* becoming more and more prominent. The climax at the end is the disclosing of the 'highest secret', 'I love thee well', so 'Give up all your *dharmas*, take Me alone as your refuge; I will set you free from all your sin' (18.66).

No doubt many modern Hindu interpreters would respond to this by saying that the Supreme is both *saguna* and *nirguna*, both 'with qualities' and 'without (or beyond) qualities'. So the distinction, they argue, is merely a matter of perception, though to move beyond the bounded particularities of the personal, describable-by-qualities, differentiable being this implies is the higher path. And there have certainly been a number of devotional poets (Kabir for instance) whose God in the end was seen as 'beyond all description'. But did they suggest that this was a higher path? Generations of India's *bhakti* theologians disagreed, and vehemently. The God we worship, they said, certainly cannot be exhausted by our ascriptions; there is a beyondness too. But there is *no higher way* than that of loving, adoring relationship with the 'One who is a treasurehouse of every

292

good quality'. It may be an 'inseparable relationship' (as Ramanuja put it so often) but to identify God as this gloriously Other who is 'overwhelmed with compassion for his creatures, his loved ones', is to find the ground for one's true identity.

What we need to grasp here, then, is both that the way we identity that Being 'than which there is no greater' (Vedanta's description of Brahman), is the way by which our own identity is shaped, and that therefore, according to these theologians of divine love, it is crucial for the *true shaping of our identity that we do not aim for or assume any absolute identity with that supreme Being*. Power-issues are at stake here too, not least the extent to which the concerned Identity, whether theistic or trans-theistic, is made the focus for community defensiveness that becomes militant. The usual assumption is that the theists - Vaishnavas and Saivas - were the community-minded ones. There is some truth in this, but Sankara's monastic followers were equally capable of forming themselves into semi-military bands, when self-defence was quite capable of becoming aggression. Such commitment to protect the boundaries of community identity seem somewhat in conflict with the grounding vision of such communities. For all these interpreters of the way of liberation, *casting off false identities, false conditioning, and finding our true identity is the ultimate aim*. Ultimate aims, though, always have to reckon with historical accommodations.

Chapter 14
Hindutva's Religious Nationalism
(& Minority Responses)

Even when discussing a religion's more metaphysical struggles, we find we cannot entirely steer clear of institutional conflict. So we turn to a contemporary ideological and politico-cultural movement in India that many see as a crisis threatening to make India's self-identity unrecognisable to her modern admirers. This is the movement encapsulated in the term *Hindutva*. Those who urge us to differentiate carefully between Hindu religion and the Hindutva movement are quite right. It is undeniable, though, that some of the most potent advocates of Hindutva's more belligerent political stance have been sacrally empowered leaders of traditional Hindu communities. There has been a politicising of the saffron-clad, and a saffronising of politics.

Many streams have flowed into this now deep-running river within Indian political and cultural life. The setback in the national parliamentary elections of 2004, with loss of power for the alliance in which Hindutva-supporting BJPdominated, may indicate some waning of interest in religion-based politics. Such a judgement would be premature, if only because the feeder streams are so widespread. It is also a mistake to isolate, as many commentators do, any one of these causal influences and see that as the one crucial factor creating the unexpected political power wielded by those who have identified themselves with the Hindutva project.

(1) There is what is felt as the humiliating legacy of *alien invasion, conquest and rule* - first Persian and Mughal Muslims, then European Christians. This thousand-year period is still deeply traumatic to culturally and nationally conscious Hindu identity. There were no doubt very different forms of conquest and rule. The British colonisers, for example, never took on an Indian identity in the way the Muslims did. Yet, this whole period is inevitably as conquest from outside. There was, in different ways, the loss of indigenous political control and of economic resources that affected everyone, though felt most by previously dominant classes. More important perhaps, the continual undermining of self-confidence and pride in

294

Hindu cultural value-systems seemed almost integral to the history of both periods. Their rule was resented as demoralisingly alien.

(2) There is, then, the perception - more common in conservative Hindu community - of a continuing invasion of *dislocating and debasing cultural life* from the West. This links with the fear, ambiguous though this may be, of the economic neo-colonialism of rapidly accelerating globalisation. That elite Hindu classes profit most from the 'liberalized' economic policy adds paradox here, but does not change the perception among the lower middle classes comprising the bulk of Hindutva support.

(3) There is in the Hindutva mind (as with Muslims) the *associating of Christian and western missions* with this invasive economic and cultural market, while Hindu tradition is portrayed as having been never self-assertive, always tolerant, but now called upon vigorously to resist the aggression of others. Arun Shourie, a vigorous proponent of the Hindutva position, argues that Christianity is at its core both 'self-obsessed' and essentially aggressive towards others. Its world mission is of a piece with imperialism (Shourie 1994, 2000).

(4) There is the consequence of colonial and orientalist *'inventing'* of Hinduism. That is, a reshaped self-identity effected both by the colonialists' humiliatingly negative criticisms of what they perceived as 'Hinduism', as well as the portrayal by orientalist scholars too often reflecting their own pre-conceived imagining of what religion should be. Either way, a greater *uniformity of Hindu self-identity* emerged that, again paradoxically, neo-Hindu nationalist movements unconsciously appropriated. Propounding this theory in terms of the creation of a a hitherto non-existent Hindu consciousness grossly overstates it. There was a very long history of Brahmanic incorporation preceding modern colonialism. But the upsurge of numerous new and vigorous forms of Hindu identity, from early in the 19th century onwards, does form a shaping continuity with the present resurgence.

(5) There was, in the 1980s, a growing *political vacuum*, with the populace at large feeling that the highly moralistic nationalism of the Congress movement had lost its momentum and its moral status, and therefore needed to be replaced by a more pure nationalism, by a new unifying force - moral, religious, cultural and national. There was the loss for a while of a focal figure of national devotion within

Congress, provided by leading figures in the Nehru dynasty up to the asassination of Rajiv Gandhi. Attempts by Congress to push Italian-born Sonia, Rajiv's widow, into this semi-divine role were ridiculed by the Hindutva-party. Yet, in the end it seems in part to have been the mystique of Sonia Gandhi's presence, along with her politically emerging son and daughter, that helped turn the tide for Congress.

There was, too, the failure of the BJP-dominated government to translate the rhetoric of 'shining India' and its liberalised economy into the reality lof improved conditions for the poor. The widening gap between middle-class affluence and lower-class (especially rural) poverty was no doubt the clincher in the unexpected victory for Congress and more socialistic candidates for government. People's expectations were high.

(6) There has been the perception that the prevalence of the *discourse of secularism* (see chapter 7) has dominated the attitudes of the English-speaking intelligentsia seen as wielding power in urban centres of India, marginalizing more indigenously religious modes of thinking and discourse.

(7) Along with the perceived threat of globalisation, cultural and economic, there is its converse, the large numbers of the *Hindu diaspora* throughout the world, daily facing the strangeness of alien cultures and the trauma of being 'othered', and often continuing to nurture sentimental notions of the purity of their homeland and nostalgic longing for the rich culture they (or their forebears) left behind (Kakar 1995: 183-89).

(8) There has been the powerful *re-invigoration of the Muslim world* even within India, especially in what are seen as alarmingly militant and totalitarian global forms. This resurgence is feared as a very direct threat to Hindu self-identity. Again, this is not merely a religious and cultural threat, but political, economic, and military. The horrifying trauma of partition remains an unhealed wound, regularly re-opened by internal clashes, and by eruptions of military conflict with Muslim Pakistan on borders relatively close to India's capital. The tension was greatly heightened with the emergence of Pakistan's success (along with India) in acquiring the competence to build and use nuclear weapons. The daily performance of ritualised

guard-changing on both sides of the border check-post makes wonderful drama. But the tragedy of partition cannot be forgotten.

It is significant that it is in Gujarat, from which great numbers of India's global merchants have gone out, and where Muslims have established such effective commercial contacts overseas too, that the most fierce attacks on Muslims have taken place. Militarily, though, it is the Kashmir conflict that feeds the flames most intensely, with constant reports of atrocities against Hindus by Islamic insurgents, probably encouraged from within Pakistan. That the very large Muslim majority in Kashmir has been continually and often viciously harassed by Indian troops is still not seen by nationalist Hindus as good reason for Muslim agitation there.

In 2004, even under the Hindu nationalist government, there have been unexpected moves for peace and for a settling of the Kashmir conflict. Intense USA pressure is presumed to lie behind this change of manner. It now remains to be seen how the new Congress-dominated government will handle this new opportunity for a settlement of the dispute, and thereby, for an easing of the threat of nuclear conflict.

(9) There is the marked increase in *aggressive missionary activity* by evangelical Indian Christians, often backed financially and ideologically by western supporters. Not infrequently this support is strengthened by illegal proselytising while visiting on tourist visas. Even apart from such illegalities, it is extraordinary that the official number of missionary workers in India today is far higher than it was at the time of Independence. There are other quite different reasons too for conversion being such a highly sensitive issue in Hindu-Christian as well as Hindu-Muslim relations, but this new missionary vigour is undoubtedly one of them, with conversion being seen by Hindutva militants in socio-political rather than in religious terms.

(10) There is the upsurge - part of a global movement - of *newly realised selfhood* and the demand for rights by long-oppressed peoples at the margins of life in India, viz. *Dalits and Tribals* (see chapters 10, 16-18). It is the liberation movements within these groups that are often vigorously supported by NGO aid agencies and by both Christian and Muslim bodies, again usually backed by organisations from outside India. Land-owning and other powerful

Hindu castes fear loss of traditional status through the structural social and economic changes these movements herald. Violent clashes and revenge attacks are frequent. One instance of this fear of loss of an elite status was the violent backlash against the policy of reserved seats further confirmed by the V.P.Singh government. Significantly this was just before Hindutva came to power.

(11) Taking the above one step further, there is the perceived threat to the unity of the nation by *insurgent movements* among 'tribal' people often aiming at seceding from the Union, movements associated with Christian and other 'alien' influences by Hindutva nationalists.

(12) There is the *new mobility* available to huge numbers of 'lower middle-class' people, making possible pilgrim travel to sacred centres all over the country, and reinforcing the perception of all India as a sacred land, as one individed *punya-bhumi*.

(13) There have been the highly effective strategies for local grounding and mobilisation of the Hindutva movement carried out by the Rashtriya Svayamsevak Sangh (founded mid-1920s) and its related organisations. RSS claims to be merely a movement for cultural renewal, but its political impact is very clear. RSS strategies include not only gaining control of personnel in key institutions such as the police, regional media, teaching, legal and other professions, but even revising educational textbooks in line with their particular version of history. In particular, the accepted theory of secular historians that there was once a conquest of indigenous inhabitants (often identified as Dravidians) by invading Aryans, and it is from the latter that Vedic and Brahmanic religion developed, is anathema to Hindutva militants - as well as to conservative Hindu tradition generally. In 2004 the new 'secular' government rescinded these revisions, the main pro-Hindutva ideologue responsible for them actually having lost his seat in the election.

In large part this organisation's success derives from its appropriation and political use of religious symbols and imagery that resonate with deeply felt passions within the consciousness of India's wide-ranging 'middle classes'. The most politically potent such symbol was, for some time at least, the Rama-temple the Hindutva movement has vowed to build in what is believed to be Rama's birthplace, Ayodhya, on the site of the Muslim Mosque destroyed by RSS volunteers in the early1990s. Many other uses of religious symbolism could be listed. There was also the rise to powerful positions - Prime Minister and Home Minister - of two contrasting and therefore complementary leaders (A.B.Vajpayee and L.K.Adhvani), both well grounded in RSS doctrine and strategy, and together able to attract a wide range of support. By late 2004 their stars had waned.

(14) Finally, there is the global surge, in which Hindutva surely shares, of movements asserting self-identities believed to be under threat from the *homogenising tide of modernity*, identities expressing their distinctiveness in ethnic, religious and nationalist terms. Such movements may express fears because of fragmentation of previous political unities, however these may have been created, and open the doors to extremist mythic assertions of the glorious unity of an earlier age.

Violence Against Minorities

Each of these inflowing factors calls for much more elaboration than is possible here. All contribute in some way to the creating of a felt need for a more unified Hindu identity. A few provide insight into the reasons (far from justifications) for the long list of violent acts perpetrated by militant Hindutva-supporters in recent years. Generally, though, unscrupulous politicians, or pseudo-political local leaders, exploiting a critical situation have to be the prime suspects. Within the movement there is great ambivalence about the violence. It is consistently argued by BJP supporters - as with the murder of the Australian Baptist missionary working among leprosy sufferers - that these acts of violence have been carried out by one or other anti-BJP body, usually pro-Pakistan Muslims. (Globally, activist Muslims too are often 'in denial' concerning acts like 9/11). Although atrocities against Muslims in India have been in far greater numbers and intensity than against Christians, in some ways anti-Christian acts are the more significant precisely because the political connection is far more tenuous. And Christians are little more than two and a half percent, Muslims five times this number.

Investigations by governmental authorities generally lacked rigour. Usually there seemed little intention of bringing perpetrators to justice. There have been many cases where the police have merely turned a blind eye actually in the presence of anti-Muslim and anti-

Christian violence. This was especially the case in the horrific massacre of several thousand Muslims in Gujarat in 2002, with the victims being targetted with systematic ruthlessness. The ostensive reason for the carnage was the burning of several dozen Hindutva supporters on a train returning from Ayodhya. The official government report on this Godhra incident, presented in January 2005, contended that the fire began accidentally inside the train. Forensic evidence did not point to a deliberate arson attack, as had been argued throughout by the BJP-dominated government, state and central, without any careful examining of the evidence. There was, however, clear evidence of both carefully pre-planned and widespread killing of Muslims after the initial event, and gross collusion with the perpetrators by politicians, police and even the military. In any case, the great majority of those many Muslims who were slaughtered were completely innocent of the burning or of any other violence against Hindus.

Again, though, we need to be reminded that great numbers of Hindus throughout India were appalled both by the burning and the subsequent slaughter. Rather than focus on the gruesome details of anti-minority atrocities, we need rather to be critically aware of underlying factors pertinent to questions of identity and changing identities. Yet, the very fact of a long Hindu tradition claiming tolerance and non-violence as essential to its life gives pause for thought. When politically motivated and manipulated with the clever use of sacred symbols, this same peace-loving identity can be made to take very different shape and erupt in violent rage against 'enemies' within who are seen as threatening their very being as Hindus.

Cultural Aliens?

One of the problems as perceived by nationalist Hindus, then, is that all Muslims are Macca-oriented and all Christians identify themselves with originating bodies in the West. Both - in Hindutva's imagination - are still sustained culturally and emotionally by that unbroken umbilical cord binding them to one or other alien country and its culture, and so to its political interests. This completely ignores the many Muslims who shared the long struggles of agitation against the foreign raj and for an independent India. It ignores the remarkable contribution of large numbers of outstanding Muslims to India's pluralist cultural life, of which for example, Asghar Ali Engineer has written (Karlekar 1998). It also ignores the centuries in which the great majority of India's around 120 million Muslims have lived quite amicably side by side with their Hindu neighbours in many parts of India, very clearly seeing their ethnic roots as *Indian, not alien*. That there have from time to time been points of community conflict (as between Hindu sects also) is part of the picture too of course.

Then, to perceive Christianity as being nurtured primarily by its western origins is to ignore, for example, the existence of that vibrantly strong Christian community in Kerala, the Orthodox-related churches, which have a history in India at least thirteen centuries longer than Indian churches with any western origins. When Indian-Christians express in some specific cultural symbolic form the Indianness they actually feel, many find it painful then to be accused by militant Hindus of merely 'stealing' their cultural symbols, or of blatantly pretending to be Hindus as a guise for stealing converts. No doubt not all attempts by Christians to be more indigenous have the pure intention of expressing their Indianness in more authentic ways. The urge to convince others of the truth of their faith and the perfections of their Lord is a strong streak in Christian self-identity. Too often this takes the form of a proselytising spirit. But to reject all efforts at being more indigenously grounded as hypocrisy, an insincere mask, a mere strategy for making Hindu converts, hardly does them justice. In fact the most eager inculturators among Indian Christians are usually the least evangelical.

There is, though, an inevitable consequence of Hindutva's condemnation of Christians as essentially 'alien'. As a community they are now more self-consciously 'Christian', less confident of themselves as an integral part of Indian life. Questioning another's identity - especially by a dominant group - itself reshapes that identity. If this minority community, or family of communities, is to respond appropriately at this time of such great tension, then with whom they identify, and how they in turn identify the 'other', is all-important.

It has, unfortunately, become dangerously common for Christians mistakenly to identify Hindutva with Hinduism and the Hindu community. No doubt the pervasive impact of the Hindutva programme has been very great, especially through the highly effective local strategies of the Sangh Parivar at many different levels and within many different institutions of Indian life. Obviously, too, organisations such as RSS and VHP are part of the Hindu historical reality, just as militant fundamentalist Christian groups who despise everything Hindu are also part of the Christian historical reality.

Yet, very careful discrimination is needed here. For one thing, as Sudhir Kakar's psychological analysis of the 'new Hindu identity' points out, most Sangh Parivar leaders - K.B.Hedgewar, M.S.Golwarkar, for example – have not primarily been products of Hindu tradition, however successfully they use symbolism from that tradition. They are rather 'decidedly modern....individuals who have turned their backs on their own Western education' (Kakar 1995). Even the most influential of earlier RSS leaders, V.D. ('Veer', 'Hero') Savarkar was a 'cultural' Hindu, having little personal commitment to Hindu practice and faith. His was essentialy the nationalist stance of a politically minded 'modernist'. Does this account for his loathing of Gandhi's approach to the liberating movement, and the increasing evidence of a very close connection between Savarkar and the Mahatma's murderer, Nathuram Godse?

Community Identity; God-Naming

The question is - confining ourselves for the moment only to a Christian response - with whom, among the diverse identities being presented within our increasingly complex world, do Indian Christians find themselves identifying? With which human community do they most completely feel they belong? With anyone who is named 'Christian', whatever their attitude to Hindus and the faith of those not 'Christian', just because Christians belong to 'our community'? Can this faith-community claim to transcend prior human communities such as caste, or regional/linguistic identities? Or do Christians - maybe led by compulsions within their faith as much as those of the pluralist 'secular' consciousness of their time - find themselves identifying with those - Christian, Hindu, Muslim - who share their human values, their aspirations for a more just world, their hopes for the healing of the ills of the world and its creatures? What are the possible dynamics of the 'naming' of a Christian God? When is such naming quite rightly the basis for primary identity? And will any God-naming that shapes new identities always entail community exclusiveness?

Here, again, we surely have to discriminate between differing kinds of God-naming, and certainly between an identity shaped by self-transforming religious *believing* and a nominal identity consequent to community *belonging*. But the common assumption that the more intense the believing the more exclusive the community belonging is far from the way things actually work out in religious life.

There is a strand of militant Hindutva that pays ostentatious lip-service to the name 'Ram', but gives significance to such God-naming only insofar as this creates communalist intensity. The name is a useful means to creating a unified consciousness. True, there is an important strand in Hindu tradition that relativises divine names ever since that ancient and famous Rigvedic text, 'They call him Agni, Indra....What seers have seen as one, they call by many names'. So, we find one major strand of Hindu faith concluding that if the self is to be truly free, all names - even divine names - have to be transcended. Ultimate Being is unknowable and therefore unnameable, indescribable.

Other Hindu interpretations find our ultimate freedom in some very specific naming of God. Sometimes this has led to an exclusive community spirit, sometimes not. Both the naming of Rama and of Krishna has led their devotees in these divergent directions. In any case, naming, identifying the Focus of faith in specific ways - even if multiple ways - and thereby identifying with particular ways of envisioning that Focus, has been crucial to almost all religious life in India through the centuries. The Name is the focal point of identity - the identity of the Focus of faith, and the identity of the believer. Naming in multiple ways does not negate this. Indeed, the 'Name' in Indian faith (in Sikh devotion especially) often means the *character*, the transcendent Focus for maybe countless descriptively identifying names, with one name elevated above all others.

Religious faith will always provide the basis for a certain kind of exclusiveness. A distinctive shared vision is not necessarily communalistic though. For intrinsic to the incorporating Name itself may well be an *inclusive* stance towards others. What, then, has been characteristic of Hindutva and its religious nationalists? In most regions of North India (Hindi and Rajasthani-speaking especially), public affirming of the name of Ram has been a powerfully symbolic rallying point. India is to become *Ram-rajya*, the realm of this great Avatar of Vishnu. Yet it is Krishna that is generally the more popular in the South, East and even in strife-torn Gujarat. Some commentators have seen an anomaly here. But 'Ram' can be just a quite general name for God - as with Gandhi's dying exclamation, 'Ram, Ram'. It is this very non-specific meaning which is intended usually by Hindutva's exponents. In terms of Hindu tradition as they see it, an inclusive Hindu-dom is looked for. It excludes, they claim, only those alien traditions that will not accept that inclusiveness. Christians and Muslims are seen as the excluders, especially in not being open to and respectful of 'Hindu' traditions.

And as we have seen, one prominent strand of Christian identity - in part as a response to the newly militant Hindu identity - has provided ammunition for this judgement. That vigorously militant forms of 'fundamentalism' (see chapter 8) increasingly mark the religiosity of one prominent strand of recent Christian worldview is undeniable. There are, though, very different responses that witness to a far more *inclusive* attitude to 'Hinduism': the elegantly eirenic writings of the Kannadiga Christian, Stanley Samartha, for example, or his successor at the World Council of Churches, the Sri Lankan Wesley Ariarajah, and earlier the eco-sensitive writings of the Malayali Orthodox Bishop, Paulus Mar Gregorius, or the more contemporary dialogical witness of the mission-oriented Tamil Christian, Selvanayagam Israel, to name but a few non-Catholics. Among Catholics in India, over the past half-century the question is where any such list would end, so prolific has inter-faith dialogical writing been. Mention can be made, however, of such disparate writers as Ignatius Hirudayam, Ignatius Puthiadam, John Chethimattam, Raimundo Panikkar, Subhash Anand, Richard De Smet, George Gispert-Sauch, Sarah Grant, Anand Amaladas, Michael Amaladoss, Ishanand Vempeny, and many more.

Yet, more typical of recent Christian feeling is a document issued by the National Christian Council of India following a Consultation on 'Religious Liberty and Human Rights' in 1999. The context was the violations of human rights perpetrated by Hindutva extremists against Dalits, Tribals and against Christian missions working among such disadvantaged minorities. There is every reason to make public the 35 points listing violations of Christians' human rights. They are, though, formulated in terms that make 'Hinduism' and 'Hindu dharma' the culprits. Then this document, in general negating a dialogical approach, has a concluding section urging the need for 'dialogue' with people of other faiths. This latter looks very much like lip-service reluctantly tacked on.

It is inevitable, and justly so, that the social traumas of their history should lead Dalits, following Ambedkar's lead, to speak in sweeping terms of the evils that 'caste Hindus' have perpetrated. There can never be a just transforming of what are very real evils in society without naming those evils. The reality is, too, that Hindu communities have done far too little even to alleviate the struggles and suffering of disadvantaged groups, let alone systemically transform their status. Yet, for the Christian community in its representative institutions to name 'caste Hindus' as the enemy 'other' in this indiscriminate way, cannot but exacerbate the tension, and endanger the life of the wider community that independent India has been struggling for. If Christians identify the militancy of Hindutva with Hinduism *per se*, inevitably the hate and fear of others that this programme has inspired will continue to intensify. The perceptual walls of mutual alienation will be built even higher.

So I return to my earlier point: our need to differentiate between Hindutva and the Hindu people. Identifying needs to be discriminating. The fact that the proponents of Hindutva function from within one or other Hindu community, and use Hindu imagery, even that a few traditional Hindu Acharyas are part of Hindutva militancy, does not mean that the religious heart of Hindu tradition activates their programme.

Hindutva's Three Symbolic Themes

Three concepts, deeply embedded in religious discourse generally, rise to prominence in the symbolic language of Hindutva: *sacred land* and *blood, sacred myth* and *scripture, unifying dharma*. Each *can be* a dangerous factor in identity-shaping, unless re-visioned and re-iterpreted:

(i) *Sacred Land & Blood*: Many of the wars thickly dotting human history have been based on one or other of these three themes, broadly interpreted. But territorial conflicts have been the most common. Violent conflict and the shedding of blood on and for their land itself intensifies the sense of identity people have with that land. Blood-drenched land is felt to be sacred land. The sense of belonging is immeasurably intensified. A people's identity is felt to be even more irrevocably bound up with what thus becomes even more a *sacred* place. Within Hindu tradition there are uncountable earthing-points for this sense of *Bharat* as a *punya-bhumi*. Originating as very local sacred spots belonging to one or other sect, many of them over the years have become pilgrimage centres for all Hindus, and especially with the recent rapid growth in tourist travel. So they have functioned as places of unification for Hindus. The concerned temple may well have been built by a ruler who intended precisely that this sacred place become both a symbolic centre for his dominion and thus a unifying factor, even if he had identified himself with one or other sectarian cult and traced his genealogy by naming sacred figures of that cult. And the concept of 'this sacred land', with its corollary that from this sacred earth all those who do not accept it as sacred have to be cleansed, along with appeal to the blood of martyrs of the past and for further blood to be sacrificed - all this has become an intrinsic part of Hindutva rhetoric. But it can also (according to the findings of Susan Bayly, in Marty & Appleby 1994; see chapter 15 below) become a key concept in the sense of identity of Christians, as is the case with Christians of Kanyakumari who feel themselves beleaguered.

(ii) Then there is the appeal to the power of sacred all-embracing *myth*. Each sacred place is already identified by recounting its particular mythic origins. India-wide the great epics, Mahabharata and Ramayana, have become the stories of the nation, the grounding history of Mother Bharata. It is no mere coincidence that it was immediately subsequent to the long weekly showing of these stories, during which the whole nation was enthralled by every instalment week by week, that there occurred a great upsurge in support for the Hindutva project . It was no lucky accident that L.K.Adhvani, setting out on his 'pilgrimage' to Ayodhya, was portrayed as a Rama-figure, complete with divine bow and seated in his royal chariot. (Some local power-bases prior to this, for example M.G.Ramachandran's role for ADMK in Tamil Nadu and N.T.Ramarao of the Telugu Desham in Andhra, reversed this process: it was actors who had established themselves as divine figures on screen who then were able to duplicate this role in the political world, by still making use of the symbols of those mythic figures they had enacted).

However, the apologetic use of scripture in the past century has increasingly tended to emphasise its literal truth, its historical and scientific accuracy, which seems thoroughly out of tune with the way scripture functioned for Hindu devotees of earlier ages. It is difficult to avoid the conclusion that this is a case of the fundamentalism of some Christian and Muslim exegetes being imitated by Hindus. Among the more 'intellectual' and 'spiritual' Hindus, though, ever since the 19th century - as we saw earlier - it is the Bhagavad-Gita (part of the Mahabharata of course) that has been affirmed as the great unifying scripture, itself seen as intrinsically bringing together so many apparently disparate streams of Indian religious tradition, and being primarily concerned with inner transformation.

(iii) Hindutva also emphasises a common *dharma*, which is seen as the formative and unifying factor in Hindu cultural life. It is worth noting that the RSS, for example, opens its membership to all castes, claiming to transcend all forms of discrimination, even though leadership is mainly in the hands of those from Brahmin communities. From time to time in recent years efforts have been made by emissaries of Visva Hindu Parishad (now a rival to RSS) and others to appeal to Dalit people. There is clearly some recognition - belated though it may be - that treatment of Dalits in the past has been reprehensible. Yet (as I discuss more fully in chapters 16-18) the existence of caste as such is seriously questioned by very few devout Hindus, however much its discriminatory excesses may be lamented when these are actually recognised.

It is the *cow* that stands as the focal symbol of Hindu cultural life, the protection of the cow having been seen for a very long time as that dharmic deed by which Hindu religion and culture will stand or fall. The cow herself traditionally symbolises such standing and falling: in this increasingly corrupt *kali* age of our time *dharma* is depicted as tottering on but one leg, so she is less able to fulfil her role as *kama-dhenu*, the fulfiller of all desires. Sudhir Kakar believes that a fruitful way to analyse the 'constructed revival of Hindu identity' (1995:197) is to look closely at the highly effective oratory of Sadhavi Rithambra, as expressed in a pro-BJP speech given throughout India in 1990-91. It is significant that at the highly emotional climax of her speech appeal is made to the protection of the cow. 'If you do not awaken (and 'Hindu *jagaran*' is another name for the whole Hindutva programme), cows will be slaughtered everywhere....(the) catastrophes of history will say Hindus are cowards.' And then, rapidly moving from appeal to the manhood of her Hindu audience, she humorously draws out sharp contrasts between Hindus and Muslims, again sharpening the Hindu sense of self-identity. In her long list of such differences, she concludes by ridiculing Muslims: 'The Hindu worships the cow, the Muslim attains paradise by eating beef....Whatever the Hindu does, it is the Muslim's religion to do its opposite. I say to them: "If you want to do everything contrary to the Hindu, then note that the Hindu eats with his mouth: you should do the opposite in this too!"' (*op.cit.* 211-213).

This public oratory may be humorously put, but the polarising passion underlying it is strikingly effective with a crowd of Hindu people. So much greater, then, the need for countering voices of interpretation from within the Hindu community, whereby blood on the land, the power of myth, and the dynamic of *dharma*, are given new visionary orientation, a new inclusiveness for the whole human community.

Chapter 15
'Pressure on the Hyphen' of the Indian-Christian

Questions of identity, then, thrust themselves upon us from many quarters. No thinking Christian in India can be unaware of the *anomalies,* certainly the *perceived anomalies,* of being an *Indian-Christian.* Abroad, an Indian identifying herself/himself as a Christian meets surprise: 'I thought Indians were Hindus'. At home a more likely result is suspicion, even if this is politically engineered in the main. Kiran Sebastian, Professor of Theology in Bangalore, rightly contends that the dynamic character of an Indian-Christian identity rules out any simplistic understanding of what being an Indian-Christian means. Rather, 'the ambivalence which lies at the core of Christian identity in the Indian context needs to be both recognized and exposed'. There are great 'pressures on the hyphen' for the Indian-Christian ('Pressure on the Hyphen: Aspects of the Search for Identity Today in Indian-Christian Theology', *Religion & Society,* Dec 1997, p.37).

If for no other reason, such critical self-reflection has been forced on Indian Christians by the varied range of recent attacks by Hindutva extremists on Christians as well as Muslims, that we noted in the last chapter. It is the authentic Indianness of Christians that is questioned, and therefore their right to remain on this sacred *punya-bhumi* of Bharat. To live on Indian soil and be fully part of Indian life, all Christians, as well as any other minority community, should - according to militant Hindutva - openly declare themselves to be culturally and patriotically 'Hindu', whatever their private devotions may be focussed on. Rashtriya Sangha Sevak leader, K.S.Sudarshan, early in October 2001 (a month after 9/11) clearly implied that Indian Christians are, potentially at least, legitimate targets for anti-terrorist action, just as are Muslims. Addressing 21,000 RSS Volunteers in Delhi, Sudarshan was adamant that, being a foreign religion dependent on a foreign missionary presence inevitably prevents it becoming truly Indian. Not only should all such support systems be thrown out of India immediately, but the Christian Church should be taken under governmental control just as the Church in China had been by the totalitarian regime there. When this kind of militancy, along with a glorifying of the 'Hindu nuclear bomb', erupts within a tradition renowned for its peace-loving tolerance, clearly it is not only Christians who have a crisis of identity.

I have already attempted to probe some of the historical precedents - political, religio-cultural, socio-economic - as well as the current dynamics underlying such aggressive claims. All sides will, eventually, need to be thoroughly self-critical about this. For now, though, we look briefly at Christian identity-consciousness.

It was my Bangalore colleague, Christopher Duraisingh, who first wrote in the early 1980s of the 'hyphenated' being and identity of Indian-Christians. Their consciousness is 'co-constituted': the worlds of both Judeo-Christian and 'pan-Indian' traditions in their corporate memory merge creatively in their Indian-Christianness. In this 'doubly determined' identity, their Indianness entails a distinct form of being Christian, and their being people of Judeo-Christian faith entails a distinct mode of being Indian.

Critics have suggested this binary analysis over-simplifies the dynamics. Neither the Judeo-Christian nor the Indian streams are as one-dimensional as this model could imply. Any such static, non-fluid view of the process, though, is the exact opposite of what Duraisingh intended. Then, too, this was written at a time just before the real breakthrough in general theological consciousness in India of the distinctives of, and compulsions for, a new Dalit identity as an inescapably significant ingredient of Indian-Christian identity. Duraisingh, in line with the great majority of those who had come to be typified as 'Indian-Christian theologians', had pointed to one of the traditional classical systems as a kind of paradigm. Ramanuja was taken as an earlier Indian model of such hyphenated consciousness, for in this Hindu theologian too a fusion of Vedic and vernacular *bhakti* streams can be discerned.

From within the same theological institution (and both going on to formulate their thesis at Harvard) Sathianathan Clarke has asserted that Duraisingh's 'pan-Indian' perspective 'is highly vulnerable to being co-opted by caste Hinduism' (Clarke 1998: 14 - but I refer more fully to this work in the chapter below on a new Dalit consciousness). It is in reworking this concept of the hyphenated character of Indian-Christian identity that Kiran Sebastian points to the immense 'pressures on the hyphen'. The tensions are precisely because of this interpenetrative meeting of diverse identities moving across from one side to the other. But at such an interface there is also the power 'to reconstruct and reconceive' (*op.cit.* 32-33).

Indian-Christian, Dalit-Christian

Dalit Christians in particular - as we see in the chapter on Dalit issues - resent the manner in which until very recently it was the writings of those who converted to Christian faith from dominant castes that were assumed to be the most significant forms of 'Indian-Christian theology'. Robin Boyd's *Introduction to Indian Christian Theology* (first edition 1969), that has become something of a classic, does not refer to a single Dalit theologian. It turns exclusively to those from the 'higher' communities whose Christian faith naturally interacted with more classical expressions of Hindu faith. Indian Christians of Protestant traditions, such as M.M.Thomas and S.J.Samartha who reflected in the 1970s on this phenomenon of Indian responses to Christ, in their distinctive ways also tended to look to the dominant castes as providing the most significant material for Indian-Christian theological reflection (Thomas 1970; Samartha 1974). Like a majority of Catholic India-Christian theologians up to very recent times, taking *advaita* as in some sense paradigmatic for Christians, Samartha's turning to those with a classical Hindu background is to be expected. But even with his far greater emphasis on human liberation within the context of Indian socio-cultural and secular life, Thomas still turns to Hindus from 'higher' caste backgrounds for examples of those touched by the 'Acknowledged Christ of the Indian Renaissance'.

Clearly, there was a serious imbalance here that may well be described as a form of 'hegemonic' dominance, to use Sathi Clarke's words (Clarke 1998). Three points, though, should be noted in defence of earlier faith-interpretation by 'higher' caste Indian Christians, such as the Tamils P.Chenchiah, V.Chakkarai, A.J.Appasamy, the Bengalis K.M.Benarjee and Brahmabandhav Upadhyay and many others, including more contemporary Catholic writers (See e.g. A.J.Appasamy's *Christianity as Bhakti Marga*, 1928; V.Chakkarai's *Jesus the Avatar*, 1932).

Firstly, we should not lose sight of the importance of their standing critically against the stream of the dominant western missionary interpretation of Jesus and his liberative way. They uncover important insights concerning possible meanings of Jesus and of Christian faith that only inculturated Indian faith could, even if it does arise from the inculturated experience of those from 'higher' communities.

Secondly, their stand should not be seen solely as a response to the earlier 'Brahmo demand for a National Christianity', as Clarke argues at one point, quoting M.M.Thomas (Clarke 1998: 37). Their inculturation sprang, rather - as Clarke himself suggests - from their 'burning desire to express their own caste Hindu-Christian constitudedness'. Their theology, therefore, is best seen in terms of a creative internal dialogue, 'the dialogue between Christianity and the Brahmanism within themselves' (again, quoting M.M.Thomas). The authenticity of that internal dialogue should be given due recognition, even if at that time it often did not directly reflect the concerns of those Dalits who became Christian - who eventually far out-numbered caste converts.

Thirdly, there still remains the need for Christian faith within an Indian context to be aware of, actively to explore and to respond creatively to what I have called the 'Hindu theology's forgotten struggles' (Selvanayagam 2002). These 'struggles' take many forms. Not least is the tension between a *dharma*-based establishment worldview and the more *dharma*-transcending thrust of indigenous ecstasy, with its central theme of love as the ultimate value. Here, though, is not the place to take this point any further. I merely quote from the closing paragraph of the essay mentioned above (*op.cit.* 83):

Cultural impact is never merely one-way, and along with the unexpected outposts of resistance and insurgency that remain, there are surprising insights to be found within the larger systems. The task remains, therefore, of uncovering these struggles and thereby countering all our cultural assumptions.

Indian-Christian Diversity & Tensions

The neglect of Dalit and Tribal forms of Indian-Christian faith, and the imbalance in favour of expressions of faith from 'higher' caste converts, is now being vigorously rectified in theological circles in india. Such changing attitudes are reflected in anthologies of Indian-Christian and Asian Christian writings (e.g. Sugirtharajah 1993 and 1993a). Critical reflection on social issues has become paramount, following the lead given by Christian journals such as *Religion and Society*, published by the Christian Institute for the Study of Religion and Society (established in the 1950s largely by the efforts of P.Devanandan and M.M.Thomas) and by publications of similar Catholic organisations responding to the liberationist movement. Now there are other pointers. The great preponderance of articles in long-established journals such as *Bangalore Theological Forum* (published by the United Theological College, Bangalore) and, a little less markedly, the Jesuit Catholic *Vidya Jyoti* show increasing focus on the experience of Dalits and Tribals, with rapidly decreasing dialogue with classical Hindu belief-systems and spiritualities.

In fact, the tension among Catholic Christian theologians on this Sanskrit-Dalit divide is not difficult to detect even in *Vidya Jyoti*, especially significant as this is the community that has made more attempts than any others, especially since the pioneering writings of Pierre Johanns in the 1920s and 1930s, to explore Vedanta and the classical Hindu theological systems ways to more authentic Indian-Christian self-expression. The tension is clearly less in the *Journal of Dharma*, published from a seminary for non-Latin Eastern Catholics, originating largely from 'high'-caste communities of Kerala, also with a strong traditional grounding in classical Indian philosophy and culture.

The writings of K.M.George are representative of the creation-sensitive spirituality of strands in the Orthodox (Syrian) tradition of India, also found in George's earlier mentor, Paulus Mar Gregorius (Mar Gregorius 1988). Another theological teacher originally from that 'Syrian' background, K.P.Aleaz, still writes extensively of the creative possibilities of re-experiencing Christian faith within a non-dualist metaphysical framework, as classically formulated by the eighth century Hindu philosopher-theologian, Sankara (e.g. Aleaz 1996). Similar interpretations of a genuinely Indian-Christian identity are expressed by a number of Catholic leaders through their Ashram-based spirituality, such as the Bede Griffiths tradition at Shanti Vanam, Tamil Nadu, or that of Vineet Francis, with an Ashram in Karnataka. A Christian *advaita* was also explored with considerable skill by Sr Sara Grant (member of the Christu Prema Ashram, Pune) in her Teape lectures of 1989 (Grant 1989).

These various forms of Indian-Christian acculturation and reflection have made little impact on the radical social orientation of recent liberationist and Dalit theology. Yet, we should not doubt the great significance of the inner dialogical journey of Indian-Christians for whom the wide-ranging classical Sanskrit traditions have been a major identity-shaping factor. 'Hindu Christian', or 'Hindu Catholic', were the terms used of themselves by the 19th century Bengali nationalist Christians, K.M.Banerjee and Brahmabandhab Upadhyay. Their's was an impressive struggle to integrate their strongly held pro-Indian worldview with their equally fervent devotion to Christ. Brahmabandhab, although baptised into a genuine sharing in Christian sacramental and ecclesial life, and clearly attaining an outstanding sense of communion with Christ, still continued to be nurtured by images and spiritual instincts from his earlier Hindu rootage. The volatility seen in the changing ways he expressed his faith, as well as their remarkably creative insights, show clearly just how complex that 'Hindu-Christian' identity was (Lipner & Gispert-Sauch 1991).

There was, then, a ferment of 'hybridised' (to use Foucalt's term) cultural interaction during that period (especially the late decades of the nineteenth century) of nationalist Hindu response to Christian critique of old tradition and affirmations of a new vision of life and of God. This ferment threw up many similarly volatile characters whose core identity still remained 'Hindu'. Many, like Brahmabandhab's friend and early mentor, Keshab Chandra Sen, would have called themselves 'Christian-Hindu' (rather than 'Hindu-Christian'), perhaps just 'new Hindu', in that most never took the step of initiation into the Christian community. Yet, new insights from the Christian belief-system, and therefore also from western education, made a deep impact on their way of seeing the world (Samartha 1974).

For a number of Hindu intellectuals, although the cultural ferment of those times brought challenges to older and hitherto unquestioned identities, the resulting sense of Hinduness was more sharply focussed, more consciously integrated and therefore even stronger than before. Reformers such as Dayanand Sarasvati - again in the second half of the nineteenth century - vehemently rejected all Christian claims and aimed to return to the true roots of Hindu religion: 'Back to the Vedas' was his integrating slogan. This meant doing away with mythology, ritual, doctrines, sectarian deities, as well as many socio-cultural traditions that were believed to have grown up after that early age of pure Vedism. Theirs, they believed, was a far more authentic Hindu-ness.

What became the dominant neo-Hindu position, however, was the more inclusive, and less decisively interactive, way of Vivekananda, Radhakrishnan and others, for whom 'all paths to God are equally valid'. For them, though, it is the elevated path of non-dualist Vedanta that most fully allows for the many levels of spirit at which humans find themselves. In the end, in other words, there is still a critical perspective to such inclusiveness.

Such 'inclusiveness' fails to provide the creative form of critical interpenetration that the reflective Indian-Christian will expect. For, clearly it is of great importance to recognise the non-static, fluid character of Indian-Christianness. It is not only its hyphenated character that is subject to 'pressures'. There is also great ideological pressure on both sides to see Christians and Hindus in terms of single, clearly identifiable traditions and communities. Such homogenizing is not only a major danger to the pluralism of the Indian nation. Pressures to conform to such constructed norms inhibit the liberative potential of religious life within the nation's life. In whatever particular stream either of Indianness or of Christianness the Indian-Christian is located, the emerging identity entails a new configuration of what it is to be 'Indian' as well as what it is to be 'Christian'. The crucial question is, though, what distinctive and authentic forms of Indianness are called for that can draw out those distinctive forms of Christianness that are also authetic?

Authentic 'Fundamentalist' Christianity?

Again, *diversity* is crucial to authenticity. There are many ways of being an Indian Christian, just as there are many ways of being Hindu. A recent study of 'fundamentalism' among Christians in the deep south of India, by Susan Bayly (Marty & Appleby 1994), is considerably enriched by providing the perspective of social anthropology. It is as an inevitable response to and even emergence out of features of Hindu fundamentalism that Bayly sees much of the increasingly hardening Christian exclusivism and mythic demonising of Hindus and their culture. Her argument is that most of the basic features of Christian fundamentalism in the South are thoroughly indigenous to Hinduism, at least in its rural Indian form.

Finding *continuities* in this way is invariably helpful ; accounting for such vigorous, seemingly spontaneous movements. There are, though, aspects of Bayly's argument that we need to question rather critically. Not least is her apparent assumption that any form of emotionally charged, self-protecting activist movements with religious overtones (such as the fishermen's struggle for justice in the South) can be labelled 'fundamentalist'. The liberationist fishermen's movement may have some features in common with what can properly be dubbed 'fundamentalist', but it hardly makes for clarity to use this term for the movement as such. But I have already taken up (in chapter 8) some of the problems in discussions about 'fundamentalism'.

There is also the claim (in Bayly's account) that recent developments among southern Christians is primarily by way of *imitation* of fundamentalist forms of militant Hinduism. No doubt the history of Hindu sects offers many examples that contrast sharply with the peace-loving tolerance of the Gandhian type. And no doubt too the raw materials of any 'fundamentalism' emerging in India will have Indian roots of some kind - the emotionalism, the absolutism, the other-worldliness, the heightened veneration of a particular scripture, certainly forms of exclusivism, are all possible to sectarian Hinduism. Yet the way those forms of South Indian Christianity with much more clear 'fundamentalist' features echo so closely southern American fundamentalist vocabulary, doctrine, strategies and even preachers' garb (usually double-breasted suit and flamboyant tie) and life-style, make it clear that no one should blame militant Hindus for seeing a western connection, even if is not quite as politically sinister as they suspect. The imported imagery is unmissable.

The contrast with an authentically indigenous Indian-Christian devotion, even evangelical commitment, can be seen in the life and witness of (both Telugu Dalits as it happens, both once known well to me, but almost unknown outside their locality) such men as Sadhu K. Ratnam (now deceased) and K.Azariah. In these Indian-Christians and in countless others like them, there is a gentleness, a personal humbleness, a lack of concern with 'success', a quiet confidence in the reality of their Christ-based vision, a commitment to sharing this vision, yet a faith that 'can respectfully embrace the faith of others in the great spiritual landscape which is India' (Rowe 1994: iv; also Lott, 'Faith and Culture in Indian Christian Identity', in Premasagar 2002:1-35).

But 'indigenous devotion' is in no way uniform. And, by way of contrast again with the gentle Indian-Christianity of Ratnam and Azariah, I also agree with Susan Bayly that mainstream Christian leadership in India has usually failed to reckon with the persisting power of more primal forms of religion - ecstatic spiritism, invoked in drum-led dance, miraculous healing, the power and authority of charismatic leaders, the singing of hypnotically repeated popular songs, for example. Its Christianised forms are to be found especially in urban vernacular congregations. By way of example of a 'charismatic cult leader' Bayly describes (*ibid.*) the religiosity of the remarkable late 19th century Malayali Christian prophet, Justus Joseph, also known as Vidwan Kutti, 'the learned youth'. At a time when:

...the Saint Thomas Christians' old ecclesiastical structures had been thrown into disarray by a series of crises over leadership and episcopal succession, this ordained Malayali Brahmin convert broke with his Anglican missionary sponsors and proclaimed the imminence of Christ's second coming. Beginning in 1875, he acquired a following of ten thousand to fifteen thousand...mostly Saint Thomas Christians who danced and sang in a secret Celestial Language, revering their self-professed messiah as a composite incarnation of Jehovah, the Hindu Ram, the biblical Joseph, the Muslim imam and martyr Ali, and the nineteenth-century Anglican evangelical bishop of Calcutta, Daniel Wilson.

This movement, claims Bayly, was 'typical of the region's tendency to generate wildfire millenarian groups', as is also the 'return to expressions of guru-centred revivalist Christianity' since the late 1980s or so, in which charismatic healing, the exorcising of demons and speaking in unknown tongues are prominent as signs of being truly in touch with divine things. The mainstream churches are denounced as led by 'figures of weakness and uncertainty in the contested terrain of Hindu raj and militant communalism'. Militant believers despise what they see as their ecumenical compromises, interfaith syncretisms, weak-kneed lack of struggle with Satan. their view of Christ as mere secular liberator, and above all their lifeless formalising of worship and devotion,

Bhakti & *Sakti* as Authentic Christian Spirituality

What we are describing here is essentially *sakti*-religion, the worldview of those for whom the 'power' (envisaged in female form)

can break through at every moment of crisis. Another classifying term for this religious form could be *bhakti*. The passion and ecstasy, certainly the single-minded focus (*ekantika*), typical of various forms of India's *bhakti*-faiths may not always be as wildly counter-cultural, as compelled by power-goals, as *sakti*-faith usually will be. But there has been much overlap; and both seem to be more characteristic of the local traditions of non-Brahmanic indigeneity. Often the more love-compelled, love-drenched faith of the *bhakta* is more innate to an Indian Christian religiosity not yet conforming to and constrained by the religious style expected in urbanised middle-class life. In many ways, too, *bhakti*-faith incorporated much of the non-conformist, ecstatic features of *sakti*-religiosity. Drum and dance were as much part of many 'love'-movements, and an essential part of *bhakti*'s primal streams, as of the 'power'-tradition. It was often a dancing God - especially Nataraj Siva and Krishna - who evoked the passion of the *bhaktas*. Tamil Vaishnava *bhakta* Nammalvar, for instance, rin his 1000 stanza Tiruvaimoli rarely leaves the theme either of Krishna's exhilarating dance or the dancing feet of his liberated devotees. (I have reflected more fully on the the liberating image of the divine dancer in my Cambridge Teape lectures for 1999, 'Set Free by a Dancing God', yet to be published).

Gradually a wider circle of Indian Christians (not only the Mizo people noted in chapter 10), especially those with Dalit origins, begin to recognise the cultural alienation they have been subjected to by the absence of drum and dance from their liturgical and spiritual life.

Unfortunately, Christian *bhakti* has in other circles now begun to take harder fundamentalist forms - bibliolatry, a fierce protection of what is perceived as the threatened marks of Christian identity, an aggressive posture towards other faiths and an uncompromising rejection of their values and cultures. Even Christians who are not of the same sectarian persuasion are fiercely condemned as hypocrites.

It could no doubt be argued that *bhakti*-religiosity, with its intense and absolutist focus on the saving efficacy of one divine figure, has always held the seeds of such fundamentalism. Hindu claims of eternal tolerance towards all faiths is not without some basis, but ignores great swathes of historical reality. Even in the *bhakti* movements themselves we can see glimpses of this more confrontational reality, for there we often find sentiments such as this verse of Nammalvar, the Tamil Vaishnava saint of perhaps the ninth century:

> Other than his form in Kurugur, there is no lord......
> All you Saivas, Jainas, Bauddhas,
> Cease your endless argument,
> Only praise the Lord who stands in Kurugur
> (Tiruvaimoli IV.10 - cp. trans. Bharati &.Lakshmi 1987).

As well as the total rejection of both 'mainstream' church life and all other faiths, there is another interesting phenomenon found in South Indian Christianity. Large numbers from traditional churches - St Thomas, Catholic, Church of South India, Lutheran - while still remaining members of their original churches, are caught up in this more charismatic religiosity, and profess to find more authentic worship and fellowship in charismatic, perhaps pentecostal meeting places. They may not use this language, but they find ecstatic religion more directly gives expression to their self-identity.

Lionel Caplan (Marty & Appleby 1994; cf. also Caplan 1982) has described this growing phenomenon of ecstatic Christianity in South India as a 'counter-cultural' movement of resistance to what would otherwise dominate them. As I contended above, there is non-Indian impetus here at work also, especially in the particular *exclusivist doctrines*, the language and other features of the culture the ecstasy becomes locked into. The influence of writings, preaching, and other forms of support from America and elsewhere is all too obvious in the language used. But the indigenous resonance this arouses is clearly not alien.

Earlier mainstream missionary leadership so often assumed that most of these primally indigenous ways of being religious can be and must be wiped clean from the convert people's consciousness. The religious reality is very different: wiping a consciousness clean, even if it were desirable, is not such a simple matter. At the other geographical extreme of the subcontinent, as we noted in chapter eleven, during times of all-engrossing and intensely emotional spiritual revival in Mizoram and the North East regions, the drum and dance that had long been banned from worship, came back in the spontaneous eruption of a religious form deeply embedded in tribal consciousness (Kipgen 1997; Lalsanghkima 1998).

Indigenous Worship Forms

Indigenous forms of Christian worship can raise hackles in widely varied quarters. As one rather deeply involved in attempting to develop what at United Theological College, Bangalore, we called 'intercultural' worship (Lott 1986), I have from time to time been asked to guide research by students from other countries. Invariably their starting point will be: what indigenous forms may appropriately be borrowed from Hinduism, without thereby betraying authentic Christian tradition? It was the kind of question I myself would once have asked. But, properly to understand the process a very different view of faith-consciousness is required. For, when Indian-Christians seek authenticity - in worship, theology, ethical positioning, or whatever - their concern has to be, not 'what can we properly appropriate?', but,' how can we best be true to that distinctive experience that is ours within a more inclusive Indian-Christian consciousness?' It is a question, again, of authentic identity.

As seen in the previous chapter, recent polemical attack from the Hindutva front shows a similar misapprehension. Attempts of the past three or four decades - and there were very significant attempts much earlier - to give expression to the Indianness of Christian ecclesial life and worship are fiercely condemned as 'copying', even 'stealing' from Hindu tradition (while at the same time accusing Christians of not being 'Hindu' enough!). Christian motives for being more indigenous will inevitably be mixed. For some, being more 'Indian' may well be a ploy to soften resistance by others to the Christian message. Was this the case with the remarkable Italian Jesuit, Robert de Nobili, in the early seventeenth century, whose indigenous ways among the Brahmins of Madurai in South India have at times been held up as a pioneering model? Or did he recognise that there was just no other authentic way for people from a high-caste background to be religious? Motives for fiercely rejecting this principle of inculturation will be equally uncertain.

Once a measure of alienation had been established by the western conformities expected in early ecclesial strategy (and Christian indigenous critics agree with one side of the Sangh Parivar polemics at this point), there are bound to be points of anomaly in Indian-Christian struggles to discover and give expression to more authentic forms of self-identity.

(i) There is the 'Indian Mass', seeking eucharistic union with Christ in ways that echo Hindu Upanishadic, Agamic and *bhakti* religiosity, and (in spite of constraints from the Vatican) now well-established at the (Catholic) National Biblical, Catechetical, and Liturgical Centre, Bangalore (though not authorised by Rome for use outside the Centre).

(ii) There are the more inclusive, more contextualised 'intercultural' liturgies developed at the (non-Catholic) United Theological College, Bangalore, clearly responsive to wider social and cultural impulses in contenporary India (Lott 1986).

(iii)There is the 'Alternative Liturgy' authorised by the Synod of the Church of South India in 1985 (see my 'Faith & Culture in Interaction: The Alternative CSI Liturgy', in Sathi Clarke (ed.), 1989, *Reflections (Essays in Honour of the Rt Revd Sundar Clarke),* Madras; also Westerfield Tucker, K. (ed.) 1996, 'Historic Tradition, Local Culture: Tensions and Fusions in the Liturgy of the Church of South India, in *The Sunday Service of the Methodists (Studies in Honour of James F.White*, Nashville: Abingdon), which in its central eucharistic prayer is clearly indebted to wide-ranging Indian tradition as well as to the rehabilitated eco-vision of modern times.

(iv) Other liturgical expressions are the thoroughly Tamil-style sung liturgies of Tamilnadu Theological Seminary, Madurai, where there have also been explicitly 'Dalit liturgies' (*Vazhipaduvom*, Madurai: TTS Dalit Resource Centre, 2000). Apart from preparatory communal acts, and the use of traditional folk-Tamil forms of song for the sermon, these latter liturgies are mostly statements of Dalits' socio-economic oppression and aspirations to fuller life. There is little 'cultural-anthropological' input. Elsewhere there has been greater effort to explore Dalit cultural identities, with (for example) vigorously rhythmic drumbeat and folk-dance as intrinsic to the liturgy. Similarly, in the North-East there has been (but see chapter 10 above) the Mizo Drum-Dance; and (in both Catholic and Protestant circles) faith expressed through the adapted classical dance-forms of Bharata Natya. Then, there are the highly significant (and internationally noticed) iconographic paintings and sculpture of artists such as Jyoti Sahi, drawing on primal and classical imagery, often in essentially contemporary style (Sahi 1986).

All these and many more divergent ways in which both Indianness and Christianness are expressed inevitably bewilder those faithful who want to be sure that their identity today is not only sharply defined, but is just as it was yesterday. There is too in this process of change in Indian cultural life the impact of (post)modernity, which at points can transcend westernization, even if inevitably they are bound up together. This means that liturgies aiming to engage with life can never remain in some pristine purity of classical form. They will necessarily explore ways in which the fusion of past and present, tradition and modernity, Indian and Christian, culture and faith, already take place and can do so in further new ways of worship as well as in life. To a large extent it will be the particular local cultural community providing the nurturing background to faith that will determine the Indian-Christian's way of worship, as of other forms of self-articulation. But that nurturing background too will never be static.

Such explorations may well be confusing to anyone - conservative Christian or militant Hindu for example - looking for a simple identity for Christianity, especially if looking for an uncluttered alienness. The depth, the diversity, the richness of the Indian cultural traditions within which the transforming dynamic of Christian faith seeks for authentic embodiment make it inevitable that the Indian-Christian search for selfhood will throw up more complex and more intense culture-faith questions than anywhere in the globe. The conjoined newness of hyphenated Indian-Christian being can only find expression in a self-identity that is a long process of post-missionary, post-colonial self-discovery. Such identity can never be merely the repeating of patterns already given, either by Indian or by Christian tradition. It is this which means that anomalies and ambiguities are inevitable. Yet, this constant critical reflection on inherited ways of being both Indian and Christian opens up the potential delight of creative self-discovery.

Chapter 16
Caste Identities & Faith's Reforms

In traditional Indian society the identity most clearly defining people has been the caste-community within which they were born. Hence a common term used for caste, *jati*, 'that to/in which (one is) born'. The older traditional term was *varna*, meaning 'description, nature, colour'. Some scholars find this last connotation significant, in that in general people of 'higher' caste are markedly lighter in colour than the so-called 'lower' orders. Even in the Rig Veda certain lower orders, called *Dasas*, 'menials', 'slaves' are described as dark-faced savages, in contrast to the light-skinned 'noble-ones' (*Aryans*).

Caste's Origins in Aryan-Dravidian Divide?

Ideologues of Hindu nationalism are, as we saw, made very irate by the theory of an *Aryan invasion*. Held for many years by modern scholars - now a little less confidently - this theory proposes that there was a period some three or four millennia ago when the Aryan tribes, perhaps from central Asia, came pouring in through the north-west of India and subdued the indigenous peoples of the Subcontinent. Those hugely important archeological findings of the 1930s onwards in the Indus Valley (now mostly Pakistan) make it clear that the earlier civilisation there was not destroyed by military invasion as once assumed. Catastrophic geological changes and ecological decline seem to be the cause of its fall, including the drying up of the great river previously watering that part of the huge 'Indus Valley'. Was this the legendary Sarasvati river alluded to in Vedic literature?

And, was this ancient civilisation the originating source of the Dravidian cultural stream of South India? For the non-Aryans are usually identified in this theory with the Dravidians who were forced to retreat to the South. Their separate ethnic origins are reflected in the obviously distinct languages and cultural life of the South, compared to the more Sanskrit-related languages ('Indo-European') further North. Even political life in post-Independence Tamil country was for several decades dominated by the issue of Dravidian as against Brahmin/Sanskritic identity, with rigorous efforts made to purge Tamil language of all Sanskrit accretions.

In other words, for all the oversimplified versions of this theory, in terms of present identities in India that ancient past leaves indelible markings. For there is also the *legacy of the caste divisions* also resulting in part from that ancient process of intermingling of distinct ethnic and cultural communities. Issues of purity and of power can be seen too, however subtle the assimilations involved. 'Aryan' purity was believed to be there in the identities of sacred Brahmins, ruling power in the warrior Kshatriyas, economic power in trading Vaishyas - though originally Aryan identities may have been a simpler duality: sacred ruler-priests, and artisan-workers. In the complex social structure eventually to emerge, it was the conquered 'Dasas' who served as artisans, serfs and menials of the lower castes.

'Hindu' Fusion of Diverse Streams

Naturally, modern Hindutva militants find it impossible to accept a theory that sees the origins of Hinduism's Brahmanic religion in an invasion of immigrants from some debatable alien location. Nor is caste, they claim, other than the recognition of differing functions.

There is no doubt that earlier interpretations of the process by which non-Vedic (the term 'pre-Vedic' is offensive to many Hindu apologists) and Vedic religious streams merged in later Hindu India have been greatly oversimplified. Yet, divergent types of cult and worldview can be identified. A number of scholars have seen the focus of early Vedic (and therefore Aryan?) religion in household and sacrificial *Fire* (Agni), with corresponding high deities of the heavens - especially various forms of the Sun and his movements through the sky - linked by a number of powerful gods of storm, wind and war between, especially the great Soma-drinker Indra. In this worldview male gods dominate, though we do find a few female earth-related deities too. But in the religion of the 'Indus Valley' the sacredness of *earth and earth's waters* are central. Ritual bathing places provide the focus for cultic life, with the bull (and other animals), 'proto-Siva' with yogic pose and erect phallus, and the female earth-mother also prominent (see my 'Religious Faith & the Diversity of Religious Life in India', in Das 1987).

Significantly, in the Hindu religious life that was to emerge in later centuries after the fusing of these two streams (along with others too), features of those non-Vedic, Indus Valley (Dravidian?) forms of religion become massively prominent. That the last of the four Vedas, which was added quite a long time after the other three, looks less 'Aryan' and more 'folkish' could be merely because the fusion was already underway, especially among the less 'established' classes, and the fourth Veda represents this lower-order, folkish religious stream. The religion of 'lower' caste people today is generally characterised far more by this folkish religion. And to add to the con-fusion of religious streams, much everyday religion and culture even of 'higher' castes today actually bears little resemblance to pure Vedism. In other words, while there are diverging streams of religiosity, with 'lower' and 'higher' communities differing in how they see the world and express their faith, those streams cannot be identified easily and clearly. Caste-wise, religious identities seem con-fused.

Religious Grounding of Social System

Caste identities, though, do have a religious grounding, even if they can be categorised as largely 'sociological'. In the first place, the identity of some castes is based on their distinctive religious faith and practice. Sectarian allegiance can become caste allegiance, as with the Lingayat community of South India for example. Their beginnings as a faith-group castigating all caste identity is now a very distant memory. The Ayyangar Brahmins also of the South are mostly very serious about maintaining caste status. Their community faith is that of Sri Vaishnavism, in which at least God is believed to look to the heart's love rather than caste status in accepting those who approach him.

Then there is the *famous Rig Vedic text* that gives an early account (though in the last section of this Veda) of caste division: the Purusha Sukta, or Hymn concerning the primal Person. When the gods sacrifice this mysterious primal Person, his limbs become divided. From his mouth come those who utter sacred words, the Brahmins; from his shoulders come strong warrior rulers; from his thighs, those who travel for trade; from his feet lowly serfs and servants. In other words, caste divisions are given a sacral basis, divine legitimation, and the sacrality of this hierarchy became fundamental to the Brahmanic worldview. But although the later sacred law-books too assume this four-fold division, the communities of the Hindu social structure have never been so simply identifiable.

As K.M.Panikkar and others pointed out long ago, caste relationships are far more *complex*. The gradations even within the different sub-castes of Brahmins are considerable. Within the hundreds of groups classed as Sudra, those gradations of status are sometimes very great indeed, and relate to sacral identity, to degrees of purity or pollution, as much as to differing degrees of political and economic power. Some writers assume a continuity between the more lowly Sudras and those groups once deemed 'untouchable', now identifying themselves as 'Dalits'. This, though, does not sufficiently recognise the very distinctive social disabilities suffered by 'untouchables', and the alienation to which their presumed pollution has condemned them historically.

Theories of Caste's Origins

This raises the difficult question of *sociological theory* concerning the origins of caste distinctions. Quite a sharp debate has been going on among social anthropologists as to whether caste has to do mainly with the purity/pollution divide, with a power-structured hierarchy, or with more economically based transactional relations.

(i) Cambridge anthropologist, J.H.Hutton (1963), looked to key features of primal cultures for the origins of caste distinctions. Almost universally in primal communities we find belief in the dynamics of *mana*-power and *taboo*, often functioning within some kind of totemic worldview too. Given this belief-system, the occupations of particular groups are seen as inherently involving the mysterious power of '*mana*', as the Melanesians called it. *Mana* is both enabling and dangerous, and so incurs various degrees of *taboo* in relation to other groups. The special skills developed and handed on within a community, and the rituals and artefacts used in the process, were jealously guarded. Those possessing and passing on these skills themselves were assumed to possess *dangerous potency*. Thus, untouchability, certainly carefully graded forms of interaction, become endemic in the dynamics of such a worldview. And in India these were worked out in the caste system, with its very clear rules as to who can relate to whom and in what ways. Not only have taboos been legion within the caste system, but a complex and carefully observed hierarchy was the inevitable outcome. However, that only in Indian society did taboo became hardened into the complexities of caste must be attributed to some further historical factors.

(ii) Rather like Hutton, though not speculating so much regarding primal origins, Louis Dumont (1970,1998) believed the big key for

326

unlocking the mysteries of Hindu society lay in the issue of *purity* and *pollution*. There is not only the simple principle of the higher the caste the greater the purity, and the lower the caste the greater the pollution. There is too the highly complex network of differing occupations and patterns of behaviour, each of which either *absorbs* pollution (as clothes-washers, dirt-sweepers, farmers, soldiers, etc) and thus helps protect the higher castes, or *avoids* pollution and thus enables the proper offerings (by the most pure, the Brahmins) to be made to the gods from whom the world's needed blessings come. Each community's identity is determined by the degree of purity or pollution destined for that community within this system of mutual interdependence.

(iii) MacKim Marriott (1960) on the other hand, while not disallowing that the caste system was one of mutual interdependence, explained its working in terms of transactions between communities with differing degrees of *food-providing power*. Those who provide and are served are always ranked above those who receive. The hierarchy is thus in terms of resources, and the ability to dominate or be dominated thus becomes a key to identity. In some ways this is not far from a Marxist analysis, even if there is no overt ideological intent.

(iv) Those who point to the'ecological significance of caste', as do Gadgil and Malhotra (Guha 1994), also shed further light on the system's functioning. Based on analysis of the traditional interdependence of a number of communities in West India, it becomes clear that their utilising of specific resources in shared and overlapping territory makes caste (there at least) analogous to biological species finding their evolutionary niche. Centuries of experience had led to carefully controlled exploiting of the environment by each caste according to its own tradition. That interdependent resource-sharing was fatally dislocated by British colonial policies regarding natural resources. Uncontrolled demands on the raw materials needed to feed the empire's growing economic needs created competition for diminishing resources, and led to inter-caste rivalry rather than mutual interdependence. Modern independent India continued and further developed massive state utilising of resources. Gadgil and Malhotra conclude that in this new environment the caste system is a 'maladapted' handicap to coping with the nation's modern needs.

(v) There are numerous other theories, put forward by scholars within India as well as elsewhere. Hindu ideologues tend to argue that the system was primarily *functional*, based on different and necessary occupations, and that it was quite *flexible*, with considerable mobility from one caste to another, at least up to the last few centuries. More recently it is claimed to be solely a sociological phenomenon, not essentially religious. Certainly nationalists such as members of Vishva Hindu Parishad argue that caste distinctions are not essential to Hindu religion and culture. And therefore the radical reform of caste, that will eventually remove every trace of the discriminations of the past, in no way affects the continuing life of Hinduism as such.

Structure & Attitude

Much weight is given by Hindu 'modernisers' generally to the Bhagavad Gita's point that the true Brahmin is one who lives in a certain way, a person with purity of character, not one who happens to be born into a Brahmin community. Escaping structures, though, is not always that easy. Identities become deep-rooted and corporate egos become tied almost irretrievably to the status given by the past, however 'invented' that identity. Being so systemically grounded, unless there is a strategy of deliberate action for structural change - as has been governmental policy since Independence - those caste structures will very likely persist in determining how people feel, think and act at many different levels.

Perhaps such 'political' strategy should not be expected of religious bodies. In any case, with religiously motivated reformers, the most usual position is to preach what is to be aspired to, if possible to practice this personally, perhaps within the concerned religious community, but to leave wider structural change to the policy-makers in the course of history. Only more 'totalitarian' religious regimes have attempted to enforce a more absolute standard on everyone. It is perhaps for this reason that within Hindu reform movements of the nineteenth and twentieth centuries there was considerable ambiguity regarding what to do about caste. Most reformers agreed that many aspects of caste were unjust, especially social and economic discrimination against lower castes. And they were no doubt quite sincere in finding resources *within Hindu traditions* for the theological and social changes they advocated.

Historically, though, it is impossible to ignore the self-criticism and the *new religious movements* at least prompted, though not necessarily created, by the impact of outside influences. There was Islam (as much earlier the impact of Buddhism). And for many caught up in the more modern spirit of reform, the immediate stimulus was the impact of Western secular and Christian missionary teachings, often their scathing and humiliating attacks on what they saw as the 'obscenities' widespread in Hindu faith and practice, its ethics as much as its theology. Even the relatively appreciative account by J.N.Farquhar, written in 1914, of reforms within Hinduism written (Farquhar 1914) is throughout laced with descriptions of Hindu customs as 'filthy and disgusting' (e.g. p.9). But a critique of caste divisions as such was actually rarely at the centre of these outsiders' attacks. The British were themselves tied to a class system of such rigid structure that in some ways it differed little from caste. Generally, though, Protestant missionaries (influenced by 19th century social reforms in the West) did at least *aim* to remove caste distinctions from the communities they founded, as against acceptance of those distinctions by Catholic missionaries, especially those from southern Europe. In the next chapter we look at the account of these differing attitudes written by a socially astute Jesuit Catholic, Walter Fernandes.

There is another external factor to reckon with. For there is some truth in the point made by post-colonialist historians, as well as by pro-Hindutva writers, that *colonial rule*, with its census-taking, and the accompanying need to list people in easily identifiable groups the better to control them, was crucial in the *hardening of caste attitudes*. Many new identity-boundaries were created, and old ones hardened, during that period. Obviously this included Hindu self-perceptions as well as the perceptions of others concerning 'Hinduism'. That these identities were thereby created *de novo*, or indeed that no identifiable realities exist other than those which dominant image-makers create, is another sort of claim altogether and simply not believable.

19th Century Reformers

The first of the *nineteenth century Hindu reformers* was Ram Mohan Roy, founder of the Brahmo Samaj, here meaning the 'Society of Theists'. Western (and often Hindu) comment has tended to lose sight of the fact that Roy was responding initially to the challenge he felt from exposure to Islamic Sufi spirituality. True, it was not long before Roy was writing enthusiastically about the moral excellence of Jesus - as opposed to the theological distortions to which he believed Christian tradition had subjected the Jesus story. And the style of his calm polemic against idolatry and suchlike forms of Hinduism (including the doctrine of *karma* and the cycle of rebirths) is very much that of the rationalist unitarianism that was growing in Britain at the time. On caste, though, while seriously critical of what it entailed, he made no moves to break with its structures as such, either in his personal and family life, or as part of his reform programme. Actively renouncing caste (as against criticising it orally) would at that time no doubt have meant the breaking of many channels of communication with most of his fellow Hindus.

Within the Samaj, ambiguity about caste later became the major cause of an open rift. In part the break was due to the very differing personalities, the differing spirituality, perhaps even the caste background, of the two leading figures in the second half of the century. *Debendranath Tagore*, a Brahmin of devoutly serene even if patriarchal spirit, seemed to many of his contemporaries like an embodiment of an Upanishadic seer. He was given the title Maharishi. *Keshab Chandra Sen*, on the other hand, not a Brahmin, was more volatile, more intent on radical change. Though the rules of the Samaj stipulated that no-one officiating as minister at the worship of the Samaj should wear the sacred thread identifying him as one of the twice-born, at one point Tagore, clearly not too happy about this rule, began to permit the sacred thread to be worn. In effect this was a declaration of the sacral validity of caste distinctions, though veiled by Tagore's lofty indifference to such systems. In any case, Sen and his supporters protested. There had already been disagreement over the issue of marriage between people of different castes as well as on other matters of social reform. Though in no way an orthodox Brahmin (he had no time for the doctrine of *karma* and the cycle of the soul's rebirth), Tagore was far less critical, more conservative, on social issues than was Sen.

Within a short time, in spite of attempts at reconciliation, Sen (still only 24 years old) broke away and formed another organisation. We need not refer to the various further crises in his spiritual journey, including the question of whether or not his obvious devotion to the person of Christ led him at any point to 'become a Christian'. Insistence on identity here in terms of the formalities of membership and belonging would be misplaced. What we should note is the extent to which Sen, from very soon after his break with Tagore, encouraged his followers to express their devotion in the passionate *bhakti*-form of public *sankirtana* typical of his fellow-Bengali Chaitanya, with fervent singing, drumming and dancing in procession through the streets.

Vaishnava *bhakti* was in fact the tradition of Sen's own family, so this more passionate style of religiosity will have been innate to his consciousness. Was it this 'memory' that provoked the more radical response to the issue of caste and the distinctions based thereon? Not that we can assume a common form of outworking of such innate strands of human consciousness. Nor that fervent *bhakti* is the only basis for a socially critical stance. But it has often been the case in Indian religious history that when the Focus of faith has been a tradition-transcending, love-evoking, perhaps taboo-breaking personal Being - such as Krishna, or Siva , or Rama as more popularly worshipped - there may well have been at the very least a flouting disregard of the taboos of caste in the practice of that faith.

This is not the place to assess each reformer's attitude to caste. Certainly in some regions the *Arya Samaj* of the fiery Dayanand Sarasvati, for a while influenced by Keshub Chandra Sen, has made a considerable impact on Hindu views of caste. Dayanand's main aim was to re-establish the kind of Vedism he expounded, and his polemic was directed primarily against image-worship, the corruptions of Puranic religion, child-marriage and such corruptions of what he saw as true Vedism, and especially the killing of the cow (central to his fierce condemnation of Islam and Christianity). True, he was also strongly critical of contemporary views about and practice of caste. The Samaj, as Hindu religion generally, is to be open to all castes. Yet he still accepted what is innate to the doctrine of *karma*: the births (into whichever community) we pass through are caused by our past merits or misdeeds. Even so, in more recent times missionaries of the Samaj, along with activists of Rashtriya Svayam-sevak Sangha, have been active among people of 'lower' caste and among Dalits. Those who had converted to Islam or Christianity have been encouraged to return to the Hindu fold, a cleansing ceremony (*suddhi*) being performed to receive then back. In itself, of course, this does not imply a critical attitude towards caste structure as such.

Radical Rejection of Caste's Structures

Two other much earlier figures looming large in Indian religious history whose movements challenged Brahmanic tradition and, implicitly at least, the structures of its society were *Mahavira* and *Gautama Buddha*, both Kshatriyas by birth. The more radical way was Mahavira's extreme rejection of any form of violence against living things, linked with the other rigorous ways of self-denial held to be part of soul-purifying. It is often fogotten just how widespread was Jainism throughout India, including the South, up to the medieval period. But it was the Buddha who proved to be even more attractive to the general populace, again up to the time of Hindu medieval resurgence. Today again Buddhism draws significant numbers of Dalits into its fold, even if the *political* dimension of such moves is as dominant a motive as any. There are revolutionary implications for society as well as for personal living in the Buddha's teachings.

Yet, through the centuries what has drawn people has often not been so much the cool maxims of his 'Aryan'(Noble) Eight-fold Path', or the 'middle way' between being ascetic and sensual. It has rather been the power of 'great compassion', the sheer attractiveness of the Buddha's own person. It is on that Person that devotion-like meditation has been focussed, the practice of which is to uproot the cause of distress, and so lead to desireless nirvanic tranquillity. Devotion to the Buddha's person is especially strong in the 'Great Vehicle' form of Buddhism that has proved so popular among the 'common people'. But even in the more ethics-oriented way of the 'Elders', for many it is the power of the Buddha's person - as supreme teacher, as perfect example, and even as sacred presence - that serves as devotional Focus.

Indeed, there are those who argue that the change in Indian religion from Vedic altar to Puranic image, from costly sacrificial fire to simple offerings of love, from sacral priestly action to popular bhakti, or loving devotion centred on a personal Focus, was a revolutionary change sparked by the place held by the Buddha in the affections of common people as they made their love-offerings of flower and fruit at the feet of their beloved compassionate one.

There is good reason to see the 'Gospel of Hinduism', the Bhagavad Gita, as a Brahmanic response to the enormous challenge posed to their sacred status by the rapid spread of the 'Gospel of the Compassionate One'. Not that this need invalidate the Gita's innate power of its own to attract people of diverse caste background.

As we have seen, then, actively working for the changing of social structures has not often been part of a religious group's programme. Religious people generally are more concerned about *attitude* and personal behaviour towards others. Even a spiritually and morally sensitive politician such as M.K.Gandhi, at one time the Mahatma (Great-Soul) in the affections of so many, though sincerely intent on improving the life of those until then called 'untouchables', even refusing to enter a temple unless those of Dalit communities were freely admitted too, is now bitterly resented for failing to address the *structural* sources of their humiliating conditions. More specifically Dalits who have opted not to be Hindu recall that Gandhi openly insulted them by denying their ability to discriminate between one religion and another. Such changes, he wrote, are 'conversions of convenience' (Webster 1992: 114-15). That he re-named them 'Harijan' is now taken as a further insult by Dalits, in that this was also the name given to the children of Devadasis, women dedicated early to God, and often then sexually available to patrons and priests. Spiritual awareness does not always lead to historical and 'structural' awareness.

On the other hand, the softly, softly approach to the issue of caste on the part of Hindu reformers was to be expected. Though they did at times succeed in influencing (British) governmental legislation - e.g. Ram Mohan Roy in relation to widow-burning, voluntary or not - few were in a position directly to change social structures. Certainly very soon after Independence, legislation was introduced making it a crime to act in any way in which there is clear discrimination on the basis of caste.

Over fifty years later, the self-identity of huge numbers of people is shaped by secular factors other than caste - profession, political party, local voluntary body, educational establishment, governmental department, economic status, and so on. And large numbers of people increasingly identify themselves in terms of one or other wider religious community - Hindu, Muslim, Sikh, Christian. Yet, within these secular and religious identities, *caste still plays an important determining role*. Even within those religious communities which ostensibly renounce caste, differences of status as well as of loyalty on the basis of caste are still endemic and sometimes strong. In recent years it is especially in the Christian church that Dalit groups have expressed their sense of oppression *within the very community* they originally expected to find freedom from caste discrimination. In India the reshaping of identities that have for so long been based on caste grouping is no simple task

Chapter 17
The New Dalit Consciousness

The struggle in India for a new *Dalit self-identity,* especially during the last half of the nineteenth century, is in many ways as momentous as the struggle for national freedom that culminated in India's Independence at the end of the first half of the century (i.e.1947).

Dalit liberation is a crucial part of the unfinished business in India's freedom from alien rule. Being part of this nation-wide movement for liberation from all earlier structures enslaving mind and soul as well as body and corporate life, inevitably it is a movement that will take several generations to reach the freedom it seeks.

The Experience of Being 'Dalit'

'Dalit', meaning *broken, crushed, down-trodden*, is the self-designated name now used by those who once were called 'outcaste', 'untouchables', and then, by Gandhi, 'Harijan'. Politically they have become 'scheduled castes', those whose status warrants special governmental compensations. Dozens of distinct and disparate groups throughout the Subcontinent make up the more than 200 million Dalit people. All share the stigma of having been subjected to an ancient humiliation - having been branded a polluted people and treated as inferior humanity. They were condemned as much by birth into a polluted community as by subsequent life in one or other polluting occupation, such as being sweepers of refuse and human wastes, tanners of skins, washers of soiled clothes, and so on. In reality many existed as labourers in any capacity available to them. Those with regular employment all too often were little more than slaves to landowners. Being usually beef-eaters intensified their perceived pollution.

The record of the forms of humiliation to which Dalits were often subjected in order that their touch, or vessels they have touched, even their shadow, may not taint others, makes for distressing reading - or listening. It is impossible to imagine the psychological wounding that resulted from having to wear a spit-pot around one's neck, or carry a broom for wiping out one's footprints, on record as demanded of some Dalit groups (R.Enthoven,in *The Tribes and Castes of Bombay,* Bombay 1922, is but one account of such treatment). Their sense of self-identity has been so shaped by hierarchies of purity/pollution that self-worth even among such outcaste groups was given pathetic boulstering by identifying other 'untouchables' as on an even lower rung of the identity-ladder.

Diverse Responses to being Dalitised

That individuals worked out strategies enabling them to escape their 'crushed' status is undeniable. At times outstanding outcastes broke through by the power of personal charisma - at times even being accepted as God-touched, perhaps as inspired gurus by people who, according to the normal rules of *dharma*, were to keep them at a distance because of their dangerously polluting presence. Some managed to upgrade by other means. Sexual 'misalliance' was usually subject to cruelly severe punishment, but did not always result in complete disaster. Mythic genealogies speak of new lower to mid-ranked communities emerging. And with the greater mobility of recent decades, some individuals and families have been able to escape by the covert adoption - in localities where there families are not known - of more acceptable caste identities.

There are, too, the fruits of liberated India's legislation against caste discrimination in general and untouchability in particular. Were not Dalits, such as B.R.Ambedkar and Jagjivan Ram, key nationalist leaders at the time of Independence? Has not a Dalit become President of the Republic and have not large numbers of influential local leaders been Dalits? Even if not in rural areas, at least in the cosmopolitan life of the great cities to which millions of Dalits have migrated, and as part of the rapid changes demanded by industrial bodies, have not large numbers of Dalits found new freedoms, the beginnings of a less stigma-scarred identity? In spite of the obscenity of this strand of human history, the picture is far from all doom and gloom.

There have, too, been desperate, valiant and sometimes effective acts of resistance by whole communities. In a moment we look at one such. Yet, we deal here with structures that lie embedded very deep in the *corporate psyches* of Dalits as much as non-Dalits. They are structures of community *consciousness* as much as of community organisation. The self-perceptions, the societal assumptions, the fears and animosities that are all part of our ways of seeing the world can hardly be wiped clean by the efforts of one or two generations.

There are Dalit self-interpreters who speak of the need to heal the corporate *pathological* condition their people have been scarred with. M.Azariah, earlier CSI Bishop of Madras and ardent advocate of the need for a new Dalit self-assertiveness, also sopke of their 'wounded psyche' (Massey 1994: 320). A.P.Nirmal went further, and - in his inaugural lecture as Professor of Dalit Studies at Gurukul, Madras - spoke of Dalit people's *pathos* as the existential and therefore theological starting point for their resistant self-reflection (Nirmal 1990; also J.Massey 1994: 214-30). To others though, any such negative image demeans Dalit self-identity.

Legislation against atrocities, compensatory discrimination, as well as other such political and economic steps for change have very obviously been necessary. But as other Dalits have pointed out (e.g. Massey 1995), a change of consciousness - for oppressors as well as oppressed - calls for more than external enactments of this kind. On the other hand, the criticism that compensatory discrimination merely perpetuates and intensifies a separate victim-based identity carries little weight in view of the structured nature of the cruel victimisation already endemic to the Dalit world. When social and economic structures are skewed against Dalits, the least to be done is a period of reverse skewing. In any case, whatever they may-take as their existential starting-point, Dalits themselves feel the need to move beyond this overwhelming sense of inherited victimhood. How is this to be achieved?

Conversion to one or other world faith was one important path to a new sense of self-identity and self-worth, though only some 10% of Dalits have taken this path. Finding a new identity based on an explicitly non-Hindu faith is not the only way they have declared their non-Hinduness. Many, similarly asserting their independence of Hindu *dharma*, and so a distinct self identity, have done so by way of more explicit *political* ideology. We look at some of the prickly issues related to conversion in the next chapter. And in a moment we shall also see that Dalits, within their own indigenous traditions, were far from lacking all cultural and spiritual resources for coping with their 'crushed' state. Invariably their religious life has interacted in differing ways with other dominant traditions, and especially with Hindu tradition.

Earlier Dalit Faith-Movements

So, we find Dalit groups, within one or other specifically *Hindu* movement - usually a *bhakti*-type of devotional spirituality - who have been able to break through the bondage of an imposed inferiority of selfhood and discovered a newly empowered corporate psyche. Among Marathi-speaking Mahars, before 80% opted to become Buddhist in the mid-20th century, there had been a remarkable *bhakti* movement. Among the Chamars of Punjab from the mid-1920s there was a similarly striking Sikh-like movement with one of its grounding-sources being the songs of their fellow-Chamar, Guru Ravidas, also worshipped as a divine figure. In Chamar rural settlements their's was a *panthik* ('the Path') style of religious faith, similar to a key strand of the faith of Kabir and Nanak. Calling their faith 'the original *dharma*' was in tune with the claim made by a number of such movements that their original and true identity was lost, but is now rediscovered (Juergensmeyer 1982; Khare 1984; Webster 1999)..

The Bala Shah movement among the Chuhras, also of Punjab, in its eclectic inclusion of strands of Islam, may be atypical for Dalit people. In this case the role of personal divine Power lacks the immediacy and dynamism of other Dalit faith-movements. Yet, as Webster concludes, their faith gave them a self-esteem that enabled them to say they 'were not simply who other people said they were....They took refuge in God as the One who had given them an identity more noble than that assigned by society and who would vindicate them at the end' (Webster op.cit.15-25).

But there were local movements of a similar kind in most other regions of India through the centuries. Far too little research has been done on these faiths and the new self-confidence they inspired. Even within the Dalit movement itself, including Christian Dalit self-expresssion until very recently, Dalit ideology was almost exclusively based on sociological and political discourse. Abraham Ayrookuzhiel, as we see below, was one of the first pro-Dalit writers to point to the 'religio-cultural dimension' of human experience as the needed starting-point for Dalit self-reflection.

Converson to Buddhism

Although they were but 10% of the more than twenty million Dalit people, those who took the more radical step of becoming Buddhists, Muslims, Sikhs, Christians, constitute a highly significant section. The motives for such moves have been variously interpreted by those trying to plot the path of Dalit history. The conclusion reached by

Webster, and endorsed by other historians of Dalit experience, is convincing. Conversion was both a search for a self-identity endowed with greater human dignity and an act of self-expressive social defiance.

Small numbers of conversions to Buddhism were taking place even by late in the 19th century, with the theosophy-related movement led by Iyothee Thass among Tamil Dalits (Aloysius 1998). As would be expected in a Buddhist movement, Brahmanic rituals and Veda-based doctrines are rejected. The emphasis was, first, on *right consciousness* (for example, negatively, polemic against Hinduism was essential to their identity formation; positively, their true Tamil identity was to affirm that 'we are the original settlers of this land'). Then, there was *right conduct*, with Buddhist ceremonies used to bind them together in celebration of the rites of passage and the cycle of life and nature. Typical of oppressed people was their far greater emphasis on *celebration* rather than the individual contemplation more prominent in classical Buddhism, and on *movement* - the 'organisational vehicle of the oppressed' (Aloysius p.11) rather than on institution.

It was, though, the impact nearer the mid-20th century of B.R.Ambedkar - now given almost sacred status by many Dalit activists - that was to lead to the movement in which many thousands of Dalits declared themselves Buddhist. Ambedkar - in spite of his key role in the nationalist freedom movement - was adamant that Hindu *dharma* has nothing but bondage to offer Dalits. Not entirely rejecting, but not favouring Islam and Christianity as viable options for Dalit liberation, his logic led to Buddhism, and so the neo-Buddhist movement was really under way.

Dilemmas for Christian-Dalit Identity

Even though *Christian* Dalits are not recognised as 'scheduled caste' Dalits by the Indian government, we look in this chapter mainly at issues struggled with by this large community, with its more theologically articulate leadership. It has been the belated recognition of the significance of the Dalit presence within Christian communities - Catholic, Orthodox, Protestant, Pentecostal - that has been the chief single cause both of a more radical liberationist stance towards the world around and of more critical self-reflection concerning its own ecclesial life. For, the very institution that originally was seen by

Dalits as a place of hope, by belonging to which a new identity was ensured, has itself frequently proved to be caste-bound. On the basis of his sociological research, Mumtaz Ali Khan concluded that the famous (or infamous if you hold an opposing viewpoint) conversions to Islam of 287 families of Dalits (a few of whom were Christians) in Tamil Nadu's Meenakshipuram in 1981 were prompted by the greater equality found within Islam than within the Christian church (in Oddie 1991).

This is especially ironic in view of the main argument used by politicians in the 1990 debate in parliament, when it was decided *not to allow Christian Dalits a Dalit identity* and so to deny them the right to access scheduled caste privileges, no matter what their continuing social and economic needs. Christians, it was said, must be caste-less, for that is what their faith teaches. The social reality is that liberation from the stigma and humiliating alienations of their 'untouchable' past was at best but partial, even within this 'body of Christ'. The argument based on a religion's theoretical non-acceptance of caste differences could equally be used of Buddhist and Sikh Dalits. But this is ignored in their case, the argument then being that those religions are home-bred, even part of 'Hinduism', much to the annoyance of Sikhs, in spite of the special compensatory status granted their Dalit groups.

Strength of Caste-Identity in Christianity

Dalit theologians have little hesitation in countering emphases on the complex character of our identities in the modern world by pointing to *caste as the only identity* that in the end counts. No matter what one's status in terms of education, affluence, cultural prowess, or even political success, the Dalit view is uncompromisingly focussed: 'In reality caste is the one and only criterion for identifying anyone in today's caste-ridden society.' (P.Mohan Larbeer, 'Dalit Identity - A Theological Reflection', in Devasahayam 1997: 376. Larbeer has been, since late 1990s, Principal of the Tamil Theological Seminary, Madurai). Dalit ideology too positions itself similarly. V.J.Rajasekhar, for instance, (Christian) radical editor of *Dalit Voice,* has argued that, for Dalit Christians, 'if there is conflict between their religion and Dalit identity' they must opt for their Dalit identity. Their identity 'cannot be compromised', though religion can be (March 1990, see Webster *op.cit.*164).

Dalits within the Catholic church point to the strength of caste-group identity with equal conviction. In the *Dalit International Newletter* (edit. Webster) of October 2000 Nandi Joseph writes: 'In India caste identity is stronger than religious identity', and the Church's fine rhetoric about 'universal brotherhood, liberty and equal opportunity....does not apply to caste reality' ('The Dalit Reality of the Indian Catholic Church'). The extensive list of complaints - along with the recognising of a few victories - that then follows is inevitably a one-sided account. Victims are not usually given to cautious balancing of the record, and why should they? But the account makes clear that the struggle for a new status, a new identity, for Dalit Catholics within their ecclesial life has only just begun. The theological rhetoric has been heard for some time; the reality in power-sharing has still a long way to go.

In Protestant ecclesial life, both the egalitarian views of a number of 19th century evangelical British missionaries critical of caste discriminations, and a greater commitment to the democratising process in church life, did make an impact, though critics such as J.Massey find little difference between Catholic and non-Catholic attitudes either among 19th century missionaries or today's church. Jesuit scholar W. Fernandes (Fernandes 1996:160-64; this article makes extensive use of the historical research of G. Oddie, H. Grafe and D. Forrester, especially Oddie 1978), writing cogently about attitudes to caste among nineteenth century missionaries and Christians in the South, comes to a somewhat different conclusion. It is worth noting just how fierce was the struggle even then:

The (southern European) missionary's framework of 'saving souls' and his feudal background that failed to consider social equality a fundamental human value, combined with the upper caste Christian refusal to recognise the new converts as equals and (denied these) 'untouchable' converts the liberation from caste oppression they had come in search of.....the new (Dalit) Christians who viewed Christianity as a higher caste identity, were not prepared to accept separation of castes within the Church....Most Protestants, particularly Anglicans, emphasised equality while Catholics maintained separation within their churches....Christianity served to consolidate and organise caste Identities that had hitherto been loose-ended....(It) was coopted into the traditional social hierarchy....By the late 19th century when Dalits entered the (Catholic)

Churches in large numbers, these caste identities within the Churches had been consolidated already. As late-comers, Dalits found themselves the targets of discrimination, despite some missionary support....most Churches were forced to allot separate seats for them at the back of the building....After some time many Protestants too compromised with caste. Evangelical motives got precedence over egalitarian ideology. When the Anglican bishop (of Tirunelveli) ordered the suppression of identification of Christians according to caste names....the Nadars threatened to join the more conservative Catholics or Lutherans, (and) many Protestants came to accept that caste solidarity helped rather than hampered conversions....The attempts by some Protestants at creating a casteless Christian community by forming a Caste Suppression Society, holding inter-caste meals and dropping caste names, made little impact....Even the present conflict is in reality a new phase of (Dalits') search for a new identity.

The struggle for a new Dalit identity in earlier periods does throw light on present realities in both Christian and wider community life. In those regions or churches where only small numbers of non-Dalits are Christian, ecclesiastical discrimination because of Dalitness naturally is unlikely to be found. There may well, of course, be intra-Dalit rivalry, which on the surface can appear to be more vigorous than that between Dalits and non-Dalits. Yet, this competitive rivalry does not carry the same humiliating sting of alienation. Where there are sufficient numbers of non-Dalits for ecclesial power to be mainly in non-Dalit hands, most likely it will remain firmly held by them.

The fact that nationwide those from Dalit backgrounds comprise something like 65-70% of the Christian community has not been reflected either in the numbers holding key positions in the community's institutions - i.e. positions of power - or in the theological style and content of writings identified as 'Indian Christian'. In Robin Boyd's 'classic' textbook on Indian Christian Theology, used extensively as a primer for three decades in India's theological colleges, there is no mention of even one Indian Christian Dalit as having anything significant to say by way of distinctively Indian reflection on Christian faith. And this directly reflects what has generally been the Church's theological attitude until quite late in the 20th century. Until the late 1970s I have to confess with some shame to echoing these assumptions in my own thought and writing, in spite of my living among and working with Dalit Christians as close friends from 1959 to 1976. Even a faith that holds all people as equally God's children can remain unaware of the realities of social and political power.

Forcefully made aware, by the mid-1970s, of this replicating of caste injustice within its own institutional life, inevitably the Christian community's sense of its identity has had to be rigorously re-examined. At least there is now in most ecclesial and theological quarters a new *awareness* of the issues, awareness of the systemic injustices that permeate all our human structures, including the church, unjust structures that force various vulnerable groups to the margins of any kind of wider community sharing. And while awareness may merely give birth to rhetoric, and tokenism, and more skilful masking of reality, it will inevitably also entail a new sense of self-identity, a new vision of what we should be and can be. An irreversible momentum has been created. Of the many writings on Dalit Christian issues now available (see bibliography), Webster (1994) still remains probably the most thoroughly researched history, introducing clearly many Dalit issues - ecclesiastical, social, political, religious - as they have developed over the past two centuries.

We need to differentiate between *urban* and *rural* India in this matter of caste discrimination. Village India has by long tradition located the various Dalit communities either on the margins or at some distance from 'caste' communities. The patronage practised by the privileged in rural communities has no doubt at times made for a sort of security and interdependence, skewed though it is, that urban life makes impossible. Economically, too, the disparities between affluence and slum-life in cities can be far more obscene. Socially, though, it is in rural life that the divisions are more obvious. The greater mobility and dynamism of urban life gives more scope for social mix, however strong caste assumptions remain..

With the more clear rural demarcations, the less spatial defining of urban life should mean that within any village where Dalits have become Christian, 'higher' caste people are unlikely to follow. This has not always been the case though, as the research of G. Oddie (a 'secular' historian, not a missionary apologist) has shown conclusively (Oddie 1991: 99ff). In a significant number of villages there were ('non-Brahmin') caste converts who became Christian originally as a result of Dalits' witness and life-changes. Even so, there is no escaping some degree of caste tension, either overt or hidden, within Christian communities both rural and urban.

The very *location* of Dalits in rural areas, then, expresses very clearly their precarious, marginalised, sub-altern identity. Much of the form and self-perception of that identity is given by others, by dominant groups within the social and economic order. Though functionally essential to the life of others, because of the ancient perception of their polluted and therefore polluting being, the boundaries between their presence and others must be clearly drawn. So, it is not just where they are to live, but - as we noted earlier in this chapter - their very birth that has determined who and what they are. An all-embracing system of sacred belief - including inescapable cycles of past *karma* - and system of ritual is used to confirm their separate status.

We need to beware, though, of concluding that Dalit self-identity is created *solely by others*, that they have been led to perceive themselves and their world only in terms of the polluted ones, not worthy of the touch of others. At one point this became a central thesis of pro-Dalit ideologues concerning Dalit self-identity. More recently there is a dawning recognition that, however powerful the impact of caste attitudes on Dalits' self-perception and sense of their culture, this identity has not been reduced solely to a feeble parrotting of what they have been told to believe about themselves.

The Power of the Paraiyars' Drum

What is 'indigenous' to, what provides *resistant resources* for at least one tragically oppressed Dalit group in Tamil Nadu has been perceptively drawn out by Sathianathan Clarke (1998) in his analysis of the role of the drum and the goddess Ellaiyamma in the religio-cultural life of the Paraiyar people.

Clarke probes the significance of the drum in the cultural life of the Paraiyars, whose name literally means the 'drum-people'. Even in English, though, their name has come to mean a person identified socially as the lowest of the low, to mix with whom would somehow be polluting - a 'pariah'. The term is even used widely for a wandering, uncared for scavenging dog! Of all communities of Dalit people the Paraiyars have been for countless generations subjected to what may well be human history's most systemic social stigmatising. To the outsider this seems strange, in that their specialist occupation, drumming, seems far less intrinsically demeaning than that of some other Dalits: 'night-soil' removers, for instance. Sathi Clarke takes their identifying symbol, the drum, and after a rigorous cultural-anthropological analysis, explores ways in which its meaning for the Paraiya people can be understood christologically. Is Christ the Drum for them? Does the drum function for them as a 'christic presence'?

In the religious life of the Paraiyars, the drum is the crucial heart-beat. It is closely linked with, and is essential to, their relationship to their community deity, Ellaiyamman. The drum functions in many different ways and communicates a variety of meanings. In processions, at times of wedding, for example, or when an auspicious and purposive journey is being made, the drums clear any dangers that may threaten, they drive away the demons, and entice the Goddess to bless and empower. For, life-power, *sakti*, is her essence. The drums are also essential at the time of sacrifice to the Goddess - in order to invoke and even invigorate her, inspiring her to manifest her power so that the evil powers also attracted at such times are confronted and destroyed.

Thus, the drum is essential to the exorcising of evil , and by extension, this is the drum's role at times of funeral - a dangerously polluting time. The spirit of the dead is contained and sent off to its proper habitation, and demons who are disturbed and awakened by death are driven away. But it is not only Paraiyar people themselves who are dependent on the drums for this liberating work; caste communities too are equally dependent. The drum is also used to make important announcements to the community, as well as to provide the rhythm to which dancers move, in relaxed celebration and as release for stress at the appropriate time during funerals.

The drum, however, is also a symbol of the degraded status to which the Paraiyars have been reduced. Made of calf-skin - a taboo substance - the drum is therefore seen by caste-communities as dangerously polluted and polluting. Yet, for these Dalit people it symbolises far more than an identity of polluted outcasteness. It is, for one thing, a symbol of their resistance to this ancient de-valuing by others. To the Paraiyars, the drum communicates divine power, and a power that those who despise them are also and openly dependent on. The drum has thus become a counter-image to the

Brahmanic sacred Word, itself known as *sabda*, or resonating 'Sound', but that from which the Dalit is alienated by that Word's strictures on their polluted status. The drum enables the Dalit to retain a sense of positive identity, keeping the incessantly infiltrating power of the caste community's culture from being completely overwhelming. The reverberating sound of the drum penetrates the boundaries imposed by caste regulations. For that drum-sound - whether in celebrative or afflictive mode - constantly confronts the caste community, affirming the being of a people whose cultic power they in fact fear.

Not only is the drum a symbol of this 'emancipatory resistance'; it is also reconciliatory, in that it ensures a positive place of recognition for the Paraiyars, as least as a necessary group in the wider community, and mediates to others the power of their Goddess. Clarke argues that in this way the drum's symbolic role has been a kind of 'christic presence' for the Paraiyar people.

And at this point we need to note that substantial numbers of Paraiyars converted to Christianity, mostly in the first half of the twentieth century. 'The Christ dynamic of emancipatory reconciliation is concretized in the drum.' (*op.cit.* 282). And so Clarke sees a particular correlationship between the drum of the Paraiyars and the functioning of Jesus in the latter's role as 'Deviant', one who deliberately put himself outside of normal society, placed himself with the displaced, one who violated the lines accepted as distinguishing the pure from the polluted. Yet he was one who was found to mediate divine power. Moreover, there is a common context of suffering. Both Jesus and drum are seen as representing a way of suffering. It is Jesus as Deviant who provides the transforming clue that God affirms the Sufferer, and vindicates the suffering as a way to restoration and resurrection.

Responding to Clarke's Account
Following the Harvard theologian Gordon Kaufmann (in turn influenced by the South Indian social theologian M.M.Thomas), Sathi Clarke interprets the significance both of Jesus and the Paraiyars' drum in terms of 'humanisation'. Crucial though this may be as an interpretive category, does it not neglect what is surely a significant dimension of the drum/Goddess tradition of the Paraiyars as of all drum-linked cultures, i.e. its eco-inclusiveness? In one form or

another, this eco-dimension is intrinsic to the cultural life of all primal communities over against the destructive anthropocentric de-naturing of our cosmic being that has been so characteristic of western modernity. Here too there are encouraging signs that we are beginning to see that true humanness is itself an *eco-category*, even finding it easier to be caught up again in the rhythms of the drum! (I explore this theme in an essay on 'The Primal Drum', in *Sri Andal's Contribution to Culture*, Sri Ramanuja Vedanta Centre, Madras 1983). This multivalent archetypal symbol invariably has some reference to the *human community's earth-grounded life*. Not that the relationship of drum or of Goddess to human earth-boundedness is explicit and obvious in either mythic or cultic expressions of the Paraiyars. But it is innately and deeply embedded there.

Earth, symbolised in feminine form, is in a number of ways closely bound up with all South India's goddess figures - the very name of the Goddess, Ellaiya(-amman), for example, literally means 'All(-mother)'. Strangely, this is so in a number of Indo-European languages, though there is little direct etymological link between them and the Dravidian family of languages. Some Paraiyars themselves believe the name of their Goddess refers to the 'boundary' - as she is the one who not only protects, but is the embodying boundary of the village. In spite of what I see as a missed opportunity in Sathi Clarke's interpretation of the drum, his work is an important breakthrough.

Today very few young men of the Paraiyar community wish to learn either drum-making or drum-playing; in part because it is precisely this which has identified them as Paraiyars. It is the very symbol of what is perceived by others as their polluted and degraded status. A similar paradox once faced the Indian classical dancer, in that even Bharata Natya in the 19th century became identified (colonial British influence here no doubt) with the sacred prostitution of the Devadasi and the 'indecencies' of the 'nautch girl'. That which had been, in their cultural life, the means of exultant liberation came to be seen as the means of their humiliating degradation. The Christian might say that, in view of the donkey's head with which the second century Romans depicted the crucified Jesus, the symbols of their faith too has been subject to similar humiliating paradox.

The invasiveness of a caste Brahmanic/Sanskritic worldview cannot be denied. Sathi Clarke analyses this in terms of *hegemony*, the key critical principle elaborated by the Italian neo-Marxist ideologue, Antonio Gramsci. 'Hegemony' is the process by which a dominant class aims to control subaltern communities in a pervasively comprehensive way. So the class struggle is understood not only as between capitalists and the people, or owners and those who actually produce things, but also involves 'cultural and religious conflict over which values and beliefs will dominate the thought and behaviour of people.'(Quoted, *op.cit.* 41). Not that the dominant class will always try *directly* to impose its own belief-system on those it seeks to control. There is a more subtle and dialectical relationship than this. Existing institutional forms are used as part of this process, so that what emerges as the controlling instrument is a 'symbolic pattern that appears inclusive, universal and normative for all', and the 'dominated participate....in their own domination'. There are, though, argues Clarke, ways in which 'subaltern communities creatively construe counter-hegemonic procedures' (p.42).

Up to the quite recent emergence of a more assertive Dalit consciousness, 'Indian Christian theology' has been, according to Clarke's account of it, subjected to a similar hegemonising process. As we noted, it was converts from the 'higher' caste communities who determined how 'Indian-Christian theology' was articulated, as against the traditional European forms established by missionaries and perpetuated by less questioning Indian disciples. But at least it stood against and was a counter to the powerful stream of western theological dominance. It needs to be applauded as such.

At times, too, most of these 'Indian-Christian' theologians had trenchant things to say about caste. Even so, it is undeniable that they needed far more self-critical awareness of the systemic character of caste-power, and that 'Indian Christian theology' needed actively to encourage authentic interpretation of Dalit Christian experience. At least they were attempting to give genuinely inculturated expression to the meaning for life they had discovered in their new hyphenated identity as Indian-Christians.

However much in leading theological circles the focus may have been on this form of 'Indian-Christian theology, throughout India in countless homes and vernacular congregations, in the praying, preaching and daily witness of Dalit Indian Christians - when not under the theological control, direct or indirect, of western authority - their faith was actually being expressed in very different terms. I myself had frequent glimpses of this when, even in the presence of 'the missionary', rural Dalit preachers with this authentic touch communicated a faith that in substance and style was far from a faint echo of the usual missionary message. (O.V.Jathanna's response Sathi Clarke's analysis was along these lines: Clarke p.53, n.34).

In line with this Clarke allows a brief footnote to admit that there are 'continuities' between Dalit and caste Hindu religious life. But interlinking patterns of cultural and religious life are far more than a mere footnote to a long hegemonic history of Brahmanic control strategies. Yes, the divide between is deep, but deeply rooted too are many shared ways of seeing and doing - the result of a shared folk-rootage, sometimes even a shared religious experience - especially in *bhakti* other such counter-cultural movements. Then there have been the long millennia of pre-Brahmanic primal rootage, in common for Dalits and caste Hindu communities, that has been the most binding cultural link, and through the ages effected such great changes of religious outlook from early Vedism to later Hinduism. The power of such deep-rooted indigenous cultures is such that hegemonic movements are never completely one-way. The binding structures of society, however, and therefore caste identities, have remained largely unbending, perhaps becoming even more unflexible by the early modern period. While *bhakti* religion, with its regular instances of charismatic low-caste leaders (one of Ramanuja's gurus for example), need not be seen merely as Brahmin-led 'opiate of the people' (as some Marxist history contends; D.D.Kosambi for example), the reality is that the ecstatic breakthroughs never actually broke down caste structures. If anything, in time they hardened.

Dalit Religio-Cultural Roots: Ayrookuzhiel & Others

A great strength of Clarke's analysis of Dalit experience is the crucial role he allows for the religio-cultural dimension. In an earlier essay about sources for a new Dalit identity, Abraham Ayrookuzhiel too had argued that while their battle for a changed economic and political identity can be waged within the broader framework of the present Indian democratic and secular constitution, in recent years

Dalit writers increasingly 'draw inspiration from some of their own primeval myths, symbols, gods and heroes to rebuild their distorted religio-cultural identity' ('Chinna Pulayan: The Dalit Teacher of Sankaracharya', in Fernandes (1996: 63). He then analyses an indigenous song to the local spirit-god, often a ludic figure, Pottan, accompanying dance found in the Theyyam worship of the Pulayan people of northern Kerala, whose history we look at again in relation to conversion. The song shows remarkable resistance to higher caste discrimination, almost entirely on the 'rational' grounds of a common humanity: 'When your body or ours is wounded, it is blood that pours out of both. Why then quarrel over caste?' Or, 'the (high-caste) Chovar dances holding the bronze image, we dance holding pots of prawns. Why then quarrel over caste?'. (There is also an interesting and detailed comparison of the human body with a Pulayan hut). Ayrookuzhiel sadly died just as he was beginning to explore this dimension of Dalit rootage more seriously, and to that point he remained, in the words of Clarke, 'only a social scientist....unable to reflect theologically on his finding that Dalits exhibited a "counter-culture"'.

In contrast to this emphasis on the religio-cultural dimension of Dalit experience, for some time pro-Dravidian writers have been arguing (as to some extent Ayrookuzhiel does above) for the 'rational' and 'humanist', even trans-religious, culture of 'Dravidian' tradition, especially as expressed in the early Tamil work, Tiru-kural. And some Dalits - again, as Ayrookuzhiel did too - now claim identity with this pre-Brahmanic Dravidian strand of South Indian culture. However much Dalits may wish to distinguish their roots from the Brahmanic sacral world, it is difficult to see continuity with this imagined non-religious cultural past.

Another form of pro-Dalit polemic is developed by a political philosopher, Kancha Ilaiah, at Osmania University in Andhra Pradesh, who with great dialectical vigour argues for a radical distinction between the 'superior' ways of relating to and knowing the world found among 'Dalit-Bahujan' ('oppressed-common people/masses') and that of the 'Brahmanical' system. (Shah 2001:108-28). Dalit knowledge of things is said to arise from empirical experience of nature and their day-to-day interaction with nature. It is based on an authentic materialism, so that their consciousness is in harmony with the processes of nature. The Brahmanical worldview, on the contrary, is the result only of the *consuming* of nature, for their concern is only to produce their own Brahmanical self 'constructed around supernatural forces', grounded in a self-centred and moribund idealism that lacks any basis for 'progressiveness'. Again the 'rationalism', 'humanist' and properly 'secularist' outlook of Dalits is stressed, along with an essentially antipathetic view of 'religious' faith and practice.

Only a few of those seeking conceptual grounding for Dalit-ness, then, have sought to discover resources within indigenous faith-systems. In the search for a new common identity, able to unite and empower their many deeply divided communities, the great majority of Dalit ideologues and activists have focused almost exclusively on the social, economic and political deprivation of their people. In differentiating their people from the dominant system, there are of course frequent references to the 'evils of Brahmanic Hinduism', a central theme in the writings of that all-important leader of the Dalit movement, B.K.Ambedkar, so politically/constitutionally influential around the time of India's Independence. Ambedkar recognised the power of a shared religion in creating a common identity, and decided it was Buddhism that provided the Dalits with the most effectively liberating new identity. In line with Ambedkar's intentions, in recent days some Dalit leaders have used, or threatened to use, mass conversion to one or other non-Hindu religion as a political lever against militant Hindutva. Others, as we saw, have given up completely on religion - 'a plague on all your houses' - and turned to a secularist worldview, even if contending that this will be a distinctively Dalit secularism.

The Dalit as Oppressed Victim

Inevitably and necessarily, though, by far the most common theme is the shared experience of oppressed victimhood. The long, long story of cruel humiliation is the sustaining narrative. There may be allusions to Dalit cultural values by way of contrast with traditional 'Hindu' values (as in Ilaiah above), but serious exploration of cultural and religious roots is rare. An exception that at one time became a prominent form of liberative action was the forcing of Hindu temple authorities in key centres to open their doors to Dalits. For those - like the followers of Narayana Guru in Kerala - who willingly accept a Hindu religious identity, this is no doubt an important liberating moment. But critical analysis is mostly focused on the social-economic-political conditions that oppress and dehumanise Dalits.

When Christian Dalits interpret their experience of Dalitness, their brokenness, they too most usually depict that continuing history of *victimhood* in the light of biblical narratives instancing similar stories of injustice, alienation, slavery, and the signs of liberating hope to which these stories also point. The periods of slavery and exile from which the Hebrew people were set free, and the central Christian story of Jesus as liberator for those marginalised by unjust social structures - whose own victimhood finally became a way of ultimate release - are taken as models of hope and liberating action. So too are the many other allusions to God's 'option for the poor and oppressed' in the remarkable writings of the Hebrew prophets. For the Dalits' own suffering is their necessary existential starting point.

A.P.Nirmal, for example, in his (early 1990s) inaugural lecture as Professor of Dalit Studies at Gurukul Lutheran Theological College, Chennai, took *Dalit pathos* as the epistemological basis for a distinctive Dalit theology. A community's whole consciousness, its God-consciousness too, is shaped by such a history of suffering; it is in a sense a pathological consciousness. 'It is in and through this pain-pathos that the sufferer knows God...(and) knows that God participates in human pain' (in Nirmal 1991, 'Doing Theology from a Dalit Perspective', esp. p.141). Nirmal even exalts the role of servanthood, as 'servitude is innate to the God of Dalits', 'brokenness belongs to the very being of God....He is one with the broken. He suffers when his people suffer. He weeps when his people weep. He laughs when his people laugh. He dies in his people's death, and he rises in his people's resurrection'(*ibid.* 70).

Thus, the *Jesus-story and the Dalit-story converge*, for dalitness is the key to understanding the divine and the human in Jesus. As Webster points out, for Nirmal, and quite rightly, 'Dalit Christian theology, like all people's theologies, is a theology of identity' (Webster 1992: 231). Nirmal even speaks of the need for Dalit 'exclusiveness' - at least as an interim stance. Non-Dalits may believe that the stronger the distinctive sense of a community's identity, and the more the history of special pathos and victimhood is stressed, the greater the stresses on wider community bonds - whether within the Christian church, indigenous region (language), Indian nation, or even of common humanity. Yet, without a common recognition of the wounding injustices of our past, a recognition of the stresses already experienced by communities such as Dalits, there is little possibility of genuine shared humanness. Being able to celebrate such wider identities depends upon awareness of the ways those identities have been cruelly denied to fellow-humans in the past. In terms of Nirmal's Dalit theology, only when we share the brokenness of their God can we share such wider new life and its more inclusive identities. Meanwhile, though, we are left with some serious institutional tensions, and certainly not only within the Christian church, as inner expectation and institutional reality diverge.

Chapter 18
'In Search of Identity'
through Conversion

It is the contention of many Hindus, and not only militant nationalists, that *conversion is a primary cause of religious conflict in India*. Cause of conflict or not, it is a fact that issues relating to change of religious loyalty are debated throughout India with greater intensity than any other religion-based topic. Sebastian Kim's recent *In Search of Identity* (2003), the most systematic and sympathetic account to date of *'Debates on Religious Conversion in India'* (his sub-title), rightly points to the way this now fiercely argued issue uncovers differences of religious understanding at the heart of Christian-Hindu encounter.

Yet, we should not overlook the equally important fact of divergent viewpoints also *within* the Christians and Hindu communities. Even those who believe in leaving open the possibility of change of faith may have very different reasons for this and also may envisage a very different process. For some it will be a valid form of protest by the oppressed. Conversions of Dalits, for example, are often justified by their proponents on this basis. For others, to be free to work out one's faith is basic to authentic spirituality, perhaps even an essential human right.

A number of these issues, more indirectly, arise also in a rather different recent publication, *Religious Conversion in India: Modes, Motivations, and Meanings*, edited by Rowena Robinson and Sathianathan Clarke (2003). This is an important collection of essays in social history and therefore provides a more sociologically sophisticated stance than that of Kim. So, while the present conversion *debate* is not so directly discussed, here too the diversity of 'modes, motivations, and meanings' relating to change of community faith-loyalty in India emerges very clearly.

A perspective that is more pastoral and theological is found in Andrew Wingate's earlier *The Church and Conversion* (1997), perhaps the most useful introduction for the general reader to many of the issues relating to conversion. Here too the diversity of stance on what conversion means - even among Christians over the years - becomes obvious. Wingate neatly summarises much of the discussion beyond India, and beyond social science, determinedly anti-reductionist in giving weight to what converts themselves believe their experience means.

Recent Conversion Legislation

The conversion debate impinges, sometimes explosively, on recent *political* debate. Late in 2002 rigorous new legislation against conversion from one religion to another 'by force, allurements, or fraudulent means' was introduced by the government of Tamil Nadu in S.India, the state that since Independence has been one of the most progressive and tolerant in the Subcontinent. Within days of loss of BJP-support in Tamil Nadu (as in most states except for Karnataka) in the election of May 2004, this Bill was rescinded.

A very similar Bill was about to be introduced into Gujarat, a state with much less easy communal relations in recent years. Here too, 'force' and 'allurement' are taken to include any possible form of threat or inducement - presumably even the promise of spiritual benefit or improved life, which rules out 'conversion' altogether as usually understood. For, every religion speaks of the blessings that accompany faith/insight/initiation, and may well also speak of the negative consequences - not necessarily by way of explicit threat - when people fail to live according to the 'true way'. And, in this recent legislation, when conversion from one religion to another is anticipated, the local magistrate has to be informed and that officer's permission taken. The progress of this Bill in Gujarat remains to be seen, following loss of BJP power at the centre.

On the face of it the aim to rule out force, allurement and fraudulent means to win converts from one religious community to another seems thoroughly laudable. Indeed, the Constitution - along with affirming every person's freedom to practise, profess and also to propagate his/her religion - already insists that there shall be no form of coercion, threat or inducement accompanying such religious self-propagation. Critics of the attempted new legislation believe this qualifier already guards sufficiently against misuse of the religious freedom provided by the Constitution. The 'anti-conversion Bill', argue its critics, would merely open the way for prejudiced local officers to deny virtually all freedom to change one's religion, or to prosecution (with a possible 4-year jail sentence) after conversion, as it will be all too easy in every act of conversion to accuse those involved of some kind of 'allurement'.

Conversion is particularly associated with Christian mission, though many of India's present population of over a hundred million Muslims were also originally converts from communities claimed as 'Hindu' by recent nationalists. As Buddhism is seen by neo-Hindus as indigenous, even as a form of Hinduism, the surge of Buddhist converts in recent years agitates Hindu militants much less. It should be noted that the freedom to propagate one's religion - making conversion a possible outcome - had been included originally at the insistence of Christians, who claimed this missioning stance as an inalienable part of Christian self-identity. Certainly Christian leaders in Tamil Nadu found the briefly introduced new legislation very threatening, and believed that it contravened basic facets of religious freedom the Constitution aimed to protect. Even back in the 1940s, though, we can see the seeds of the fierce debates that have burst out from time to time ever since.

Or is it the case that this constitutional provision has for too long been improperly exploited by the more aggressively mission-minded faiths of India? That certainly is the claim of those attempting to introduce the new laws. A long series of group conversions across the state, in particular the Meenakshipuram conversions to Islam and culminating in the more recent conversion of 250 rural Dalits near Madurai by the vigorous evangelism of Seventh Day Adventists, was said to be the immediate provocation (Wingate pp.152-64).

The Power-Context

More serious, though, is the *power-context* in which the practice, profession and propagation of a religious faith - as well as resistance to the dominant power - takes place, though such awareness has to be double-edged. There is the fact that all life now is lived globally, which inevitably entails linkages with powers outside India - political, economic, religious - powers still seen as imperialist in intent. There is then also the struggle, a just struggle if ever there was one, for new forms of sharing in power by Dalit and Tribal people within India.

Undeniably, too, the conversions debate is in part prompted by the continuing *struggle for power* in rural regions and in land-based economies; local power-politics are prominent in the picture. In Tamil Nadu, for example, there is the blatantly power-seeking alliance between the party of present Chief Minister Jayalalitha and the militantly pro-Hindutva party that has been (until 2004) dominant at the Centre. If the intention of the latter is followed through, many more states will in time enact similar anti-conversion laws. The unexpected triumph of Sonia Gandhi's Congress Party has certainly for the time being changed the direction of conversion-talk as of many other matters.

Conversion Asserting Community Self-Identity

Conversion, however, is *never merely a political* matter. Kim convincingly argues that on both sides of the divide - in this case militant Hindus and defensive Christians - perceiving the conflict primarily in *political* terms has been a major reason for being unable to engage in fruitful debate on conversion. It is, too, 'ironic that both....accuse each other's practice of conversion of being politically motivated' (2003: 179). In reality, there are sincerely held religious and theological factors that need to be engaged with, though these are inevitably bound up with the socio-political and economic context at the same time, made very clear both in Robinson & Clarke (2003) and Wingate (1997) from their quite different perspectives.

The central issue again is essentially that of *self-identity,* with *community* identity being an inescapable dimension of how we perceive ourselves, how we perceive our destiny. Certainly in a tradition-rich civilisation such as India, identity is primarily *community-based.* It is not individual belief or behaviour, but being part of a community tradition that most directly identifies a person. Yet, as we have seen, moving on to a new identity transcending such community-based life has for millenia also been possible in Indian religious traditions. 'Conversion', therefore, is almost invariably taken to mean a change of community allegiance, a different outward affiliation. The act of converting may well entail the verdict, 'you are no longer one of us'. Within Brahmanic *dharma* - that all-inclusive social/cultural/religious ordering of Hindu life - a person is most clearly and decisively defined by the community of caste and sect s/he belongs to, with even that dharmic defining able to be transcended once ultimate self-liberation (*moksha*) is attained. So there is a way of breaking through the boundaries of community (i.e. becoming a *sanyasi* or renouncer) that is acceptable even to the *dharmic* tradition.

Threat to Coherence of Community Identity?

However, breaking those community boundaries, and the religious life undergirding them, by converting to another religious faith, and declaring allegiance to another religious community, entails not only breaking of caste, but denial more fundamentally of that *dharmic* faith and order on which the Hindu community is based. In Islam, once allegiance to the Muslim community, the *Umma*, has been affirmed, then remaining part of that body, the body of true believers, is probably even more important than in Hinduism. Accepting a variant belief-system and life-style is for orthodox Islam even more threatening, warranting not just ex-communication of the apostate, but - formally at least - death.

So we find the strange anomaly that when in 1852 the gifted Hindu mathemetician, Ram Chandra, became baptised as an Anglican Christian in a very public rite in Delhi attended by many high-ranking British officials, the Muslim community was even more agitated than the Hindu. We should note, though, that even before his conversion Ram Chandra was seen as anti-Hindu in that he argued publicly as an anti-faith rationalist, and in doing so he had often also been engaged in debate with Muslims. A well-known high-caste surgeon, Chinman Lall, was baptised with Ram Chandra, and it was his conversion that created more opposition among the Delhi Hindus. Though the immediate agitation died down, it was only five years later that the terrifying rebellion of 1857 took place, in which Chinman Lall was killed and Ram Chandra just managed to escape (See Powell, 'Processes of Conversion to Christianity', in Oddie 1997: 27-9; also Powell 1993).

The intense rage of Hindus and Muslims that burst out in 1857 was not all about the greasing of sepoys' bullets with a taboo substance, whether the fat of cow or pig. Nor was it solely resentment of an alien imperial power - though we should note the supportive presence of key British officials at the Delhi baptisms, even though neither East India Company nor the Imperial Raj were officially in favour of making changes in people's religious allegiance. Resistance, then, surged up from a wide-ranging sense of threat to the very bases of Indian community, Muslim as much as Hindu. And conversions, especially if connected with imperial power, were symptomatic of that threat.

Mass Movements as Social Protest?

It is, though, *mass movement* from one affiliation to another that has become the more critical point. The key question politically (religiously too) is: under what conditions is a change of religious identity justified? It makes little historical sense to argue that religious changes, movements from one faith-identity to another, should never occur. The reality is they have taken place regularly throughout India's long history. There have been movements from tribal cult to inclusion within a wider tradition such as the Brahmanic or Sanskritic, and before that probably the Dravidian. Similarly there have been movements from Saivism to Vaishnavism, or from primary allegiance to Surya, or Narasimha, or Brahma, to a cultic group that proved more powerful. There have been huge movements into Jainism and Buddhism - and it is too often forgotten just how dominant these two were up to the tenth century even as far as deep into southern India. In all these a decisive switch of faith-identity is involved.

Then, too, the millennia-long process of incorporating countless tribal groups in this way should surely be seen as a form of converting. Rowena and Clarke discuss the question of whether such movements can also be termed 'conversion', pp 7-13. Frykenberg too, in a 1981 review of Oddie 1977 (1991), argues for a more precise, though wide-ranging, definition and analysis of 'conversion' than he believes Oddie's work provides. The problem is, over-precise definitions immediately exclude, especially if we stress *discontinuity* as necessary to conversion, which Frykenberg does - see also Wingate p.251 (I take up this issue more fully below).

The view of militant Hindutva, though, is that all these movements in earlier Indian history occurred within the wider 'Hindu' family, so that conversion today in any direction other than as a 'return to the Hindu fold' is a socially disrupting evil. In particular, the conversion of communities of people to such 'foreign' religions as Islam and Christianity will, it is claimed, lead inevitably to social dislocation, cultural debilitation, moral depravity, and political imbalance. When liberationist Christians, Catholic and Protestant, claim that conversion movements of Dalits and Tribals are mainly acts of socio-political protest, though ideologically at the opposite pole from Hindutva, in terms of their functioning the movements are seen in a similar way. They are signs of socio-cultural change, seen either as necessary resistance to present oppression, or as undesirable disruption.

It may well be the communities controlling the land and local economy (perhaps formally being upgraded members of the huge Sudra group of castes) that landless rural people feel most directly resentful of. But even the land is locked into the Brahmanic system; the land-economy has its religious undergirding. It may, for example, be said to belong essentially to the deity of the village for whom the local land-owners are hereditary stewards. Those brought to feel the oppressive squeeze of such an all-embracing system, having suffered under it in their casteless, landless, powerless condition for many generations, may believe that the only form of protest available to them is to declare themselves other than 'Hindu', and to align themselves with a faith-option at least officially claiming freedom from the oppressions of caste. Mass conversion can indeed be seen as an act of social protest.

Continuity-Discontinuity

Even so, it has to be (as Wingate, Kim and others argue) far more than this. One of the key points made by the South Asian historian G.A.Oddie in a number of writings concerning change of religious faith in recent centuries is that *continuity* of worldview is inevitable. Yet there are also - as Oddie points out - also points of *discontinuity*, and it is the dialectic of these two aspects of the process of conversion that is crucial.

But first a look at some of the facts relating to conversion. Census statistics make it clear that mass conversions have been frequent since the late mid-19th century. In 1881 there were less than two million Christians in India, and the majority of these were from one or other caste background. In each subsequent decade there was an increase of around 30%, the great majority of whom were part of Dalit or Tribal mass movements into Christian faith, so that by 1981 there were over 16 million Christians, and by 2001 there were close to 25 million who identify themselves as Christian, perhaps more than two thirds of whom are from Dalit or Tribal backgrounds. The rate of increase among those identifying themselves as Buddhist has actually been even greater during this period.

And what were the social effects of these movements? The accounts missionaries wrote back to their sponsors concerning changes in the life of converts suffer from two distortions. On the one hand they were all too ready to exaggerate the dramatically improving effect becoming Christian had on communities previously 'benighted in their heathen darkness', as though baptism (and breaking with the symbols of past cultic life, as was invariably expected by the missionaries) transformed both self-image and ways of living almost immediately. Contrasting 'before and after' pictures were needed to satisfy home supporters, and exaggerated accounts were inevitable. The opposite distortion was because 19th century missionaries had strongly predetermined views of exactly how converts should change. When they in fact developed a different kind of identity - i.e. not in the missionaries' own image - this could be found problematic. But more on this point in a moment.

In any case, the claim by some critics of conversion that the results are an unmitigated evil has to ignore undeniable evidence to the contrary. The contention (in *The International Review of Missions !*) by an RSS ideologue that 'conversion always means moral depravation' is a piece of polemics with little historical basis. We noted in the previous chapter how Oddie cites well-documented accounts of such impressive changes in the life of some converted villages that even neighbouring higher caste people also asked for baptism. In other cases, inevitably, the opposite was true. Not only was there strong opposition from neighbouring caste groups; there was no convincing evidence of 'moral' improvement among the converts.

A Case-Study: Conversion from Theyyam-Culture

One instance of this, according to J.J.Pallath's field study (1995), concerns the Pulaya community of South West India. The Pulayas have been called 'one of the lowest ranking untouchable castes', considered 'tribals' until the official declaration during the Emergency of 1974 that they were a 'caste'. (Incidentally, this is an example of the movement from 'tribe' to 'caste' probably typical of the caste-system historically, even if each such caste-creation may occur in different context and different conditions). This is a community whose cultural history includes *theyyam*-worship. *Theyyams* are ritual drama-dances - famous for the magnificent masks put on by the dancers - by which 'their spirit world is conceived and religious life celebrated' (*op.cit*.59). The dancers become manifestations of a wide range of spirit-beings, legendary heroes, powerful sources of bane and blessing (4). Even the Pulayas' social structure and caste position is 'identified in relation to *theyyam*' (*ibid.*).

The consequences of the change of identity were great for the significant numbers who became Catholic Christians from 1938 onwards. Pallath gives great weight to the replacement of their *theyyam*-based cultic life with the less dramatically potent and less cosmically pervasive Catholic symbol-system as a major reason for the loss of self-identity many seem to have suffered. On the other hand, he argues, it was their oppressed caste-status and the low self-esteem this entailed that led to conversion in the first place - though the *theyyam* cult itself had functioned as 'an embodiment of protest' (pp.96-123). In making this break with their past, however, even though there have been economic and educational advantages, the imposition of a liturgy to which they found great difficulty in relating, made the symbolic discontinuities too great. In particular Pallath sees the liminal and ludic dimensions of that previous cult, and the greater sense of integration due to their role as vigorous actors in the dance-ritual, as disastrously missing in the priestly Mass that took the place of the *theyyam*. With an inadequate cultic structure in its place, a weakened and confused community identity was the result. Oppressed and humiliated socially though they were previously, according to Pallath (who was brought up as a neighbour among them) the Pulayas' richly symbolic *theyyam* life provided ways of coping with the trauma of their Dalit status.

Disorientation from Imperial Rule

Even so, loss of community cohesion, perhaps an increase in social problems, loss of personal integrity and mutual trust, and a weakening of obedience to previously accepted ethical norms, may well be caused not by the change to Christianity as such (or Islam or Buddhism as the case might be), but by the very loss of cohesion, continuity and conformity that either precipitated the conversion in the first place, or that was taking place in the wider community for other reasons - social, cultural, political.

There is little doubt that one of these was the disorientating impact of imperial rule in India especially felt in the second half of the 19th century. There was the obvious challenge to the systemically integrated and interdependent social/political/religious traditional life of India that had evolved over many centuries. And there were also in particular disrupting economic policies introduced by the British, causing that interdependence to break down in ways which, as usual, hit hardest those whose lives were most vulnerable, those with least resources to fall back on. There are, of course, opposing ways of looking at such dislocation. When a community's 'location' is that of polluted 'untouchable' in the first place, and its only basis is servile dependence on more privileged groups, little wonder that more radical critics see at least the social dislocation involved as a boon rather than a bane.

The mass movements may not have been directly sponsored by, or even offically encouraged by, the imperial powers. They did, however provide the overarching power-context within which the movements occurred. And while these mass conversions were in general not worked for directly even by most missionaries, nor in general were converts blatantly offered material benefits (Pickett's conclusion that the slur of 'rice Christians' is unwarranted was based on extensive even if not unbiased research), important group conversions had direct economic links.

For example, the Madigas in Andhra who became Christian around the time of the great famines of the 1880s were part of the missionary policy of providing work for the hungry. Educational benefits and hospital treatment at mission centres did have converting effect in some cases. And it was even official ecclesiatical policy in some regions for material recompense to be given to those undergoing training for baptism. Many of these mission agencies were not actually British. Little wonder, though, that Hindu nationalists find it irksome that the foreign power causing dislocation in the first place, then - through its religious missions - invited the dislocated to change their religious affiliation and join Christendom.

Multiple Factors Shaping Community Identities

So, then, the effects of conversion on community identity depend on many different factors: on the situation pushing the concerned community to convert, on the extent to which previous cultural life provided a sense of community identity (perhaps even empowerment to resist the oppressive encroachments, economic as well as cultural, by other communities), and especially on how effective the converting agents were in providing either creative continuity with previous cultural life, or an alternative that could prove sufficiently integrative in its place (see too Wingate 1997: 211-31). The effects have never been uniform. There is ample evidence that there has often been, whether immediately or more slowly, a *strengthening* of community morale and an *empowered sense of self-identity*. But, in that conversions - individual or corporate - necessarily entail the re-formation of self-identity, and the 're-locating' of that person or group in relation to their peers, their neighbours of other communities and castes, their whole context, then there may well be a period of some dislocation and confusion, perhaps even a *crisis* of identity. Unless, though, there was already some crisis of identity, it is hardly likely that conversion will be seen as an option at all.

The shaping of a strong new identity, then, depends on various factors. The role of guiding mentors in the new faith is crucial. If they are insensitive to the need for *continuities* as much as change in the faith of the converts, if they fail to grasp the dynamic role of *symbols* in establishing a new consciousness, and if there is inadequate identity-confirming nurture ('pastoral care' to use Wingate's terms), then a confused self-identity, a weakened identity, can hardly be avoided. A community's sense of selfhood will obviously become confused if the previous symbol-system is deliberately destroyed and that put in its place is unable to create an inclusive faith-world, a new cosmos. Communities are sustained by their identity-shaping symbols.

Protestant Unawareness of Cultural Dynamics

Among mass-movement Protestant Christian communities, in general few leaders were adequately aware of the socio-cultural dynamics. Nineteenth century European evangelical criteria for authentic Christian faith were assumed by the great majority of missionaries to apply to Indian converts. Indian assistants to the missionaries often took over these same assumptions.

Three qualifiers are needed here though. First, there is the fact that most often it was Indian testimony that was far more persuasive in effecting conversion than was the preaching of foreign missionaries. Genuinely indigenous imagery and motifs sprang up in Indian preachers' interpretation of faith, in spite of missionary guidelines.

Then, there were the devotional lyrics composed in thoroughly vernacular *bhakti* style by Indian Christian devotees, perhaps especially in the South Indian languages. These wonderfully expressive lyrics were to become deeply embedded in indigenous Christian consciousness. Significantly, the Basel missionaries in Karnataka, convinced that new converts should be totally protected against any influences from their previous culture, banned all such lyrics and insisted that only translated German hymns should be sung.

Thirdly, there are several instances of converts - especially from caste cultural backgrounds - refusing to accept missionary strictures on cultural continuity, and insisting that they be allowed more freedom to express their Christian faith in what seemed to them more authentic Indian forms.

A Convert's Resistance

A striking, if complicated, example of this can be seen in the conflict (in the 1840s and 50s) between G.U.Pope and the renowned 'Tanjore poet' Vedanayagam Sastriar, whose father had been a Catholic convert (see Antony Copley's essay in Oddie 1997). Though Pope was a fine scholar in Tamil, and even translated poetry of some of the God-impassioned Saiva *bhaktas*, he was a difficult man - authoritarian, irascible, often harshly unfair, intolerant and disrespectful even with fellow-missionaries, certainly with Indians, whether Hindu or Christian. Nor was Vedanayagam given to meekness of manner.

Crucial in their mutual antipathy was the question of caste. Pope accepted the hardline policy of the Anglican church at that time: public breaking of caste must be made the mark of Christian communion - literally, in that it was at the eucharistic communion that there was to be clear expression of converts' casteless new life by their eating and drinking together, even from the same cup. This, though, was but one part of the problem.

Pope was a missionary of the Society for the Propagation of the Gospel, and therefore more catholic in outlook (on the meaning of eucharist for example) than even his Anglican sending body, far from radical Protestant, felt comfortable with. So we might imagine that Pope would be more likely to be open to cultural continuities - as Catholics were in practice, however damning their 19th century descriptions of virtually all Hindu ways. Even two centuries earlier, at the time of the remarkable Italian Jesuit Robert de Nobili's deeply inculturated missionary approach to Madurai's high-caste people, few other Catholic missionaries appreciated his stance.

Continuities in Converts

So, we should not overstate the notion that 'Catholic' means an accepting of continuities between pre- and post-baptismal life. Yet, Pope's Anglican junior colleague, the Revd Holden, speaks of 'Romanist' practice as 'little more than the substitution of the saints for the Swamis and the romish chapel for the heathen temple. I have seen even the heathen marks made of the holy ashes on the face....' This young man did recognise, though, just how crucial to popular Indian religiosity are rites and symbols, even if Hindus refer to such as 'sport'. Naturally, he said, they find it difficult to give this up for a religion 'which imposes a spiritual worship, adapted to the nature and character of Him who is the object of it' (quoted by Copley *op.cit.* 218-19, but see whole article173-227).

Geoffrey Oddie contends that during the second half of the 19th century Christians in this southern region in many ways were 'little different from Hindus', such were the cultural continuities after conversion. A little further north, in Andhra Pradesh, Carman and Luke's 1968 research (*Village Christians & Hindu Culture*) revealed a similar situation (Both Wingate and Kim rightly suggest that the discontinuities are also significant). The continuities in ritual and symbolic life implicit in inculturation were *not* what missionaries were hoping to see in the life of their converts.

My own experience in Andhra (in the same once Muslim-ruled Telangana region in which Carman did his research) both agrees with and diverges from this. For example, the very first time, in 1960, it was arranged that I go to visit a Dalit *basti* in the large area for which I had pastoral oversight, and there give my first rural speech in Telugu, we found on arrival that the Christian young men had long-standing other plans - no doubt astrologically arranged - plans that the village catechist had not respected. They were that same night to give their annual dramatic performance of the Hindu epic Ramayana, in Telugu referred to as 'Sita-Rama-Nataka'. At the time this clash of programmes (and personalities as it happened) was all unknown to me. In the event, quite large numbers of Hindu Caste people from the village came to see and hear the new 'White

Dora'; while many of the Christian Dalits went to the 'Hindu' drama their young men were putting on. It was not, though, that they were all merely nominal Christians. They were, for example, enthusiastic in their weekly group singing of *kirtanas* in praise of Jesus. Yet, part of their identity seemed to make it natural to them to produce their own performance of the 'Hindu' story of Rama and Sita.

No doubt the 'pressures on the hyphen' there were very complex, and at the time I did not probe what was happening in the way I now would. There may well have been economic pressures - for they were largely dependent on local Hindu landlords. Certainly there will have been socio-cultural pressures to assimilate, to affirm an aspiration for oneness of identity with the dominant Hindu communities, as a non-confrontational way of reducing their sense of alienation and outcasteness - the exact opposite of a perhaps more usual religious strategy of asserting an identity of otherness. And in any case, even if we leave aside the so-called 'higher' religious forms such as the Ramayana (the basis of the Rama-Sita story, seen by today's liberationists as a tale of Brahmanic conquest of indigenous Dravidians), Dalit Christians shared a great deal of 'folk' animistic religiosity in common with all Hindus, as Carman and Luke found. In common with Pallath, too, we might conclude that Dalit Christians needed far more ritual drama and symbolism than was available to them in their almost puritanical Methodist-based cultic life. They did have those fine *bhakti* songs; but they were denied both the ecstatic ways of Pentecostalism and the cultic imagery - even if inadequate (according to Pallath) - of Catholicism.

Conversion of the Heart?

Those Methodist origins inevitably lead me to think of conversion in the first instance as a matter of faith-orientation, the 'strangely warmed heart' that was the turning-point experience of John Wesley, whose 300th birth anniversary fell on 17 June 2003. And this pietist view of conversion as the internalising in the heart of a response to the great Object of faith that has come to 'mean the world' to us, became widespread throughout Britain by the mid-19th century, and in the missionary movements then burgeoning. Many Anglicans, as well as the various non-conformist missions, were openly uncomfortable about what seemed to them a lack of such inner conversion in those being baptised in India's mass movements.

Conversion, they believed, was essentially a new self-identity that begins with a personal born-again experience.

Taking inner faith and personal experience, therefore, as the crucial mark of true conversion, it follows that there does not *have* to be a movement from one religious community to another? Nor has it always meant this historically in India. There have always been quite large numbers of 'secret Christians' (Wingate op.cit. 139-51). And those who have identified themselves as 'Hindu Christians' would have usually been quite content - if given freedom in matters of faith - to remain as disciples of Jesus *within* their Hindu community.

Newbigin: Community Change Essential

This issue has occasioned fierce debate at various periods among Christian leaders in India. So, it is the *nature of conversion* that is really at issue. Church of Scotland missionary Lesslie Newbigin (for a number of years a Church of South India Bishop in Madras, then a leading global ecumenical figure) represented the conservative position. Conversion might be unnecessarily disruptive of communities at times, but faith in Christ must mean belonging to the body of Christ, an essentially visible and therefore identifiable community. A new community allegiance is unavoidable. While he did not exactly subscribe to that maxim of fourth century Cyprian, then affirmed by Rome, that 'outside the church there is no salvation', for Newbigin, as for the majority of missionaries, there was no authentic Christian identity without active church membership.

The pastoral needs of socially and culturally vulnerable converts figured large in his reckoning. But the decisive point was his contention - here agreeing with the influential missiologist Hendrick Kraemer - that there has to be an essential *discontinuity* between Christian faith and other faith, between life in Christ and life outside Christ (see Jathanna 1981: esp.111-119, for a thorough exposition of Kraemer on this issue). In the thought of Newbigin conversion must involve a movement from one faith-group to another.

In his late 1980s-early 1990s 'Gospel and Culture' project Newbigin went on to try to point the way to a distinctively Christian cultural enfleshment of Christian faith. To him this meant not only recognising and attempting to purify our cultural milieu of its secularist assumptions, but also the creating of a distinctively Christian cultural life, seemingly free too of any indebtedness to, any shared perspectives or values with, other faith-based cultural life (see *The Gospel and Contemporary Culture*, edited Hugh Montefiore, Mowbray 1992). Discontinuity and uncontaminated uniqueness - perhaps typical of his conservative Reformed tradition - were central to Newbigin's view of authentic Christian identity.

Counter-Calls for Continuity

Such an emphasis on a radical break with earlier nurturing faith and tradition would have been anathema to such 'Hindu-Christian' Catholics as Brahmabandhab Upadhyay in the second half of the 19th century. Among Protestants caste converts too this opposing view had already been argued by the Madras-based *Rethinking* group (esp. Chenchiah *et al*, 1938), led by caste converts such as the lay theologians V.Chakkarai and P.Chenchiah. For them, strands of *continuity* with Hindu faith and culture was of the essence. Mission is not to aim for a separate community, but is a movement within 'the Hindu social fold' (p. 44). Further north, Manilal Parekh, though baptised himself, even more vigorously denounced efforts to 'proselytise' and thus divide converts off from Hindu society. In the 1960s, reflecting on the meaning of baptism, even the church's professional theologians (e.g. Russell Chandran and the then young Christopher Duraisingh) began to propose a new interpretation of this act not as setting apart, but as making for a more inclusive social stance. In particular, baptism 'into Christ' meant solidarity with all those seeking a new humanity (Wingate pp.188-210; also more recently Kiran Sebastian's essays on baptism).

Radical Danish missionary historian, Kai Baago, believed the organised church in India to be so irrevocably part of an imperialist age that *any* notion of conversion from Hinduism to Christianity will miss the true meaning of faith in Christ. If Christ transcends all cultures then he certainly needs to be set free from the bondage of the Christianity created by western imperialism. His argument could well be that of a Hindu nationalist: Why should people be converted at all? 'Do they have to be incorporated into church organizations which are utterly alien to their religious traditions?' Faith in Christ is to be developed *within* Hindu cultural life (In 'The Post-Colonial Crisis of Missions', *International Review of Missions* LV/219 (July 1966), 322-32). Naturally, this radical critique of missions was anathema to theologically orthodox ecclesiatics such as Newbigin, whose faith-perspective and sense of Christian identity were little changed by his many years in India.

The question of how discontinuous cultural life is to be for a 'convert' was, as we noted above, raised in a seemingly more secular context too. The American historian, Robert Frykenberg, in his critical review (in *Indian Economic and Social History Review,* 17, 1981: 121-38) of Geoffrey Oddie's analysis of the conversion process within Indian society, argued that a more radical break with past cultural life was essential if we are to use the word 'conversion' meaningfully. No one can deny the pertinence of Frykenberg's call for more systematic analysis of how religious communities emerge, of why some develop a strong sense of self-identity and others do not, and indeed of the powerful dynamics by which religious change occurs. Can we, asks Frykenberg, construct a 'typology of phenomenological elements and factors which, to one degree or another, can be expected in all conversion movements?' More doubtful are the rather sharp boundaries set by his own definition of conversion: 'Conversion is a change....from one view of life to another; from one set of beliefs or opinions to another; from one party, religion, or 'spiritual' state to another' (*op.cit.*129). With this definition of 'conversion', is there sufficient room for strands of *continuity* with previous life and its view of the world? The stress on discontinuity is too strong. As Wingate puts it: 'It is the balance between continuity and discontinuity that may be the vital factor in the development of a conversion movement' (1997: 251). Though Wingate's is a more pastoral and theological perspective, it is probably the case that a recognition of both tendencies is vital to proper *sociological* understanding too.

The 'Humanisation' of M.M.Thomas

It was dual theological-sociological stance of M.M.Thomas - for many years Director of the Christian Institute for the Study of Religion and Society, based in Bangalore - whose prolific writings provided what came to be (until the hardening attitudes of the 1990s) the more dominant mainstream Christian official account of Hindu-Christian cultural and social continuities. That it was 'dominant' is far from meaning that it was an integral part of the majority of Christians' self-understanding, or even integrally part of the theology taught in the many regional colleges. Here is another point at which official *rhetoric* and felt *reality* have been poles apart. Thomas' liberationist stance looked to collaborative Hindu-Christian 'nation-building', for him a primarily *secular* meeting-point in which the Christian gospel is essentially concerned with 'humanisation' in its fullest sense. Asia is modernising, and the Christian faith, with its commitment to newness and change, is an essential part of the new hope that modernity offers all Asian people (see my critique of Thomas' view of modernity in Das 1987).

In the first place - said Thomas and others - it is the *Christian church itself that is called to conversion*, conversion to an inclusive social commitment. As a re-interpretation of conversion's meaning, this was a point argued from the 1980s onwards by Catholic social theologians such as Walter Fernandes and Wilfred Felix in the even more politically sharp-edged socio-economic position that Christians are to see their identity in terms of aligning with and taking a fully active part in movements for the transformation of the marginalised (*Indian Missiological Review* 1983-4).

Thomas' main point was not dissimilar, but was somewhat less confrontational, more positive about what God is already doing through the transforming revolutions taking place among the people of Asia. Sacral boundaries and ecclesial identity were perhaps less deeply embedded in his worldview. No doubt it was easier to find all revolutionary changes as part of God's 'new creation' to which Christian faith is to witness. True conversion, from this perspective, is being in tune with that transforming mission of God, its scope being far wider than 'the church' and its identifiable boundaries. Such conversion means identifying with a 'common humanity' that is 'open to the insights and inspiration of all faiths, both religious and secular'.

In other words, in spite of important points of overlap with Newbigin (for there are 'Barthian' strands, differently configured, in both), for Thomas socio-cultural continuities - even if critically perceived - are central to true Christian faith. Collaboration with all 'humanising' endeavour is central to the identity formed by faith in Christ, and to the conversion that is part of the identity-shaping process. Indeed, a distinctly separate 'Christian' identity is not essential to his position (Thomas 1969; 1971) Interestingly, both Baago and Thomas were later appointed to state office by their respective countries - Baago as Danish ambassador to India, Thomas as state governor in Nagaland.

Unresolvable Anomalies

Kim sees unresolvable anomalies, 'given the Indian context', in an attempt by the Commission on Conversion convened by the National Christian Council in 1966 to harmonise views based both on the continuities and discontinuities of the above approaches. This not only affirmed that conversion entails the 'transition from one faith to another', 'public confession', distinctive 'patterns of behaviour', and a 'continuing visible companionship'. It also claimed that movement from one community to another is not essential to the process, and that a 'turning to the Lord' is as necessary to 'Christians' as to anyone else. True, conversion of any kind has in part been problematic because of social realities in India. Already sharply divided identities and defense mechanisms within the Hindu caste system were further sharpened by aggressively critical 'Christian' attitudes and practices. These social realities made it next to impossible for there to be Hindu-Christian 'companionship' (especially if Christians were of lower caste origins), or for conversion to Christian faith not to result in the felt-need for a new community allegiance, a movement in some sense away from the Hindu community and into the community of Christians. The Commission was correct, though, that socially and culturally such a community switch can hardly be understood as *essential* to Christian faith.

Internalising Symbols of Faith as Primary

In the first place, then, *conversion has to be understood as a 'turning' to God*, as the taking on of a new vision of life and reality, a newly directed destiny. And some such 'conversion' is expected within almost every religious community. Even those born into the tradition in many cases are expected to experience some kind of renewing 'birth'. Islam, its radicals included, sometimes play down the notion of being 'born-again' within Islam - though conversion into Islam from outside obviously involves a kind of 'new birth'. Generally, though, nurture within the Islamic community is seen as integral to spiritual growth, even when that includes periods of crisis. Yet, Muslims on Hajj do claim just such a sense of new birth, and it is clearly important in Sufi experience.

It is just this internalising of the symbols of faith that is primary even when 'conversion' entails a turning to some other path of faith.

For all the anti-conversion rhetoric in India today, such movements from one faith to another have, as we noted earlier, happened in very large numbers throughout Indian religious history: becoming followers of the Buddha or Mahavira, turning to faith in Siva, or Rama, or Krishna, finding a new vision of things through Guru Nanak, or Swami Narayana, to name just a few 'converting' faiths that emerged largely within India, apart from instances of new-found self-identity in response to the message of Christ or the Prophet.

Conversion, then, has eventually, even primarily, to do with the *internalising of new-found faith*. Yet, it is its communitarian consequences that prove far more problematic. For, with any new faith-orientation, conversion inevitably results in some kind of new community identity. This can be, though, an identity that is very loosely framed, and that will have variously configured relationships with wider society and its structures. The faith-sharing necessarily entails *some* form of identifying with those belonging to the community of that faith, if only as an initial means of nurturing in the new faith.

It may, though, be a highly *critical* relationship with that community. There may be rejection of much which that institutionalised community has come to stand for. There is, therefore, no reason to see that community (in any faith-system, perhaps especially Christian) as the *primary identity*. For it is not that external community which is definitive of, or the primary focal point of the new identity. So, as we saw, a 'convert' from within Hindu tradition to faith in Christ has not always found it necessary to move from one community to another. Such converts as have been permitted by their 'non-Christian' families to remain as Christian devotees within those families, in spite of obvious points of tension from time to time, bear witness to the fact that such Christian-within-Hindu life is not impossible.

Caste Realities Inescapable

The 'social realities', however, take us far beyond such familial accommodation. There is the hard reality of caste division, a divisive social structure that led some missionaries, especially evangelical Anglicans, to stress the need for an open break with a self-identity based on caste-identity. And this often entailed finding a new identity in a new faith-community. What they aimed for was not so much a

373

denial of all caste differences in every aspect of social life, but that at least within ecclesial life, and especially at the 'Table of the Lord', there shall be no sense of 'higher' and 'lower', and especially no lingering belief in untouchability. The particular demands made by European evangelicals in the symbolic break with caste-identities were not always very enlightened, either socially or theologically.

Particularly irksome must have been the anomaly of the racist attitudes and sense of inherent superiority missionaries usually showed in their relations with Indians, whether Christian or Hindu, and their demand at the same time that high-caste converts give up their sense of superiority. Caste, though, was/is but one issue in the new life to be expected of those whose world is 'turned', whose self-identity is changed, because of their new faith. The ethical dimensions of faith, the social structures that impinge on faith, are far from peripheral.

No Fixed Course for Conversion

What few involved in the process of conversion have been able to accept, though, is that there are no fully worked out, no readymade blueprints for the social and ethical life of faith in every place, every situation. Conversion has to be a life-long period of growth in insight and commitment, even if patterns for the new identity are set up from the moment of initial commitment. Sathi Clarke, too, in summing up the historical research of others, emphasises both the *fluidity* ('a fluid process of changing affiliations of religious beliefs and traditions with a range of possibilities', 2003: 8) and the *ongoing* effects of the converting process (a 'dynamic process' whose prospects extend also to 'an anticipatory future', p.288). The *internalising* mentioned above will depend any many different factors.

If, though, the convert is taught from the outset to see all prior identities as demonic, all previous relationships as expendable, all indigenous cultural life as requiring rigorous exclusion, we can expect little genuine spiritual growth, just static complacency. Such a position is tantamount to making the identity of the new faith-community more absolute than the sacred Object of the faith of that community.

Conversion to Buddhism as Social Protest

Those of us who stress the more piously devotional dimension of faith can easily make assumptions about the conversion process that may be very different from the realities experienced at those 'frontier'-points of mission, mainly among Dalit and tribal communities. There, the act of conversion is often, almost as a matter of historical necessity, a *symbolic act of protest* against their people's poverty, social humiliation and impotence, and the oppressed conditions of their life of which they have now become aware. Is such 'resistance' not a basic human right? The compulsion to see the new faith primarily in socio-political terms can become almost irresistible. It is precisely, too, because group conversion is seen by dominant powers as so objectionable that oppressed groups are the more likely to turn to this as their perhaps only possible act of protest. For Dalits a clear ideological focus has emerged: they seek to resist the oppressive dharmic tradition of Brahmanic Hinduism. For them at this juncture there is little concern for issues of religio-cultural continuity, or for the 'hyphenated' nature of faith-identities.

In November 2001 there was a mass conversion event in New Delhi. At a rally of some 50,000 Dalits, perhaps as many as 8,000 were given initiation (*diksha*), not as Christians or Muslims, but as Buddhists. This was the culmination of a six-month national campaign by Ram Raj, chairman of the All India Confederation of Scheduled Caste and Scheduled Tribe Organisations, encouraging Dalits publicly to assert their separation from Hinduism. Ram Raj himself was the first to convert, taking the new name Udit Raj.

Opting for a Buddhist identity, rather than Christian or Muslim, follows the precedent set by the great hero of the Dalit movement, 'Babasaheb' Ambedkar, almost fifty years earlier. On the one hand, for Dalits to affirm a Buddhist identity takes much of the religio-cultural and even political sting out of such a public disaffirming of Hindu identity. Hindutva sees Buddhism as indigenous to India, and therefore still part of 'Hindu' culture and society. On the other hand staging such a public converting event made it painfully clear that many Dalits wish no longer to identified as 'Hindus'. The event, therefore, engendered no little agitation nationwide. In spite of receiving High Court permits for the event, the Dalits found their way to their chosen site - the spacious Ramlila grounds, near Parliament building - blocked by the police. Posters appeared falsely claiming the event to be cancelled. Eventually the organisers were able to rearrange the event at the Ambedkar Bhavan.

These (and other) details are not irrelevant: mass conversions of this kind are politically explosive. But so are the social conditions experienced by Dalits that make conversion of some kind seem necessary, if only as a political gesture, an act of defiance by which an oppressed but not totally impotent people assert at least this much resistance to what they see as a dominant and oppressing community.

The question is, how much more than a 'political gesture', a symbolic 'act of defiance', is such conversion? Interpretations by the media and its commentators varied: *The Tribune* called it a 'farce', a political non-starter. For, rather than be weakened by such a 'nominal change of religion', caste is more 'deeply entrenched', more powerfully locked into political life, than was the case in Ambedkar's day. *India Today* also described it as largely a political stunt. Other newspapers saw it as symbolic of the felt fact of caste oppression, and therefore a significant 'slap in the face of the Sangh Parivar' (*The Statesman*). *Frontline* picked up the way in which the Vishva Hindu Parishad claimed the event masked a Christian conspiracy, in that conversion is pre-eminently and invariably a Christian ploy to gain power and weaken Hinduism, however devious the strategy. It is a fact that various Christian leaders did support the conversion ceremony, it being an accepted argument that conversion, however perceived as socially and culturally disruptive by Hindus, is one of the few means left to Dalits to express their defiance and their freedom of choice.

All this makes it very clear that acts of mass conversion have all manner of ramifications. They may not be solely symbolic acts of social and political protest, though the politicising of such events - by both sides - obscures the faith dimension. For, both among Buddhist and Christian communities, the new self-identity created by such mass conversions has entailed significant changes of inner orientation - visible in terms of a new self-confidence, a new sense of destiny, a new spirit of faith.

Conversion's Ambiguities Call for Critical Self-Appraisal

This *ambiguity* between political symbol and faith-identity makes the questions of motivation raised by Hindu activists understandable, even valid. This is not only because Christian missions, and indeed most other missions too, have historically included various forms of social work - educational, medical, local industries, etc - as an intrinsic part of being missionary. And the critic naturally sees this solely in terms of conscious or intended 'allurement', even if this fails to understand the fundamentals of Christian faith and its inescapable sense of vocation to world transformation. Equally inescapable, though, is the charge that *global 'mission' forces* are at work here, and that this mission operates within an imbalance of global power - cultural, economic, military - that in reality contradicts elements fundamental to Christian faith. Part of this 'imbalance' is the unpleasant fact that very large amounts of money come in from abroad, thus injecting an alien and artificial factor into the situation. The polemics of the Arun Shouries of Hindutva are not totally without basis.

That missions, along with their works of charity, do also aim for some form of 'conversion' in itself is not the problem. Hindu missions also receive significant monies from abroad, and Hindu counter-missions are also active making intensive efforts to make converts, or as they see it, to 'bring back those who have strayed form their original fold', perhaps through a ritual of 'purifying' (*suddhi*). This counter-missioning complicates, but does not substantially affect the key issues surrounding conversion.

I conclude, then, that the ambiguities from all sides surrounding group conversions make honest and critical self-appraisal from all sides urgently necessary. As a response to acts of violence against Christians - specifically to the horrendous murder in Orissa in January 2000 of the Australian Baptist leprosy missionary, Graham Staines - the Indian Prime Minister Vajpayee's statement that there must be a debate on conversions was far from adequate to the occasion. It was especially inadequate in the context of several hundred acts of often well-organised persecution perpetrated by those claiming to represent the majority community against a minority community of less than 2.5%. (In the months following this atrocity there was also bitter criticism of an inadequate police response. By September 2003, however, a dozen or so men had been arrested and convicted either to long terms of imprisonment or, in the case of the ring-leader, to death. It was touching to find the widow of Graham Staines pleading for the condemned killer's life).

But, however deplorably inadequate the official response from Delhi, it is precisely such a self-reflective debate that Christians do need to carry out among themselves. Christians need not deny that their self-identity is inseparably bound up with this phenomenon of conversion. Nor need they deny that it is impossible to imagine a Christian faith in which there is no expectation at all of some kind of converting experience, involving a 'turning' to faith in Christ, a sharing in the life of others with such faith, and ways of affirming to others the reality of that faith. Yet they also cannot deny that the milieu in which conversion takes place in India carries with it such intrusive non-faith factors - political histories, economic pressures, even the new global imperialisms - that Christians need openly and critically to 'debate', among themselves and with people of 'other' faith, just what being part of a Christian identity means. Far too few Christian leaders seem willing to engage self-critically in such a debate, preferring instead to sloganise, just as the Hindutva party does, but from the opposing viewpoint. Oppressed peoples may well have the right to use conversion as a weapon against the dominant. Unfortunately, in such a politically charged context the faith-dimension and life-turning that genuine conversion calls for have been obscured. So, this term 'conversion' functions at numerous different levels: clarifying what is meant is itself one reason for the needed debate.

Conclusion
When Faith-Identities are Dangerous

In spite of the increasing emphasis on the constructive power of the human self and its imagining - the ability even to create selfhood and self-identity - we cannot escape the bonds implicit in the givens in our humanness. No self emerges wholly free from its historical grounding and biological configuring. Our 'boundaries' are shaped first by birth and genes, by race and ethnic tradition, by family and other group ties, by the cultural ambience of childhood, even by an environing landscape. Both genetic nature and early nurture shape the particular identities by which we define our humanness

Then, there is also the self's ongoing encounters and interaction with further conditioning contexts - social, national, global - and the 'othering' this entails. This interacting too helps shape the subjectivity that makes us aware of our own selfhood. Not that this always creates a sense of freedom able to plan and make decisions, able both to respond to others and exercise power in relation to others. The experienced realities of power-relations may build up little but bitter resentments. Either way, there is an inescapable conditioning to how we place ourselves as well as how others place us.

So, the givenness in this identity-shaping process, its corporate and cultural dimension, finds its focus in that inner personal awareness of who we are and where we belong. And these conditioning determinants *can* become the means by which we attain a sense of self-determination. Selfhood emerges out of forms of social experience, though these two foci of human identity will perhaps always exist in some measure of tension.

The impact of *religion* on this identity-shaping process in human history has been and still is immensely pervasive. The symbols, myths, rituals, beliefs and institutions of our religious traditions, have often been the most prominent factor in the dynamics by which whole communities, as well as individuals, have understood who they are, where they belong. That corporate remembering which, for long millennia, has shaped people's ways of seeing themselves and others, has invariably been itself religion-shaped. Even more potent has been the impact of faith in individual self-identity and in the distinctive self-understanding this produces.

My first point, then, is a very simple one: It is dangerous, from numerous perspectives, *when secular ideology does not recognise, or seeks to counter with its own belief-system, the reality and power of the religious dimension in our corporate human identities.*

As children of both tradition and modernity, though, we have to qualify this simple emphasis on religion in two ways:

(a) Our world, and therefore our identities, have become increasingly complex - the result of rapid change, of increased mobility, of easy exchange of ideas, and especially the result of modernity's questioning of received cultural values. In the resulting complexity of modern life, we become in differing ways citizens of multiple worlds, living out multiple identities. One of our present imperatives has become the search to integrate our diverse identities in some workable way.

This brings a two-fold danger. There is first the danger of the inner worlds making up our selfhood becoming so fragmented that we lose any enduring sense of belonging, of continuity. Further, fragmented identities are prone to take refuge in the apparent strength of some new mythic identity. This strident new identity may well appropriate features from a religiously structured past, but the re-creating will often be by those who, claiming messianic status and the goal of empowerment of their people, may well be intent on the control of their weaker fellows. Ambition for power is all-pervading in the configurating of our self-identities.

(b) There is no denying that especially the past two centuries have increasingly seen dynamics other than those of religious tradition, other ideologies, other enchantments, powerfully at work in re-shaping the way people see their world and group themselves. In western Europe primary identity consciously based on institutional religion (though not faith *per se* according to repeated polling) is now found in only a very small minority. American culture diverges on this. A majority still attend one or other church and seemingly accept its worldview, though finding ultimate commitments here calls for closer analysis. Just how central are the inner compulsions of 'Gospel-faith' in that culture, as against the compulsions of economic pressure and national status?

At an unconscious level even in the hardline secularity of Europe, of course, the imprint of age-old religious tradition may still be found. Durkheim may have been right. Was Marxism, for example, merely a radically new form of the eschatological strand of Judeo-Christianity? Perhaps corporate moments of heightened emotion in western life - football matches, the extraordinary scenes of mourning for the young 'people's princess' and suchlike highly charged occasions - are still religiously patterned. It is not difficult to finding patterns of 'implicit religion' in modern life. At least overtly, though, in the cradle of modern capitalist technology, we find Max Weber's gloomy 1930 prognosis rapidly coming true: there is a relentlessly increasing secularist view of things in which institutional religion has seemingly lost its power to create a sacral world of enchantment.

That, though, is far from how things are in much of the non-European world, including those many nations previously making up the great communist bloc and now struggling to reshape their corporate identities. There is an explicitly strong religious dimension to their new-found nationalist feeling. Many westerners, in fact, point to the religious factor in the violence found in global hotspots - the Balkans, Chechnya, Kashmir, Sri Lanka, Indonesia, parts of Africa, Northern Ireland and aim to place the blame squarely on religion as the world's real trouble-maker. Perception and reality may well be far apart here; but the power of religion to create or to reinforce strongly held identities is undeniable. Little, for example, needs be said about the strength of religious identity in the wide-spread world of Islam or in the vigorously expressed nationalism of Hindu India in recent years.

Not that the seemingly sacral rules out ways of being secular - as T.N.Madan, Gauri Vishvanathan and others have noted within Hindu tradition. *Yogis* and *Bhaktas* can also be very world-conscious. The saffron-garbed are, indeed, at the heart of much recent politics, in particular the violent conflict raging around Ayodhya. Yet, the saffron swamis are far from merely rabble-rousing leaders of attacks on Muslims and their sacred places. Subsequent to the Gujarat massacres in 2003, for instance, at least one large group of Hindu 'renouncers' is reported to have pledged itself to protect the Ayodhya Muslims against attacks they fear might be engineered by the globally militant Vishva Hindu Parishad.

Motives here may well be mixed. The point is that our faith-systems, East and West, are often world-related; and for better or worse these faiths have been and still are pervasive and powerful. Not least is their power to create a strongly coherent sense of self-identity within the complex multiplicities of human life. But faith's potency can be socially creative, as well as destructive, in many other ways too. To label disparagingly as 'fundamentalist' *every* movement in which faith-based conviction leads to social action is in effect to try to eliminate from human life deeply rooted resources for human transformation.

The reverse of 'faith-based conviction' is to be found too: people who aim primarily for political or commercial gain, or for social status, are quite capable of *using* religious dynamics to achieve those ends, perhaps even to legitimise crude ambition or avarice. East and West, there has been ample evidence of such exploiting of religion for ends that may have little to do with that religion's professed higher goals or the dynamic of its inner life. Not that we can assume that religious life is not genuine unless there is high-mindedness and purity of motive. Our faith-systems are far more complex than this. Each often itself acknowledges that there is a diversity of goals to be found among its adherents, even if some life-goals are given higher spiritual value than others.

So, then, while the potencies of religious tradition can be utilised to dangerous effect, there are even more disastrous consequences likely when hardline secularists ignore, or even seek to eliminate, religious faith as a pervasive and powerful reality in human self-identity, personal and corporate.

Secondly, it is imperative for people of faith as well as faith's opponents to recognise the *double-edged character of our religious traditions*. Religion can often act merely to *reinforce identities* given by structures that are largely social, cultural, political - perhaps expanding and intensifying these identities, perhaps gently moderating them. When faith reinforces and legitimates a corporate identity that is essentially unjust to certain human groups, then faith is being utilised to evil ends. At such points faith-based identities are ethically and humanly dangerous. Yet, it is plainly ludicrous to assume, as some secularists seem to, that all affirming of given forms in our traditions will serve to negate human good.

But there is also the other, more 'cutting edge' of faith. At its heart is also the *potential to counter, to be radically critical of our socially, culturally, and politically given identities*. It is imperative for the authentic life of religion, for the free flowing of its dynamics, that this critical cutting edge be not blunted. It is, for example, essential for the health of Christian faith in India that it challenge many western secularist cultural and political assumptions, as individual prophets within Indian Christianity have done boldly and vigorously. Yet, Christian interpreters - East and West - have too often made their uncritical peace with the life-identities that go along with many of these secularist assumptions. Of course there is much to be learnt from lively engagement with post-Enlightenment westernised values. Yet, secularist identities are potentially just as dangerously inhuman as the dark violence that religious identities can create.

It is imperative, too, for the health of Hindu forms of faith that not all Hindu groups allow themselves to be seduced by the recently dominant Sangh Parivar culture that finds its primary identity in militant religious communalism. The Hindutva programme may appear to many Hindus to strengthen Hindu faith; in reality it endangers key elements in that faith, just as any militantly nationalist grouping - whether in the Balkans, Britain, Germany, Israel/Palestine, Sri Lanka, or wherever - has endangered the inner life of the very religion it may claim to protect.

Exclusively *ethnic* grouping too can serve to weaken faith-potencies. Where ethnic groups have found the historical need to take on board the dynamic of a 'world faith' (Buddhist, Hindu, Christian, Muslim), an ongoing faith-culture dialectic is vital, for the danger of an enfeebling loss of ethnic cultural tradition is also great where this is obliterated by the adopted faith and the culture accompanying it. Faith's dynamic calls for interpenetration with the cultures that have made people what they are, or both faith and inherited culture become dangerously distorted.

It is imperative, too, that Muslim communities be enabled not only to respond critically and take up a resistant stance to western ('Christian'?) globalising moves, but also to look self-critically at the sharply defined identities found in exclusive Islamic militancy. Minorities in militantly Islamic countries in recent decades too often find themselves demonised and persecuted, even when not innately anti-Muslim. The history of clashes between Islamic nations makes it clear that any claim of Muslims that their Islamic loyalty always transcends ethnicity and even nationalist loyalty is far from a political reality. Even so, in many hardline Islamist countries there is a monolithic merging of religious, cultural and nationalist identities, in spite of claims to transcend in peace all cultures and nationalities.

The reality is, then, that the merging of identities in such 'Islamism' is very similar to that seen in their arch-enemy Hindutva, though generally the faith-dimension in Islamism is more consciously dominant than is the case with the Sangh Parivar. Whether this is the case or not, when an institutionalised faith-identity, intensified by the powerfully emotive symbols of that faith, but not necessarily by the faith itself, makes absolute claims upon our loyalty, it is not only the perceived 'enemy' who is endangered. The life of the faith itself is in danger. In the Israel/Palestine continuing conflict, to hear leading Imams in televised Mosque sermons passionately urging the congregation instantly to 'kill, kill, kill any Jew' they meet, and finding orthodox Jewish leaders inciting to similar kinds of violence, makes it clear that - whatever the provocations - central claims of those two faiths, Muslim and Jewish, had been smothered by the immediate claims of identities based on other emotive institutional factors. .

Thirdly, there can be grave danger *when people of religious faith forget this dark side lurking within our faith-traditions*. Believers may think of the Source and the Goal of faith as pure goodness and light 'without the slightest shadow of turning' (to use a biblical phrase) - and countless Hindu, Christian, Muslim and other texts employ just such language for the pure character of God. Yet, even within these same scriptural sources, there is little difficulty in finding other material that seem disturbingly ambiguous in terms of human and moral values. Faith will, of course, usually find ways of interpreting these ambiguities. The Jewish-Christian scriptures are replete with stories from which expositers have a hard time wresting spiritual value.

From time to time, though, it is precisely these dark scriptural passages and the least humane elements in our histories that are seized on as defining sources for groups perhaps on the periphery of our faiths, yet still claiming continuity within the tradition. From the Thugis of earlier Indian history (a history no doubt skewed by imperialist accounts on which interpretation has depended) to the overtly racist 'Christian' thugs (the Hindi form is the original) to be found in parts of America and Europe today, religion has provided the mythic grounding for a tightly knit sense of group identity, and a distorted sense of group power, viciously alienating itself from the rest of the human community. In every case of course there are other socio-political factors also part of the dynamics accounting for the alienation.

For, it is in response to an aggressive secularist ideology and cultural life that aggressive forms of 'fundamentalism' are most likely to arise. From a secularist perspective - no doubt Muslim and Christian too - post-independence India has been far too 'Hindu'. Others see the situation differently. For there has undeniably been a strong strand in dominant political and cultural discourse and its undergirding ideology that has ignored religion's role in the life of India's people. In spite of very different grass-roots feeling and practice, officially it has been the language of liberal modernity that has most loudly echoed in the discourse of India's varied corridors of power. It is a way of thinking and speaking that runs counter to the way the great majority of Indian people (whether Hindu, Muslim, Sikh or Christian) actually feel and act, especially at times of crisis.

Thus the identity imagined by this dominant discourse was so out of tune with the sense of self-identity held by peoples of many different traditions, that the situation was ripe for new forms of extremist religious identity to emerge. It is when (among other factors) there is a strongly felt perception that our group identity is overlooked, that a dangerously exaggerated, mythically distorted form of that identity is likely to be born. An identity vacuum is always dangerous. But when such interpretive insights leave out, even deliberately belittle, religious and cultural dimensions of human experience that have unmissably pervaded community experience at every level for millennia, how can we not expect that there will be repercussions of some kind?

Two obvious rejoinders to this kind of criticism include, first, the query as to how it would have been possible for India to be anything but 'secular', in the limited sense intended by the founding fathers (and one or two mothers). 'Secular' meant that from the point of view of the Nation-state - very soon declared a Republic - followers of all religions would be treated equally, none would be discriminated against, and no one religion would be given special favours by the State.

But there is a broader objection to reckon with here. Unless a modern nation takes on board the grounding assumptions of secularism as a worldview, and speaks the language of that secularised world, is it possible for that country to exist as a collaborating equal within the global community of nations? Even within itself, if the grounding discourse is Islamic, how can Hindus and Christians live as equal citizens within such a state? If the grounding discourse is dominated by Hindu ways of thinking, how can others be equals? The answer lies in how we understand the needed relationship between a faith-based identity - of whatever faith - and the other identities to which one is party within the human community. A sense of the legitimacy of other faith-identities, furthered by continual dialogical interaction that enables re-defining and re-directing of one's own faith-identity, would seem to be the only viable path, difficult though this may at first seem for some, but not all, of those with strong commitments of faith.

It is only within those traditions as they interact with others, and by drawing on their potential resources for enhancing relationship with wider worlds, that the 'dark side'also lurking within can be dealt with.

Fourthly - taking further the preceding point - there is the imperative for people of faith to be *aware of the dangers of power* and the *manipulative use of power*. Power, in the human realm, has to do with ego, personal and corporate. Power has to do with our human need for status and the exercise of dominance. Human institutions of all kinds - despotic or democratic, political or private, scientific or cultural, even those oriented to social service or the weakening of strangleholds of power - are, in their differing ways, structures of power and control.

Nor is it merely in the overtly human and political domain that power is a dominant reality. Our religious systems, though, have at their centre distinctive ways of perceiving the reality of power and of seeking to respond to that reality. Indeed, *power* - the dynamics of power-relations, the ambiguities of power, the hidden and uncanny springs of power, attunement with, enhancement by, control of, even the turning around of this power, and above all, what constitutes ultimate Power - is the stuff of our faith-systems, as that remarkable Dutch phenomenologist G. van der Leeuw emphasised some 65 years ago. We must reckon with the *distinctive* ways in which religions perceive and respond to this elemental potency within human existence. For all the overlapping with other factors better described in terms of psychology, sociology, anthropology, at many points the distinct dynamic of our identity-creating religiousness, is crucial to understanding human life, certainly India's life.

We have to take a step further. *It is dangerous not to be aware of the interactive power-contexts within which our corporate religious identities emerge.* So, having begun by insisting on the need for the religious dimension to be taken seriously, I now have to concede that there is a danger in naively exclusive religious explanations of things. Historical realism can so easily lose out to the wishful thinking of our mythic worlds, though it is often not religious faith as such that creates those mythic worlds.

The critical perspective of our post-Marxist and late modernist world has made it clear in a new way - and in doing so has enhanced faith's self-understanding - that all forms of discourse take place within some kind of structured power-context. The institutional life of culture and religion, as much as the arena of politics and economics, is irrevocably power-based. All our human words and actions in relation to others are seen as transactions by which we negotiate our power-position, however our power over or subordination to that other may be structured.

As we have seen, power-*countering*, power-*resistant* moves are also to be found at the heart of much religious experience. Even so, the realities of social power have to be reckoned with. And not solely in institutional religion where the sense of who we are, which group we belong to, what that group's status, and what our own position within that group, has very much to do with power-positioning. Much personal religious aspiration too can have to do with the extension of personal influence, control over others as well as over life's circumstances. In itself such aspiration may not be intrinsically evil. But motivational tensions, both within believer and faith-community, are inevitable, calling for continual self-critical awareness. It is in this ego-countering search for a self-critical stance that faith's resources become essential.

Tensions too are rather obvious between faith-based identities and wider human identities. A society structured on the basis of class - feudal, post-industrial, or merely divided by disparate incomes - is as much power-based as is that traditional ordering and identifying of people by their caste-birth. As we saw, this ancient Indian way of ordering society seems almost as endemic to Christian and Muslim as to Hindu communities in the Sub-continent, even though only the last provides legitimation through sacred myth and scriptural decree.

No doubt almost every religious tradition has inherited a problem-area making very clear that institution's need for the most rigorously sustained re-formation, or *aggiornamento* as good Pope John and the Catholic church's second great Council called the multiple tasks of re-directing their institutional life and its power-structures. The relentless reversal of this re-forming process by Pope John Paul and his close associate Cardinal Ratzinger has to do as much with power-issues as with the re-establishing of divinely revealed *truth* - the typical claim of entrenched conservatives. For Hindu society and its ethics, even for its faith-systems and spiritualities, addressing the power-inflating, power-denying structures of caste is surely the great task of the day. Power-issues are at the centre of all religious life in one form or another.

Again, both Marxist and postmodernist thought have helped us recognise these realities. In postmodernism, the emphasis is more often on disconnections and disparities between communities of discourse. The mode of discourse and thus the effective dynamic that operates in one structure-context cannot be related to that of another context. What is said and done is relative to that particular context, making the positing of absolutes and universals not only nonsensical, but dangerously hegemonic. Globalising of any kind is just a way of seeking to control by incorporating others into our group's world-view and value-system.

Gayatri Spivak, for example, has (rightly?) criticised the western-style education she was nurtured in. This assumed that it alone embodies a truly *humanist perspective,* either implying or openly declaring that all other value-systems are not based on universal human values. It is the universalising of one's own belief-system that is seen as the cardinal sin by the thorough-going postmodernist. At this point, of course, we are at the opposite extreme from Marxist faith in absolutes and universals. But do not all religious teachers too at some point universalise their faith? In spite of what most neo-Hindu interpreters say about all faiths leading to the same goal, and all paths being equally valid, particular faiths invariably take on an absolutist character for their adherents.

When postmodernist theory takes its relativist stance to nihilistic extremes, rational discourse becomes impossible, and discourse between divergent communities meaningless (Larrain 1994). Yet, the emphasis on there always being a structured power-context for our differing ways of discourse is crucial. Christian evangelists, for example, may speak of 'the power of the gospel', 'the power of the cross', and be quite oblivious to the fact that in conversion, other power-factors are in reality far more dominant, even if unconsciously, as much in the hidden agenda of their own missioning community as in the minds of their hearers. The slogan of that early communications guru Malcolm Macluhan, 'the medium is the message', still rings true. If the evangelist bears the marks, for instance, of a way of life loaded with western symbols of affluence or neo-imperialist arrogance, there is no way that the crude power of the dollar will not play a part in *how* the message is heard, indeed in *what* message is heard - especially if the messenger typically thunders on in triumphalist terms about the success that comes to those who have his kind of faith ('her' is very rare for a conservative evangelical preacher, even though there have been movements in which women have been the key communicators of converting faith, at times as public preachers too).

This recognition of the part played by structured power-context was equally true of the message of missionaries during the period of British rule. However much a number were deeply critical of aspects of that rule - though others saw it as within the providence of God - the fact that they were British, or even western, directly impinged on the way people heard their message. However much they may have avoided offering direct inducements to convert - and many did try to avoid allowing their famine-relief and other charitable works to become inducements - the faith of which they spoke had become re-conditioned by a power far from the 'power of the gospel' that was their ostensive message.

This, however, fails to take note of the power-contexts of those within India who were listening to this message. The fact that large numbers of those converting to the Christian and Muslim religions, especially in the past two centuries, have been from socially oppressed and economically deprived communities does not only mean that they were the most vulnerable to outside political influence and material inducement, as Hindu militants have so often argued. It also reflects the despair of these 'broken ones' in their contextual powerlessness and their latent hopes for a new social identity. It is their 'search for a new identity', a changed status, that is the strongest single motive in Dalit conversions. Change from their powerlessness has seemed a possibility. And in any case movements to a new identity always imply some deeply rooted dissatisfaction with the way things now are.

All this still leaves us with the anomalies of power on the side of the Muslim and Christian converting agencies. To argue that in the periods of Muslim and then British rule the great majority of conversions were neither 'by the sword' nor by direct material inducement carries little weight with the new Hindu militants, and is not in any case really the issue. Those political incursions from outside which were the cause of conversions, introduced power-factors that undoubtedly led considerable numbers of weaker communities to believe that it was in their interest to convert and thereby acquire a new identity.

Such incursions of power from outside, and subsequent changes of identity, have of course been typical of human civilisations for millennia, in Europe, in the Subcontinent, everywhere. We may bemoan this continual overpowering of the weaker by the strong, but it is an inescapable historical reality the consequences of which are reversible only by the most tenacious resistance by people of vision working within what they will see as the new directions for their histories, their new destinies.

Fifthly, it is dangerous, faith contends, not to recognise *the provisional nature of all our institutionally inherited identities*. Within religion itself we find challenges to an *absolutising of our conditioned self-identities* and their empowerments. True, religions have often absolutised their sacral institutions. They have, too, even reinforced the absolutising of such 'secular' institutions as the nation, its monarchy, its military power, its legal system and so on. That, though, is but one part of religion's complex story, even in the most ancient of our traditions.

An important strand in the Upanishads, as we saw - and even more clearly in a Buddhist vision of things that emerged around the same period - is the calling into question of all our given corporate identities, any sense of belonging we may have either by nature or nurture. It was an Upanishadic insight that *all such conditioning potentially can lead to a dangerously mistaken identity*. The names we are given, the roles we play, the forms we assume, are all part of a *nama-rupa* provisional level of existence that needs to be transcended by awareness of a higher Identity. The meaning of this insight was worked out in differing ways by later generations, so that varying degrees of reality and value were found in those lesser identities. All, though, accepted the the need for transforming attunement with that higher Identity.

In other differing ways, too, religious faith invariably points to the danger of making empowerment of by any of those lower self-identities an absolute good. That they are essential to our humanness is equally a given. Often, therefore, we find the struggle for people's empowerment by way of a heightened sense of both corporate and personal self-identity, and thereby their struggles for a more just sharing in power at every level, being encouraged from within religious life.

Not always, of course. And in any case at the centre of all faith is this challenge to any assumption that empowerment by a strong sense of identity, whatever the grounding of that identity, is *ultimate good*. It is especially our sharply defined community identities that can prove dangerous, and from more than one perspective. If our dominant self-identity serves, for instance, to distance, to demean, to demonise, to seek to destroy the other, even if there is a weakening of wider human community, rather than the opening up of possibilities of enhanced relationship with the other, possibilities of peace and corporate healing, and thereby the denial of human inclusiveness, how can we but conclude that such an identity is dangerous and undesirable? Precisely the same question can be raised concerning any identity by which inclusive relationship with the non-human communities of earth-life is not enhanced.

And yet, our global history today makes it very clear that the most fiercely fought liberation movements all over the world are those in which an intense sense of group loyalty drives people to use even extreme violence in the struggle to express that group identity. That many of these liberation struggles are linked with religious loyalties makes the sense of identity the more compelling. Liberation becomes a sacred duty, legitimated by divine sanction. Clearly there considerable tension drawn here between what may seem to be the conflicting demands springing from the one faith. Between what is necessary and what is acceptable there are very fine lines drawn.

So, when from the *point of view of faith* does an identity become 'dangerous'? The insider view in matters of religious identity will see dangers normally only in that which hinders or weakens faith, or that which distracts from the most complete possible loyalty to the Focus of faith. It is in such matters that, for example, the language of Jesus becomes unusually harsh, exclusive, even violent: 'If your hand or foot proves an obstacle (in your aim to enter God's new realm), cut it off'. Even the Vaishnava woman God-lover, Andal, spoke of 'tearing off' her breasts and throwing them at Krishna if she was not granted a more unambiguous vision of his presence.

Even the family bonds by which our identities are normally given such clear boundaries, are relegated by Jesus to levels of identity as good as dead: 'Let the dead bury their dead', was the reply to a son postponing discipleship until his duties relating to his father's death had been completed. A harsh-seeming response. But other loyalties, more absolute, are called for. And the hindrances to such loyalty will likely include various other forms of identity. The whole point of the passion of the *bhakti* movements is that ultimately love for God, devotion to God, is the one essential in life. Nothing else, it would seem, matters in comparison. Even the other great givens such as those dharmic principles by which social identities are so sharply delineated, are transcended in the *bhakti* movements, often in ways reminiscent of the New Testament's identity-questioning.

The claims of faith, though, are not always so (seemingly) alienating from other community relationships. Liberated spirits such as Basava in the South, Tukaram in the West, and Kabir in the North again and again point to common features of being human, as well as of being God-related, that bind people together in basic human as well as faith-loyalties. The faith-loyalty they envision breaks many religion-based norms, yet springs itself from within that religious life.

Thus, transcending the normal is far from the whole story of faith, as we have seen again and again. Other relationships do stake their claims, even on the grounds of central dimensions of that same faith. What does become clear, though, is the manner in which faith can counter so vigorously our assumption, often found in writings on society and culture, that any strong sense of identity must self-evidently be good. Giving absolute value to self-identity *per se* is constantly challenged. The fact that communities as well as individuals are motivated and empowered by a strong sense of identity in itself is not sufficient to endow that empowerment a value above all others.

Sixthly, another 'dangerous' possibility in the formation of religious identity is the notion that *diversity is the enemy of true faith and of a faith-centred identity.* Here is another characteristic of 'fundamentalist' faith: the truth must result in uniformity, and the faithful are bound by sacred duty to struggle for that exclusive goal. Even violent means to overcome the enemy to the Truth becomes legitimate. There is a sense in which those committed to a pacifist way (Mennonites, Brethren, Hamish, Shakers, Jehovah's Witnesses, Quakers/Friends, Jains who have taken the 'great vows', as well as monks belonging to various other orders) could also be called 'fundamentalist'. They renounce violence on the grounds (perhaps a literalist interpretation) of what they see as fundamental texts. Few pacifist believers, though, are literalists. Their non-violence is integrated with a whole peace-loving way of life. This life-style may in one sense be exclusive of others, but it rarely seeks to exclude others aggressively or eliminate them violently.

There is a commonly held assumption that this obsession with control of the boundaries of the way we are religious, indeed the way we are human, is typical of the strictly monotheistic faiths, especially Christianity and Islam. Only when you believe strongly in One God will you go on to assert that belief in that one true God, ways of worshipping, the institutions and life-behaviour based on that belief and worship - all should be uniform. Fundamentalist intolerance, it is usually thought, goes hand in hand with dogmatic religion, religion that sees the Truth in terms of beliefs and doctrines. The corollary to this is that Eastern religions are said to have no such divisive commitment to doctrinal systems as the basis for their identity-formation. More intuitively based experience of self-realisation is all.

It is, however, just not true that eastern religions are not doctrine-based. No one can deny that there are marked differences of ethos and emphasis between the belief-systems and the institutional religious forms of the East and those of the West and Middle East. Political exploitation of religious commitments, too, have largely been different. In seeking political control with the help of religious loyalties, the positions taken up by the pro-Buddhist Asoka (third century before Christian Era) or the leaders of later mini-empires who were more pro-Jaina or pro-Hindu, were all different from that of Constantine, with his presiding over Christian councils in which the exact definition of divine identity was seen as a matter of political as well as spiritual life or death. India never had the precise equivalent of the Spanish Catholic Inquisition (identity factor?) or the forms of intolerance towards any who were not of their narrowly defined faith typical of at least three centuries of Protestant history. The function of doctrine then *is* rather different in these traditions.

Even so, Indian religious history provides ample evidence of aggressive intolerance of those whose identity was other. Only a thoroughly blinkered view of that history can ignore the violence that from time to time has characterised relations between different religions and sects, quite apart from the violence between Muslims and others. Jains, Buddhists, Saivas, Vaishnavas, and various cultic groups have all at times been involved in fighting each other, armed both with fiercely held doctrine and weapons of death. Even the communities of world-denying Sadhus, those whom more than anyone we would suppose to be above concern for community identities and their boundaries, have in fact often been at the fighting edge of opposition to others. The saffron-robed Sadhus who so vigorously demolished the Babri Masjid were not merely acting out some wild aberration. The role of such renouncers from time to time has been exactly along these lines for a long, long time. Endless easy-going and inclusive tolerance has not been the dominant religious identity of India, however useful such a mythic self-narrative has been in the modern national struggle to create such an identity. When our mythic identities deliberately obscure other identities undeniably part of our own histories, there is dangerous self-deceit, as some within all these religions have always been able to see.

Having reluctantly said this, I am now much more happy to affirm that Indian religion, and the Hindu traditions in particular, also have a remarkable history of permitting and even creating great *diversity* of identity. And this has been its strength. In the end it will be dangerously weakening of Hindu religious life if the trend to work for uniformity and a uniform identity continues. One prominent factor in this move towards greater uniformity and the downplay of diversity is the perceived uniformity of the 'others', Islam and Christianity. Pronouncements of the Pope or the World Council of Churches are seen as carrying absolute sway over the whole of Christendom. Vishva Hindu Parishad - the World Council of Hindus - is seen as an appropriate response to such global bodies as WCC, and as a means of creating not just a single authoritative voice for all Hindus, but as creating a uniformity comparable to that of Islam and Christianity.

The historical 'reality' in both these two 'communities' is quite different, for there is an immensely wide range of ways of being Muslim and ways of being Christian. Both, though, themselves can frequently speak of their own community identities as though there is little of significance separating the many constituent sub-groups. We can hardly doubt that this self-perception communally and doctrinally as cohesive, homogeneous bodies helped create the way they then spoke of Hindu religious traditions, an 'othering' that in time so decisively shaped Hindus own perception of themselves. Recent historical opinion - influenced increasingly by postcolonial thought - can even go to the extent of asserting that 'Hinduism' did not exist before the nineteenth century, a position that etymologically may be correct, but ignores hugely significant continuities of faith, of ethos, of practice.

Whatever may be nineteenth century historical realities, there is clearly a growing tendency towards uniformity of Hindu self-perception. Militants who interpret what is believed to be the necessary oneness for a strong national ethos and identity, claim to speak on behalf of essential Hinduism. And however much we distinguish cultural, nationalist Hindutva from Hindu religion, from

Hinduism in its diversity of religious communities, there has been a clear impact on all Hindu perceptions of Hindu selfhood. For one thing it is more self-confident, more self-assertive. And in itself this can hardly be resented.

However, identifying Hindutva in terms of nationalist selfhood and culture narrows the boundaries of Hindu identity in a self-damaging way. As soon as there are defining characteristics brought out as to what constitutes this Hindutva, there is an inevitable narrowing of self-understanding. To qualify as Indian, every citizen now (according to the more strict forms of Hindutva doctrine) has to perceive himself or herself in terms of a defined Hindu cultural tradition. Which means that the inclusive plurality of Indian national identity is lost. The diversity intrinsic to a pluralist culture increasingly becomes problematic, and we move inexorably towards fundamentalism. If the politically based interpreters continue to define the identity of 'Hinduism', the trend towards uniformity will continue. On the other hand acceptance of diversity and plurality within the Hindu community, or within any religion, should logically lead to acceptance of diversity and plurality in the *wider human community*.

And diversity surely implies fluidity, a life of faith that is never static, faith that is able at times of renewed vision to move from one position, one identity, to a new position, a new identity. Again, it is faith itself that calls for such mobility, the possibility of change. To set unbending boundaries to the Transcendent within, which the believer finds an ultimately binding identity, is to lose sight of true transcendence. Obviously, there is stability and undeviating assuredness too within the life of faith. There is the anchorage of the basic givens, the fundamentals that are intrinsic to any faith. Tradition cannot count for nothing.

Given a clear awareness of the realities of power, such fluidity from time to time will mean a change of heart, a change of self-identity - a form of conversion. No doubt, at the heart of every religious vision is the conviction that here is the true way, the door to ultimate reality. And the community that builds itself around this vision will erect boundaries that mark the people of that way off from others: perhaps as the pure are to be separate from the polluted, or as light contrasts with darkness, as truth differs from falsehood, good from evil, believers from infidels. Just how impregnable such boundaries are made does vary greatly from tradition to tradition. In some cases, of course, those judged to have been grossly unfaithful are cast out from the inner fold. Even death for apostasy might be held as a threat over those contemplating a move out from 'the true faith'. No religious community finds it easy to lose those who have been nurtured in that community, especially when it means conversion to what is seen as the 'other side', an alien faith. Yet change, including change of religious loyalty, change of nurturing community, has always been innate to human religious history.

In the case of the mass conversions that have occurred in India - to Islam, to Buddhism, but pre-eminently to Christianity - as well as the mostly much earlier 'conversions' and recent re-conversions to Hinduism - we have a far more complex socio-political process, and we have seen some of these complexities. The imperial legacy and the 'new imperialism' of globalisation; the foreign missionary presence both in personnel and through funding; the identifying of patriotic Indianness with being Hindu; the perceived lack of patriotic loyalty among the rising aspirations of Dalits and tribal people to find new identities; the resistance of middleclass Hindu and their organs of power to accept the liberating movements within the peoples they have oppressed; the surge of evangelical fervour - including missioning zeal - within Christian and Muslim communities in India, echoed in the missioning activities of Hindu groups.

All this and much more contributes to the present highly imflammable situation, a situation in which conversions, perhaps in more than one direction, will continue whatever preventive action is taken. Indeed, the more repressive the measures taken to prevent conversions, the more rapidly they occur seems to be one lesson from recent Indian history. But it is a situation in which wisdom dictates that a deeply probing debate about conversion is long overdue - a debate among Christians, as well between Christians and Hindus. Christians can no longer merely repeat the *mantra* that the freedoms of the Constitution are on their side, or that everyone has the right to opt for the religion of their choice. Other dynamics too are at work that are far from constitutional provisions, and are certainly not all gospel-based.

Seventhly, there is a wider aspect of this need for diversity. To be religious within the complexities of our modern world calls for continual *interpenetration*, a 'dialectic', between our faith-identity and the multiple identities life today presses upon us. Religion has always engaged in a variety of ways with contextual realities. Such engagement is just more complex now. This obviously poses serious threats to the integrity of the faith-identity, threats so severe that increasingly religious people are turning to static and fundamentalist forms of community identity. Interacting with the complexities of the world today seems far too dangerous to faith, and so they opt to return to the felt simplicities of an older faith-world. 'Back to the Vedas', 'Back to the Bible', the purity of 'Hindutva', 'stand against Satan'.

No one committed to the reality of faith will despise rigorous critique of the corrupting seductions, the blinkered greed, the hidden oppressions, the destructive dominance of many aspects of our world today. Faith-identities, though, have never been 'pure' or static, never based on and developed from the purity of divine revelation or spiritual vision alone. Faith-identities have always been shaped in interaction with the dynamics of social, cultural and political worlds. Even the strategies and structures of power that were part of these worlds have in differing ways impinged on faith-identities.

Failures of faith abound, even though they have at times wonderfully transcended and challenged such power-worlds. But it is the dialectic and the dialogue that are the key to understanding how faith-identities have changed. Such dialogical interaction today has to extend at every level to other faith communities. In reality this was often the case too in the past, even if unconsciously. If the 'other' faith remains merely the product of our mythic demonising, the faith of the demoniser is endangered as much as the life of the demonised. Either way, our faith-identity, however strongly focussed, does not remain some unchanging entity untouched by those other worlds, perhaps worlds of faith that we fear. Either way, there is a continual moving on; we are pilgrims on the way.

It is, then, of essential to viable faith that it *relate to the wider human community* and the even wider *communities of ecological life*. This criterion - relating to wider worlds - is certainly not artificially brought in from the worldview of liberal humanism. God-consciousness has always been, potentially and often in practice, relational-consciousness, a newly based identity so enhancing of old identities that earth's life as well as the whole human race becomes an essential part of the identity. If any religious tradition has lost these potential resources for enhancing such wider relationships, then that religion is in dire need of re-formation. That all religions throughout much of their histories have been primarily concerned with self-nurture and self-identity, even to the extent of demonising the other, in no way denies that they also may have the potential for enhancing relationship as a central feature of that self-identity

Eighthly, then, it is imperative for the health of any faith community that it develop a *self-critical* stance. Religion's role in creating self-affirming attitudes, in creating precisely the strong sense of self-identity this discussion has been all about, is crucial to our humanness. Yet, any religion that takes on a merely self-legitimating role and lacks the ability to see, as Jesus put it, 'the log in our own eye' while condemning 'the speck in your brother's eye' (Matthew 7.1-5) is unfaithful to essential dimensions within its own life. It is the vision of the perfect fatherliness of God that, in this saying of Jesus, is the reference point by which we are to see and judge ourselves - as persons, as communities - just as rigorously as others. Such transcending yet life-impinging vision is precisely the kind of resource within our religious life that can enable the self-critical perspective we need. But what happens when the centrality of the otherness of God, or whatever Focus faith envisions, with all its potential for self-questioning as well as self-enhancement, is taken over by the 'otherness' of a demonised faith-community seen as a competing enemy? A complacency ensues that is as disastrous for the spiritual wellbeing of that demonising community as it is for relations with those demonised.

Finally, for any of the above prescriptive criteria to be realised, what is very clear is the crucial role of *interpretive leadership* within each religious community. (See Appleby and Marty 5: 491) Those responsible for reflecting on the meaning of faith within a community - theologians, acharyas, gurus, imams, itinerant preachers and suchlike - have not only to be well-grounded in the cultic-mythic-matrix of their own tradition; they need equally to be aware of the claims of wider humanity. They need to be inclusive visionaries, or they will have little chance of serving even their own community well.

I emphasise again that the claims of a particular faith need never merely be accommodated to the perceptions and claims of either other faiths or secular worldviews. If, though, there is dynamic faith it will continue to engage with other worlds dialectically, dialogically, giving and gaining, changing and being transformed. Much of this, of course, takes place within a faith-community quite apart from the line taken by interpretive leaders. Even so, the role of interpreters remains crucial in determing if a community is to remain self-destructively intraverted, or is to engage with the world in ways that enhance the life both of the believing community and those 'other worlds' with which it engages. For, however great the need for people of faith to resist some of the hegemonising assertions of a secularist world, to make their heroic stand in defence of values they believe in, however vital it may be for communities whose essential self-identity is threatened to resist the oppressions of the powerful, for socially and ecologically-conscious faith to continue its stance against those whose ways are unjust to the weak and destructive of the earth - in spite of all these imperatives, if religious faith fails to realise its peace-making and healing potential, the consequences both for the world and for faith will be disastrous.

Interpreting faith and its meaning in relation to the life of the world is crucial to faith itself (Lott 1987). Faith's *meaning* is necessarily worked out in those wider relationships. And this crucial but difficult hermeneutical task is especially necessary in inter-faith relationships. If we believe our faith in some way puts us in touch with ultimate realities, then engaging in dialogue with people of similar conviction, even if their faith and its community loyalty identifies them as 'other', is an essential part of the dialogical life faith calls for. Given the crises of our times, and the frequent violence between religion-based communities, there can be few more urgent tasks than that of dialogical interpretation.

Epilogue:
An 'Ecstatic' and Inclusive
Christian Identity

Finally, we look briefly at a shaping of identity fitting to Christian faith, fitting to a follower of the radical prophet Jesus, reckoning with the central grounding themes distinctive to that faith:

(i) A 'Christian' identity is inextricably bound up with the identity of Jesus. Problems abound in trying to delineate sharply between the Jesus of history and the Christ of faith. Faith itself expects that the original identity retains an element of mystery. As Albert Schweitzer concluded in his 'Quest' a century ago: 'He comes to us as One unknown, without a name (but saying) "Follow me"....'

Yet, the grounding story, the Gospel record of who and how Jesus was, has to be a crucial part of 'Christian' faith. Jesus saw things in a distinctively Galilean way, with its ingrained rebellious spirit. This still leaves him deeply rooted in the faith and tradition of the Hebrew people, in spite of his decisive divergence from the Jerusalem elite - from priestly scheming for power and pharasaic legalism alike. Nor is there serious evidence that the forms of anti-Roman militancy of the messianic rebels of Galilee persuaded him. True, he was identified as a 'Galilean'. And there were mounting tensions in his relations with 'my people Israel'. Even so, a common grounding faith-identity with those people of the Covenant is found in all we know of his words and actions throughout that brief but momentous ministry. No doubt the tension is inbuilt. As a Galilean from the North, Jesus could never have been fully identified with Israel's leadership in the South.

Already, then, there is a counter-cultural factor here. Already, too, we see how cultural and political power-groupings impinge on visionary life. He is an outsider, leading a people's ecstasy-marked movement of those largely alienated from the institutional powers concentrated in the South. What he said and did continually broke through the boundaries of what was expected by the establishment. To them his identity as a true Israelite was suspect.

However much, though, those caught up in the fervent popular response to his healing and preaching saw themselves as the true 'people of God', inheritors of the identity God gives 'my people Israel', very soon it was the *rootlessness* of his own and his followers' status that gripped his consciousness: 'The Son of Man has nowhere to lay his head' (Matthew 8.20). He was - the story suggests for much of his brief ministry - 'on the road, up to Jerusalem', moving inexorably to rejection and death. A pilgrim prophet on his way to seeming failure. For followers of Jesus, then, given cultural and communal identities may be inescapably important, but such identities are not primary. Rarely, in fact, are they primary for people of faith.

(ii) One reading of the sources for understanding the identity of the followers of this homeless Son of Man gives the impression that membership of his faith-group gave a sharply defined identity strongly over against those who opposed Jesus. For most evangelical Christians this will be the defining boundary: 'Those who are not with me are against me' (Matthew 12.30): 'There is no other Name whereby we can be saved' (Acts 4.12). They ask but one question: Do you accept Jesus alone as Lord and Saviour? If not, then some degree of distancing, even antagonism, is seen as inevitable. If Jesus is the 'Light of the World', it seems to a strict evangelical that all other lights must delude, and lead into darkness.

Fred Pratt Green, a poetic and rather saintly Christian pastor who died at the ripe old age of 97 just days before this lecture, wrote many fine hymns. In one, though, he wrote of those 'who reap the holocaust'. He seemed naively unaware of the painful offence this would cause, and later willingly changed the offending line. Another hymn affirms: 'Christ is the world's Light, He and none other', each stanza asserting again, 'He and none other'. Pratt Green's inclusive spirit makes it unlikely that he actually believed this in its stark exclusiveness. His intention was no doubt in tune with those many theologians of our time, such as the Catholic faith-interpreter, Karl Rahner, with an inclusive Christology that accepts the historical reality of many lights, many points of spiritual revelation, all of which find their ultimate source in that transcendent Christ who is the One 'who illumines everyone (coming into the world)' (John 1.9) . The problem is, Christian inclusivists then have to recognise the right of other people of faith to make similar claims for the Light in their own revelatory tradition, as they indeed do.

In any case, there are many hints within the Gospels that belonging to those who say, seemingly with sincere faith, 'Lord, Lord, (open the door to us)', cannot be taken as the more crucial defining boundary. In the concerned text (Matthew 25.11-12), 'I do not know you' was the unexpected response. Indeed, it is the unexpected sources of divine truth, surprising locations for the divine presence, that is made so frequently clear in the Jesus-story. There seem few fixed identities. Elsewhere in the story there is the equally surprising assertion that our personal being, our humanness, is not to be defined by religious practice: 'The sabbath is made for man, not man for the sabbath'. And 'faith' was gladly recognised in those who were not part either of the community of Israel or of his own following.

This is not to say that people's response of faith (or rejection) to the mission of Jesus as it unfolded before them was anything less than crucial. And the 'I am' sayings in John's Gospel are every bit as central to the Jesus-story as are the 'I am' identity-texts in the Upanishads. It is made very clear, though (Matthew 25.31-46) that it is never even conscious discipleship which ensures that one belongs to the realm of the 'Son of Man'. It is, rather, ministering to 'these the least' of his brothers and sisters. Otherwise there is that fearful word: 'You do not belong'. Admittedly, we can debate the identity here of those 'least brethren' with whom the Son of Man is to be identified; maybe it is already an ecclesial boundary that defines who is to be shown Christ-like worth. Other factors, other stories, hint at a much wider vision in the consciousness of Jesus.

(iii) One such prominent factor in the ministry of Jesus is the identity of those who were seen as worthy recipients of his healing touch and powerful word. Not only are they those whose ethnic and cultural roots placed them outside the identifiable community of God. There were even those believed to be far beyond the pale, even downright polluted (by disease, by occupation, by gender, by treacherous deeds). Not that there was no tension in the Gospels concerning the anomalies of this mission. Was he not 'sent only to the lost sheep of the house of Israel' according to one strand (Matthew 15.24)? How can he 'take the children's food and give to the dogs'?

The Evangelists hold differing perceptions of the mission of Jesus at this point. Even in the account of Matthew - more bound by a Jewish identity - the boundary is not allowed to stand unbroken.

Just as true faith is not so bounded, neither is healing, the dynamic signs of the inbreaking of God's new realm. The old identities are to be replaced by a far wider sense of belonging. Now, too, no one is the 'enemy'. Those previously seen as such are to be 'loved', their well-being 'prayed for', an unguarded cheek offered to them if they should attack. Identities are turned upside down for those who are faithful to this 'prophet of Nazareth'.

(iv) Another key dimension is added to the identity of Jesus-followers by the dominant Gospel image of Jesus as Healer. *Ecstasy* is a key term here, in the sense of 'standing outside' the normal boundaries of ego, those set by others and assumed to be normal, and so being able to break through the boundaries within which demonic powers were presumed to operate. Such ecstatic boundary breaking was so closely linked to these healing acts that to call Jesus' healing work 'shamanistic' (Davies 1995) is not wide of the mark. Such is the emphasis on confronting and overcoming demonic powers, setting free from their tyranny, commanding wholeness of soul and body, that the shamanist style of this Healer is unmissable, even if the power of his direct word - free of touch and other shamanistic methods - makes Jesus a noticeably different sort of Healer.

Indeed, the original biblical terms for the earth-including 'salvation' promised through God's Anointed (Messiah), which the Gospel-writers clearly believe are being fulfilled, are the same as 'health' and 'wholeness'. Whatever tensions between soul and body there may be, once there is commitment to the transcending obligations of the new 'realm of God' that is breaking in, that new God-realm is intended, it seems, to initiate a new freedom for the whole earth. Even the sea, home to powers that can destroy, is now to be calmed; those paralysed by guilt are forgiven; the disabled are empowered to dance, and even death is held at bay.

No wonder this Healer insisted on feasting and drinking in celebration of this new era that had dawned. No wonder, too, such taboo-transcending confidence provoked fierce resistance from those whose identities were already hardened by a less open tradition. To one dominant strand of Jesus-followers, though, their Healer was now the centre-point of a new creation, the One by whom and through whom all things came to be and cohere together in unity. Eco-consciousness is inherent in the vision of Jesus. And this too calls for a kind of ecstasy.

(v) All this, though, does imply the acceptance of a new transcendent identity, the claims of which are absolute. Yes, the old binding identities are gone, as they were for Jesus. For instance, when told that his mother and brothers had come for him, making their claim on him after a period of frenetic ministering to the needs of the crowds who 'flocked' to see and hear and receive his touch, Jesus replies: 'Who are my mother and brothers? Are they not those who learn of God's way and follow it?' (Mark 3.31-35). There is even the challenge to renounce family bonds, to 'hate' even father, mother, sister, brother if the bond with them stands in the way of the higher claims of God (Luke 14.26). The sacred bond of blood and family relationships, then, is now made subordinate to this new transcendent claim.

And this new identity makes claims in the other direction too. The 'other', the 'enemy' is no longer to be hated in the way always expected of those with an opposing identity. The 'enemy' is to be loved whatever the consequences (Matthew 5.43-46). Similarly, those previously absolutised identities shaped by loyalty to the nation and its sacral Law, to the temple and its priestly cult, and certainly to Caesar and his imperial peace, were radically relativised. Inner transforming, and the resulting new relationships, in response to the transcendent inbreaking, was now the key to the new primary identity.

Different words may be used, but second generation followers of Jesus were similarly aware of their new identity. For Paul, who introduces some striking new interpretations of the Jesus-vision, the primary new identity is to be 'in Christ', or to be possessed by Christ, by his Spirit. The apostle's old identity, based on Hebrew lineage and purity of what India would call dharmic life in strict observance of the sacral Law, he claimed to 'count as garbage' (Philippians 3.3-9). Indeed, Christ himself is now his primary identity: 'I live, yet not I....Christ lives in me'. 'I am resolved to know only Christ, and him crucified', for 'I am crucified with Christ' (Galations 2.19-20).

In countless similar passages it is claimed that the life of Christ, a life offered up in death, is to become the believers' life. And this clearly entails a radical relativising of all other identities. That primary identity are all-absorbing, its claims are absolute. Of course, the Apostle's position here raises the enormous question of what he means, what we are to mean, by such an exclusive Christ-identity. How do those other identities actually relate to the new Identity? What kind of absolutism does this entail? And just how far was Paul in reality liberated from his earlier grounding identity and its cultural norms?

(vi) When the Apostle makes Jesus' death by being crucified the foundation of the Christian's sense of the inbreaking transcendence of God, we are led into an upside-down new sense of what God is and does among us. In turn this leads - in spite of all manner of anomalies and continuities, some enriching, some not - to a radically new sense of self-identity, worked out from within a grounding in prior cultural life and being. The Apostle's interpretation of the Cross was strikingly new to that first-generation of Jesus-followers. There is little doubt, though, that the death itself, so deeply traumatic, was already dominant in their consciousness. So it was not surprising that this belief in the transforming efficacy of this death - made so by equally dominant faith in God's resurrecting power - became literally 'crucial' (cross-shaped?) to Christian discipleship. It is not surprising that the Cross became the great symbol of Christian identity. To 'wear the cross', to 'take up the cross', means to be a Jesus-follower. It also means, literally, to be a 'crusader'.

And yet, being in tune with the teaching, the character, the spirit, the behaviour, the form of mission, and especially the dying of this faith-figure surely entails a life-stance directly the opposite of crusading militancy. The Crucified who is to be followed negates such violence or any form of aggression towards others in either act and word. Engaging in the same liberating, healing and eventually dangerous mission as he did is certainly called for as part of 'following Christ'. But proselytising as a means of increasing the numbers of those to be identified as 'Christian' entails a quite different stance.

The essential mark of Christian identity, then, is the inner transformation resulting from that cross-identifying and from 'dying with Christ'. The 'old human (Adam)' within cannot be simply wiped away, but becomes transformed into the 'new human'. Continuities are inevitable and essential. But there is a new direction, and a necessary turning away from what may once have been absorbing life-goals. There is a sense of liberation from the past and the embracing of a life in which self-centredness is 'crucified'. The ego and its hunger for self-empowering is to be redirected, re-centred. Power, personal or institutional, is now part of a very different vision of life. For, 'dying with Christ' calls for the loss of one's own identity-status by identifying with those themselves 'crucified' by any form of cruel oppression, or impoverished thereby. Power is now seen in what the 'world' may see as weakness. A share in this newly visioned Power is sought for those hitherto denied it. This is what is entailed in opening oneself to the Spirit of that same cross-marked Christ. The self-offering *love* of that central figure of devotion is to 'overflow in the hearts' of his followers.

Contradictions between this vision of a new identity and the realities of the Jesus-follower's life and character will abound, as too in the life of the community of Christians. Faith will be sorely tested at times even to see any such transforming process. But that is the nature of faith.

Tensions are inevitable, too, between loyalty to the person of Jesus and to the wider claims of the God-realm that so obviously extends far beyond that historically identifiable figure. The change to the less history-bound name 'Christ' indicates something of the mystery (for Christians) of how God works well beyond the range of Jesus-followers. Yet, their identity remains grounded in that history. It is that Jesus-story which sets for Christians the decisive narrative, the paradigm pointing to how evil is to be confronted with good, hatred by love, enmity by an unchanging concern for the wellbeing of the other. And for all Christian concern with the 'Body of Christ' (another key concept in the Apostle Paul), their overwhelming emphasis is to be on the living, inwardly empowering Spirit, for ever placing the believing self 'outside' its normal ego-boundaries in ec-static self-transcendence.

The identity of the followers of Jesus, therefore, can never have a once-and-for-all fixed character, an immutable 'body'. Systems and institutions will of necessity be created to serve the transforming intentions of the great Lover; none but that Lover's Spirit, though, can be absolutized. The Christian's grounding givenness is in those clear marks of the character and mission of Jesus the Gospels reveal;

but that Christians are to be people of the Spirit of God, the Spirit of Jesus, means this givenness can never be more than a revelatory starting point, a continually meaningful reference point, but not a pre-given identity.

With the Cross as the literally 'crucial' centre-point of this givenness of Christian identity, with this kind of symbol as the basis for inner transcendence and life-transformation, it is little wonder that a radically new, ever-changing identity becomes imperative to those who follow the crucified One. Yet how far from this reality are the community fears, the worldly ambitions and the class/caste loyalties that so often become the basis for our Christian identities! At least there is little doubt, with the Cross as the originating source of our faith, that some Christian interpreters will be able to lead us to that self-critical stance without which we cannot move forward.

To follow Jesus is to set out on the road to a continually new-born identity. And a life of journeying, moving on, with no ever-fixed position, engaging critically with the many cultures, ethnicities, societies, political systems that make up the life of humankind, in turn makes diversity inevitable. Do not, urged Jesus, identify God's realm too easily, saying 'Look, here it is; or, there it is!' Just be assured that in the struggle to identify and embody that realm of divine power, it is indeed already 'among you' (Luke 17.21).

There is not just a dying to the old self that is called for. There is also the promise of a rising to new life, new selfhood. There will, therefore, be many different ways of being 'Christian', many different levels at which people respond to this Christ who dies, rises again and calls people to share his spirit of ego-effacing, life-transforming love. Some responses will be a faithful conforming to that Spirit. Some, tragically, will be so warped by non-faith compulsions, especially compulsions to personal and institutional power, they become nothing less than the enemies of the Christ-Spirit. Yet, as long as the pilgrimage of faith continues, the possibility of growth in that Christ-Spirit remains. And this means that interpretation is of crucial import to the faith-pilgrim's living and believing.

Select Bibliography

Abraham, K.C.(ed.), 1990, 1995. *Third World Theologies: Commonalities & Divergences*, Maryknoll: Orbis, Tiruvalla:CSS.

Ahmad, Aziz, 1999. *Studies in Islamic Culture in the Indian Environment*, Delhi: OUP.

Alam, Javeed, 1999. *India: Living with Modernity*, Delhi: OUP.

Aleaz, K.P., 1996. *Christian Thought Through Advaita Vedanta*, Delhi: ISPCK.

Allen, Douglas (ed.), 1993. *Religion and Political Conflict in South Asia*, Delhi: OUP.

Aloysius, G., 1998. *Religion as Emacipatory Identity: A Buddhist Movement among Tamils under Colonialism*, Delhi: CISRS.

Amaladoss, M., (*et al: eds.*), 1981. *Theologizing in India*, Bangalore: TPI.

Amalorpavadass, D.S.(ed.), 1982. *Indian Christian Spirituality*, Bangalore: NBCLC.

Anderson, Benedict, 1983. *Imagined Communities*, London.

Anderson, B.W., 1978(3rd ed.). *The Living World of the Old Testament*, London: Longman.

Appasamy, A.J., 1928. *The Gospel as Bhakti Marga: A Study of the Johannine Doctrine of Love*, Madras:CLS. Armstrong, Karen, 2001. *Islam: A Short History*, London: Phoenix.

Armstrong, Karen, 2000. *The Battle for God*, New York: A.A.Knopf.

Askari, Hasan, 1977. *Inter-religion*, Aligarh: Printwell.

Aulen, Gustaf, 1953. *Christus Victor: An Historical Study of the Atonement*, London: SPCK.

Baillie, John, (1939), 1963. *Our Knowledge of God*, London: OUP.

Barker, Chris, 2000. *Cultural Studies: Theory and Practice*, London: Sage.

Bellah, Robert N., 1985. *Habits of the Heart: Individualism and Commitment in American Life*, Berkeley.

Berger, Peter L., 1969. *The Sacred Canopy*. New York: Anchor.

Bharati, S. & Lakshmi, S. (trans.), (n.d.). *The Tiruvaimoli of Nammalvar*, Melkote: T.B.Music Education.

Bharucha, Rustom, 1993. *The Question of Faith*, Delhi: Orient & Longman.

Bharucha, Rustom, 1998. *In the Name of the Secular: Contemporary Cultural Activism in India*, Delhi: OUP.

Boyd, Robin, 1975 (rev.ed.). *An Introduction to Indian Christian Theology*, Madras: CLS.

Breuilly, John, 1993. *Nationalism and the State*, Manchester.

Caplan, Lionel, 1982. *Towards a Sociology of Christianity in South India*, University of Madras.

Caplan, Lionel, 1989. *Religion and Power*, Madras: CLS.

Carman, John B., 1974. *The Theology of Ramanuja: An Essay in Interreligious Understanding*, New York: Yale University Press.

Carman, John B., 1994. *Majesty & Meekness: A Comparative Study of Contrast and Harmony in the Concept of God*, Grand Rapids: Eerdmans.

Chakkarai, V., 1932. *Jesus the Avatar*, Madras: CLS.

Chaudhuri, B.(ed.), 1992. *Tribal Transformation in India*, Vol.III, *Ethnopolitics and Identity Crisis*, New Delhi.

Chaudhuri, Nirad C., 1996. *Hinduism: A Religion to Live By*, Oxford: OUP.

Chenchiah, P., Chakkari, V.(et al), 1938. *Rethinking Christianity in India*. Madras: Sudarshanam.

Clarke, Sathianathan, 1998. *Dalits and Christianity: Subaltern Religion and Liberation Theology in India*, Delhi: OUP.

Connor, Walter, 1994. *Ethnonationalism: The Quest for Understanding*, Princeton University Press.

Copley, Antony, 1997. *Religions in Conflict: Ideology, Cultural Contact & Conversion in Late Colonial India*, Delhi: OUP.

Coward, H., 1983. *Religious Pluralism & the World Religions*, Madras: Univ.of Madras.

Coward, H., 1988. *Sacred Word and Sacred Text: Scripture in World Religions*, Maryknoll: Orbis.

Coward, H.(ed.), 1989. *Hindu-Christian Dialogue: Perspectives and Encounters*, Maryknoll: Orbis.

Cracknell, Kenneth, 1986. *Towards a New Relationship: Christians & People of Other Faith*, London: Epworth.

Cracknell, K. 1995. *Justice, Courtesy and Love: Theologians & Missionaries Encountering World Religions, 1846-1914*, London: Epworth.

Das, Somen, 1987. *Christian Faith and Multi-form Culture in India*, Bangalore:UTC.

Davies, Stevan, 1995. *Jesus the Healer: Possession, Trance and the Origins of Christianity*, London: SCM.

de Bary, W.T., 1972. *The Buddhist Tradition in India, China and Japan*, New York: Random.

Downs, F.S., 1994. *Essays on Christianity in North-East India*, Delhi: Indus.

Devasahayam, V. (ed.), 1997. *Frontiers of Dalit Theology*, Madras: ISPCK/ Gurukul.

Dumont, Louis, (1970)1998 (rev.ed.). *Homo Hierarchicus: the Caste System and its Implications*, Delhi: OUP.

Durkheim, Emile, 1915, 1971. *The Elementary Forms of the Religious Life*, London: Allen & Unwin.

Eck, Diana L., 1993. *Encountering God: A Spiritual Journey from Bozeman to Banaras*, Delhi: Penguin.

Eisenberg, Evan, 1998. *The Ecology of Eden: Humans, Nature & Human Nature*, New York: Picador.

Eliade, Mircea, 1958. *Patterns of Comparative Religion*, London: Sheed and Ward.

Embree, T.Embree, 1989. *Imagining India*. Delhi: OUP.

Erikson, Erik, 1951. *Childhood and Society*, London: Imago.

Erikson, Erik, 1960. 'The Problem of Ego Identity', in Stein, M.R.. (ed.), *Identity and Anxiety: The Survival of the Person in Mass Society*, Illinois, Free Press of Glencoe.

Farquhar, J.N., 1914. *Modern Religious Movements in India*, London: Macmillan.

Ferguson, Niall, 2002. *Empire: How Britain Made the Modern World*, London.

Fernandes, Walter (ed.), 1996. *The Emerging Dalit Identity*, Delhi:ISI.

Fernando, L., 2002. *Seeking New Horizons (Festschrift in honour of M.Amaladoss, S.J).*, Vidyajyoti & ISPCK: Delhi.

Forward, Martin (ed.), 1995. *Ultimate Visions: Reflections on the Religions We Choose*, Oxford: Oneworld.

Forward, Martin, 1997. *Muhammad: A Short Biography*, Oxford: Oneworld

Fraser, J.N. & Marathe, K.B.(trans.), 1909, 1983. *The Poems of Tukarama*, Delhi: Motilal Banarsidass.

Fuller, C.J., 1992. *The Camphor Flame: Popular Hinduism & Society in India*, Princeton:Princeton University.

Gadgil, Madhav and Guha, Ramachandra, 1993. *This Fissured Land: An Ecological History of India*, Delhi: OUP.

Gadgil, Madhav and Guha Ramachandra, 1995. *Ecology and Equity: the Use and Abuse of Nature in Contemporary India*, London: Routledge.

Gandhi, Leela, 1998. *Postcolonial Theory: A Critical Introduction*, Edinburgh: Edin.Univ.

Gellner, Ernest, 1983: *Nations and Nationalism,* Oxford: OUP.

Giddens, Anthony, 1990. *The Consequences of Modernity*, Cambridge: Polity.

Giddens, Anthony, 1991 (with annual reprint). *Modernity and Self-Identity: Self and Society in the Late Modern Age*, Cambridge: Polity.

Girard, Rene, 1977. *Violence and the Sacred*, Baltimore: Johns Hopkins University.

Gosling, David, 2001. *Religion and Ecology: in India & Southeast Asia*, London: Routledge.

Grant, Sara, 1989. *Towards and Alternative Theology: Confessions of a Non-dualist Christian,* Bangalore: ATC.

Guha, Ramachandra, 1998. *Social Ecology*, Delhi: OUP.

Hallman, D.G.(ed.), 1994. *Ecotheology: Voices from South & North*, Geneva: WCC.

Hansen, T.B., and Jaffrelot, C. (eds), 1998. *The BJP and the Compulsions of Politics in India*, Delhi: OUP.

Hardy, Friedhelm, 1983. *Viraha-Bhakti: The Early History of Krishna Devotion in South India*, Delhi: OUP.

Hardy, Friedhelm, 1994. *The Religious Culture of India: Power, Love, Wisdom*, Cambridge: CUP.

Harris, Elizabeth (*et al*), 2002. *Spirituality Across Borders*, London: Way Publications.

Hastings, Adrian, 1997. *The Construction of Nationhood: Ethnicity, Religion & Nationalism*, Cambridge;CUP.

Heim, S. Mark, 1996. *Salvations: Truth & Difference in Religion*, Maryknoll: Orbis.

Hess, L. and Singh Sukhdev (trans.), 1986. *The Bijak of Kabir*, Delhi: Motilal Banarsidass.

Hobsbawm, Eric. *Nations and Nationalism since 1780*, Cambridge: CUP.

Huntington, Samuel P., 1996. *The Clash of Civilizations & the Remaking of World Order*, London: Touchstone.

Hutton, J.H., 1963 (4th ed). *Caste in India*, Delhi: OUP.

Hutton, Will, 2002. *The World We're In*, London: Little, Brown.

Jathanna, O.V., 1981. *The Decisiveness of the Christ-Event & the Universality of Christianity in a World of Religious Plurality*, Berne: Peter Lang.

Jathanna, O.V., 1999. ' "Religious Pluralism": A Theological Critique', *Bangalore Theological Forum*, Bangalore:UTC.

Juergensmeyer, Mark, 1982. *Religion as Social Vision: The Movement Against Untouchability in 20th-Century Punjab*, Berkeley: University of California.

Juergensmeyer, Mark, 1996. *Religious Nationalism Confronts the Secular State*, Delhi: OUP.

Juergensmeyer, Mark, 2000. *Terror in the Mind of God: the Global Rise of Religious Violence*, Berkeley: University of California.

Kakar, Sudhir, 1995. *The Colours of Violence*, Delhi: Penguin.

Kakar, Sudhir, 1997. *Culture & Psyche: Selected Essays*, Delhi: OUP.

Kappen, S. 1994. *Tradition, Modernity, Counterculture: An Asian Perspective*, Bangalore: Visthar.

Karlekar, H.(ed.), 1998. *Independent India: the First Fifty Years*, Delhi: Indian Council for Cultural Relations.

Kedourie, Elie, 1960. *Nationalism*, London.

Khare, R.S., 1984. *The Untouchable as Himself:Ideology, Identity and Pragmatism amongLucknow Chamars*, Cambridge:CUP.

Kim, Sebastian C.H., 2003. *In Search of Identity: Debates on Religious Conversion in India*, Delhi: OUP.

King, Anthony D.(ed.), 1991. *Culture, Globalization and the World-System: Contemporary Conditions for the Representation of Identity*, London: Macmillan.

Kingsbury, F. & Phillips, G.E ., 1921. *Hymns of the Tamil Saivite Saints*, Calcutta: YMCA.

Kinsley, David R., 1973. 'Through the Looking-Glass: Divine Madness in the Hindu Religious Tradition', in *History of Religions, Vol. 13, 2*.

Kinsley, David R., 1979. *The Divine Player: A Study of Krishna Lila*, Delhi: Motilal Banarsidass.

Kipgen, Mangkhosat, 1997. *Christianity and Mizo Culture*, Jorhat:ETC.

Klostermaier, K.K., 1994 (2nd ed). *A Survey of Hinduism*, New York: SUNY.

Kraemer, H., 1938. *The Christian Message in a Non-Christian World*, London: Edinburgh.

Kunnumpuram, Kurien (*ed. et al*), 1997. *The Church in India in Search of a New Identity*, Bangalore: NBCLC

Lalsangkima, Pachuau, 1998. *Ethnic Identity & Christianity in North-East India: with special reference to* Mizoram

Lannoy, R., 1971. *The Speaking Tree: A Study of Indian Culture and Society*, Oxford: OUP.

Larrain, Jorge, 1994. *Ideology & Cultural Identity: Modernity & the Third World Presence,*Cambridge: Polity.

Lasch, Christopher, 1980. The Culture of Narcissim, London: Abacus.

Lipner, Julius & Gispert-Sauch, G., 1991. *The Writings of Brahmabandhab Upadhyay*, Bangalore: UTC.

Lipner, Julius, 1994. *Hindus: their Religious Beliefs and Practices*, London: Routledge.

Lochhead, David, *The Dialogical Imperative: A Christian Reflection on Interfaith Encounter*, London: SCM.

Longchar, A.Wati, 1995. *The Traditional Tribal Worldview and Modernity*, Jorhat: ETC.

Longchar, A.Wati (ed.),1999. *Encounter between Gospel and Tribal Culture*, Jorhat: ETC.

Longchar, A.Wati & Davis, L.E.(eds),1999(a). *Doing Theology with Tribal Resources,* Jorhat: ETC.

Lott, Eric, 1980. *Vedantic Approaches to God*, London: Macmillan.

Lott, Eric (ed.), 1986. *Worship in an Indian Context*, Bangalore: UTC.

Lott, Eric, 1987. *Vision, Tradition, Interpretation: Theology, Religion and the Study of Religion* (Religion and Reason 35), Berlin: Mouton de Gruyter.

Lovelock, James, 1979. *Gaia: A New Look at Life on Earth*, Oxford.

Ludden, David (ed.), 1996. *Making India Hindu: Religion, Community, & the Politics of Democracy in India*, Delhi: OUP.

Mach, Zdzislaw, 1993. *Symbols, Conflict, and Identity: Essays in Political Anthropology*, New York: SUNY.

Macleod, W.H., 1976. *Guru Nanak and the Sikh Religion*, Delhi: OUP.

Madan, T.N., 1987. *Non-Renunciation: Themes & Interpretations of Hindu Culture*, Delhi:OUP.

Madan, T.N.(ed.), 1997. *Religion in India*, Delhi: OUP.

Madan, T.N. 1998. *Modern Myths, Locked Minds: Secularism & Fundamentalism in India*, Delhi: OUP.

Mar Gregorius, Paulus, 1988. *Cosmic Man: The Divine Presence*, New York: Paragon.

Marriott, McKim, 1960. *Caste Ranking & Community Structure*, Pune: Deccan College

Marty, Martin E. and Appleby, R.Scott (eds), *The Fundamentalism Project (Vols 1-5):* Vol.1,1991. *Fundamentalisms Observed;* Vol.4, 1994. *Accounting for Fundamentalisms: the Dynamic Character of Movements;* Vol.5, *Fundamentalisms Comprehended*, Chicago: University of Chicago.

Massey, James (ed.), 1994. *Indigenous People: Dalits (Issues in Today's Theological Debate)*, Delhi: ISPCK.

Massey, James. 1995. *Dalits in India: Religion as a Source of Bondage or Liberation*, Delhi: ISPCK

Mazower, Mark, 2004. *Salonica, City of Ghosts: Christians, Muslims and Jews 1430-1950*, London: HarperCollins.

McDaniel, June, 1989. *The Madness of the Saints: Ecstatic Religion in Bengal*, Chicago: University of Chicago.

McKibben, Bill, 1990. *The End of Nature*, London: Viking.

Mol, Hans, 1976. *Identity and the Sacred. A Sketch for a New Social-Scientific Theory of Religion*, Oxford: Blackwell.

Mol, Hans (ed.), 1978. *Identity and Religion. International, Cross-cultural Approaches*, London: Sage.

Montefiore, Hugh (ed.), 1992. *The Gospel and Contemporary Culture*, London: Mowbray.

Moultmann-Wendel, Eisabeth, 1994. *I am My Body: New Ways of Embodiment*, London: SCM.

Muthunayagom, D.J., 2000. *(The) Bible Speaks Today (Essays in Honour of Gnana Robinson)*, Delhi: ISPCK.

Nandimath, S.C., 1979. *A Handbook of Virasaivism*, Delhi: Motilal Banarsidass.

Nandy, Ashis, 1983, 1988. *The Intimate Enemy: Loss & Recovery of Self Under Colonialism*, Delhi: OUP.

Naughtie, James, 2004. *The Accidental American: Tony Blair and the Presidency*, London: Macmillan.

Nietzsche, Friedrich (trans. Hollingdale, R.J.) 1979. *Ecco Homo: How One is to Become What One Is*, Harmondsworth: Penguin.

Nirmal, Arvind P., 1990. *A Reader in Dalit Theology*, Madras: Gurukul.

Oddie, G.A.(ed.), 1991. *Religion in South Asia: Religious Conversion & Revival Movements*, Delhi: Manohar.

Oddie, G.A. (ed.), 1998. *Religious Conversion Movements in South Asia: Continuities & Change, 1800-1900*, London: Curzon.

Oddie, G.A.(ed.), 1998. *Religious Traditions in South Asia: Interaction & Change*, London: Curzon.

O'Flaherty, Wendy D., 1973. *Asceticism and Eroticism in the Mythology of Siva*, Oxford: OUP.

Otto, R., 1923. *The Idea of the Holy*, London: OUP.

Pallath, J.J., 1995. *Theyyam: Folk Culture, Wisdom and Personality*, Delhi: ISI.

Panikkar, Raimundo, 1977. *The Vedic Experience: Mantramanjari*, Pondicherry: All India.

Panikkar, Raimundo, 1983. *Myth, Faith and Hermeneutics: Cross-Cultural Studies*, Bangalore:ATC.

Parekh, B., 2000. *The Future of Multi-Ethnic Britain: The Parekh Report*, London: Profile.

Parekh, Bhikhu, 2000(a). *Rethinking Multiculturalism: Cultural Diversity and Political Theory*, London: Macmillan.

Phan, Peter (ed.), 1990. *Christianity and the Wider Ecumenism*, New York:Paragon House.

Pieterse, Jan N. and Parekh, Bhikhu (eds), 1997. *The Decolonization of the Imagination: Culture, Knowledge and Power*, Delhi: OUP.

Porritt, J. and Winner.D., 1988. *The Coming of the Greens*, London: Fontana.

Powell, Avril A.,1993. *Muslims and Missionaries in Pre-Mutiny India*, Richmond: Curzon.

Premasagar, P.V. (ed.), 2002. *Contemporary Reflections on the Faith of Our Mothers & Our Fathers* (Kunchala Rajaratnam Endowment Lecture Series 2), Madras: Gurukul.

Race, Alan, 1983. *Christians and Religious Pluralism*, London:SCM .

Radhakrishnan, S., 1953. *The Principal Upanishads (edited with Introduction, Text,Translation and Notes)*, London: Allen & Unwin.

Ramanujan, A.K., 1973. *Speaking of Siva*, Delhi: Penguin.

Ramanujan, A.K., 1981, 1993. *Hymns for the Drowning: Poems for Vishnu by Nammalvar,* Delhi: Penguin.

Rashid, Ahmed, 2000. *Taliban: the Story of the Afghan Warlords*, London: Pan.

Robertson, Roland, 1992. *Globalization: Social Theory and Global Culture*, London: Sage.

Robinson, Rowena & Clarke, Sathianathan (eds.), 2003. *Religious Conversion in India: Modes, Motivations and Meanings*, Delhi: OUP.

Rowe, D.J., 1994. *Consider Jesus: Lessons from the Life & Ministry of an Indian Evangelist Called Azariah*, Bombay: D.J.Rowe.

Ruether, Rosemary R., 1992. *Gaia & God: An Ecofeminist Theology of Earth Healing*, London: SCM.

Russell, Bertrand, 1938. *Power: A New Social Analysis*, London: Allen & Unwin.

Sachs, Wolfgang (ed.), 1992. *The Development Dictionary: A Guide to Knowledge as Power*, London: Zed.

Sahi, Jyoti, 1980. *The Child and the Serpent: Reflections on Popular Indian Symbols,* London: Routledge.

Sahi, Jyoti, 1986. *Stepping Stones: Reflections on the Theology of Indian Christian Culture,* Bangalore: ATC.

Said, Edward W., 1994. *Culture and Imperialism,* London: Vintage.

Samartha, Stanley, 1974. *The Hindu Response to the Unbound Christ,* Madras: CLS.

Samartha, Stanley, 1996. *Between Two Cultures: Ecumenical Ministry in a Pluralist World,* Geneva: WCC.

Sanneh, Lamin, 1993. *Encountering the West: Christianity & the Global Cultural Process,* London: Marshall Pickering.

Santmire, H. Paul, 1985. *The Travail of Nature: The Ambiguous Ecological Promise of Christian Theology,* Philadelphia: Fortress.

Schama, Simon, 1995. *Landscape & Memory,* London: HarperCollins.

Sebastian, J.Jayakiran, 1997. 'Pressure of the Hyphen: Aspects of the Search for Identity Today in Indian-Christian Theology', in *Religion & Society,* Vol.44, No.4. Bangalore.

Selvanayagam, I. (ed.), 1995. *Biblical Insights on Inter-Faith Dialogue,* Bangalore: BTEESC.

Selvanayagam, I., 1996. *The Dynamics of Hindu Traditions: the Teape Lectures on Sacrifice,Gita & Dialogue,* Bangalore: ATC.

Selvanayagam, I., 1996(a). *Vedic Sacrifice: Challenge and Response,* Delhi: Manohar.

Selvanayagam, I.(ed.), 2002. *Moving Forms of Christian Faith : Essays in Honour of Thomas Thangaraj,* Delhi: ISPCK .

Sennett, Richard, 1977. *The Fall of Public Man,* Cambridge: CUP.

Shah, Ghanshyam (ed.), 2001. *Dalit Identity & Politics (Cultural Subordination & the Dalit Challenge, Vol.2),* New Delhi: Sage.

Shiva, Vandana, 1988. *Staying Alive: Women, Ecology and Survival in India,* Delhi: Kali for Women.

Shourie, Arun, 1993, 1997. *A Secular Agenda,* Delhi: HarperCollins.

Shourie, Arun, 1994. *Missionaries in India: Continuities, Changes, Dilemmas,* Delhi: ASA.

Shourie, Arun, 2000. *Harvesting our Souls: their Design, their Claims,* Delhi: ASA.

Shiva, Vandana & Mies, Marie, 1993. *Ecofeminism,* London: Zed books.

Smart, Ninian, 1968. *The Yogi and the Devotee,* London: George Allen & Unwin.

Smart, Ninian, 1995(2nd ed.). *Worldviews: Crosscultural Explorations of Human Beliefs,* Englewood Cliffs: Prentice-Hall.

Smart, Ninian, 1996. *Dimensions of the Sacred: An Anatomy of the World's Beliefs,* London: HarperCollins.

Smith, Wilfred Cantwell, 1962, 1978. *The Meaning and End of Religion: A Revolutionary Approach to the Great Religious Traditions,* New York: Macmillan, London: SPCK.

Smith, Wilfred Cantwell, 1981. *Towards a World Theology: Faith & the Comparative History of Religion*, London: Macmillan.

Stackhouse, Max. (ed.), 2002. *God and Globalization (vol.3)*, Harrisburgh:Trinity Press International.

Stiglitz, Joseph, 2002. *Globalization and its Discontents*, London: Penguin.

Sugirtharajah, R.S.(ed.), 1993. *Asian Faces of Jesus*, London: SCM

Sugirtharajah, R.S. & Hargreaves, C.(eds.), 1993(a), 1995. *Readings in Indian Christian Theology*, Delhi ISPCK.

Swidler, L (et al), *Death or Dialogue: From the Age of Monologue to the Age of Dialogue*, London: SCM.

Thapar, Romila, 1992. *Interpreting Early India*, Oxford: OUP.

Thomas, M.M., 1969. *The Acknowledged Christ of the Indian Renaissance*, Madras: CLS.

Thomas, M.M., 1971. *Salvation as Humanisation: Some Critical Issues of the Theology of Mission in Contemporary India*, Madras: CLS.

Tomlinson, John, 1999. *Globalisation and Culture*, Cambridge: Polity.

van der Leeuw, G., 1963 (1st pbl.German 1933). *Religion in Essence and Manifestation*, New York: Harper.

van der Veer, Peter, 1997. *Gods on Earth: Religious Experience and Identity in Ayodhya*, Delhi: OUP.

van der Veer, Peter, 1998. *Religious Nationalism: Hindus and Muslims in India*, Delhi: OUP.

Vaudeville, Charlotte, 1993. *A Weaver Named Kabir: Selected Verses with a Detailed Biographical & Historical Introduction*, Delhi: OUP.

Viswanathan, Gauri, 1998. *Outside the Fold: Conversion, Modernity and Belief*, Delhi: OUP.

Webster, John C.B., 1992. *The Dalit Christians: A History*, Delhi: ISPCK.

Webster, John C.B., 1999. *Religion and Dalit Liberation: An Examination of Perspectives*, Delhi: Manohar.

Wilfred, Felix (ed.), 1992. *Leave the Temple: Indian Paths to Human Liberation*, Maryknoll: Orbis.

Wilfred, Felix (ed.), 2001. *Jeevadhara Vol.XXXI No.181: Communities and Identity-Consciousness*, Kottayam: Jeevadhara.

Wilson, Bryan R. (ed.) 1967. *Patterns of Sectarianism*, London: Hodder & Stoughton.

Wingate, A., 1997. *The Church and Conversion*, Delhi: ISPCK.

Woodward, Kath, 2002. *Understanding Identity*, London: Arnold.

Zaehner, R.C., 1969. *The Bhagavad-Gita (with a Commentary Based on the Original Sources)*, Oxford: Clarendon.

Zvelebil, K.V.(trans.), 1984. *The Lord of the Meeting Rivers: Devotional Poems of Basavanna*, Delhi: Motilal Banarsidass.

Index of Names